Advertising and Promotion

An Integrated Marketing Communications Approach

Chris Hackley

Second Edition

Advertising and Promotion

An Integrated Marketing Communications Approach

Chris Hackley

Los Angeles | London | New Delhi
Singapore | Washington DC

© Chris Hackley 2010

First published 2005

Reprinted 2005, 2006, 2008
This second edition published 2010

SAGE Publications Ltd
1 Oliver's Yard
55 City Road
London EC1Y 1SP

SAGE Publications Inc.
2455 Teller Road
Thousand Oaks, California 91320

SAGE Publications India Pvt Ltd
B 1/I 1 Mohan Cooperative Industrial Area
Mathura Road
New Delhi 110 044

SAGE Publications Asia-Pacific Pte Ltd
33 Pekin Street #02-01
Far East Square
Singapore 048763

Library of Congress Control Number: 2009932899

British Library Cataloguing in Publication data

A catalogue record for this book is available from
the British Library

ISBN 978-1-84920-145-2
ISBN 978-1-84920-146-9 (pbk)

Typeset by C&M Digitals (P) Ltd, Chennai, India
Printed and bound in Great Britain by TJ International Ltd, Padstow, Cornwall
Printed on paper from sustainable resources

Mixed Sources
Product group from well-managed
forests and other controlled sources
www.fsc.org Cert no. SGS-COC-2482
FSC © 1996 Forest Stewardship Council

To My Wife, and My Boys

Contents

Foreword and Acknowledgements

The first edition of this book evolved from my discussions with advertising professionals and academic colleagues. It formed the basis for my advertising teaching for the subsequent four years. The new edition is substantially rewritten and updated and benefits from the feedback of many people, not least my students and colleagues at the School of Management, Royal Holloway University of London. I am especially grateful to Dr Amy Tiwsakul, Lecturer in Marketing at the School of Management, University of Surrey, for many valuable suggestions and constructive feedback on my ideas. My thanks also to Sage's excellent editorial team and their reviewers for their professionalism and constructive help.

The book is enhanced by many practical examples and I am indebted to those who gave copyright permission for me to adapt or reproduce materials. My sincere thanks go to Ayesha Datoo, BSc, Senior Account Executive at Cheil Worldwide UK. Ayesha took time out from her extremely busy schedule to help me obtain permission to adapt materials to write the Samsung Tocco case in Chapter 4. I'm proud to say Ayesha took my advertising course on her way to graduating from Royal Holloway with a BSc in Management with Marketing, before beginning her stellar career. My thanks to Samsung and Cheil Worldwide for granting copyright permission to adapt the case and reproduce the images.

My thanks also go to Dr Tayo Otubanjo, Director, Strategy and Account Planning, for the Nigerian agency Centrespread FCB of Lagos. Tayo kindly facilitated my adaptation of the First City Monument Bank campaign and print ad. My thanks to FCMB and Centrespread FCB for granting copyright permission. Further thanks to Ogilvy UK and Unilever for kind permission to reproduce visual material from their Dove campaign, and also to AMV BBDO London and *The Economist* for permission to reproduce two of their striking ads. Finally, I thank Professor Arthur Kover, former editor of the *Journal of Advertising Research*, for his contribution of a case vignette along with a great deal of research that has inspired both me and many others.

Chris Hackley
Royal Holloway University of London

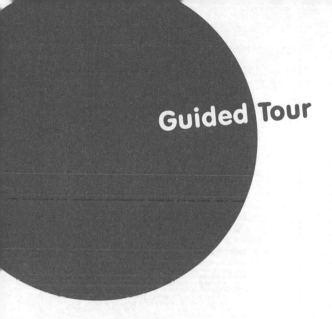

Guided Tour

Welcome to the guided tour of *Advertising and Promotion*, 2e. This tour will take you through the main sections and special features of the text.

Chapter Outline: A brief introduction and outline of what the chapter ahead will cover.

Key Chapter Contents: A clear set of key contents is provided for each chapter.

Boxed Sections: Issues and topics of interest are given through examples and critical discussions in boxed sections that feature throughout the chapters.

Picture 1 Advertising is a communication medium visible in most social spaces, as in this example of outdoor advertising in New York's Times Square.
(See the colour insert near the middle of this book for a full colour image.)

many ways we define our existence in terms of consumption. As advertising and communication make our continuous consumption of branded items a culturally normal practice, other competing cultural values that encourage abstention from consumption are relatively reduced in status. Today, at least in advanced economies, over-indulgence is the norm and waste is everywhere. Changes in cultural norms and practices of consumption (such as the move towards eating 'fast' food and away from the family-based social ritual of the home-cooked meal) to some extent reflect the influence of promotional culture. Deeply held

Colour Picture Insert: A colour insert features illustrations and further commentary on promotions and advertising campaigns discussed in the chapters. Links to these colour plates are included alongside the relevant discussions in the book.

competition all converge to form the consumer's understanding of a given brand. Include word-of-mouth and personal experience of brand usage, and it becomes clear that we cannot normally remember which particular communication or experience was significant in forming our enduring impression of a particular brand.

Brands subsist symbolically as a nebulous and mutable, yet enduring, memory of many kinds of consumer experience. Brands have a tangible, concrete reality, of course; they are created through human and technological processes, they require resources and usually (though not always, as in the case of virtual corporations) occupy office or factory space. But, most importantly, a brand also has a secret life, as symbolic abstraction. This abstraction, the brand image, acts in concert with its more tangible dimensions to frame and support the overall idea of that brand. Many brand marketing organizations try to integrate the various communications channels they use so that they act in harmony and, together, carry coherent and consistent messages about the brand. Doing this makes possible synergy effects by which each medium can leverage the influence of the others, enhancing marketing effectiveness by projecting the brand values and personality more powerfully.

The integrated perspective of this book does not conflate disciplines or media channels that are, rightly, considered by managers to be separate and distinct. Rather, it acknowledges the blurring and convergence of communication media sources in consumers' outlook. It also acknowledges that communications act interdependently: there are synergies that, in the new global media infrastructure, can be exploited by marketing organizations. The assimilation of brand advertising and marketing into mainstream entertainment media, discussed in detail in Chapter 6, is perhaps the most powerful indication of this integrative synergy (Hackley, 2003a).

Chapter Summary

Chapter 1 has introduced the topic of advertising and outlined the key themes of the book. It has outlined major changes in the advertising environment which are driving new forms of advertising. These changes are behind a second creative revolution as advertising agencies try to think of creative responses which will keep them at the centre of the brand and marketing communications world. The changes they face focus around the impact of Web 2.0 and mobile communication, the decline in newspaper readership and the fall in television advertising revenue, and the implications for funding models which drive business revenue through advertising.

The chapter also discussed general issues of advertising concerning its economic, social and business function. Finally, the chapter looked at the

Chapter Summary: The summary helps to re-emphasize key themes covered in the chapter.

nature of brands and the importance of advertising and promotion in framing brand symbolism.

Now the topic has been introduced, Chapter 2 will look at the long history of theorizing about advertising.

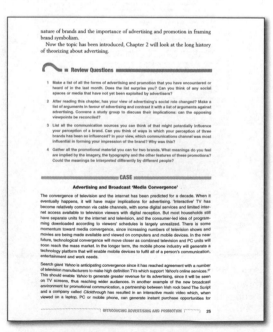

Review Questions

1 Make a list of all the forms of advertising and promotion that you have encountered or heard of in the last month. Does the list surprise you? Can you think of any social spaces or media that have not yet been exploited by advertisers?

2 After reading this chapter, has your view of advertising's social role changed? Make a list of arguments in favour of advertising and contrast it with a list of arguments against advertising. Convene a study group to discuss their implications: can the opposing viewpoints be reconciled?

3 List all the communication sources you can think of that might potentially influence your perception of a brand. Can you think of ways in which your perception of three brands has been so influenced? In your view, which communications channel was most influential in forming your impression of the brand? Why was this?

4 Gather all the promotional material you can for two brands. What meanings do you feel are implied by the imagery, the typography and the other features of these promotions? Could the meanings be interpreted differently by different people?

CASE

Advertising and Broadcast 'Media Convergence'

The convergence of television and the internet has been predicted for a decade. When it eventually happens, it will have major implications for advertising. 'Interactive' TV has become relatively common via cable channels, with some digital services and limited internet access available to television viewers with digital reception. But most households still have separate units for the internet and television, and the consumer-led idea of programming downloaded according to viewers' schedules is largely unrealized. There is some momentum toward media convergence, since increasing numbers of television shows and movies are being made available and viewed on computers and mobile devices. In the near future, technological convergence will move closer as combined television and PC units will soon reach the mass market. In the longer term, the mobile phone industry will generate a technology platform that will enable mobile devices to fulfil all of a person's communication, entertainment and work needs.

Search giant Yahoo is anticipating convergence since it has reached agreement with a number of television manufacturers to make high definition TVs which support Yahoo's online services. This should enable Yahoo to generate greater revenue for its advertising, since it will be seen on TV screens, thus reaching wider audiences. In another example of the new broadcast environment for promotional communication, a partnership between Irish rock band The Script and a company called Clickthrough has resulted in an interactive music video which, when viewed on a laptop, PC or mobile phone, can generate instant purchase opportunities for

Review Exercises: Group and individual exercises are designed to aid reflective learning and a practical consideration of the themes, cases and concepts raised in the chapters.

brands placed in the video. This is significant because of the increasing use of computers and mobile phones for viewing pop videos. The viewer can run the cursor across the screen to obtain details and/or purchasing information for any item in the video. However, viewing TV clips via mobile or PC devices is still a very small part of total television viewing. Most television is viewed on sets that are not connected to the internet and interactive services are not yet a major part of typical television viewing.

The economic impetus behind broadcast media convergence comes, on the one hand, from the shrinking audiences and advertising revenue for traditional television, and, on the other, the increasing audiences for televisual forms of entertainment via the internet and PC or mobile communication. The internet has powerful potential as a platform for television content and advertising because of its massive audience reach and its capacity for targeting, instant response, and audience measurement. The problem for internet sites is that, while they are attracting an increased proportion of advertising spend, the sums are still relatively small compared to traditional media. Internet advertising in total is experiencing rapid growth and exceeds the advertising revenue of some individual commercial television channels. Internet advertising revenue in the USA exceeded $23 billion in 2008, across banner and display advertising, sponsorship, classified and email. There is a mutual need driving convergence: traditional media need to find ways to access the huge audience traffic of the internet, while internet sites need to tap into some of the platform impact and (still) higher total advertising revenues available from television exposure.

The potential implications of convergence for advertisers, for programme makers, and for audiences, will be profound. There is an expectation that mobile advertising could take off as a massive revenue generator in the near future, but (as discussed in Chapter 10) there are still obstacles to be overcome. These include the lack of a common platform to carry video, text and audio on all mobile devices, and the fact that consumer behaviour around mobile phones currently resists receiving overt advertisements. Mobile phones are carried everywhere, they are always on and they are highly personalized, which gives them obvious potential for carrying advertising. This market is still in early development but is predicted to be worth many billions by 2011. In the longer term, the convergence of mobile and internet delivery with unified receiving devices will generate new media funding models, though it is likely that advertising will play a major part in this, some way or other.

Case Questions

1 Look up three social networking websites to see how they use click-through or banner advertising. In your opinion, could any of these sites be more attractive either to audiences or to advertisers if they were available via a television screen?

2 Television advertisements are, today, frequently broadcast on YouTube or on company websites before they appear on television. In some cases, the internet is the only media channel used. What are the advantages and disadvantages of each medium, TV and internet, for the traditional 20 or 30 second audiovisual advertisement? Are different creative approaches more suited to the TV or the internet for such ads?

Case Questions: Case questions encourage further research and consideration of the case study example and the themes it helps to illustrate.

brands placed in the video.[28] This is significant because of the increasing use of computers and mobile phones for viewing pop videos. The viewer can run the cursor across the screen to obtain details and/or purchasing information for any item in the video. However, viewing TV clips via mobile or PC devices is still a very small part of total television viewing. Most television is viewed on sets that are not connected to the internet and interactive services are not yet a major part of typical television viewing.

The economic impetus behind broadcast media convergence comes, on the one hand, from the shrinking audiences and advertising revenue for traditional television, and, on the other, the increasing audiences for televisual forms of entertainment via the internet and PC or mobile communication. The internet has powerful potential as a platform for television content and advertising because of its massive audience reach and its capacity for targeting, instant response, and audience measurement. The problem for internet sites is that, while they are attracting an increased proportion of advertising spend, the sums are still relatively small compared to traditional media. Internet advertising in total is experiencing rapid growth and exceeds the advertising revenue of some individual commercial television channels. Internet advertising revenue in the USA exceeded $23 billion in 2008,[29] across banner and display advertising, sponsorship, classified and email. There is a mutual need driving convergence: traditional media need to find ways to access the huge audience traffic of the internet, while internet sites need to tap into some of the platform impact and (still) higher total advertising revenues available from television exposure.

The potential implications of convergence for advertisers, for programme makers, and for audiences, will be profound. There is an expectation that mobile advertising could take off as a massive revenue generator in the near future, but (as discussed in Chapter 10) there are still obstacles to be overcome. These include the lack of a common platform to carry video, text and audio on all mobile devices, and the fact that consumer behaviour around mobile phones currently resists receiving overt advertisements. Mobile phones are carried everywhere, they are always on and they are highly personalized, which gives them obvious potential for carrying advertising. This market is still in early development but is predicted to be worth many billions by 2011. In the longer term, the convergence of mobile and internet delivery with unified receiving devices will generate new media funding models, though it is likely that advertising will play a major part in this, some way or other.

Case Questions

1 Look up three social networking websites to see how they use click-through or banner advertising. In your opinion, could any of these sites be more attractive either to audiences or to advertisers if they were available via a television screen?

2 Television advertisements are, today, frequently broadcast on YouTube or on company websites before they appear on television. In some cases, the internet is by no means the only media channel used. What are the advantages and disadvantages of each medium, TV and internet, for the traditional 20 or 30 second audiovisual advertisement? Are different creative approaches more suited to the TV or the internet for such ads?

Case Study: An in-depth case study is provided at the end of each chapter, linking the chapter to a relevant industry example. This is also accompanied by a set of case questions.

---

3 Design a concept for a social networking website. Current examples include YouTube, Facebook and Twitter. How would you make your concept popular, and, if you were successful in building significant traffic, how do you think you could monetize that traffic ('by selling the site to Google' isn't an acceptable answer)

Further Reading

Managerial Texts

Belch, G. and Belch, M. (2008) *Advertising and Promotion: An Integrated Marketing Communications Perspective*, 8th edn. New York: McGraw Hill.

Fill, C. (2009) *Marketing Communications: Interactivity, Communication and Content*, 5th edn. Essex: Pearson.

Percy, L. and Elliott, R. (2009) *Strategic Advertising Management*, 3rd edn. Oxford: Oxford University Press.

Pickton, D. and Broderick, A. (2005) *Integrated Marketing Communications*. London: Pearson Education.

Socio-Cultural Perspectives

Cook, G. (2001) *The Discourse of Advertising*. London: Routledge.

Leiss, W., Kline, S., Jhally, S. and Botterill, J. (2005) *Social Communication in Advertising: Consumption in the Mediated Marketplace*, 3rd edn. London: Routledge.

McFall, L. (2004) *Advertising: A Cultural Economy*. London: Sage.

Web-Based Resources

Brand communication consultancy: www.symbolism.org/about/html

A database of advertising slogans: www.adslogans.co.uk

The UK account planning group: www.apg.org.uk

The UK advertising regulator, the Advertising Standards Authority: www.asa.org

A site by branding consultancy Interbrand: www.brandchannel.com

Media resource called the National Readership Survey of Britain: www.nrs.co.uk

UK-based media research resource called the Broadcast Audience Research Board: www.barb.co.uk

University of Texas advertising teaching resource: http://advertising.utexas.edu

Duke University advertising history resource: http://scriptorium.lib.duke.edu/adaccess/

Further Reading: A list of relevant further reading is suggested for each chapter.

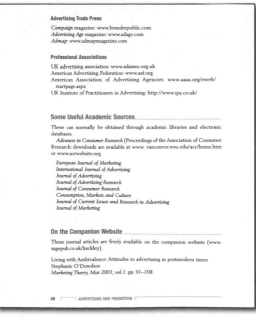

On the Companion Website: Online teaching support including extra case studies is provided at the end of each chapter.

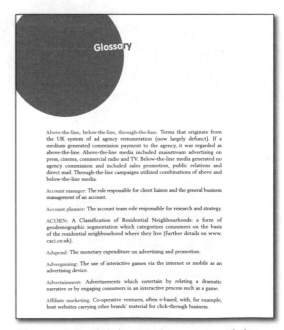

Glossary: A detailed glossary of terms is provided at the end of the book.

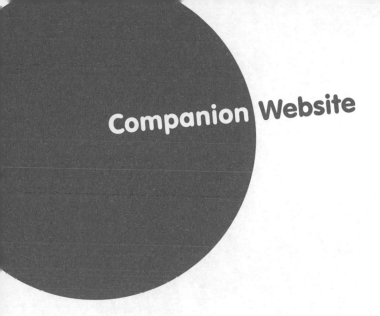

Companion Website

Be sure to visit the companion website at www.sagepub.co.uk/hackley to find a range of teaching and learning materials.

For instructors:

Password-protected instructor resources include:

- An **instructor's manual** offering guidance for teaching the book. Contents include **suggested activities**; **suggested activity feedback**; **class discussion topics**; **indicative answers/responses** for the chapter review questions and chapter case questions featured in the textbook; and **extra case studies**.
- Detailed **PowerPoint slides** for each chapter.

For students:

- **Online journal readings.**
- **Links to relevant websites** are provided for each chapter.
- An **online glossary** that covers all the relevant terms in the book.

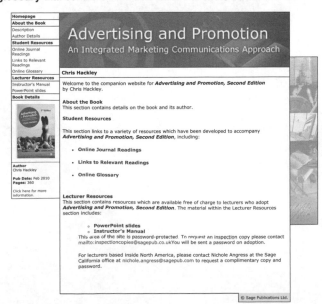

Introduction to the Second Edition

The first edition of this book, *Advertising and Promotion: Communicating Brands*, has been a successful core text for a number of under- and postgraduate courses. It was written to offer a new synthesis of literature, theory, practice and research for taught courses in the area. The book brought together the managerial focus of advertising and agency operations in the service of the brand, with a consumer cultural focus on the social and ethical role of advertising. It therefore offered a broader intellectual treatment of the subject than is typical in most managerial texts, while it also offered a managerial perspective which is typically neglected in social or cultural studies texts on advertising. The second edition retains this synthesis in an improved form, written with student needs in mind and bringing out the managerial issues with greater depth and detail. The new subtitle more accurately reflects the scope of the book. The intention is to bring out the integrated marketing communications perspective more strongly in this new edition.

The book has been updated with new practical examples and new references, sources and cases, in order to try to keep students abreast of the rapidly evolving advertising environment and its research. The main changes in the organization of the book are as follows. Chapter 1 outlines the key themes of the book and is re-written. Chapter 2, 'Theorizing Advertising and Promotion', is substantially re-written in order to try to improve clarity and progression, and to set advertising theory in a broader context of development. Chapter 3 is now entitled 'The Brand and Integrated Marketing Communications Planning', reflecting the emphasis of the book on integration in communications planning, while Chapter 4, 'Advertising Agencies: Creative Work and Management Processes', focuses on the working practices and functional roles of agencies in the service of the brand. Chapter 5, 'Promotional Media in the Digital Age', is substantially re-written to try to capture something of the profound implications for advertising practice of the digital communications revolution. Chapter 6 is re-titled 'Non-Advertising Promotion in Integrated Marketing Communication' and deals with some of the many elements of the promotional mix which do not conventionally fall under the category of advertising but which, nonetheless, are essential components of strategic and integrated communications thinking. Chapters 7, 8 and 9, 'International Advertising', 'Advertising: Ethics and Regulation' and 'Advertising Research', are updated and restructured and include many new examples. Chapter 10 of the new edition becomes 'Integrating e-Marketing and Advertising'. Most of the longer end-of-chapter cases and questions have been replaced with new material and many of the smaller case vignettes within the chapters have been updated or replaced. Each chapter also has review questions, while the sources, glossary and references are all updated. (Glossary terms are emboldened in the text.)

1 Introducing Advertising and Promotion: An Integrated Marketing Communications Approach

Chapter Outline

Chapter 1 sets the tone for the book by noting the fundamental economic, technological and commercial changes which are taking place in the advertising environment. In particular, it draws attention to developments in communications technology and the implications for media funding models which will affect the market for advertising. The chapter introduces key concepts and issues for the study of advertising and promotional communication in a global context.

Key chapter content:

- The changing global advertising environment
- The challenges facing advertising agencies
- What is advertising?
- The promotional mix
- Studying advertising: managerial, consumer and societal perspectives
- Brands and symbolism in Integrated Marketing Communication.

The Changing Global Advertising Environment

Advertising's Second Creative Revolution

As this book is being written, advertising is undergoing a second creative revolution as the industry tries to respond to new media funding models created by Web 2.0, mobile communications technology and changing patterns of media consumption. Advertising agencies are thinking laterally as never before to place their creative stamp on new forms of content which are attractive to clients. The first, somewhat mythologized creative advertising revolution of the 1960s occurred in the context of a classic media funding model. Paid-for advertising generated the revenue to fund media channels. In other words, the spot advertising in the intervals paid for television shows, while the classified and display advertising paid for print publications, with a small contribution from the cover charge. As circulation and viewing figures grew, so did advertising revenue. This funding model set the parameters for advertising, since advertisements had to fit particular genre conditions in order to be suitably differentiated from the 'editorial' content in traditional media vehicles such as newspapers and commercial television or radio shows.

Today, the traditional funding model is no longer the natural order of things. In fact, the world of old media has been turned on its head since media professionals now talk about 'content' as something which drives the consumption of advertising. 'Content' could be news, documentary, entertainment, opinion, indeed any communication form at all which has the potential to generate audience engagement. New media funding models are emerging because of various pressures, including the **fragmentation of media audiences** under the influence of new communications technology, and de-regulated media markets. Spot advertising during commercial breaks on television or radio, classified and full-colour advertising spreads in press publications, outdoor and cinema advertising all retain their high profile, **audience** reach and dramatic impact. But the advertising landscape is changing. For example, it is becoming pitted with many new **media vehicles** as digital technology reduces start-up costs for print, internet and broadcast media. There are more magazines, television and radio channels than ever before. But the audience reach of each individual media vehicle has shrunk under increased competition and changing patterns of media consumption. This trend is evident all over the world. Some of these new media vehicles are not funded by the traditional model, social networking websites being the most striking example.

Another pressure on the traditional funding model for media is the change in media consumption patterns as viewing and readership figures for traditional television, print and radio fall, and advertising revenues consequently collapse. For example, in the UK and the USA, newspapers established for over 100 years may cease to exist in the not-too-distant future as advertising revenue falls to unsustainable levels.[1] Underlying the reduction in advertising revenue for traditional media, fewer consumers are paying for print media and more consumers are viewing, and interacting with, media content on mobile phones, PCs, laptops and other wireless devices such as netbooks. We can watch television programming or read news on digital devices without having to watch the ads. Even more problematic for conventional advertising, the internet offers a massive potential audience reach for cheaply made and easily targeted 'viral' advertisements which cost nothing to place on video sharing websites such as *YouTube*. Finally, when 'convergence' is achieved between television and the internet, and the mass market begins to watch all of its TV on PC screens with a wireless broadband capability, the advertising revolution will be in full flow and advertising agencies will face a very different environment to the one in which they evolved.

All these changes mean that what we understand by 'advertising' as a genre of communication is changing, and this has as yet uncertain implications for the advertising industry. Advertising has always been a fluid creative industry in which creative 'hot shops' and talented individuals could thrive, but the core organizational actors in the advertising environment have consistently been advertising agencies. Over nearly 400 years, since the development of mass consumption print publications, advertising agencies have proved to be the most flexible and astute of organizational forms in adding skills and techniques to retain their central place in an evolving media environment. But can they deal with the challenges of new media and the digital revolution?

BOX 1.0

Advertise Yourself

Video sharing websites, especially *YouTube*, have had a striking effect on the advertising environment. The defining features of mass media advertising were once that it was paid-for, it was identifiable as an advertisement, and the identity of the sender was known. Normally, paid-for advertising was placed in designated media spaces set aside solely for the purpose, such as the intervals created in-between and during television or radio shows on commercial channels, or the classified pages or lifestyle sections of print publications. Today, many advertisements are placed on *YouTube* as well as, and even instead of, being placed on mass, paid-for media channels. A successful ad on the internet can be viewed and shared by millions of people in just a few weeks, giving an audience reach which was once only possible through television advertising. Some videos now appearing on the site have been made by advertising agencies to look as if they were made by private citizens. Even the videoed responses to these ads, called 'video blogging', have sometimes been paid for by advertisers.[2]

(Cont'd)

Not only professionals have been advertising in this way: individuals have even started to use *YouTube* as a free dating service, by recording and placing advertisements for themselves aimed at potential romantic partners.[3] Advertising has become a form of public performance and visual art which is accessible to the public in unprecedented ways through free-to-access video sharing websites. The viral possibilities of these sites mean that uploads which people like can spread to millions of viewers to offer an audience reach for advertising on a scale which far exceeds the audience figures that terrestrial television shows achieve today.

Advertising Agencies Face a Challenge

The aforementioned scenario, then, could eventually result in an advertising environment quite different from any that has gone before. Conventional advertising, in the form of a striking 30-second television spot or stunning print display, is not going away. But the dynamics of making money out of this communication form for brand clients and agencies are certainly changing.

If they want to maintain their place at the centre of the marketing world, advertising agencies have to respond to this new reality creatively by re-organizing, and by evolving new skills and techniques. For example, according to some visionaries, weblogs have become the most important source for new agency business,[4] as clients and agencies struggle to find time for the traditional **pitching** process. Blogging has, in fact, become a key marketing strategy (Hackley, 2009a: 124) and many agencies have embraced this trend in their own websites. Many others are placing digital communication at the centre of their planning process in response to the demand from internet providers for many forms of creative content. It isn't easy to generate revenue from digital content, since, as noted above, some of the most important internet business models are free-to-use and their audiences resist the presence of advertising. Nevertheless, social networking sites like *Facebook* and *Youtube* have tried to get their user traffic to accept a certain level of click-through or banner advertising. A further issue is that the internet has driven the idea of freemium[5] as a funding model, giving away a basic level of information and services in the hope that this will attract clients willing to pay for a higher level of service.[6] Many advertising agencies themselves are using such a model, offering case studies and other information sources free of charge via their websites in the hope that clients will be attracted enough to pay for a deeper engagement with the agency.

New Funding Models Needed for Web 2.0 Communication

The concept of freemium, giving away free basic content to encourage consumers to pay for enhanced services, has become associated with second generation interactive Web 2.0 applications and services. The defining feature of Web 2.0 is not new technology but new ways of understanding how the technology can be applied to facilitate new modes and models of business and communication. The term Web 2.0 is mere jargon but it has become associated with the lateral thinking required to creatively harness the interactive properties of the web for social and commercial purposes.

Social networking and video sharing websites, blogs and wikis exemplify web-based business concepts which are enriched by open access and user participation. In many cases, such sites as *Twitter*, *Facebook* and *YouTube* generate huge user traffic and struggle to monetize this other than by trying to get users to accept a certain amount of paid-for advertising. *Twitter*, for example, founded in 2007, gained 7 million users in the USA alone in two years. It is a free service which generates no revenue yet it was valued at $250,000,000 when it raised money early in 2009.[7] It remains to be seen how *Twitter* might be able to turn its audience traffic into revenue.[8] Other sites utilize the freemium concept to add value to services which can only be acquired by customers paying a premium. The advantage of freemium is that it can generate considerable audience reach through **word-of-mouth (WOM)** very quickly. The difficulty of translating this audience reach into large revenue streams is the key problem of internet business models.

Many agencies have re-organized and crossed into new areas, for example direct mail agencies such as Wunderman London[9] have expanded their service offer, even producing broadcast advertising. A few media agencies have moved into advertising and even into television production, while other advertising agencies have developed new revenue streams by re-positioning themselves as ideas companies and developing creative projects as diverse as comics, movies and stage plays.[10] There are ongoing experiments with new agency forms, such as the 'social-media' agency[11] which attempts to handle all the brand communication via the web.

From the client side, non-traditional styles of advertising are taking a greater share of promotional spend because of the need to engage consumers in ways which offer better value than spot advertising. In particular, clients need their agencies to offer an integrated communications solution which offers value and impact by using different communication channels in a single campaign. For example, this may take the form of a television advertisement supported with dedicated brand websites containing consumer forums, games and company information, and creating a presence for the brand in other areas through media coverage, sponsorship, direct marketing and sales promotion activities. Within the flux of change in the advertising environment, advertising agencies cannot be expected to be the experts in every communication channel but they are in a prime position to generate and co-ordinate new models of a creative and brand communications strategy.

Agencies Develop New Skills and New Revenue Streams

If agencies are to survive, they have to engage with new client priorities. For example, many commercial television channels outside the UK are partly funded by revenues from **product placement**. The art of placing brands in entertainment vehicles such as TV shows, movies, books, stage plays and computer games, has attracted increased attention from brand clients conscious that many consumers avoid conventional spot advertising but are happy to see brands 'embedded' within their mediated entertainment (Hackley and Tiwsakul, 2006). Music artists have been paid to sing about brands in their lyrics and brands have even been placed in TV shows after a scene has been shot through a technique known as digital product placement.[12] This branch of advertising communication is frequently handled by specialist product placement agencies, or by the media arm of advertising agencies. Nevertheless, it is a growing revenue generator which advertising agencies need to access. Not only do they need to master new skills, agencies also have new client priorities to serve. For example, in the UK, the biggest advertising budget is spent not by a global brand marketing conglomerate but by the Government Central Office of Information (COI) which spent £178 million on advertising in 2008.[13] This money was spent on 'social' marketing campaigns promoting, healthier lifestyles, road safety and other causes. Social marketing campaigns demand a different treatment to commercial campaigns, resulting in new creative challenges for agencies.[14]

What will result from the current changes in the advertising environment is anyone's guess, but advertising agencies might well retain their importance in one form or another. Since they began as brokers of classified advertising space in the early press publications, they have added many new skills and techniques such as copywriting, creative production, business strategies, brand strategies, consumer and market research and media planning. They are in a positive position to continue their evolution into the new creative and media environment. In spite of all the changes, broadcast and print advertising still retain their presence and marketing power. Advertising in general is likely to remain a major field of management, social and cultural studies, given the increased presence of mediated communication in the daily lives of billions of people, though the notion of what advertising is and how it can be understood will evolve.

What is Advertising?

Advertising and the Promotional Mix

In marketing management, promotion is one element of the **marketing mix**, the others being product, place (distribution), and price. Advertising is a sub-category of the **promotional mix**, along with other forms of promotional communication, including: public relations; personal selling; corporate communications; direct mail and other direct marketing techniques; sales promotion; exhibitions; and internet communication. Advertising itself is often broken down into further sub-categories based on the communication channel: print media; broadcast media (TV, radio, cinema); outdoor (also called Out of Home); and sales promotion. These media categories subsume a large number of promotional techniques. For example, sales promotion can refer to anything from brand logos printed on balloons and pens to in-store demonstrations or two-for-one package offers. The category of print media might refer to mass media such as national newspapers or magazines, or to an in-house publication and even a direct mail campaign. Promotional categories do not always have precise and agreed definitions, and in practice they overlap each other.

The various elements and sub-elements of the promotional mix constitute separate professional categories. For example, many marketing communications professionals spend their working life in sales promotion, or in direct mail or personal sales, or public relations. In many cases, large organizations treat these as separate functions with different departments handling, say, corporate communications, direct marketing, advertising or sales. Yet, in the new advertising environment, and from a management point of view, the logic of **Integrated Marketing Communications** is compelling. Media audiences now access more channels than ever before, and in different proportions. Newspapers and television still retain their place in the advertising scene, but they have given up a lot of ground to the internet and mobile communication. In response, brand clients want promotional campaigns to be integrated across media channels and across promotional sub-categories. Given the long-entrenched professional and organizational separation of the various marketing communication techniques and channels, the ideal of fully Integrated Marketing Communication (IMC) management remains only partially realized. As we have touched on above, there is a shake-out going on in the promotion industry which includes not only advertising agencies but direct mail, sales promotion, media and branding agencies, and even **creative hot shops** and digital agencies. The winners will be the ones which adapt most successfully, and most profitably, to the logic of Integrated Marketing Communication.

Blurring the Definitions of Advertising and Promotion

The ingenuity of advertisers and the flexibility of advertising as a communication form often render attempts to define it in one sentence trite, or tautologous. As noted in Box 1.0, the internet is creating new forms of advertising which don't conform to the old definitions. Advertising often sells something, but often does not, since a great deal of advertising promotes not only branded products and services but also political candidates and political parties, public services, health and safety issues, charities or other non-profit issues. Advertising is often an impersonal communication, distinguishing it from personal selling, but there are many ads that are eye-to-eye sales pitches delivered by actors or celebrity endorsers in a mediated imitation of a personal sales encounter. Advertising is usually paid-for, appearing in a media space set apart for promotional communication. But, increasingly, as noted above, advertisements may be put on internet sites such as *YouTube*[15] with no fee involved at all, because viewers actively search out advertisements they may find entertaining or amusing. In fact, as the website *Visit4info*[16] has shown, advertising is such a popular form of entertainment that consumers will pay to download the ads. What is more, advertising budgets are increasingly being turned to forms of promotion which are implicit rather than explicit, such as sponsorship or product placement. Consequently, attempts to define advertising in concrete and exclusive terms are usually more notable for what they leave out than for what they include.

Advertising can sometimes be distinguished by genre elements that set it apart from other forms of mediated communication. Overheated sales pitches from improbably coiffed spokespersons, deliriously happy housewives singing irritatingly catchy jingles at the kitchen sink, unfeasibly attractive models excited by chocolate confections all spring to mind as advertising clichés. But then again, many advertisements contradict advertising stereotypes. Just as Bill Bernbach created the ironic or self-deprecating ad in his iconic Volkswagen campaign of the 1960s, may advertisements now subvert conventional genres and eschew the rhetoric of over-selling in favour of postmodern irony, under-statement or a narrative designed to create presence and generate word-of-mouth for the brand, as opposed to trying to sell it.

So, a narrow definition of what advertising *is*, can obscure our consideration of what advertising *does*. We might categorize a given piece of communication as an advertisement in terms of its parallels with a vague and fuzzy mental prototype of what an ad should look or sound like (see Rosch, 1977, cited in Cook, 2001: 13), but the norms of advertising media, genres and payment methods are being revised by changes in the industry. Advertising may be a communication that at some level has a promotional motive, but this hardly prepares us for all the kinds of promotional messages we are likely to encounter. Neither can it prepare us for the subtlety of motive that underlies many hybrid promotional forms. A post-match interview with a logo-wearing sporting star, a free download of a trial version of a new computer game, free content from a magazine's website you can download to your mobile phone, a 'courtesy' phone call from your bank, can each be regarded as forms of promotional communication, or, to the lay-person, of advertising. They stretch beyond typical textbook definitions of advertising but, nevertheless, exemplify the integrated and multi-channel trend of much contemporary promotional activity. A realistic study of advertising and promotion cannot hope to put all the parts in neatly labelled packages. Advertising takes the enquirer on a journey that is all the more fascinating because it defies boundaries.

Studying Advertising

The Consumer Perspective

Take a moment to think about the advertisements you have seen or heard this week. At whom do you think were they aimed? What, exactly, were they trying to communicate? How did they make you feel? Did you rush to buy the brand? Did you tell your friends about the ad? Which medium conveyed the ads? Did you see them on a passing vehicle, on outdoor poster sites, on the television, hear them on the radio, read them in the press? Did you see other forms of promotion on your clothing, smell them in a promotionally enhanced shopping environment, see them on product packaging, on an air balloon in the sky or on the back of a bus ticket? It is difficult to remember more than a few of all the hundreds of promotions we experience each week, at least if we live in urban areas and have access to televisions and computers. Advertising has become such a feature of daily life that sometimes it seems as if we hardly notice it. Advertising often seems to pervade our cultural landscape and we carry on our lives taking it for granted, as if it were as natural as grass or trees.[17]

We are struck, then, when particular promotional campaigns become topics of general conversation or objects of public disapproval. It is then that we realize how taken-for-granted most advertising is, and we wonder how this paradox occurs. Advertising is, of course, so powerful precisely because it is taken-for-granted. There are frequent press features that reflect our puzzled fascination with the latest iconic or controversial ad. The TV show dedicated to the funniest or most outlandish ads has become a mainstay of popular TV programming in many countries. Advertising's crossing over into mainstream entertainment and the uses entertainment media make of advertising styles and techniques reflect another aspect of advertising's dynamic character as a perpetually evolving form of social communication (Leiss et al., 2005). The hard-sell ads remain, but there are also new narrative advertising forms of ever greater subtlety and variety.

BOX 1.2

New Narrative Forms of Advertising

In 2009 a series of television ads for T-Mobile showed what appeared to be a 'flash mob' of a few hundred people breaking spontaneously into a choreographed dance in the middle of London's Liverpool Street Station. Incredulous commuters reached for their mobile phones to film the event and share it with their friends. The ad has become a huge hit in its own right. The T-Mobile tune played briefly at the end and the spoken line 'life is for sharing' are the only things indicating that it is an advertisement.

In many countries, new narrative forms have been developed which depart from the traditional genres of advertising. An earlier example was one of a series of Adidas sportswear ads which looked more like short films than advertisements. One featured the iconic soccer star David Beckham and England's rugby world-cup-winning star Johnny Wilkinson. The ads are edited vignettes of a contrived kick-about session in which each tests the other's skill at their respective sports. There was no backing-track or voice-over. There was nothing to indicate that it was an ad, apart from the appearance of the Adidas name in small type at the end. The ads became widely talked about, shared and viewed. The campaign merged the marketing communications genres of sponsorship, celebrity endorsement and advertising to produce a hybrid genre, which might be called **advertainment** since the ads are presented simply as entertainments. They attracted press coverage in the UK even before they were aired and generated widespread interest and attention from sports fans, thus achieving a key objective of many advertising campaigns – to be talked about. The lack of a direct-to-camera endorsement from either sportsman merely enhanced the sense of authenticity of the brand for viewers interested enough in sport to understand the prestige of the sportsmen. The style also spoke to many consumers who felt jaded with traditional advertising and cynical toward product endorsements. The absence of an explicit message lent the ads a stronger sense of authenticity, which complimented both the brand and the viewer for their mutual sophistication.

The Social Power of Advertising

The great advantage of teaching advertising is that it is such an immediate part of daily experience it is relatively easy to get a sense of student engagement with the subject. Few people do not have opinions on advertisements they have seen. This can give the subject great resonance as a subject of study which is suitable for a wide variety of practical and theoretical treatments. Beyond the classroom, advertising can occasionally have an astonishing power to grasp widespread attention and, in a few celebrated cases, change entire markets. The legendary 'Laundrette' ad that John Hegarty of the agency Bartle Bogle Hegarty created in the 1982 campaign for Levi 501s used American provenance to revolutionize the denim jeans market in general and sales of Levis in particular for the following decade. It has been claimed that the campaign increased sales of denim jeans by some 600 per cent. Other campaigns have become so talked about they have changed language, for example when a campaign for Budweiser beer increased the market share for the brand and earned valuable free publicity simply because they added a word ('Whassup') to the vernacular of American English (and even earned a listing in Longman's *Dictionary of Contemporary English*).[18] Campaigns for Gold Blend coffee and for the Renault Clio in the 1990s earned similar fame in the UK and provided valuable PR benefits for those brands through newspaper feature articles and television comment. More recently, noted campaigns have included T-Mobile's much talked-about ads (see Box 1.2) which showed a 'flash mob' of apparently spontaneous dancers in Liverpool Street Station,[19] and the Fallon agency's[20] campaigns for Cadbury which featured a drumming gorilla in one example, and children making their eye-brows dance to an electro-funk sound track[21] in another. Ads such as these generate much comment, keeping the advertising in the public mind and adding an air of charisma to advertising as the most enigmatic of creative industries.

The Managerial Perspective

For organizational managers, advertising and promotion are tools for supporting a wide variety of marketing, corporate, or business objectives. There are many professionals on the client side, such as brand managers and planners, and brand marketing and communication executives who are deeply sceptical about the claims made for advertising as a business tool, unless they are backed up by statistical evidence of an attitude change, recall, or, preferably, sales response. Brand managers are usually under pressure to account for their advertising budgets by linking them to sales or market share in the short to medium term. They have little use for theories of advertising based on building long-term brand equity. This is understandable, because in the long term, they're in a different job, or out of a job. Many others in the marketing business feel that they have to match competitor promotion levels for fear of losing a market share if they don't. Even though much advertising activity is driven by organizational politics and competitive neurosis, there is an acknowledgement that the world's major brands would be inconceivable without advertising. Neither can it be doubted that the commercial fortunes of some brands, and in some cases the size of entire markets, have been transformed through powerful and creatively compelling advertising campaigns. Even so, there are persistent questions hanging over advertising's effectiveness and the genuine return it delivers on investment. As a consequence, the advertising budget is often the first to be cut in difficult economic times and mutual insecurity can colour the relationships between clients and advertising agencies.

The Managerial Uses of Advertising and Promotion

Industry professionals tend to regard advertising as a powerful if imprecise marketing tool, a means of persuasively communicating with (or to) millions of customers. But advertising's ability to sell can be overplayed: it is also used for other purposes, such as to match competitive activity or to build brand presence. In fact, some academics have argued that advertising almost never sells, but in most cases serves to remind and reassure existing consumers that the brand is still salient (Ehrenberg et al., 2002). One simple rationale for this might go as follows: human beings have a short-term memory capacity of about six or seven items. Most purchases are not researched exhaustively, so we will often choose from the six or seven brands of which we have heard and can recall without effort, and which are easy to find. Factor in consumer markets of many millions of people, and it seems self-evident that the most memorably, and the most persistently, advertised brands will take the top few places in the market. The problem with this informal theory of advertising is that it implies that the content of the ads is not necessarily of critical importance. There will always be examples of ads which will capture the public imagination and build a brand presence out of all proportion to their budget, but these are rare. The truth is that much advertising needs only to be good enough, and it is quite rare for entirely new brands to break into the top few places in established product or service markets. While all this is a simplification, it might help explain the popularity of some leading brands of fast food and household detergent whose ubiquitous advertising campaigns are often excoriated for their cliché ridden narratives and deplorable creative standards, and yet they are hard to forget and they seem to play a part in the success of the brand.

Of course, advertising's persuasiveness is not only used in profit generation. 'Social marketing' (Kotler and Roberto, 1989; Kotler and Zaltman, 1971) is a genre that addresses issues of social concern. Many public services, charities and government departments use advertising campaigns to try to promote their causes or to change behaviour with respect to, for example, alcohol or cigarette consumption, safer driving, sexual practices, domestic violence or social prejudice towards disability or ethnicity. Social advertising even shouts louder than brand advertising. As noted above, government-sponsored social advertising commanded the largest advertising spend in the UK in 2008. In terms of impact, it can shout louder by shocking audiences into paying attention, at least for the duration of the first ad. Social campaigns are allowed by the regulatory authorities, at least in the UK, to push the boundaries of tasteful depiction further than brand advertising, because of their ostensibly virtuous motives (also see Chapter 8).

Questions of what kinds of advertising 'work' and deliver the best value to shareholders, taxpayers and other stakeholders are perpetually researched by business academics and advertising agencies. But no one has a definitive answer. The effectiveness of a campaign invariably depends on many factors, including its objectives, its audience, its budget, its timing and media channel, the quality of the creative execution, and many other environmental factors such as market price and competitive behaviour. In Chapter 2 we examine some of the many theories of advertising which have been developed to try to find answers to the key questions which management in the field face.

The Societal Perspective

Advertising is regarded by many people as a communication form which is inherently deceitful and debased, and occasionally offensive. Yet, considering the tenaciousness with which corporations pursue profits, remarkably few ads tell literal untruths. Of course, some do, but most advertising satisfies typical social conventions of tact and truthfulness. The interaction of consumers with advertising and promotional communication is usually too complex and subtle to be thought of as, simply, a matter of either fact or fiction. If an ad implies that a man's sexual attractiveness and social status will be enhanced by shaving with a Gillette razor or deodorizing with Lynx body spray, surely this is merely preposterous rather than untrue? Who would possibly take such an idea seriously? To be sure, consumer perceptions and beliefs about brands are self-sustaining to some degree: we believe what we want to believe, sometimes in the face of contradictory evidence. Do smokers really cough less using low-tar cigarettes? Are we slimmer because we put a calorie-free sugar substitute in our coffee? It can hardly be denied that there is an important element of wish fulfillment in what we choose to believe in advertising. The advertisers provide the suggestion, and, as consumers, we complete the Gestalt. Gestalt psychology refers to the way people complete the circle of meaning from partial cues or prompts. In other words, our inference goes beyond the evidence.

'Reading' Implicit Meanings in Ironic Advertising

A peculiarity of advertising is that we are expected to be able to distinguish between untruth and humorous hyperbole, but the advertisers make every effort to blur this distinction (see Box 1.3). This is just one reason why this sophisticated communication form is rightfully a part of literary academic study. Advertising performs an essential economic function in capitalist economies but for it to perform this function well, it demands a relatively sophisticated level of discernment from consumers who have already learned the reading strategies demanded by advertising. Advertising is rarely a significant part of the school curriculum, yet negotiating a way through the advertising landscape is important to the economic and social competence of citizens. The role of implicit meanings, irony and humerous hyperbole is relatively poorly understood in advertising. We examine this topic in detail in Chapter 2.

BOX 1.3

Self-satirizing Advertising

'Lynx'-branded male grooming products are marketed with expensively produced TV ads that show male users becoming unexpectedly irresistible to beautiful women. The ads assume that the viewer will understand that it is all just a joke: the plots are clearly intended to be funny. A recent (2009) offering is a handy-sized spray deodorant marketed as an instant way to attract the opposite sex. The TV ads show a young man using it in precisely this way. Lynx is pointing at the narrative conventions of male grooming brands and laughing at them with the viewer. But the high production standards of the ads show viewers that, in fact, the marketing campaign is deadly serious. Viewers agree – Lynx is the leading brand in several male grooming product segments. Could it be that knowing the ads are not serious strengthens rather than weakens the message, that using Lynx deodorant might just make the user more sexually alluring to the woman of his dreams? According to some theorists, it is enough that audiences are aware of the implied message in an ad for the communication to be persuasive – they do not have to believe it (e.g. see Tanaka, 1994).

Controversy over Advertising

Advertising is blamed for many social evils, from eating disorders to the decline in public manners. Yet, paradoxically, advertising is also widely regarded as trivial. It tends to occupy a lowly status in our cultural hierarchy, beneath popular art, literature, movies, even stand-up comedy performers. But its lowly cultural status is belied by our fascination with it. We enjoy TV shows about the funniest ads and we often talk about the latest ads in our daily conversations. Cook (2001) notes this duality about advertising's cultural status. It is regarded as both trivial and powerful, banal and sinister, amusing and degrading. Even though advertising is a familiar form of communication in developed economies, we still struggle to come to terms with its apparent force.

Although the level of popular interest in advertising is great, there is little consensus about its role in society. Some argue that it corrupts cultural life with its insistent, hectoring presence cajoling us to buy ever greater quantities of goods and services. Organized consumer resistance to advertising has taken the form of vandalism, such as a French anti-advertising group spray-painting '*le pub tue*' or '*le pub pue*' on all the advertising posters in the Paris metro, the RATP.[22] Advertising intrudes into ever more social spaces both public (see Picture 1) and private. Many schools, especially in the USA, now accept fees to give exclusive rights to commercial organizations to advertise and sell their goods on campus. It was reported that one student was suspended for wearing a Pepsi T-shirt on his school's 'Coke Day'.[23] Even religious observance is not immune from advertising's influence. Advertising-style slogans in brash colours promoting religious observance can be seen outside many places of worship. Evidently, advertising influences the communication norms of the very culture from which it draws.

But while some have a political objection to advertising in all its forms, many people are irritated not by advertising in general but by what they see as its excesses, whether these are to do with its ubiquity or with the offensiveness of particular creative executions. Even acknowledging advertising's unique ideological force in promoting consumerism, legitimizing capitalism and framing everyday experience (Elliott and Ritson, 1997) does not necessarily imply an anti-advertising stance. Few can deny that advertising is intrinsic to the creation of wealth and many would argue that it has an equally important role in the free and untrammelled expression of ideas, a socially progressive exchange of 'ideas for living', to adapt John Stuart Mill's phrase.[24]

For many who accept the economic inevitability of advertising, its forms and styles provide particular sources of annoyance. 'Pop-up' internet ads and email 'spam' are a continuing irritation for many internet users, and unwanted junk mail annoys millions of householders daily. Roadside poster sites are sometimes accused of polluting the urban environment or even of distracting drivers and causing road accidents. Organizations are often accused of using advertising unethically for commercial advantage. There is periodic press criticism of advertising's role in children's health and moral development.[25] The rise of 'pester power' as a marketing technique and the distortion of childhood values into those of adults[26] are two of the trends that ad agencies have been accused of initiating, or at least exploiting. All these issues reflect concern with the social responsibility, ethics and regulation of advertising (discussed in detail in Chapter 8).

The diversity of views advertising attracts reflects its role at the centre of what Wernick (1991) called 'promotional culture'. Within promotional culture, we grow accustomed to spending significant sums of money on items that are not essential for survival. We associate happiness with consumption, indeed, in

Picture 1   Advertising is a communication medium visible in most social spaces, as in this example of outdoor advertising in New York's Times Square.

(See the colour insert near the middle of this book for a full colour image.)

many ways we define our existence in terms of consumption. As advertising and communication make our continuous consumption of branded items a culturally normal practice, other competing cultural values that encourage abstention from consumption are relatively reduced in status. Today, at least in advanced economies, over-indulgence is the norm and waste is everywhere. Changes in cultural norms and practices of consumption (such as the move towards eating 'fast' food and away from the family-based social ritual of the home-cooked meal) to some extent reflect the influence of promotional culture. Deeply held values and practices are undermined and finally overthrown under the influence of advertising. Advertising's apparent triviality as a sub-category of popular art should not distract us from this powerful cultural influence in framing and changing, as well as reflecting, the way we live.

According to some critics, advertising offers the illusion that one can live 'the good life' by buying material goods (Belk and Pollay, 1985). Yet advertising is also an easy target to blame for the weaknesses which have characterized humanity since its beginnings. Advertising and promotion are, in the end, necessary to economic growth, competition and consumer choice. How we manage the advertising that we make and see has deep implications for the wider world in which we live and it is incumbent on consumers, managers, advertising practitioners and policy makers to have a better understanding of the ways in which advertising wields its influence, in order to make informed choices about advertising policy, regulation and practice. Advertising is both a managerial discipline with profound implications for the wider economy and for the general standard of living, and (arguably) one of the most far-reaching cultural forces of our time.

Brands and Symbolism in Integrated Marketing Communication

The Brand and Marketing Communication

It is important to appreciate advertising's place within an inter-connected tissue of mediated communication.

Marketing communications in general, and advertising in particular, are now seen as *the* major source of competitive advantage in consumer markets (Shimp, 2009). Other elements of the marketing mix occur prior to promotional communication, yet it is the communication which stamps the brand identity on a market. In a world of near-instant communication and fast technology transfer, it is difficult for brand owners to police their global intellectual copyright. The brand has to stand out as a communication, so that consumers will recognize it and actively seek it out for the symbolic values it represents (Gardner and Levy, 1955). In this way, successful branding creates a quasi-monopoly and a basis for charging what economists call 'supernormal' (i.e. higher) prices. In a sense, it is a mere tautology to draw an equivalence between brands and their promotion. After all, many people have never owned a Mercedes, or shaved with Gillette, or walked in Jimmy Choos, but many of those people would be able to describe the brand if asked, and they might buy it if they had the means and the inclination to do so. All the totality of communication about and around a brand informs the way people think about it, and in some mysterious way this communication percolates through to balance sheets.

Decisions on pricing, design, packaging, distribution outlet and even raw materials are taken with one eye on the brand's core values and how these might be perceived in the light of media coverage of the brand. We should note that the term media coverage now includes citizen journalism, internet publications, weblogs and chatroom dialogue, as well as copy produced by professional journalists for established print publications. It is mistaken to argue that communication is all there is to brand marketing (but see Schultz et al., 1993; Wells, 1975), but it is a truism that advertising and marketing communications have assumed a key importance in the destiny of brands and their producing organizations.

Brand Engagement

Advertising alone does not make the brand but the successful consumer brand is, nevertheless, closely identified with its portrayal in advertising and other marketing communications media. The multiplication of media channels through new technology and regulatory change has meant that most aspects of brand marketing management have become tinged with a concern for the potential impact on brand communications and the integrity of the brand personality. For example, measuring 'online brand engagement' has become a priority for brand managers keen to leverage their brand's web presence to best effect, while much effort is devoted to garnering the impact of mobile communications for advertisers (Sharma et al., 2008). Consequently, understanding the symbolic communication of brands has become the key task of brand management. The brand 'image' (see Levy, 1959) has come to represent a dynamic and enduring source of consumer interest (and company revenue) which management are keen to try to shape or control.

Marketing communications do not simply portray brands: they *constitute* those brands in the sense that the meaning of the brand cannot be properly understood in separation from the consumer perceptions of its brand name, logo, advertising, media editorial, its portrayal in entertainment shows, peer comment and the other communications associated with it. Whether brand *a* is better designed, more attractive, easier to use, or more useful than brand *b* is rarely something that can be decided finally and objectively. It is usually to some degree a matter of opinion. This is where advertising acquires its sugges-tive power. It occupies a realm in which consumers are actively seeking sugges-tions to layer consumption with new social significance. Advertisers offer us material to engage our imagination and open up new possibilities for consump-tion experiences. Consumers are not passive dupes being taken in by exagger-ated claims. Advertising is so powerful because, as consumers, we are actively complicit in our own exploitation. We enjoy being sold intangible dreams. We find that life becomes more interesting when one's choice of deodorant or sugar substitute becomes a statement of personal identity and lifestyle aspiration. And of course, on a more practical level, it is the existence of advertising which enables competition and informs consumers about choices.

Functionality and Symbolism of Brands

In order to understand the role of advertising in brand marketing it is important to focus not only on the promotional sales message but also on the symbolic meanings incorporated into the brand (Levy, 1959). Brands have functionality. They do something for consumers, they solve problems. They also have a symbolism which is largely articulated through advertising and promotion. Brands communicate symbolically in the sense that they are signs or combinations of signs (words, music, colours, logos, packaging design, and so on) that convey abstract values and ideas. For consumers, the world of marketing is a kaleidoscope of communication, the component parts of which are impossible to disentangle. When commentators say that marketing and communications are inseparable (Leiss et al., 2005; Schultz et al., 1993: 46; Shimp, 2009: 4), they are making an important point. Every aspect of marketing management (price, distribution, product design) can carry powerfully suggestive symbolism.

BOX 1.4

Functionality, Symbolism and the Social Power of Brands

The functionality of a brand refers to what it does: the symbolism of a brand refers to what it means. The two are not necessarily identical. Advertising is central to the creation and maintenance of the wider symbolic meaning of brands. This wider meaning can give brands a cultural presence which goes beyond purchase and ownership. Brands such as Marlboro, Mercedes-Benz, Gucci, Prada and Rolls-Royce have powerful significance for non-consumers as well as for consumers. Branded items are recognized, and they carry a promise of quality and value. But the symbolic meaning the brand may have for friends, acquaintances and strangers cannot be discounted as a factor in its appeal. For example, a simple item of clothing such as a shirt will sell in far greater numbers if it is bedecked with a logo that confers a symbolic meaning on that item. Wearing a Tommy Hilfiger branded shirt is said to confer prestige on the wearer because of the values of affluence and social privilege the brand represents (Schor, 1998: 47, cited in Szmigin, 2003: 139).

(Cont'd)

Anthropologists have long noted the importance of ownership and the display of prized items for signifying social identity and status in non-consumer societies. In economically advanced societies, brands take this role as a 'cultural resource' (Holt, 2002: 87; see also Belk, 1988; Elliott and Wattanasuwan, 1998; McCracken, 2005) that enables and extends social communication. The influence of brands is such that even resistance to brands has become a defining social position. The 'social power' of brands (Feldwick, 2002a: 11) refers to the meaning that goes beyond functionality and is a symbolic reference point among consumers and non-consumers alike. This symbolic meaning is powerfully framed by advertising and sustained through other forms of communication such as word-of-mouth, public relations, product and brand placement in entertainment media, sponsorship and package design, and through the brand's presence in mobile and internet media.

Marketing is replete with symbolism in many forms. Marketing activities of all kinds can be seen to combine signs that resonate with cultural meanings (Barthes, 2000; Umiker-Sebeok, 1997; Williamson, 1978). The futuristic design of a Dyson vacuum cleaner or the clean, aesthetic lines of an iPod have the powerful appeal of implied values that are very important to the consumer. A Rolex watch might be a well-made jewellery item with time-keeping utility but the Rolex brand is best known as an ostentatious symbol of wealth. Rodeo Drive in Beverly Hills, California, Madison Avenue in New York, and Knightsbridge in London are home to many designer stores because these locations have become culturally identified with prestige retail outlets. The location, as well as the price, carries a powerful symbolism for the brands.

Other Dimensions of Brand Symbolism

Many other aspects of organizational activity not usually categorized as communication can carry particular meanings. Perhaps the most visible aspects of commercial communication for consumers are advertisements placed in **above-the-line** media such as TV, outdoor, the press, cinema or commercial radio. But organizations know that consumers' experience of brands is integrated in a powerful sense: consumers will not normally distinguish between different communication channels when they think of a brand or an organization. So, organizations need to be conscious of the way that their various communications can be interpreted and of how consistent these interpretations may be with those from other communication sources. This is the logic of the Integrated Marketing Communication process (Schultz et al., 1993).

When the UK airline corporation British Airways redesigned the livery on its airplanes at great expense the aim was to offer a stronger and more contemporary corporate image to support other communications and marketing activities. As consumers encounter corporate communications through vehicle liveries, and also through letterhead design, corporate advertising, staff uniforms, telephone conversations with organizational staff and press coverage of the organization's activities, they will assimilate these experiences into their overall understanding of the brand. Corporate identity is a distinct field of research and practice (Melewar and Wooldridge, 2001) but much of its importance lies in the connection consumers make between corporations and their brands in an integrated marketing communications landscape. More broadly still, in advanced economies marketing activity can be responsible for a huge majority of the images we see. The ways in which we interpret, understand and use them are central to our experience of marketing and consumption (Schroeder, 2002).

There are yet more subtle dimensions of communication to consider. In the Veblen effect (Veblen, [1899] 1970), demand for a product reacts inversely with price changes. Price signifies the quality **positioning** of the brand and this can be an important influence on demand for very expensive, prestige items. Although it is anti-competitive for manufacturers to enforce prices on retailers, nonetheless many brand owners do not like to have their product discounted because of the potential threat to consumers' perceptions of quality. The high price of prestige brands is an essential part of their brand positioning. Such brands are seldom discounted because of the fear that such an action will dilute the brand appeal and damage its market positioning. Instead, extending the brand with items of inferior quality sold at a lower price point serves to maximise the brand revenue while retaining the perception of quality.

The architecture and floor design of retail stores can also carry heavy **signification**. In the early 1900s US department store retailers were well aware of the power of impressive architecture in creating environments that inspired consumers to consume (Marchand, 1998). The interior design of retail outlets is also a powerful signifier in the marketing process. Retail organizations often commission detailed research into in-store consumer behaviour in order to help the design to cohere with the brand image of the store and to enhance sales per square foot of floorspace. For some fashion retail brands, such as Abercrombie and Fitch, every detail, from the volume of in-store music (60 decibels) to the look of the 'models' (i.e. retail assistants), is part of the brand symbolism.

As consumers, then, we understand brands holistically by assimilating meanings from many diverse channels of communication. Media editorial, direct mail shots, customer service encounters, television and press advertising and retail store displays, brand logos, product design and price relative to competition all converge to form the consumer's understanding of a given brand. Include word-of-mouth and personal experience of brand usage, and it becomes clear that we cannot normally remember which particular communication or experience was significant in forming our enduring impression of a particular brand.

Brands subsist symbolically as a nebulous and mutable, yet enduring, memory of many kinds of consumer experience. Brands have a tangible, concrete reality, of course; they are created through human and technological processes, they require resources and usually (though not always, as in the case of virtual corporations) occupy office or factory space. But, most importantly, a brand also has a secret life, as symbolic abstraction. This abstraction, the brand image, acts in concert with its more tangible dimensions to frame and support the overall idea of that brand. Many brand marketing organizations try to integrate the various communications channels they use so that they act in harmony and, together, carry coherent and consistent messages about the brand. Doing this makes possible synergy effects by which each medium can leverage the influence of the others, enhancing marketing effectiveness by projecting the brand values and personality more powerfully.

The integrated perspective of this book does not conflate disciplines or media channels that are, rightly, considered by managers to be separate and distinct. Rather, it acknowledges the blurring and convergence of communication media sources in consumers' outlook. It also acknowledges that communications act interdependently: there are synergies that, in the new global media infrastructure, can be exploited by marketing organizations. The assimilation of brand advertising and marketing into mainstream entertainment media, discussed in detail in Chapter 6, is perhaps the most powerful indication of this integrative **synergy** (Hackley, 2003a).

Chapter Summary

Chapter 1 has introduced the topic of advertising and outlined the key themes of the book. It has outlined major changes in the advertising environment which are driving new forms of advertising. These changes are behind a second creative revolution as advertising agencies try to think of creative responses which will keep them at the centre of the brand and marketing communications world. The changes they face focus around the impact of Web 2.0 and mobile communication, the decline in newspaper readership and the fall in television advertising revenue, and the implications for funding models which drive business revenue through advertising.

The chapter also discussed general issues of advertising concerning its economic, social and business function. Finally, the chapter looked at the nature of brands and the importance of advertising and promotion in framing brand symbolism.

Now the topic has been introduced, Chapter 2 will look at the long history of theorizing about advertising.

 ■ **Review Questions**

1 Make a list of all the forms of advertising and promotion that you have encountered or heard of in the last month. Does the list surprise you? Can you think of any social spaces or media that have not yet been exploited by advertisers?

2 After reading this chapter, has your view of advertising's social role changed? Make a list of arguments in favour of advertising and contrast it with a list of arguments against advertising. Convene a study group to discuss their implications: can the opposing viewpoints be reconciled?

3 List all the communication sources you can think of that might potentially influence your perception of a brand. Can you think of ways in which your perception of three brands has been so influenced? In your view, which communications channel was most influential in forming your impression of the brand? Why was this?

4 Gather all the promotional material you can for two brands. What meanings do you feel are implied by the imagery, the typography and the other features of these promotions? Could the meanings be interpreted differently by different people?

CASE

Advertising and Broadcast 'Media Convergence'

The convergence of television and the internet has been predicted for a decade. When it eventually happens, it will have major implications for advertising. 'Interactive' TV has become relatively common via cable channels, with some digital services and limited internet access available to television viewers with digital reception. But most households still have separate units for the internet and television, and the consumer-led idea of programming downloaded according to viewers' schedules is largely unrealized. There is some momentum toward media convergence, since increasing numbers of television shows and movies are being made available and viewed on computers and mobile devices. In the near future, technological convergence will move closer as combined television and PC units will soon reach the mass market. In the longer term, the mobile phone industry will generate a technology platform that will enable mobile devices to fulfil all of a person's communication, entertainment and work needs.

Search giant *Yahoo* is anticipating convergence since it has reached agreement with a number of television manufacturers to make high definition TVs which support *Yahoo*'s online services.[27] This should enable *Yahoo* to generate greater revenue for its advertising, since it will be seen on TV screens, thus reaching wider audiences. In another example of the new broadcast environment for promotional communication, a partnership between Irish rock band The Script and a company called *Clickthrough* has resulted in an interactive music video which, when viewed on a laptop, PC or mobile phone, can generate instant purchase opportunities for brands placed in the video.[28] This is significant because of the increasing use of computers and mobile phones for viewing pop videos. The viewer can run the cursor across the screen to obtain details and/or purchasing information for any item in the video. However, viewing TV clips via mobile or PC devices is still a very small part of total television viewing. Most television is viewed on sets that are not connected to the internet and interactive services are not yet a major part of typical television viewing.

The economic impetus behind broadcast media convergence comes, on the one hand, from the shrinking audiences and advertising revenue for traditional television, and, on the other, the increasing audiences for televisual forms of entertainment via the internet and PC or mobile communication. The internet has powerful potential as a platform for television content and advertising because of its massive audience reach and its capacity for targeting, instant response, and audience measurement. The problem for internet sites is that, while they are attracting an increased proportion of advertising spend, the sums are still relatively small compared to traditional media. Internet advertising in total is experiencing rapid growth and exceeds the advertising revenue of some individual commercial television channels. Internet advertising revenue in the USA exceeded $23 billion in 2008,[29] across banner and display advertising, sponsorship, classified and email. There is a mutual need driving convergence: traditional media need to find ways to access the huge audience traffic of the internet, while internet sites need to tap into some of the platform impact and (still) higher total advertising revenues available from television exposure.

The potential implications of convergence for advertisers, for programme makers, and for audiences, will be profound. There is an expectation that mobile advertising could take off as a massive revenue generator in the near future, but (as discussed in Chapter 10) there are still obstacles to be overcome. These include the lack of a common platform to carry video, text and audio on all mobile devices, and the fact that consumer behaviour around mobile phones currently resists receiving overt advertisements. Mobile phones are carried everywhere, they are always on and they are highly personalized, which gives them obvious potential for carrying advertising. This market is still in early development but is predicted to be worth many billions by 2011. In the longer term, the convergence of mobile and internet delivery with unified receiving devices will generate new media funding models, though it is likely that advertising will play a major part in this, some way or other.

 ■ **Case Questions** ━━━━━━━━━━━━━━━━━━━━━━━━

1 Look up three social networking websites to see how they use click-through or banner advertising. In your opinion, could any of these sites be more attractive either to audiences or to advertisers if they were available via a television screen?

2 Television advertisements are, today, frequently broadcast on *YouTube* or on company websites before they appear on television. In some cases, the internet is the only media channel used. What are the advantages and disadvantages of each medium, TV and internet, for the traditional 20 or 30 second audiovisual advertisement? Are different creative approaches more suited to the TV or the internet for such ads?

3 Design a concept for a social networking website. Current examples include *YouTube*, *Facebook* and *Twitter*. How would you make your concept popular, and, if you were successful in building significant traffic, how do you think you could monetize that traffic ('by selling the site to Google' isn't an acceptable answer).

■ ■ Further Reading ■

Managerial Texts

Belch, G. and Belch, M. (2008) *Advertising and Promotion: An Integrated Marketing Communications Perspective*, 8th edn. New York: McGraw Hill.

Fill, C. (2009) *Marketing Communications: Interactivity, Communication and Content*, 5th edn. Essex: Pearson.

Percy, L. and Elliott, R. (2009) *Strategic Advertising Management*, 3rd edn. Oxford: Oxford University Press.

Pickton, D. and Broderick, A. (2005) *Integrated Marketing Communications*. London: Pearson Education.

Socio-Cultural Perspectives

Cook, G. (2001) *The Discourse of Advertising*. London: Routledge.

Leiss, W., Kline, S., Jhally, S. and Botterill, J. (2005) *Social Communication in Advertising: Consumption in the Mediated Marketplace*, 3rd edn. London: Routledge.

McFall, L. (2004) *Advertising: A Cultural Economy*. London: Sage.

Web-based Resources

Brand communication consultancy: www.symbolism.org/about/html

A database of advertising slogans: www.adslogans.co.uk

The UK account planning group: www.apg.org.uk

The UK advertising regulator, the Advertising Standards Authority: www.asa.org

A site by branding consultancy Interbrand: www.brandchannel.com

Media resource called the National Readership Survey of Britain: www.nrs.co.uk

UK-based media research resource called the Broadcast Audience Research Board: www.barb.co.uk

University of Texas advertising teaching resource: http://advertising.utexas.edu

Duke University advertising history resource: http://scriptorium.lib.duke.edu/adaccess/

Advertising Trade Press

Campaign magazine: www.brandrepublic.com
Advertising Age magazine: www.adage.com
Admap: www.admapmagazine.com

Professional Associations

UK advertising association: www.adassoc.org.uk
American Advertising Federation: www.aaf.org
American Association of Advertising Agencies: www.aaaa.org/eweb/
   startpage.aspx
UK Institute of Practitioners in Advertising: http://www.ipa.co.uk/

Some Useful Academic Sources

These can normally be obtained through academic libraries and electronic databases.

Advances in Consumer Research (Proceedings of the Association of Consumer Research: downloads are available at www. vancouver.wsu.edu/acr/home.htm or www.acrwebsite.org

European Journal of Marketing
International Journal of Advertising
Journal of Advertising
Journal of Advertising Research
Journal of Consumer Research
Consumption, Markets and Culture
Journal of Current Issues and Research in Advertising
Journal of Marketing

On the Companion Website

These journal articles are freely available on the companion website (www.sagepub.co.uk/hackley).

Living with Ambivalence: Attitudes to Advertising in Postmodern Times
Stephanie O'Donohoe
Marketing Theory, Mar 2001; vol.1: pp. 91–108.

Currencies of Commercial Exchange: Advertising Agencies and the Promotional Imperative
Anne M. Cronin
Journal of Consumer Culture, Nov 2004; vol. 4: pp. 339–360.

Sustainable Communication and the Dominant Social Paradigm: Can they be Integrated?
William E. Kilbourne
Marketing Theory, Sep 2004; vol. 4: pp. 187–208.

Notes

1   In the UK, the London *Evening Standard* is facing difficulties in the face of competition from free newspapers, and was recently bought out by an owner willing to take on its debts. The decline in the financial viability of US newspapers has reached a crisis point with websites such as this one, www.newspaperdeathwatch.com/category/advertising chronicling the problem (accessed 1 April 2009). The *San Francisco Herald* is perhaps the most prominent US newspaper to face possible closure due to declining advertising revenue: www.ajr.org/Article.asp?id=4404 (accessed 1 April 2009).

2   www.businessinsider.com/2008/5/found-the-ad-agency-that-produced-those-stealth-coors-ads-on-youtube (accessed 8 April 2009); 'Found: the ad agency that produced those stealth coors ads on YouTube', by Michael Learmonth: *Silicon Valley Insider*, 28 May 2008.

3   'Love is all around', *The Independent*, Tuesday 7 April 2009, *Independent Life* supplement, p. 2.

4   http://fuelingnewbusiness.com/2008/04/21/ad-agencies-need-to-blog-for-new-business/#comment-1439 (accessed 26 March 2009). See also the rise in the awareness of blogging as a marketing strategy, in Hackley (2009a:124).

5   For example, this website expounds on the freemium concept: www.avc.com/a_vc/2006/03/the_freemium_bu.html (accessed 26 March 2009).

6   Wunderman London, a direct marketing agency which has broadened its remit to offer above-the-line advertising, gives away case material and position papers on its website to elicit client interest: www.wunderman.com/pick-our-brains.aspx

7   '@Twitter: we'd really like to buy you' by Stephen Foley, *The Independent*, Saturday 4 April 2009, p. 29.

8   See also the *Twitter* case vignette in Chapter 10.

9   www.wunderman.com/wunderman-london.aspx (accessed 26 March 2009).

10 'Beale C on advertising: the best agencies get creative in hard times', *The Independent* 15 December 2008 www.independent.co.uk/news/media/advertising/claire-beale-on-advertising-the-best-agencies-get-creative-in-hard-times-1066698.html

11 'What is a social-media agency?' *Advertising Age* adage.com/digitalnext/post?article_id=133785 (accessed 30 March 2009), blog post by Reuben Steiger.

12 www.cbsnews.com/stories/2006/04/12/earlyshow/main1491494.shtml: Digital Product Placement story 'New stealth TV ads assailed' by Brian Dakss (accessed 26 March 2009).

13 'A fiscal stimulus for advertising spending', *The Independent*, Wednesday 25 March, 2009, p. 37.

14 It would be a mistake to suppose that a social marketing campaign would be any less politically sensitive than a commercial one. A recent anti-obesity campaign for the Department of Health pictured children playing computer games, perhaps a less obvious creative strategy than pictures of them eating fattening foods. The visual was supposed to imply that exercise was preferable to gaming as a leisure activity for children. According to the magazine *Private Eye* (no. 1232, 2 April 2009, p. 9) the Department of Health campaign is supported by various industry bodies including Business 4 Life, which *Private Eye* reports is a coalition of companies that includes Coca Cola, Cadbury, Kellogg's, PepsiCo and Nestlé, but no computer games companies.

15 www.youtube.com

16 www.visit4info.com

17 It may be a mistake to suggest that grass is somehow more natural than advertising. The rolling lawns of golf course fairways or hotel grounds are often featured in advertisements and have been designed partly for their visual appeal, while fans of televised sports are used to the pristine green swathes of the sporting field being turned into advertising by the technique of superimposing a giant sponsor's logo or club crest on the field during coverage.

18 'Whassup interj. American slang word meaning "Hello", from "What's up?" used especially as a greeting to someone you know well', in Longman's *Dictionary of Contemporary English*, 2001, cited in (2003) *DDB London Works*, p. 23; published in Oxfordshire by World Advertising Research Centre.

19 View the ad on www.t-mobile.co.uk/dance/ (accessed on 29 March 2009).

20 http://www.fallon.com/

21 View the ad at http://www.guardian.co.uk/media/video/2009/jan/23/cadbury-eyebrow-ad (accessed 30 March 2009).

22 *'Le pub tue'* ('ads kill') and *'Le pub pue'* ('ads stink'): see report in UK newspaper *The Independent*, Thursday, 11 March 2004: 23, 'French charge 62 activists over war on "brainless ads"'.

23 Described in Michael Moore's book, *Stupid White Men*, Penguin Books, 2002, p. 111.

24 John Stuart Mill, *On Liberty*, Penguin Books, 1982.

25 For example, UK *Sunday Times*, 6 July 2003, '"Unhealthy" food ads for young face ban'. UK *Sunday Times*, 31 August 2003, 'Junk food ads face children's TV ban'.

26 Described on a UK BBC2 TV show, *Little Women*, broadcast on 29 March 2001.

27 'Yahoo signs deals to crack TV market', London *Evening Standard*, Thursday 8 January 2009, p. 33.

28 www.clikthrough.com/theater/video/1 (accessed 1 April 2009).

29 www.iab.net/about_the_iab/recent_press_releases/press_release_archive/press_release/pr-033009 (accessed 3 May 2009).

2 Theorizing Advertising and Promotion

Chapter Outline

This chapter is organized around two overlapping traditions of advertising theory. One tradition, labelled information processing theory, uses cognitive science as its point of reference and models advertising as if it were a mediated sales conversation. The other tradition, referred to here as socio-cultural or interpretive theory, refers to disciplines such as anthropology, sociology and literary theory for its key concepts and perspectives. The chapter highlights some of the continuing contradictions raised by advertising theory as it plays out both in academia and professional practice.

Key chapter content:

- why theorize advertising and promotion?
- different stakeholders in advertising theory
- practice-based advertising theory
- information processing theory in advertising
- strong and weak theories of advertising effect
- socio-cultural theory in advertising
- meanings and messages in advertisements
- theorizing meaning in advertising
- the context of advertising and promotion
- levels of explanation in advertising and promotion.

Why Theorize Advertising and Promotion?

Business people, marketing and advertising professionals included, rarely have much time for theory. Theory is popularly understood as a synonym for the complex, esoteric, or abstract. The term 'in theory' is often used in a pejorative sense to refer to ideas that are seen as irrelevant, impractical or obscure. But theory can be seen in another, more constructive way. It can be viewed as a form of everyday understanding that allows us a sense of control over our world and, sometimes, helps us to predict outcomes based on previous experience or well-grounded assumptions. Rudimentary theories allow us to understand our world in ways that are not possible if we are solely concerned with concrete experience. We all live by implicit theories: knowing that rain gets you wet therefore you should put on a coat before you leave the house may strike you as obvious, but it involves an abstraction from particular experiences of getting wet and it informs our behaviour. It may not be as complex as a theory of relativity but it is the kind of theorizing that most of us are more familiar with.

Practical theory guides behaviour and action in the workplace even though it may be implicit rather than explicit. In one study (Kover, 1995) creative professionals in advertising worked to differing implicit theories of communication, which guided their approach to addressing creative briefs and solving communications problems. In another study (Hackley, 2003b) account team professionals worked to differing implicit models of the consumer. These models implied quite different ways of understanding, and therefore of communicating with, consumers.

Theorizing allows us to use our imagination to move from the concrete to the abstract. We can compare and combine ideas and speculate on new ways of understanding the world. Our understanding of any social phenomenon requires some theoretical dimension in order to raise it beyond the trivial. One can say without fear of contradiction that books are made up of printed words, but to compare different books and to offer views on their qualities one has to invoke implicit theories of, say, prose style ('this book is well written'), theories of narrative ('the plot was exciting') or theories of dramatic characterization ('the characters were not believable'). We have an opinion of what constitutes good writing or effective characterization even though we may not be at all familiar with the intellectual traditions of literary criticism.

Advertising is a field particularly concerned with human communication, thought and behaviour. As we shall see in this chapter, academic theory in advertising has drawn on the disciplines of cognitive psychology, sociology, anthropology, cybernetics, mathematics, communication science and literary theory. Advertising professionals are practical people who develop experience in particular areas and know what works for them in given situations, but advertising as a category can hardly be spoken of at all without some implicit theoretical assumptions to guide us. In this book, then, theory is not considered as a byword for obscurity. At a rudimentary but decidedly non-trivial level it simply allows us to articulate the world in ways that go beyond the unimportant or the obvious.

Different Stakeholders in Advertising Theory

Advertising remains an enigma in spite of its 100-year history of practice, thought, theory and research. Its social role, for good or ill, is hotly contested. Even though most of us are very used to seeing advertisements, some advertisements still have a capacity to generate offence and provoke debate around advertising's moral values and social influence. As consumers, we do not agree about advertising. From the practitioner side, too, there are stark disagreements about how, and indeed if, advertising 'works' (see Vakratsas and Ambler, 1999); in what ways it influences consumers (or doesn't) (Ehrenberg et al., 2002); and on how advertising budgets should be spent most efficiently. Academic theories tend to complicate rather than clarify practitioner debates about advertising's practical consequences. It must be admitted, though, that the advertising industry has enjoyed global growth and influence on a huge scale in spite of uncertainty about its theoretical foundations.

There are political currents around advertising which shape the kinds of discourse, and the kinds of research, which go on. Advertising has to serve many stakeholders, including main board executives, shareholders, advertising agencies, consumers, regulators, governments and citizens. It applies in many different situations. As a communication form it is complex, since it can combine music, visual imagery and written or spoken words in a huge variety of narrative forms and on a wide range of media channels. It speaks to a variety of quite different demographic, ethnic, socio-economic and lifestyle groups. The idea that advertising 'works' in one way in all conditions is clearly an oversimplification. Practitioners seem to manage well enough without theory. Agencies, though, are always looking for a competitive edge and theory often lends itself to claims that one agency can deliver better value for the client's advertising budget. Cornelissen and Lock (2002) have argued that theoretical developments in advertising do influence practice, not always by changing it but by supplying new conceptual vocabularies to articulate practice.

Theorizing Implicit Communication and Low-attention Processing

One of the most intractable problems facing advertising theorists has been finding a popular and accessible way to theorize both its explicit and implicit elements. Human face-to-face communication has been shown to be about the gestures, vocal tone, emotional timbre, poise and gravitas, facial expression and social context, as well as about the verbal content. The speeches of American President Barack Obama have excited renewed interest in the classical arts of oratory and rhetoric, and offer contemporary evidence that the force of communication lies as much in what is implicit, as in what is explicit verbal content. Words are important; they are the infrastructure around which persuasive arguments are built. But what listeners take from such communication is not determined solely by the words, by any means.

BOX 2.0

Miscommunication in Advertising

In an oft-told story of advertising miscommunication, a 1950s cigarette brand was advertised in the UK with cinema ads. The ads featured an actor alone on London Bridge at night, mock heroically lighting up a Strand cigarette to the accompanying strapline, 'You're never alone with a Strand'. The brand failed to sell and it transpired that cinema audiences felt that the user was a lonely soul who couldn't find friends. To ad agency types familiar with Hollywood movie heroes such as Humphrey Bogart, it seemed inconceivable that cigarette smoking could be seen as anything but the act of a streetwise tough guy whose heroic destiny was to be alone. The audience decoded a different meaning from the one the agency had planned to encode into the message. The reason for the miscommunication was not known: it may have been the actor was unconvincing as a hero, or the clothes, the set or the props – all may have undermined the intended effect. Today such a mistake would be unlikely to happen. Most major advertising campaigns are carefully pre-tested on trial audiences before their launch. The story reveals the subtlety and indeterminacy of meaning in advertising communication. It also illustrates the truism that the people who make advertisements are different to the audiences at whom they are aimed.

The importance of the implicit in communication may seem self-evident, yet the concept which has dominated research in advertising has been the idea of a clear, explicit, verbalized and unproblematic 'message'. Of what, though, this message is comprised is hard to say. As noted in the previous chapter, advertising can be seen as a form of 'social communication' (Leiss et al., 2005) which operates on many dimensions. As a complex communication form, advertising can be understood not only in terms of an engineering model of 'information' transmission, but also in terms of a vehicle of meaning which is interpreted in symbolic ways by different audiences (McCracken, 1987: Sherry, 1987).

Advertising theory, both practitioner and academic, has tended to privilege the verbalized content of promotional 'messages' and underplay the elements of communication which are implicit, or those to which conscious attention is not paid (Heath and Feldwick, 2008). One reason for this is that it is, simply, easier to conceive of advertising as a verbal message which is processed consciously by individual receivers. Another reason is that acknowledging the implicit elements of advertising and promotion opens up controversial issues of 'subliminal' or hidden influence. Much advertising theory has been conceived with one eye on the latent public unease articulated by Vance Packard's (1957) idea of advertisers as 'hidden persuaders' engaged in a sinister and underhand manipulation (Hackley, 2007). A focus on the rational, the conscious and the verbal, deflects the charge of manipulation quite neatly, but at the considerable price of over-simplifying the subject matter.

This chapter offers a brief outline of the historical development of practice-based theory in advertising before discussing the two, main, overlapping theoretical traditions in the field, that is, information processing, on the one hand, and socio-cultural approaches on the other.

Practice-based Advertising Theory

'Reason Why' and 'USP' Advertising

The surprising thing about advertising theory is that, in spite of the volume of academic and practitioner research, significant elements of it have changed little in a century. Early advertising theory was based on direct experience, though informed by psychological studies. It was focused mainly on improving practice. John E. Kennedy (1904) is credited with one of the earliest attempts when he wrote that advertising was 'salesmanship in print'. Kennedy was at the Lord and Thomas agency, later to become the biggest agency of its era in the world. This was where American advertising pioneer Albert D. Lasker started the first school of advertising copywriting[1] drawing on Kennedy's principles. Kennedy subsequently developed the 'reason why' approach to copywriting (Fox, 1984), a technique which led to Rosser Reeves's idea of the Unique Selling Proposition (USP) some decades later (McDonald and Scott, 2007). The USP is the single thing that gives the consumer a reason to buy. The proposition is based around this reason to buy, and should be the unequivocal message a consumer interprets from the advertisement. The 'proposition' is still the key concept in the creative advertising development process today (Heath and Feldwick, 2008). Kennedy's (1904) analogy between (print) advertising and personal selling has proved equally enduring.

Other well-known developments in practitioner theory for advertising include Bill Bernbach's emphasis on creativity, David Ogilvy's 'brand personality' and Leo Burnett's use of dramatic realism. Creativity-based ideas about effective advertising execution form one side of a divide in advertising theory. Also known as 'soft sell', compelling creativity is thought to establish and build the brand equity, anthropomorphizing the brand in value terms which stimulate responses of affection, and perhaps loyalty, from consumers. The other side, the 'hard sell' theories, are based on the idea that advertising can sell a product in the same way as a salesperson in a face-to-face sales encounter. Hard sell theories follow the tradition of Kennedy and Reeves, and the equally noted Claude Hopkins (McDonald and Scott, 2007).

The A-I-D-A Model of Sales Communication

Practitioners in advertising soon incorporated academic work to lend a scientific gravitas to their theories. Possibly the most successful exponent was John B. Watson. Watson (1924) was a behavioural psychologist who applied his learning theory to a successful career in advertising with J. Walter Thompson and later the William Esty agency (Bogart, 1966). Watson's ideas about behavioural reinforcement may have fallen out of vogue long ago, but of all the advertising theorists, Edward Strong (1929) and Harry D. Kitson (1921) can probably claim the longest legacy. Strong's book, *The Psychology of Selling*, and Kitson's (1921) *The Mind of the Buyer* melded psychological principles to evolving work in theories of personal selling. Their work added some scientific starch to a rudimentary theory of persuasive communication which is still repeated in almost every textbook on advertising and marketing, including this one. The Attention–Interest–Desire–Action (A–I–D–A) model for personal selling, adapted to advertising, remains by far the most influential theory in the field. Before examining A–I–D–A in more detail, it is worth outlining the information processing tradition in advertising communication theory.

Information Processing Theory in Advertising

The Shannon-Weaver Communication Model

'Information processing' is a term which sums up a vast tradition of advertising theory. It encompasses not only a theory of communication but also a theory of human cognition. There are many variations on the information processing theme, but they all share key assumptions about human communication, persuasion and advertising. The information processing model was originally

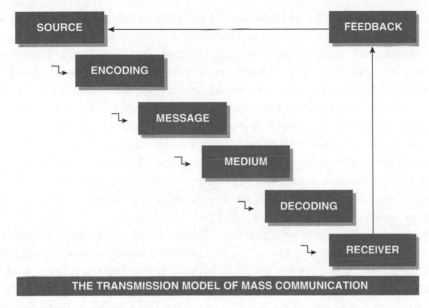

Figure 2.0   The classic transmission model of mass communication

devised to model the mathematical efficiency of technical communication channels (Shannon, 1948; Weaver and Shannon, 1963). Applied to human communication, the theory assumes that humans 'process' data in much the same way as computers or other machines. It is also called the 'transmission' model since data are transmitted to the receiver. There are many variations on the model but its basic components remain the same. There is a sender, or a 'source', and a receiver. The message is encoded into a form which allows transmission, then is sent via a medium or channel of communication to be decoded by the receiver. There is a feedback loop in the model, so that it can be determined whether or not the message was efficiently delivered. If the message was encoded accurately, and transmitted via the correct medium, the only reason for miscommunication would be 'noise', which refers to anything which interferes with the transmission or decoding/encoding process.

Whether the classic information processing model (Figure 2.0) is appropriate for human communication is a highly contested matter. Nevertheless, in most marketing textbooks and those of many other disciplines including communication studies, it is reproduced faithfully and presented as if none of its key elements nor its founding metaphor are in any way problematic.

The Transmission Model and Mass Communication

The 'transmission' model of communication was adopted and adapted by many disciplines, especially by mass communication theorists such as

Schramm (1948), Katz and Lazarsfeld (1955), Lazarsfeld (1941) and Lasswell (1948). It is easy to see how the analogy could apply to advertising. An advertisement can be conceived as a message, especially if one refers to the ideas of Kennedy and Hopkins. The message, conceived as the proposition, has to be encoded by the sender (the advertising agency creative team) into a form which will be decoded successfully by the receiver, who is of course the consumer. Encoding will put the message into a form in which communication is possible on the available media channels. In Kennedy's day, this would consist of print advertising. With the development of broadcast media it would be possible to include sound and moving pictures. The receiver has to decode the same message which the advertisers encoded into the communication in order to retrieve the meaning intended (see Figure 2.0).

The surrounding environment may have 'noise' of various forms that distracts from the message. Noise can be construed metaphorically as anything that might disrupt the communication by, say, distracting the attention of the receiver. In an aural communication it may be literal noise that disrupts the communicative process. With visual communications such as roadside advertising poster sites, noise may be all the activities of an urban road that might distract a person's attention from the poster, such as pedestrians, cars, shops, stray dogs or whatever.

This simple conceptualization has many descriptive uses. It has been a mainstay of marketing communications and advertising texts because of its economy and descriptive scope. It can be applied to almost any communications scenario and will have a degree of applicability. As noted above, the idea of the 'proposition' based on a verbalized message which the advertiser wants the individual consumer to take away from the advertisement still drives most creative briefs. As a practical construct it has proved most effective. But as a theoretical explanation for what is happening in advertising communication it has its limitations. A model is no more than a textual representation that captures by analogy some, but by no means all, of the features of the phenomenon it purports to represent. In other words, models as theoretical representations have weaknesses. Before discussing these in more detail, though, we will revisit the A–I–D–A model of persuasive advertising communication. This maps easily onto the classic information processing model of communication because of its linearity and its cognitive focus, and has generated a host of variations which fall under the category 'hierarchy-of-effects theories' in advertising.

A–I–D–A and Hierarchy-of-Effects Theories

The classic information processing model of communication provided theoretical support for Strong's (1925) A–I–D–A model of persuasion in selling encounters as mentioned above. Simply, the idea is that the consumer's

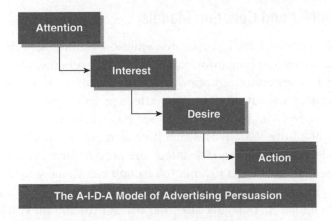

Figure 2.1   The A–I–D–A model of advertising persuasion

attention is required for a sale to take place. Following that, the salesperson has to generate interest in order to keep that attention. The next stage in the persuasive process is to elicit a desire for the product or service being sold. Finally, the action required is a sale (see Figure 2.1).

The A–I–D–A model assumes that consumers are essentially indifferent to the offer and need to have their attention grabbed. After that, they (and we) have to be pushed along a continuum of persuasion until we buy the product. When the A–I–D–A model is conceived in terms of mass communication to thousands or millions of potential consumers through advertising, this process can be seen in terms of a gradual and incremental effect. As consumers we have many communications competing for our attention. If an advertiser wants to sell us a new product or service, then on this model they first have to get our attention. This could take many attempts – we might view an advertisement many times before we find ourselves sufficiently interested to pay explicit attention to it. Once we have done that it may take many more exposures, or even many more campaigns, to elicit our interest, evoke our desire for the brand, and finally to provoke us into actually acting on the message by purchasing the advertised brand.

The logic of A–I–D–A, extrapolated from a face-to-face sales conversation to a mass advertising market, takes the human consumer as an entity which is resistant to persuasion but susceptible to a successive accretion of persuasive inputs. In other words, we are persuaded to accept the sales message as our resistance is gradually undermined by the accumulation of messages. The 'hierarchy-of-effect' represents 'compounding probabilities' (Percy et al., 2001: 36), as each step in the process is a necessary condition for the subsequent step. The 'hierarchy-of-effects' tradition has spawned many theories which are designed to improve the efficiency and effectiveness of campaign planning (Barry and Howard, 1990; see also Lavidge and Steiner, 1961; Rossiter et al., 1991; Vaughn, 1986).

Cognition, Affect and Conation Models

Some theory variations have incorporated emotion, humour or other intangible elements into an over-arching information processing scheme. One well-known generic model incorporated emotionality into purchase decisions by using a three-stage conceptualization: cognitive, affective and conative, known colloquially as 'think–feel–do' (for discussions see Bagozzi et al., 1979; Barnard and Ehrenberg, 1997; Lutz, 1977). The cognitive element persuades the consumer on a rational level by including facts about the product or service qualities. The affective dimension gets the consumer to respond emotionally to the appeal, by, say, including images of attractive, happy families or by making the consumer laugh, and therefore encouraging affection toward the brand. Finally, conation refers to the behaviour elicited by the advertisements, for example by including a direct-response coupon or telephone number for the customer to call.

Many car advertisements seem to conform to the cognitive (thinking) affective (feeling) and conative (doing) model when they picture a beautiful car to strike at the prospect's sense of aesthetics and aspiration, slot in an attractive driver or happy family to promote projective identification and elicit desire, underpin the picture with detailed information about petrol consumption and speed, and finally add a direct response mechanism for the consumer to send off for a brochure or apply for a test drive.

The think–feel–do scheme tells us why many ads combine rational with emotional appeals. It cannot tell us however which of those appeals will prove more powerful or what the right balance of rational–emotional appeal should be to create a successful advertisement. Some drivers will buy a car for its colour, some for its speed, some for its practicality. Many are influenced by the brand image, and many drivers will buy the same brand of car repeatedly even though there are many others from which to choose which will perform equally well. Clearly, there is no formula which fits every model or every buyer. As this book is being written the car industry is facing its most challenging market conditions in a century, with many major global manufacturers under the threat of bankruptcy because of a global collapse in demand for new cars. It takes more than advertising to stimulate a purchase.

Advantages of Information Processing Theory

The information processing model and its associated theories of persuasion, notably A–I–D–A and the other hierarchy-of-effect family of theories, have many advantages. One is that they allow the complexity of advertising communication to be reduced to a simplified and easily recollected model which appears to fit any communication scenario. The shared assumptions of A–I–D–A and information processing theory mean that any construct of cognitive psychology can be the subject of research into 'intermediate' advertising effects. For example, attention is a sub-field of psychological research and theory with relevance for this model. So are the psychological research fields of memory, attitude, emotion and behaviour.

Research into intermediate advertising effects focuses on the elements which, according to the information processing model, are sequentially necessary in order for persuasion to take place. For example, it is assumed that if consumers like an advertisement because of its humour they are more likely to respond emotionally to the brand, and therefore more likely to change their attitude from negative or indifferent to positive. The assumption is that a purchase is then more likely to result. Many studies are conducted on consumer memory to try to understand which advertising formats prompt the best recall scores, on the assumption that remembering an ad is a stage in the process leading to a purchase.

Advertising agencies typically conduct research on any given advertisement before they launch the campaign. They will show the ad to a selected audience. Using semantic scale questionnaires or electronic response devices they will try to measure audience or individual response on scales of attitudes and recall. If the scores are high enough, the campaign is launched. If they are not, then alternative creative executions are sought. An example of academic research in advertising which adapts the information processing metaphor of human cognition includes Keller et al. (1998) who sought to uncover the generalized cognitive mechanisms underlying the relationship between advertising and attitude, memory and behaviour. MacInnis and Jaworski (1989) sought an integrative scheme for research, using the information processing approach to study consumer responses to advertisements. Advertising science is a huge enterprise commanding vast resources. In Chapter 9 we will look in more detail at research in advertising. For the present the point to note is that the information processing approach is the metaphor governing much of this research.

Information processing models of communication originated in research into electronics and cybernetics. The metaphor between machine information processing and human cognition is compelling and has generated rich veins of theory and research, as well as supporting practice. But it also has its limitations.

Criticisms of the Information Processing Tradition of Advertising Theory

The use of information processing models of communication in advertising has been criticized on many grounds (see Stern, 1993a, for an overview). Their usefulness as a teaching device for advertising and marketing education has been questioned (e.g. Buttle, 1994) because of the extent to which they oversimplify the ways in which, as consumers or viewers, we engage with advertising.

The questionable assumption that the various elements of sender, encoding, decoding and message are self-evident and unproblematic is made without examination not only in marketing texts but also in many communications texts and theories. There is a common assumption that models of one-to-one, one-way communication can be applied unproblematically to mass communication and even interactive communication contexts. Another criticism refers to the reliance of information processing models of communication and persuasion on explicit, verbalized information and the undivided attention of the viewer (Heath and Feldwick, 2008). As we will see later in this chapter, there are theories which focus on the implicit content of advertising communication or non-attentive processing.

The Man–Machine Communication Metaphor

We have seen that information processing theories of communication and persuasion originated to model machine and not human communication. This metaphor may only go so far. Human cognition differs from machine information processing in important respects. For example, information processing models are linear and sequential. They assume that each stage of the communication process occurs in sequence, one stage after the other. Advanced research in artificial intelligence has modelled serial as opposed to **linear information processing**: computers can process input data through more than one channel at a time. Intuitively, we know that paying attention to more than one sensory input at a time is difficult for a human, but it is certainly possible. It is easy to argue that most advertising is screened out at the attention stage. But is it really? Do advertisements occupy some part of our peripheral vision and hearing, even if we are paying more explicit attention to something else?

Advertising and the Social Context

A–I–D–A and the hierarchy-of-effects models of advertising persuasion tend to focus on a single advertisement seen by an individual consumer, which is not surprising given that they were developed from a model of face-to-face sales communication and later adapted to mass advertising communication. Some authors have pointed out that advertising is seldom viewed by an individual in an experimental viewing booth. More typically, advertisements are seen in social contexts, in the company of other communications and, often, in the company of other people. What is more, they are often the subject of social interaction. Indeed, one of the key elements of success for advertising is to make an ad that is talked about (Dichter, 1949, 1966). Consequently, some researchers have argued that advertising is better understood as a social, rather than a cognitive phenomenon (Ritson and Elliott, 1999).

The Passive Consumer and One-way Communication

Another much-criticized aspect of the information processing model is its assumption that advertising communication occurs mainly in one direction towards a passive consumer who will accept or reject an unambiguous message. This leads to another criticism, which is that, in information processing and hierarchy-of-effects theories of advertising persuasion, the message and the meaning of the advertisement are synonymous. In other words, there is no theoretical scope for consumers to interpret the ad in unexpected ways, or in ways which vary between consumers. Finally, there is a key assumption that the object of any advertising campaign is a sale. As we have noted, sales, at least in the short or medium term, may not always be the best measure of a campaign's success. Some of the socio-cultural theories of advertising discussed later respond to some degree to these criticisms, though they suffer from being far less accessible than the information processing theories.

Strong and Weak Theories of Advertising Effect

Before discussing socio-cultural theories, there is another informal theory of advertising which is relevant here. The distinction between advertising and promotion which is designed to sell product, and advertising which is designed to build brand presence, has been expressed in terms of 'strong' and 'weak' (Jones, 1990). A popular analogy we have already noted expresses the same idea in terms of 'hard sell' and 'soft sell'. Theories of advertising which assume that its main purpose is to persuade a potential customer (a 'prospect' in sales jargon) to buy, are called strong theories. This category refers to the information processing models and A–I–D–A. Theories which assume that advertising cannot usually persuade a non-buyer to become a buyer but, instead, can build the brand equity and create a competitive presence which reassures existing buyers, are called 'weak' theories.

For many clients, a campaign only works if the sales graph spikes upwards within a few days of the campaign launch. This direct, causal relationship between advertising and sales is what is implied in the strong theory metaphor. Campaigns do often result in sales increases, but the causal link between the advertisement and the sale can never be proven definitively, even though the circumstantial evidence that advertising caused the sales increase may seem compelling. There will always be other possible causal variables influencing purchase patterns, such as seasonality, changes in disposable income and topical events. What is more, there may be a considerable time-lag between the campaign and the sales increase.

Advertising as Publicity

Many contemporary ads eschew the 'strong' sales pitch format in favour of a less direct narrative which is designed to build long-term brand equity, and to remind or to reassure existing customers. Ehrenberg et al. (2002) have suggested that advertising seldom actually persuades a non-buyer to buy in the short term, but more typically acts like publicity to reassure existing buyers that the brand remains relevant and current. It is easy to see how this could translate into sales through mass communication to markets of millions of people. As we have noted above, short-term memory only accommodates six or seven pieces of information, so consumer choice sets are limited. Brands have to ensure that they have a place in this choice set by reminding consumers that the brand remains salient and relevant to their lifestyle. Many car brand ads for, say, BMW or Mercedes-Benz, evince general brand values because consumers may only buy that car brand once or twice in a lifetime, if at all. They need to be consistently reminded of the brand's relevance and values for the time when they might be in a position to buy.

A great deal of theory in advertising has been devoted to understanding persuasion (O'Shaughnessy and O'Shaughnessy, 2004). But there is a question of what persuasion in advertising entails. Does it entail directly changing someone's attitude or behaviour through the force of reasoning? Or does it mean presenting brands in a generally persuasive light by inferring that they enhance personal lifestyle and frame social identity (see Elliott and Wattanasuwan, 1998)? Weak theories of advertising assume that the advertising cause and the sales effect are far less directly linked than strong theories. Ads may exercise influence over long periods of time, they may be designed to influence parties other than buyers or potential buyers (such as shareholders or employees) and they may be intended simply to remind consumers that the brand is still around and still relevant. In many consumer markets, the only way a brand can hope to compete is to match competitors' advertising expenditure (or **adspend**). If they do not, the consumer might infer that their brand is somehow second-rate or less serious than the more heavily advertised brands.

An important function of branding is that it is a badge of reassurance for the consumer (Feldwick, 2002a). Consumers are often insecure about making difficult purchase decisions. None of us wants to get our purchase home to find that it is defective in any way or that our peers regard it with disdain. Brand names offer reassurance for the consumer that the purchase we have made is safe in the sense that the brand is credible and the quality good. Brand advertising, then, supports this sense of reassurance by reminding consumers that the brand is current, relevant and successful.

The Limitations and Advantages of Mediated Communication

The power and the limitations of ads need to be understood in terms of the intrinsic limitation of mediated communication to directly persuade individuals. Individual consumers seldom leave their living-room immediately after seeing an ad to buy the product at the nearest store. Advertising simply places a brand in the consumer's **awareness** in association with certain contrived values and qualities. In this weak role, advertising may portray brands in persuasive ways but their main task is not persuasive: it is to provide reassurance.

This weak, reminding role is important since advertising does not engage with consumers singly but collectively. Advertising is, in many senses, a social experience (Ritson and Elliott, 1999). It draws on cultural reference points that subsist in interactive social contexts. Large numbers of consumers are exposed to ads. It is statistically likely that a proportion may be thinking of purchasing a particular category of product or service. The brand then has a positive presence in the consumer's set of choices when they are next in a position to buy that product category.

BOX 2.1

Whassup with Weak Advertising Appeals?

Anheuser-Busch has used various creative approaches to promote their Budweiser beer brand, for instance with ads that emphasized the brewing process and highlighted the intrinsic quality of the beer ('King of Beers'). They have also drawn on its American provenance to position the brand in an heroic light. More recent campaigns have shifted the positioning somewhat to broaden the appeal. One campaign placed the beer as a minor set prop in a narrative form that appeared to be more like a movie clip than a TV ad. One execution had a set of apparently Afro-American friends going about their domestic business and greeting each other with an increasingly loud cry of 'Whassup?!'. The characters are in a variety of situations familiar in TV domestic dramas or situation comedies: watching TV, working at a computer, bringing shopping home (a bag of Budweiser), talking to a lover on the telephone. The brand was implicated in the plot as the choice of working professionals of any ethnic origin but with an authenticity coming from their use of street slang, street clothes and love of TV sport. The ads hinted that the brand itself had the same authenticity as the characters ('Budweiser. True').

(Cont'd)

'Whassup' became a popular catchword attracting much media comment and coverage, extending the audience for the brand. A website was set up to exploit the popularity of the advertising and to allow people to download ads and screensavers. While beer ads generally seek out an audience of 18–50 year old males, the creative appeal of these particular ads clearly included but reached beyond beer drinkers. They showed an awareness that a brand is a social construction in the sense that it has a cultural meaning which is not confined to its target audience, but is informed by the ideas and associations brought to the brand by non-consuming social groups.

Socio-cultural Theory in Advertising

While the information processing communication theories and hierarchy-of-effects tradition have been the most influential, advertising agencies also make considerable use of socio-cultural theory in their practice. Many agencies employ **account planners** and researchers with backgrounds in cultural anthropology, sociology or ethnography, and these academic disciplines have contributed some insightful research studies in the field (e.g. Cronin, 2008; Ritson and Elliott, 1999; Sherry, 1987). Campaign strategy or the choice of creative execution still, often, has to be justified to the client with statistical evidence from experimental or survey research, though the socio-cultural research can also play an important role, particularly in the development of creative ideas. As for academic research into advertising, the same domination of information processing approaches is seen but there is also a strong tradition of research into advertising which is conducted from a theoretical basis of literary studies and linguistics, semiotics and art history (e.g. Mick and Buhl, 1992; Scott, 1990, 1994a; Schroeder, 2002; Stern, 1993b; Tanaka, 1994).

For example, as previously noted, the implied passivity of the consumer as a receiver of a one-way advertising message has been a criticism of the information processing models. This assumption is left unstated in 'transmission models' of mass communication but nevertheless implies that audiences 'receive' information, much as a computer receives data. In contrast, reader response theory, applied from literary to advertising texts, shows that advertising audiences often actively re-interpret advertising (e.g. O'Donohoe, 1994; Scott, 1994a). The one-way model of advertising communication seems particularly unequal to the task of theorizing the two-way advertising environment of Web 2.0 and mobile.

Interpreting Consumers

The idea that, as consumers, we are not machines but individuals who respond to advertisements in widely varying ways has also been noted. It is accepted in linguistics and media studies that the medium influences the way the message is interpreted (see Cook, 2001; McLuhan, 1964) but it is widely assumed that the precise influence is too subjective to be predicted with accuracy. When we read an advertisement inserted in a quality magazine we might interpret it differently than if we read it in a down-market publication. Likewise, we might interpret the meaning of a print advertisement differently if we saw it on an outdoor poster site or read it in a magazine.

Critiques of the passive consumer assumption have engaged with the transmission model of communication so prevalent in advertising theory. For example, Stern (1993a) undertook a thorough critique of static transmission models of communication in advertising, arguing that the model over-simplifies the communication process. Other work which has indirectly opposed the idea of a passive consumer posits the consumer as an active reader of text, as noted earlier (Scott, 1994b), or an interpreter of signs (Mick, 1986). Researchers working from the standpoint of linguistics have pointed out that what is implicit in communication is often more persuasive and telling than what is explicit. When this principle is applied to advertising communication, the limitations of a focus on explicit messages become all too apparent. For example, Tanaka (1994) analysed advertisements in detail to illustrate the rhetorical force of implied connotation and denotation in advertising. These studies, though very different, offer radical alternatives to theories which suppose the consumer to be a passive receiver of information.

Economic Rationality and Mood-motivated Buying Behaviour

A further criticism of linear models of advertising persuasion is that they risk overplaying the role of economic rationality in the consumption of advertising. Subsequent models have incorporated stronger elements of consumer emotionality not as a mediating influence but as a guiding motive in the buying process (Elliott, 1998; Holbrook and Hirschman, 1982), reflecting the often irrational and quirky motivations behind consumer behaviour (review in Dermody, 1999). Many of us go shopping when we feel down. Buying things can be therapeutic. Rationality plays little part in addictive or mood shopping. Of course, this implies that promotional communication may not always be particularly effective as a persuasive sales pitch, a point made forcefully by research that emphasizes the 'weak' theory of advertising effects.

Meanings and Messages in Advertisements

Information processing models focus on communication as the transmission of a message. Socio-cultural theories of advertising communication focus on meanings, not messages. The difference is important since the idea of a message emphasizes the power of the sender, while the idea of a meaning emphasizes the power of the receiver. Advertisements carry meanings which may be interpreted differently in different situations, or by different consumers. Advertisements can have many different meanings.

Polysemy in Advertising

Polysemy refers to the potential of a social text such as an advertisement to have many possible meanings. This perspective, of course, is not really compatible with the linear model of communication and its implied emphasis on a single, unequivocal message. The meaning of some ads is indeterminate: none of the meanings in a given ad is necessarily prior to, or stronger than, the others. There is an interpretive space through which consumers can engage creatively with the ad. This gives advertising a particular power. It is us, the audience for advertising, who impose particular meanings on a given ad, helped, of course, by the cues placed in the ad by the creative people. This freedom to interpret advertising and to use it creatively in our own lives gives advertising a dynamic character as communication. Advertising agencies, far from being limited by the complexity of advertising meaning, exploit the ambiguity of advertising (Pateman, 1983, in Forceville, 1996) to create an intimate and personal engagement with consumers. They create advertisements with many possible meanings, but the advertising design nevertheless does have a carefully considered strategy and the meanings are not entirely arbitrary. They are, rather, artfully designed so that the curiosity of a designated target group of consumers is excited.

Polysemy as a Creative Technique to Encourage Consumer Engagement

Ads that are deliberately obscure can seem inaccessible to older consumers and, by implication, aimed at younger consumers. Ambiguity of meaning in ads can be used as a deliberate strategy to engage a target group by allowing them to feel part of an in-group who 'get' the ad. In addition, carefully coded ads can create a sense of conspiracy by communicating in a way that excludes non-targeted groups. One way of signalling the desired market segment in an ad is to be seen to be excluding other segments. A TV ad campaign for Frizzell insurance in the UK deliberately deployed a creative execution using intertextual references to 1960s television news footage that would mainly be of interest to older viewers. Frizzell wanted to signal implicitly that younger consumers were not the primary target audience, because the desired market segment was older consumers who are less price conscious and, from a car insurer's point of view, carry a lower risk because they drive more safely than younger people.

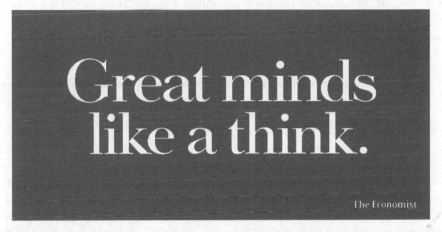

Picture 2   This billboard ad by AMV BBDO made use of the well known aphorism 'great minds think alike' to suggest that *The Economist* is a magazine for readers who like to be intellectually challenged.

Reproduced with kind permission of *The Economist* and AMV BBDO.

(See the colour insert near the middle of this book for a full colour image.)

Picture 3   This print ad by AMV BBDO asks readers whether they can afford not to keep abreast of current events in economics and management by reading *The Economist*.

Reproduced with kind permission of *The Economist* and AMV BBDO.

(See the colour insert near the middle of this book for a full colour image.)

In a more recent example, *The Economist* magazine was promoted in a series of advertisements created by the largest UK agency, AMV BBDO (Pictures 1 and 2). One ad used an intertextual reference to a well-known phrase and then adapted it to make people who looked at the ads think about them. The other example was a simple and eye-catching visual and the bald statement 'I never read *The Economist*' attributed to a 42-year-old management trainee. The irony of this statement would be immediately obvious to the intelligent reader, so the ad spoke to its desired audience segment by implying that *The Economist*'s target readers are sophisticated enough to reject ingratiation but would appreciate irony.

BOX 2.2

Diesel Ads Exploit Polysemy

The Diesel brand has a long tradition of polysemic advertising, and it tends to show the same ads all over the world. Its website, www.diesel.com has, at the time of writing in early April 2009, no mention of clothing but a series of short movies, some featuring Pete the meat puppet. The movies are entertaining in an off-the-wall, genre-subversive way. The Diesel spring 2009 men's print campaign[2] continues the edgy, polysemic style begun in the 1990s which made use of both polysemy and intertextuality to try to draw the consumer into a deeper engagement, and at the same time to signal the quirky, witty, but irreverent values of the brand. One ad (in the 1990s series) featured an enigmatic scene of bodybuilders wearing white sailor caps and bathing briefs. The scene included scientific equipment and puzzled spectators viewing from behind a red rope, as if they were at an exhibition or performance. The only direct reference to the brand was a brand name logo in small type in the corner.

Such ads are visually intriguing because they challenge our preconceptions about images and visual context. The viewer wants to make connections between the images: humans actively try to make sense of data, even where there is little to be made. Perception is subject to a Gestalt impulse whereby humans try to complete visual cues to form a coherent whole. In polysemic ads that mix visual cues drawn from unconnected discourses, this impulse draws us into the ad as we try to make the visual cues into a story we understand.

A long series of similar Diesel print ads used bizarre visual intertextual references drawing on cultural texts as diverse as museum attendance, public health advertising, educational announcements, British seaside beauty contests, soccer reports, shoot-'em-up movies and news reportage of war zones. Short, inappropriate passages of copy were imprinted on the posters to make the scene even more puzzling. The effect was to provide an entertaining visual puzzle which consumers could try to figure out. Of course, there was no definitive answer to the meaning of these ads. The creative people at the agency were just having fun in the interests of the brand, playing with cultural meaning. Underlying the apparently incoherent images was a clear advertising strategy. Viewers were expected to infer that the Diesel brand, like the ads, challenged convention in a quirky, youthful and irreverent yet cool way.

Theorizing Meaning in Advertising

'Ostensive' and 'Covert' Communication

The presence of both explicit and implicit elements in advertising communication has, as noted above, complicated the task of theorizing advertising. Forceville (1996: 105) refers to a distinction made by Tanaka (1994: 41) between '**ostensive**' and '**covert**' **communication** in advertising. This distinction allows us to theorize what is implied in ads, as opposed to what is clearly and unambiguously claimed. The ostensive communicator makes the intention of the communication clear. The covert communicator does not. The Diesel advertisements mentioned above fall into the covert category. An example of ostensive communication might be, say, a typical McDonald's advertisement. Many other ads combine ostensive (or explicit) and covert (or implicit) elements. Advertisements under industry regulation are strictly constrained from making claims that are untrue or preposterous. They get around this inconvenience by implying covertly those claims that could be seen as ridiculous or would open them up to criticism if they were made explicitly. The Lynx campaigns mentioned in Chapter 1 make absurd claims about how men's sexual attractiveness is increased by using the product, but this is implied in the narrative of the advertising, not stated explicitly as a feature of the product. In this particular case what is implied is clearly intended as a joke, although, as Tanaka (1994) notes, even if a claim made about a brand is absurd, the fact that it is understood makes it persuasive on some level.

Advertising cannot compel us to believe particular claims or to accept that certain values are embodied in a given brand. Rather, advertising suggests, implies and hints. It places images and words in a suggestive juxtaposition to imply that consuming a given brand will symbolically confer certain qualities and values. If you use a Gillette razor you are enjoying 'The Best A Man Can Get' (at least, according to the ads), and you might even acquire some of the characteristics and lifestyle of the actor in the ads. Driving a prestigious motor-car brand such as a Toyota Avensis will (we are invited to infer from the TV ads), confer a symbolic social status on us that reflects our success and desire. The ads don't actually say these things: they merely imply them, hoping that viewers will read the desired implication.

Ads frequently imply that consumers will be more sexually attractive, more powerful or will appear more materially successful if they consume a given brand. Much advertising acquires a persuasive force through its non-explicit suggestions, rather than just through its explicit claims. Where branded products are juxtaposed with images of attractive, happy and successful people, the link between the two is implied but not stated. Most importantly, it is not necessary for the advertising audience to believe these implied suggestions for the theory of covert communication to hold. It is only necessary that the audience can retrieve the meaning implied. We can see what ads are suggesting even where we neither trust the advertiser nor believe the covert implications. We know that a deodorant brand will not make us sexually attractive. We also know that the ads are implying that it will.

Visual Rhetoric and Metaphor in Advertising

Covert meaning is often conveyed in advertising though pictorial, auditory or linguistic metaphor. If a branded bottle of alcoholic drink is pictured juxtaposed with scenes of fit, young, affluent people, then the metaphoric link is clear. For example, Martini used to be advertised in the UK as a drink enjoyed by swimsuited young men and women diving from a yacht moored at a tropical island. The juxtaposition of a branded alcohol drink with apparent wealth, attractiveness and physical fitness is exactly the opposite of what one might reasonably expect, since alcohol drinking is quite likely to make exponents fat and unfit, and may also make them poor if they drink enough. The covert communication in this campaign was preposterous but was nevertheless clear. The Martini brand was used as a metaphor for sexual attractiveness and the good life. It matters little that the drink may often be consumed in social contexts that are, on the face of it, as far from the good life as one might wish to be.

BOX 2.3

Guinness Advertising and Polysemy

Guinness advertisements are often media events in themselves. The brand has created a strong tradition of creatively flamboyant and often expensive advertising that does not carry a sales message as such. The famous 'White Horses' ad produced by London agency, AMV BBDO, portrays a group of middle-aged beach bums on an exotic island waiting for and finding their perfect surfing wave. The creative strategy exploited the frustrating fact that ordering a pint of Guinness in a bar entails a fairly long wait while the beer settles. The voice-over states that 'he waits, and he waits …' until the perfect wave arrives. There is no explicit (or ostensive) marketing message, other than a brief shot of a pint of stout to help those completely in the dark about the identity of the manufacturer generously funding this lavish entertainment. Guinness (or the brand owners, Diageo) is well aware that its famous stout is an unusual, acquired taste. They are, it seems, content that their legendary creative advertising tradition is polysemic in that it can often be interpreted in many ways, including the interpretation that it means nothing at all.

However, campaigns such as 'surfers' keep the brand in the public domain and lend mystique which, when you think about it, is quite an achievement considering the pro origins of the product they have to work with. A quirky local beverage with a history of be the tipple of choice of working-class Irishmen does not, on the face of it, have great poten as a global brand. The prominence of the brand can be attributed in no small part to its tradition of creatively striking, intriguingly entertaining and confusingly polysemic advertising.

The Guinness advertising campaigns remind us that consumption is, significantly, not only a verbal phenomenon but also a visual one. We need a different theoretical scheme to conceptualize the visual. For Schroeder (2002), there are powerful lessons from the disciplines of art history and aesthetics which can help us understand the complex ways in which advertising communicates visually. Schroeder argues that we do not only consume the branded products and services that are advertised; we also 'consume' the visual images of advertising and promotion.

For example, many perfume ads in lifestyle and fashion magazines make no direct reference to the odour; instead, they juxtapose sensuous images with an enigmatic strapline or slogan that evinces some abstract notion of the brand. The visual organization of image and copy is carefully designed to rhetorically support the implicit claims made about the brand. A UK press ad for an Estée Lauder perfume portrayed a woman with flowing hair against images of waves, scattered flowers and sunlight with the copy 'Introducing the new fantasy in fragrance' and 'Beyond paradise' with the explanation that it offers 'an intoxication of the senses'. The ad had visual impact: it made a striking image when placed in a double-page section[4] immediately inside the magazine cover. By its size and page location the ad was rhetorically declaring that its subject matter was important, more important, perhaps, than the magazine's editorial. The woman's face engages the reader eye to eye with a questioning and provocative expression that seems to be asking 'Dare you join me in paradise?' The face rhetorically supports the idea that this brand transports the ordinary woman from the everyday to a different world in which she can be free to be any self she chooses. The French brand name draws on the cultural idiom of style and sophistication to imply that the perfume has those qualities and so, by association, will the reader who buys the brand. Of course, consumers will decide if they like the odour, but the odour is designed to be pleasant. Once again, the powerfully suggestive aspect of this ad is not only in its message but in its creativity. The ad is rhetorically organized to support certain implied meanings.

Visual Ads as Persuasive Rhetoric

The visual rhetoric of ads is not, then, confined to the copy. An ad is an argument, a persuasive communication. Every part of it must support the main argument, it must be persuasively suggestive. A press ad for Retinol Activ Pur face cream used a clever visual metaphor to support a claim that the cream reduced facial wrinkles. The ad featured two juxtaposed images of a beautiful (Caucasian) woman. She was wearing what seemed to be a white robe, folded over one shoulder like a Roman toga. In the background was a pure blue sky and a suggestion of white pillars, of the kind found in a Greek temple. One picture was cracked, like the surface of an old oil painting. The other was smooth. The metaphoric reference was clear: the cracks suggested wrinkles, but in an elegant way that was complimentary, not demeaning, to age. Old paintings are things of classical beauty, but the paint does tend to crack with age. The ad was designed to draw the eye across aesthetically appealing images while giving the reader heavy hints about the classic beauty they might aspire to if they were to consume the brand.

However the levels of meaning in advertisements are theorized, acknowledging their presence lends a new dimension to the analysis of advertising as persuasive communication. It brings to light some of the subtlety and complexity of advertising design, while also allowing us to draw an intellectual connection between the various artificially differentiated categories of marketing communication.

Cultural Understanding and Decoding Meanings in Advertising

In principle, any communication is open to varied interpretations since meaning itself is rooted in culturally-based forms of understanding. Once the incorrigibility of meaning is acknowledged, the complexity of the task facing marketing communications specialists can be understood. Creative professionals in advertising overcome the problem of the indeterminacy (or polysemy) of meaning in advertising by hinting through a suggestive juxtaposition that certain values are associated with certain brands, rather than by making claims which, if taken literally, would seem ridiculous. More importantly, advertising agencies put up claims that, if they were made explicit, would open them up to criticism or censure. It is a measure of a poor general understanding of communication when advertising regulation and legislation focus on the ostensive content of ads and largely ignore the implied or covert meanings that ads carry.

Polysemy of meaning creates the space for consumers of advertising to use some license in reinterpreting ads creatively according to their own cultural reference points and reflecting their own sense of identity. The text of advertising, its *prima facie* meaning, can sometimes be its least interesting aspect because consumers may reject marketing strategies that seem too contrived or obvious. They may, however, use advertising and the brands that are advertised in ways that subvert the marketing text but reflect the consumers' own values and social strategies. For example, UK consumers once mocked ads for the Skoda car, inventing jokes at the brand's expense. Skoda improved the quality of their products and then exploited the fact that their brand had become so well known by creating ads that referred to its poor public image with strap lines such as 'It's a Skoda – honest'. Consumers knew that the brand was mocking their poor (and flawed) perception of it, but the manufacturer gambled that consumers would enjoy the joke at their expense and understand that there was a serious point: that Skoda cars were much improved.

A further important issue in the way that advertising meaning is interpreted is its context.

The Context of Advertising and Promotion

Advertising as Social Construction

Developments in cultural psychology have suggested that constructs such as memory and attitude cannot be understood only in terms of private, inner processes (Potter and Wetherell, 1987). Our cognitive understanding of the social world is not only private: it is also inherently social. Meaning can be understood as a social construction in the sense that it is produced in an engagement with each other and the world. Our preferences and attitudes are culturally primed, and we choose them from a range of possibilities presented to us in our own cultural field. We understand advertising as part of our cultural landscape. It is simply there, like road signs, newspapers and TV shows, and conversations in bars and cafés. All are normal parts of our social world. As a normal feature of social life advertising reflects and reveals values and social practices. The ways we interpret advertising, and the attitudes we form of the brands portrayed, are not only our own; they are also views borrowed from the social worlds which we encounter.

If a brand is popular, such as Nike or BMW, its consumers are well aware that they are not the only people who understand the meaning of this brand. Indeed, they will very likely have an idea of the kind of other person who likes the brand. They may well have gained this impression from advertising. Our senses of discernment and preference are not fixed or given by nature. They are culturally learned in an interaction with our social worlds.

BOX 2.4

Nike as Social Construction

The Nike sportswear brand was developed through its proprietor Phil Knight's obsession with designing running shoes. Knight's original running shoes were endorsed by track star Steve Prefontaine. The brand acquired another dimension when it became fashionable street wear in Los Angeles. What had been a brand associated with sporting excellence and promoted through a policy of personal endorsement by sports stars acquired new connotations of street authenticity, toughness and resistance to conformity. The Nike 'Swoosh' is one of the most universally recognized icons of twenty-first-century culture. Although its connotations are controlled by Nike, to some extent there are elements that are beyond their control because a brand within public discourse has a self-sustaining momentum. Nike became a feature of urban culture as well as a marketed brand: the values and connotations inspired by its association with sporting performance have become inseparable from those of street coolness and an opposition to authority. The brand's marketing has been able to exploit its street authenticity, but arguably it did not create that authenticity. It is a good example of a brand as a social construction, since its cultural meaning is bound up with wider discourses (in this case, those of class, ethnicity, urban identity and the American sense of individuality).

Brands as social constructions are then no more or less than what we as consumers think they are. If Volvo is seen as safe, Rolex as prestigious, Marlboro as tough, Body Shop as environmentally conscious, such perceptions are produced by consumers in interaction with each other. Brand marketing organizations try to influence this brand discourse through their brand and communications policies (see Holt, 2004 on 'cultural branding').

Advertising Does Not Only Do Things to Us – We Also Do Things to Advertising

Advertising is not merely a force acting upon us. We actively use it in our own social lives. Research studies have drawn attention to the ways advertising is actively used in social life (O'Donohoe, 1994) as well as being passively consumed in some contexts. Advertising research often emphasizes the individual encounter with an individual ad (McCracken, 1986) when, in fact, we usually consume ads socially in the sense that we often view them in the company of others and we discuss our interpretation of them and modify it in the light of other views (Dichter, 1966). Ritson and Elliott (1999) showed how important advertising can be in the everyday conversation of adolescents. By expressing preferences and finding certain ads funny or enjoyable the researchers found that the adolescents were also expressing their sense of social identity and group membership. As blogging (including videoblogging) about advertising has become common, our use of advertising as a form of social communication through which we can express our own views, opinions and sense of identity, becomes more apparent.

Brands as Social Constructions

Advertising's meaning, then, draws on the cultural environment within which it is framed. Our understanding of ads and the brands they promote is formed in the light of the social contexts within which such communications subsist. This inherently social aspect of human understanding reflects a broader concern with the socially constructed character of social reality (Berger and Luckman, 1966) and of individual psychology (for introductions see Burr, 1995; Nightingale and Cromby, 1999). In important respects we maintain that brands and their advertising cannot be properly understood simply as self-evident entities. They must also be understood as entities that exist in the realm of social interaction, sustained through the way they are talked about and used. In other words, brands can be seen as social constructions.

A great deal of marketing activity can be seen to have a socially constructed character (Hirschman, 1986, cited in Hackley, 2001: 47) in the sense that it has an existence that is sustained in the social world beyond the tangible realities of product features, packaging and price. A brand's meaning as portrayed or implied in advertising subsists in the social space between the organization, the advertising and its **interpretive communities** of consumers.

Advertising Text and Context

Advertising acquires meaning not only by its content but also its context. Appreciating the context of communication is an important part of understanding the way meaning is construed. For Cook (2001) the contexts of advertising include the following:

- the physical material or medium which carries the text (such as the cathode ray tube, newsprint or radio waves)
- the music and pictures that may accompany the text
- the gestures, facial expressions and typography that constitute the 'paralanguage' of the text (in the UK, TV ads for Nescafé Gold Blend instant coffee featured romantically linked characters who created a sexually charged atmosphere, while interacting in settings that suggested affluence and social poise)
- the location of the text in time and space, on an outdoor poster site, in a magazine or during a commercial TV break
- the other texts that connect to that text such as the other ads in the same magazine or the other brands appearing or mentioned in a TV show

- the connections with other social **discourses** implied in the ads (for example **intertextuality**)
- the participants, that is, the intended audience, the apparent originator or sender of the ad and their respective assumptions, intentions and communicative idiom (Cook, 2001: 2) (ads sometimes have a particular 'voice' designed to confer authority, such as when ads for children's toys feature adults speaking the voice-over in the tone and patois of children).

BOX 2.5

Advertisement Context and Advertising Regulation

A good illustration of the importance of the context of advertising for the meaning we construe from it can be found in a UK campaign for a perfume brand. A magazine ad for Yves St Laurent's Opium perfume featuring model Sophie Dahl, apparently naked, elicited little comment. Such ads are common in lifestyle and fashion magazines. When the print ad was blown up into a poster and featured on roadside billboards it elicited the largest number of complains the UK Advertising Standards Authority (ASA) had ever received for a single ad, along with outraged press features and comment on British TV. The magazine ad was, presumably, seen as sensuous and witty in the context of many such ads for perfume in fashion and lifestyle magazines. The same ad on posters was widely considered to be obscene. The complaints to the ASA were predominantly from young women, exactly the readers of the magazines in which the press ad had featured. The meanings we impute to ads are, it seems, highly influenced by the interpretive context in which the ad is placed.

Clearly, this list of the contexts of advertising implies that research studies which analyse the recall and attitude of an individual consumer to a single promotion by exposing the consumer to the ad in a viewing booth risk ignoring some of the most powerful influences on how ads are interpreted and understood. Given the many features of communication which impinge on the consumption of advertising and promotion, it is not surprising that advertising professionals have learned to exploit the persuasive potential of this complexity. Ads that have no evident meaning, or ads that seem to carry numerous potential meanings, are far from uncommon. Ads that have no determinate meaning can be useful because (as noted above) they can draw consumers into a communicative engagement as they try to puzzle out the enigma of the ad. Just what is it saying? Similarly, ads that have many potential interpretations can exploit this polysemy to create consumer interest and enhance the force of communication.

Advertising and Semiotics

Semiotics deserves a brief mention because of its considerable influence in studies of advertising (Mick, 1986; Mick and Buhl, 1992). Semiotics is the study of signs and their meaning. American influence (particularly that of Charles Sanders Peirce) has broadened the field from the study of linguistic signs, also called **semiology** (de Saussure, 1974), to include the study of any signs whatsoever (Peirce, 1958; introductions in Danesi, 1994; Hackley, 1999a). Advertising and marketing have attracted much attention from semioticians (Barthes, 2000; Williamson, 1978). Ads are seen as 'strings of signs' (Umiker-Sebeok, 1997) in the service of the brand. Such signs (copy, typeface, soundtrack, positioning, image, colour, objects) rhetorically support the sub-textual or covert meanings that are central to the persuasive force of advertising. The meaning of a given sign depends on the context, the receiver and the communication codes that form the cultural expectations of the sender and receiver.

The sales message, if one can be discerned among the cacophony of signification in many ads, is only one part of the complex process of communication that is going on when a consumer engages with an ad and attempts to interpret its meaning. For example, another way of analysing the Diesel ads mentioned above is to look at the signification properties of each part of the ad. These will include the copy and the other visual elements; colours, print quality, actors, props in the scene, the clothes, the juxtaposition of images, the intertextual references, and so on. Semiotics seeks to recover the communicative codes through which we receive messages from word, visual, auditory or other signs.

As noted in Chapter 1, marketing as a whole is a rich source of symbolism (Sawchuck, 1995) that reaches into the most intimate areas of our lives to transform the meaning of everyday signs. The acts of shaving, washing, even personal cleanliness are superimposed with marketed values. Advertising lies at the fulcrum of marketing's semiotic mechanism, symbolically articulating the brand values contrived by the strategists.

We will return to some of these concepts as the book progresses through its account of the advertising and promotion field.

Levels of Explanation in Advertising Theory: Cognitive, Social, Cultural

In this book we hint at the vast range of theory in advertising. To conclude Chapter 2 it is worth briefly discussing the role and purpose of theory in the context of social science, given that scholarship and research in advertising are concerned both with managerial issues and matters of social policy. The difficulty of this is that theory and research in management and business are derivative. They do not have their own theories and methods but borrow them from social science. This creates problems of ecological validity. To express this with an example, why should a theory of emotion developed in general psychology be appropriate for advertising (Hosany and Hackley, 2009)? All too often, social scientific theories are bolted on to advertising contexts without any adaptation. The marketing field in general has a tendency to use theories without reference to their original context. It has adapted, and often bowdlerized, theoretical and conceptual developments in many other social disciplines, such as economics, psychology and sociology (Foxall, 2000; Gronhaug, 2000; Hackley, 2003c, 2009a; O'Shaughnessy, 1997). Theoretical work in advertising has, as we have seen, similarly adapted work from other fields. Much advertising research draws on assumptions from mass communications research which had, in turn, borrowed ideas such as linearity and the concept of the internal mental state from early research in artificial intelligence and computing. We have also referred to much research into advertising that has drawn on the arts and humanities, for example, literary theory (Scott, 1994a, 1994b), feminism (Stern, 1993b), anthropology (Sherry, 1987), ethnography (Ritson and Elliott, 1999), applied linguistics (Cook, 2001), critical theory (Elliott and Ritson, 1997), and so on.

All this diversity begs the question of whether one can fairly evaluate a social theory without also understanding the assumptions about the audience for the research and the rightful aims of that research. To try to accommodate something of the diversity of theory in advertising in a way which reconciles the different kinds, it will be useful to draw on the notion of 'levels of explanation' in social research, which has been used in social psychology education (Stevens, 1996) to integrate differing kinds of theory.

The Cognitive Level of Explanation

Advertising works at a cognitive level in that it influences the individual cognitive functions of perception, memory and attitude. Theories that focus on the cognitive levels of explanation also emphasize rational, conscious consumer thinking. The scope of explanation in such theories extends to the internal mental state of the individual and the assumed connection between those internal states and observed (consumer) behaviour. Copy-testing, experimental research designs and attitude research attempt to isolate the internal mental states that act as causal variables which motivate consumers to act on the advertising they see. This level of explanation offers succinct and measurable results, but its weakness is that it risks distorting the way consumers engage with and understand advertising to fit a set of convenient research methods.

Much cognitive research into advertising has taken the individual consumer as the unit of analysis (Hackley, 2002: 214; Holbrook, 1995: 93, citing McCracken,

1987: 123; Ritson and Elliott, 1999: 261). Unlike computers, humans depend heavily on social interaction for meaning. People born blind who have sight restored in middle age have to learn to perceive structures and images from a jumble of visual sensory data. In other words, they have to learn how to see. People who are raised in social isolation cannot naturally learn speech and people who live in a culture without mediated communication cannot 'read' advertising. The way that we understand advertising is deeply informed by the cultural understanding we can only acquire in social interaction. The experimental research paradigm that attempts to isolate individual physiological or attitudinal responses to advertising cannot easily capture this dimension.

The Social Level of Explanation

The social level of explanation offers an account of advertising that accommodates its social character. Advertising is not encountered in a social vacuum but in a given social context, and it occupies a place in public discourse. How we think about advertising is strongly influenced by what we hear others say about it. How many times has someone asked you if you have seen this or that ad? As ads become part of social discourse they assume the characteristics of social constructions, in the sense that Berger and Luckman (1966) described. Research and theory that focus on internal mental states (such as memory or attitude) fail to grasp the essentially malleable nature of these states. One's attitude towards an ad is not arrived at in isolation but is constructed in a social context. Social constructionism (see also Burr, 1995; Hackley, 2001) disputes the validity of the internal mental state as a construct and suggests that such states subsist in social discourse. In practical terms, this implies that it not sufficient to measure memory or attitude in experimental laboratories; rather, advertising research needs to look at consumer thinking and behaviour in its normal social context, in interaction.

It is hugely significant that advertising agency professionals understand this intuitively. But politically, many agencies still struggle to justify this form of understanding to clients and account managers who are concerned with measuring consumer attitudes to advertising. This fundamental difference of mentality is a central issue in advertising and promotional management (Hackley, 2003d), but many existing research approaches perpetuate the differences instead of providing possibilities for reconciliation.

The Cultural Level of Explanation

We have seen that advertising can be regarded as a form of cultural text. It takes the symbolic meanings and practices of non-consumer culture and recreates them in juxtaposition with marketed brands to suggest contrived brand values and to portray a brand personality. For advertising to be construed in this way there needs to be a symbolic aspect to the way consumers engage with advertising. We must understand advertising in terms that transfer symbolic meanings from our broader cultural experience to advertised brands (Belk, 1988; Mick and Buhl, 1992). This level of analysis broadens a socially constructed notion of advertising to accommodate the wider cultural influences that are the preconditions for local social discourse.

At this level of analysis power is an inevitable part of the picture. Brand marketing corporations have the economic and political power to impose contrived meanings upon cultural practices. Brand advertising, cleverly designed and expensively produced and exposed, can work to normalize particular **consumer practices** (such as cigarette smoking, alcohol drinking for females, fast-food consumption for children) and invest these practices with symbolic values such as personal independence, power and coolness. In this way advertising can be seen to operate as an ideology (Eagleton, 1991) or, indeed, as the 'super-ideology' of our time (Elliott and Ritson, 1997).

An exposition of advertising as ideology lies beyond the scope of this book. It is worth pointing out, though, that an intellectually viable appraisal of how advertising works is incomplete without an understanding of advertising's ideological power to render consumption practices normal and everyday in an infinite variety of appealing portrayals, to invest these practices with rich cultural significance and to place the interests of brand marketing organizations at the forefront of social life. If marketing as a whole can be seen as a vast semiotic vehicle constituting experiences and identities (Brownlie et al., 1999) then advertising is its engine, providing a continuous stream of new images, ideas and portrayals of consumption in juxtaposition with marketed brands.

Chapter Summary

This chapter has outlined some important elements of two contrasting traditions of theory in advertising: the information processing tradition, and the socio-cultural tradition. It reviewed practice-based advertising theory some of which is still well established, such as the idea of the Unique Selling Proposition and the A–I–D–A model of persuasive communication, and variations on the 'hierarchy-of-effects' principle of advertising persuasion. The chapter reviewed some theoretical weaknesses of the information processing model, focusing on the limitations of the man–machine analogy, since information processing theory was developed to model machine communication rather than human communication. The chapter then discussed socio-cultural theory. The socio-cultural category embraces a very broad range of advertising theory from disciplines which include anthropology, sociology and literary theory.

The chapter also discussed a distinction between hard sell or 'strong' theories of advertising and soft sell or 'weak' theories. The extent to which typical advertisements might fall into either category depends to some extent on regional variations in advertising and consumer culture. In some cases, and in some cultures, the direct sales appeal has greater relevance. For example, as a generalization, much US advertising contrasts with that of Europe, Australasia and parts of Asia in the direct style of its sales appeal. US consumers may be simply more accustomed to this style of advertising and, perhaps, more receptive to its method. Furthermore, the 'strong' or 'weak' advertising appeal may not be mutually exclusive. Even though the sales appeal may be direct, the ad can still carry important values and connotations that contribute to long-term brand-building and maintaining the communications objective. And ads with an indirect appeal may sometimes coincide with the contiguous purchase behaviour that immediately follows on from exposure to the ad.

 ■ Review Questions

1 Choose three print advertisements and three TV ads. For each, construct descriptions that distinguish the covert from the ostensive meanings in the ad. Compare your interpretations with colleagues: do they differ?

2 What is meant by polysemy? What is its importance in advertising? Collect several magazines: can you find ads that appear to be polysemic?

3 Choose one print ad and form a group with three collaborators. Try to pick out all the individual signs that might carry meaning in the ad. These might include the copy (the words, the position of the copy in the visual and the typeface or font that is used), the models, the props in the set, the background, the relation of objects and bodies to each other, the gestures, the quality of paper and use of colour and the other brands advertised in the magazine. What is the meaning of each in it's context?

4 What is a message? To what extent is meaning carried unequivocally within an advertisement? Compare three ads to discuss this.

CASE

Intertextuality and the Interpreting Consumer

Advertising is 'parasitic' (Cook, 2001)[3] in the sense that it draws from, and refers to, other discourse forms. Julia Kristeva's concept of intertextuality refers to the idea that no text is entirely original but consists of references, conscious or not, to other texts. The idea of intertextuality, originating with Kristeva and the French poststructuralists, has been adapted to advertising by O'Donohoe (1997). Intertextual references reflect advertising's parasitic nature by evincing other, non-advertising discourses. For example, television ads have evoked the discourse genres of, say: scientific reports (with a white-coated, male actor as 'objective' spokesman for the proven qualities of the brand); the face-to-face sales pitch (delivered by a man in a loud tie and check jacket); and the confidential piece of advice from the older woman experienced in household management to the younger (examples are taken from Cook, 2001: 194). Intertextual references in advertising tend to be implicit, they are there to be noticed, or not, by an interpreting consumer. They have an effect because consumers actively 'read' advertising 'texts', much as we read other texts.

In research with young British consumers, O'Donohoe (1997) has shown how advertising can use intertextuality to engage particular audience groups. Advertisements evïnce certain values by linking the brand with the discourses of, say, sport or movies. Ads for Fosters lager parodied the Australian *Mad Max* movies (and ads for Carling Black Label lager parodied the Foster's ads parodying the *Mad Max* movies). Other ads evince analogies of TV quiz shows, news announcements, fashion photographs, courtroom dialogue and TV situation comedies. In many cases, ads deploying intertextual references are then featured on compilation TV shows of funniest ads, completing the circle by drawing ads into mainstream entertainment. The intertextual references are 'read' by the target audience who recognize that the brand is speaking to them.

Creative professionals may use intertextuality as a tactic to try to engage consumers with points of shared cultural reference. Intertextual references are often used in a spirit of parody to break down consumer resistance to advertising appeals. In such cases the marketing message is predicated on the target consumers getting the reference and appreciating the wit. In one example a car chase from the movie *Bullitt* was reproduced with the car digitally replaced with a Ford Puma, driven by the laconic star Steve McQueen. The ad mocked the sporty pretensions of the Puma but in a way that might be appreciated by its audience, since it broke the advertising cliché of earnestness about the brand. Ads that subvert the genre of advertising itself have become common, trying to attain a sense of authenticity with a sophisticated audience. There is no sales message as such, merely an assumption that consumers will understand that the self-mockery is as insincere as the earnestness of stereotypical advertising. The assumption behind such creative work is that advertising audiences will interpret and think about advertising with reference to the broader cultural context.

 ■ **Case Questions**

1   Choose any three print or broadcast advertisements. Can you identify the intertextual elements in each? What does this tell you about the intended target market segment?

2   What kinds of cultural knowledge do you feel are required in order to identify the intertextual elements in your chosen advertisements?

3   Is one implication of intertextuality that advertising cannot be interpreted in the same way by people from different cultures? If this is so, how can you explain, for example, the global success of the Diesel brand, which often uses the same campaign globally without any adaptation?

■ ■ Further Reading ■

Introductions to Interpretive Concepts and Methods

Arnould, E. and Thompson, C. (2005) 'Consumer Culture Theory (CCT): twenty years of research', *Journal of Consumer Research*, 31: 868–82.

Danesi, M. (2006) *Brands*. London and New York: Routledge.

Hackley, C. (2003e) *Doing Research Projects in Marketing, Management and Consumer Research*. London: Routledge.

Hackley, C. (2010) 'Theorizing advertising: managerial, scientific and cultural approaches', in P. MacLaran, M. Saren, B. Stern and M. Tadajewski, (eds), *The SAGE Handbook of Marketing Theory*. London: Sage. pp. 89–107.

Holt, D. (2004) *How Brands Become Icons: The Principles of Cultural Branding.* Boston, MA: Business School Press.

Lee, N. and Lings, I. (2008) *Doing Business Research: A Guide to Theory and Practice*. London: Sage.

On the Companion Website

These journal articles are freely available on the companion website (www.sagepub.co.uk/hackley).

Advertising Theory: Reconceptualizing the Building Blocks
Xiaoli Nan and Ronald J. Faber
Marketing Theory, Jun 2004; vol. 4: pp. 7–30.

Beyond Visual Metaphor: A New Typology of Visual Rhetoric in Advertising
Barbara J. Phillips and Edward F. McQuarrie
Marketing Theory, Jun 2004; vol. 4: pp. 113–136.

A Cybernetic Communication Model for Advertising
Chris Miles
Marketing Theory, Dec 2007; vol. 7: pp. 307–334.

Notes

1 www.anbhf.org/laureates/lasker.html (accessed 21 January 2009).
2 frillr.com/?q=node/10514 (accessed 8 April 2009).
3 Cook (2001) maintains that advertising is no different in its 'parasitic' character from any other discourse form. Intertextuality can be discerned in culturally valued discourse forms such as classical art, drama and literature, as well as in 'low' or popular cultural forms such as movies, comic books and popular theatre, in addition to advertising.

3 The Brand and Integrated Marketing Communications Planning

Chapter Outline

The brand is the central concept of consumer marketing, and Integration is the key theme of contemporary advertising. Advertising creates, sustains and reflects the brand. This chapter describes the integrated marketing communications process in relation to the brand. It explores the distinctions between marketing strategy and advertising strategy, and it examines the ways in which communication can support marketing objectives.

Key chapter content

- Marketing and communication planning

- Integrated communication and the brand

- Integrated Marketing Communications planning

- Limitations and qualifications to IMC.

Marketing and Communication Planning

In Chapter 3 we turn from the complexities of theorizing advertising to the uncertainties of planning advertising. Planning is the area where the art of advertising is reduced to a management tool used in the strategic or tactical interests of the brand. A plan represents a template which can help to guide, control and co-ordinate the many tasks which are involved in the management of a brand's marketing and communications. In Chapter 2, we noted many theoretical perspectives on advertising which illustrated how difficult it is to impose meaning on an individual consumer through an advertisement. Part of the enigma of the advertising business is that we may not fully understand how it works, but it does, nevertheless, seem to do so and there are many striking examples. Indeed, it is impossible to conceive of the world's most prominent brands without advertising. It is important to analyse advertising, but if it is to be used as a management tool to achieve something, it is also useful to have a plan.

Integrated Marketing Communications

The phrase 'Integrated Marketing Communications' (Schultz et al., 1993) (also known as IMC) reflects managerial interest in co-ordinating different media channels to optimize the effectiveness of brand marketing communications programmes. If brand communications reflect implied values and imagery that are consistent throughout differing media channels, then clearly these channels act in a mutually reinforcing way with each successive consumer engagement. Interest in IMC has developed because of the view that marketing communication offers the 'only sustainable competitive advantage of marketing organizations' (Schultz et al., 1993: 47). Consequently, all points of contact between an organization and its audience can be utilized as possible communications channels through which all forms of communication may be used. The end goal is to influence the attitudes and behaviour of targeted audiences (Shimp, 2009).

Although advertising agencies consider traditional advertising to be their core activity, the larger, **full-service agencies** are increasingly finding that clients expect them to offer expertise across the marketing communication disciplines. Consumers, moreover, do not generally mark a strong distinction between the differing media that carry advertising. As Percy et al. point out, 'people generally look at all marketing communications as "advertising"' (2001: v). The rise of brand marketing makes the advertising medium secondary to the brand personality, an entity that can be expressed through many differing forms of creative execution and communicated through different media. Indeed, it is recognized that an explicit, paid-for advertisement placed in a mass medium may have no greater impact for a brand than a carefully integrated product placement in a movie or a high-profile sports sponsorship deal. It is no longer unusual for public relations or direct mail to be used as the main, strategic arm of marketing communications effort. Integrated advertising campaigns utilize the qualities of different media in a communications onslaught designed to project consistent brand values regardless of whatever communication source the consumer encounters.

This blurring of the lines between marketing communications disciplines is part of a radical change in the media infrastructure coming from developments in electronic communications technology and the rise of global business. Global brands now cross borders and resonate with consumers in many countries. Mass media, above-the-line advertising is often regarded as the strategic element of marketing communications, the one communication technique that can transform the fortunes of corporations, create brands and change entire markets. Although there are still good reasons for holding this view, there is also a strong case for managers to consider advertising from a strategic and integrated perspective which acknowledges that the rationale for brand communications drives the pragmatic development of integrated creative executions and media strategies.

Distinctions Between Marketing Planning and Communication Planning

Some important distinctions are worth noting at this point. There can be confusion between brand clients and advertising agencies about what, exactly, can be achieved through advertising communication. There is certainly some overlap between marketing and communication, but they are not the same. For example, a marketing plan might set an objective of achieving a 3 per cent increase in the market share over two months. A communication cannot deliver a market share, because it is a communication. What it can do is to support the marketing objective by, for example, motivating consumers by giving them a reason to buy the desired brand instead of its rivals. Exactly how it might do so would depend on the consumer target group characteristics, the product or service market in which the brand is operating, the distribution channels, ·the current competitive conditions, and so on. The relation between a marketing objective and a marketing communication objective is important and closely linked, but it can be subtle.

As an example, in one long-running campaign for the car manufacturer VW, a London agency, DDB Needham, devised a campaign based on the creative idea that Volkswagen cars were not as expensive as people thought. The **qualitative** research revealed that consumers perceived VW as high quality, and commanding a high price. In fact, the prices of the models were competitive with their rivals in each car class. The marketing objectives were to increase the market share by 3 per cent in each class (family saloon, small car and executive saloon) across Europe, and to refresh the brand. The communication objective was to persuade consumers that they could have VW reliability and prestige without having to pay a high price. The advertising strategy had to put across the idea that VWs were not as expensive as people thought. The agency found amusing and low-key creative executions which informed consumers that, in fact, VWs were indeed less expensive than they thought. The market share increase was achieved and the campaign ran for many years, winning many industry awards for creativity and effectiveness. In this case, the marketing objectives, the communication objective and the advertising strategy were not exactly the same but they were mutually supportive. Naturally, the objectives would not have been achieved if the other elements of the marketing mix, the product (including service and after-sales, warranties, reliability, image and performance) and the distribution through the service centres had not been up to scratch.

BOX 3.0

Brand Positioning and Integrated Communication

Positioning refers broadly to the values and associations, both tangible and intangible, that are linked with a given brand. This positioning differentiates the brand from its rivals. Many major brand marketing organizations take great care to articulate the positioning of brands so that the necessary values and associations can be reproduced through all levels of communications and marketing. Some, such as Unilever, undertake detailed analysis to delineate a brand's 'essence'. The components of this essence include: an analysis of the competitive environment; the target consumers; the key insight that makes the brand distinctive; the consumer benefits (tangible or intangible) conferred by the brand; the values and personality of the brand; the way the brand supports those values and why consumers should believe them; the features that differentiate the brand from its competitors; and the single concept that sums up the brand 'essence'. Unilever would need to draw out these issues for brands such as Colman's mustard, Pot Noodle snack food, Birds Eye processed foods, Surf detergent, Domestos bleach and numerous others. Each would differ depending on the brand positioning and the competitive conditions in each particular market. All major brand organizations use similar brand planning conceptual frameworks to emphasize the distinctive characteristics of each brand they market, and to enable them to maintain the same brand values and positioning through all their integrated communications.

Strategic and Tactical Planning

Another distinction in advertising planning which can confuse is that between strategy and tactics. Broadly, strategy refers to longer-term objectives which demand significant resources, while tactics refer to short- or medium-term objectives demanding less resources. However, the distinction between strategy and tactics is not always so clear cut. Promotion is one quarter of the marketing mix,[1] along with physical distribution, price and product, but it can command extensive resources and can also be the most important element of competitive success in some circumstances. Management is, after all, as much an art as a science, and the use of terms is far from precise or universally agreed. In the VW example above the use of advertising clearly had a strategic implication since it represented a major investment and helped achieve strategic corporate goals on the European market share. The distinction between strategy and tactics is typically based on the timescale and importance to the overall profitability of the organization. It is a mistake to assume, as some marketing texts do, that all promotional effort is merely tactical just because it is promotion. Advertising and promotional campaigns have, in many cases, attracted substantial resources and achieved strategic objectives for brands and for whole companies.

For example, a marketing strategy might be to achieve market dominance by being the high quality supplier, and the marketing communications would have to find a way of supporting that. A marketing tactic might be to spoil a rival's promotional campaign by having a short-term, 10 per cent price discount offer. Again, the communications would have to support the price-based promotion.

In many organizations, the ideal plan would have strategic aims and objectives operating at the level of the corporation, with operational plans designed for each individual product market. The various levels of business and marketing objective would, ideally, dovetail into each other. So, for example, if the corporation was dealing in motor cars and positioned itself as the innovator in the market, then the various car brands it sold in each motor car segment (family saloon, small car, utility sports vehicle, etc.) would have different plans tailored to their particular target market and competitive conditions, though all would need to have a degree of fit with the overall corporate strategy. Honda and electronics giant Sony have become known for their expensive, entertaining and high profile advertising campaigns which focus on the corporate brand values of quality and innovation, while they also have individual campaigns for particular models. The corporate level of communication sets the tone for the product-brand level of communication in advertising.

Consistency between Marketing and Communications Planning

There is a great deal of scope for confusion and misunderstanding between the marketing plan and the marketing communication plan. This is one reason why client–agency relations are such a fraught advertising area. The problems can be managed if there is frequent dialogue and a mutual appreciation of the differences between marketing and communication. As noted in Box 3.0, one of the key elements of integration in marketing communication is to ensure that all communications portray consistent and coherent brand values throughout all media and across all product ranges. So it is essential that the marketing planning and the communications planning do not conflict. For example, if an advertising campaign builds a high level of awareness and anticipation for a new brand launch in the chewing gum market, all that effort and resources will be wasted if the chewing gum has not made it into the stores by the time the campaign is launched, as happened in one instance. As another example, if the brand is positioned at the low cost, low quality end of the market, it would not be useful for the advertising to imply that the quality is excellent. Finally, any communication campaign needs to be targeted at the relevant consumers. A marketing plan might be well thought through and effectively executed, and the advertising designed to convey the right positioning values with the desired market segment, but if the advertising and promotion appeal to the wrong audience, or if they are placed in media channels which the desired market segment does not access, then the effort may be wasted.

Integrated Communication and the Brand

Brand marketing management entails artful and detailed planning. As we have noted above, one key area is to manage the way that the brand values are portrayed in all communications. The rise in importance of the brand as an entity which has value in itself (often expressed as brand 'equity') is one of the reasons why the integration of marketing communications has become so important.

A brand is often described in terms of four main dimensions: it is a *badge* of origin that entails a *promise* of quality and performance which *reassures* the consumer and may transform their *experience* (Feldwick, 2002a: 4–9). These elements collectively differentiate the brand from others. It has been said (Aaker et al., 1992) that advertisements can lend many qualities to a brand in the form of perceived attributes which can confer upon it a brand 'personality'. The notion of brand personality, well-established in professional brand management (and associated with the advertising guru David

Ogilvy), personifies the brand and reflects the attempt to generate a sense of affinity between consumers and brands. In the planning process, this is achieved by anthropomorphizing the brand, giving it human characteristics (a 'personality') in order to stimulate emotional responses from consumers towards that brand.

BOX 3.1

Integration and WCRS

Many advertising agencies preach integration without necessarily incorporating it into their working methods. Leading agency WCRS of London claim to have done so with their 'Engine' group.[2] WCRS's clients include BMW, Sky, Bupa, Weetabix and many more.[3] The Engine group includes agencies specializing in brand strategy and consulting, public relations, digital marketing, experiential marketing, direct, corporate and music and entertainment marketing, data-driven marketing and reputation management. The aim is to offer clients a comprehensive cross-channel and strategic brand communication service,[4] all under the umbrella of WCRS.

Given that the cultural status and longevity of brands are still something of a mystery to marketers, some will resort to lyrical paeans when they try to describe the phenomenon of the brand. They are 'gods' with 'personalities' (Feldwick, 2002a: 3). Brand **discourse** might seem overblown at times but this need not mask the substantive and important effects of brands on competitive markets and for organizational success. These effects are arguably unimaginable in the absence of advertising communication and can be seen to continue in spite of pockets of organized consumer resistance to brand marketing.[5]

Brand Communication and Differential Advantage

Communication through advertising and promotion can make consumers choose a given brand over its alternatives. This confers significant market power on popular brands. In competitive markets it is difficult to make a product or service appear distinctively different from the rest. Innovations of design, process, pricing, distribution and manufacture can be quickly copied. Manufacturing technology or service operations can often be transferred to countries with lower labour costs and overheads. This means that a tangible competitive advantage is hard to achieve and even harder to sustain over long periods under competition. Intellectual property and patent rights confer some protection on innovators but rival businesses can succeed in making their offering appear to be identical to that of an innovator in important respects. In many countries, intellectual property rights are difficult or even impossible to police. Furthermore, in developed economies consumer markets are increasingly sensitive to the actual or perceived links between public events, personalities and news stories, and brands. This makes the brand vulnerable to unexpected changes in public taste.

For these reasons and others, advertising communication is an essential component of brand marketing. A brand lives on through consumer perceptions which are formed in an engagement with advertising communication. The distinctive positioning, segmentation and targeting that are so difficult to achieve and sustain through other means can be achieved symbolically through advertising and promotional communication.

The point that communication is integral to how consumers understand and engage with marketed brands does not necessarily imply that a brand is all about superficial 'puffery' and short-term publicity. 'Puffery' is the name given to advertising copy that is so clearly hyperbolic that no reasonable person would take it literally. It is also sometimes used as a derogatory term for advertising in general. Most advertising conveys something about a brand's values and characteristics, but this is not all there is to brand marketing. Brand managers will normally argue that communications are like the tip of an iceberg, just visible above the waterline with a far more substantial structure, unseen, beneath. This invisible structure includes production, staffing, training, operations, logistics, supply and material sourcing, and all the other activities without which a branded product or service could not reach a marketplace. The communications dimension, the tip of the iceberg, is all that the general public can see and that is why it is so important. Most brands have a concrete existence as businesses with plant, machinery and personnel, but they also have another existence as an idea in the collective public mind. Some brands, such as Virgin, exist primarily as an abstract entity covering diverse businesses.

Brand advertising and communication, then, should not be thought of as a trivial or superficial activity in a marketing context. It is central to success in consumer, and increasingly industrial, marketing. For consumers the brand image or personality, the values and associations linked with the brand, the way the brand is talked about by friends and acquaintances, the way the brand is represented in press editorial and TV coverage, and the memory of personal experience of consuming the brand are all aspects of an holistic engagement with this entity, the brand. A consumer brand is a fine exemplar of the notion of social construction (Berger and Luckman, 1966) since a brand is more than the sum of its parts, it is the ways in which it is understood, perceived, and talked about. What is more, perceptions of a brand become reality in the world of mediated communication, just as, in Berger and Luckman's (1966) example, a book can become something else through the way it is perceived and talked about. Influencing the way this abstraction is thought and spoken of is clearly a task in which communication is a primary tool.

Brand Positioning and Consumer Benefit

'Positioning', introduced in Box 3.0, is one of those marketing terms that can be invoked in various different senses. It normally refers to the abstract psychological attributes and associations that a brand may evoke for consumers. It may also refer to the more tangible characteristics of a brand that ostensibly differentiate it from others, such as the logo, packaging colour, frequency of and reason for use, and any other characteristic.

Positioning is linked to the benefit, tangible or intangible, the manufacturer wishes to associate with consumption of the brand. For example, the chocolate 'countline' Kit Kat has been positioned for many years as a reward for hard work, epitomized in the famous strapline 'Have a break – have a Kit Kat'. In contrast, rival countline brands such as Bounty bars or Cadbury's Flake are positioned as sensuous indulgences, not rewards for hard work but rewards for just being you.[6] The differentiation is echoed in all advertising and brand communication since it is this differentiation which is essential to maintaining the brand's market share.

Positioning and the Marketing Concept

Positioning is fundamental to the marketing concept. Marketing as a business function cannot, of course, be wholly innovative as well as satisfying consumer needs. Consumer needs satisfaction must be reactive, while innovation requires leadership. By emphasizing the intangible benefit as well as the tangible qualities of the brand, marketing reconciles this contradiction. Advertising is often the major element in suggesting benefits to consumers. In this sense, it is through advertising that marketing can symbolically realize the ideal of consumer orientation. Motor-car manufacturers started putting more cup-holders in more cars because consumers said they wanted them. The Sony Walkman, in contrast, was an innovation that initially received negative reactions from consumer research because consumers could not envisage the benefit. They had never seen anything like it and had nothing to compare it with. Once the Walkman was marketed, consumers themselves learned that it solved the problem of boredom on walks or long journeys. If Akio Morita, the inventor of the Walkman and CEO of Sony, had enjoyed a large advertising budget he might have taught consumers the benefits of the Walkman through an advertising campaign. What he did have was an established retail distribution chain, so it made sense to simply put the Walkman on the shelves and let consumers discover the benefits for themselves. They did.

Positioning and Usage Occasions

Positioning can also refer to the usage occasions appropriate for a brand. For example, advertising can be used to signal to consumers that a brand can be used in an alternative way or by different people in relation to the previous norm. The chocolate snack Mars Bar was advertised for many years with the strapline 'A Mars a Day Helps You Work, Rest and Play'. This reflected the brand's positioning as a tasty snack that gave one enough energy to cope with a busy life. Like many chocolate snack ads it was presented as a solitary pleasure rather than a social one. A later advertising campaign showed a group of happy-go-lucky young people pushing a broken-down car to a garage, cheerfully chomping on Mars Bars, thus repositioning the brand's somewhat dated image for a younger and more socially-oriented consumer. Mars Bar consumption was now positioned as a social event and re-positioned to appeal to a younger audience. The breakfast cereal Kellogg's Cornflakes was the subject of an ad campaign that showed people enjoying cornflakes in non-breakfast scenarios. A couple enjoyed a romantic late-night bowl of cornflakes, and another consumer used the brand as a TV dinner. The aim was to increase sales to existing consumers by showing that you could eat cornflakes at any time. The brand was thus re-positioned as an anytime snack as well as a breakfast cereal.

Advertising Communication and the World's Most Recognized Brands

Advertising has helped to develop an international presence for the world's most well-known brands. If one tries to think of an internationally known brand, names like Sony, Marlboro, McDonald's, Levi Strauss, Nike, Disney, Kodak, Gillette, Mercedes-Benz and Coca-Cola are likely to come up. Advertising was not solely responsible for the success of these brands, since brand management is more complex and substantial than mere advertising. But it is hard to deny that such brands' status is inconceivable without advertising, in its various forms. Indeed, for a great majority of people this advertising supplies the only knowledge of the brand they will ever have. Millions of consumers have never owned a Mercedes, do not smoke cigarettes and rarely drink carbonated beverages. Nevertheless, if asked, many of these consumers could offer a fairly detailed description of the values and ideas they associate with Mercedes-Benz, Marlboro and Coca-Cola. Even brand names such as Prada, Gucci and Yves St Laurent are well known among consumers who have never owned any of their products.

The World's Most Valuable Brands[7]

The top 25 global brands by value in 2006 were:

1	Coca-Cola	14	American Express
2	Microsoft	15	Gillette
3	IBM	16	BMW
4	GE	17	Cisco
5	Intel	18	Louis Vultton
6	Nokia	19	Honda
7	Disney	20	Samsung
8	McDonald's	21	Dell
9	Toyota	22	Ford
10	Marlboro	23	Pepsi
11	Mercedes-Benz	24	Nescafé
12	Citi	25	Merril Lynch.
13	Hewlett Packard		

Which of these brands do you think owe most to advertising for their success?

The influence that advertising and promotion wield over non-consumers of brands is not trivial or incidental. Many global brands have acquired a cultural meaning which extends beyond buying or usage (Holt, 2004). You don't have to drive a Mercedes, wear a Rolex or drink Coke to understand that those brands have a distinctive cultural meaning. Prestige brands, in particular, convey associations of success and status so that it is central to their appeal that non-consumers understand these associations. This means that advertising that conveys the brand's values, presence and personality to non-consumers may be far from wasted. Indeed, the power of a given brand to signify particular values and impressions depends as much on the view of people who have never consumed it as upon the views of its regular consumers. Internationally known brands have a symbolic presence in social life that reaches beyond mere product consumption: they become part of the social vernacular. Advertising is normally intrinsic to building popular awareness and creating key associations for such brands.

The world's top brands spring readily to mind. There are countless brands in existence. Why have a small number of these acquired such a powerful presence in the consumer culture of so many countries around the world? One important reason is that over many years, and on a huge scale, these brands have invested in advertising. In many cases they have benefited from the striking creative work of talented advertising agencies which have made their campaigns and their brand distinctive and memorable. It is impossible to conceive of these brands in the ways that we do without advertising communication.

What Advertising and Promotional Communication Can Do for Brands

Advertising's role in marketing is often under-emphasized. It is easy to see why. Advertising and promotion are, too often, the very last things marketing or brand managers think about, after product development, market testing, business analysis, production planning, material sourcing, distribution, and so on. Yet it is a mistake to assume that the sequence of managerial activities involved in bringing a market offering to the consuming public reflects their relative importance. Advertising and other forms of marketing communication are not in themselves sufficient for successful consumer brand marketing, but in most cases they are necessary to the success of the venture.

From a managerial perspective advertising and promotion are the final step in bringing an offering to market. From a consumer perspective advertising is often the only step that they see before consumption. Advertising is the typical consumer's point of entry into the long chain of brand marketing planning and co-ordination. The advertising helps to establish a set of assumptions that the consumer will bring to all other aspects of their engagement with a given brand. Advertising is also important for the confidence and morale of other parties who have a stake in the success of a brand, such as shareholders, sales staff and other employees, and suppliers. Advertising provides tangible evidence of the financial credibility and competitive presence of an organization. Corporate communication is a distinct discipline in itself. But in a broader sense every ad is a reflection on the corporation that sponsored it because of the cumulative influence on its commercial credibility. Tangible benefits from this credibility might include longer supplier credit periods, greater influence over suppliers' prices, better employee retention and more effective recruitment, and greater confidence among stockmarket players. Advertising's corporate influence can spread far beyond the brand.

As a device of marketing strategy, advertising can also be both subtle and precise. Advertising is persuasive since it draws on values that obtain in non-marketing culture and attaches these values to marketed objects. Designer clothes, prestige motorcars, executive homes, upscale holidays and so on, all impute a social status to objects whose only social value is that constituted within a marketing culture. In turn, brands generate an emotional response from consumers as we wonder at the aesthetic beauty of advertising images, laugh at the wit of copywriters or realize our fantasies about own attractiveness and power vicariously through owning the right brands. Advertising is an important part of the creation and maintenance of the contrived brand values that make particular brands distinctive, memorable and, above all, desirable to their target groups.

The UK IPA claims[8] that among other business aims, advertising can:

- Defend brands against own-label growth
- Effect change internally as well as externally to the company
- Increase the efficiency of recruitment
- Transform entire businesses by generating new markets for a brand
- Revitalize a declining brand
- Reinvigorate a market
- Stop line extensions cannibalizing existing sales
- Change behaviour
- Influence the share price
- Make other communications more cost-effective
- Generate rapid sales increases
- Increase the growth of a mature brand in a declining market
- Address crises in public relations.

With creative ingenuity and careful targeting advertising can support many differing kinds of marketing objective. It must be remembered that advertising itself is communication: ads cannot sell anything as such, neither can they in themselves create a successful brand. What they can do is place particular ideas in the public realm to make consumers aware of brand offerings, create a favourable predisposition towards a brand, explain things about the brand and tell a story of uniqueness about the brand. Advertising can also support more closely specified marketing techniques such as positioning and repositioning, market segmentation, launch and relaunch, raising brand awareness or rebranding, and fulfilling corporate communication objectives.

Segmentation and Advertising Strategy

Advertising agency research performs the essential marketing activity of sorting and categorizing consumers. The resulting campaigns reinforce those categories, making membership seem attractive to certain targeted groups.

Marketing management texts have popularized the term 'segmentation' to refer to this need for categories of consumer to be broken down for easy identification, surveillance (through consumer research) and targeting. We consumers are often complicit in this categorization (Hackley, 2002), since we will eagerly seek out ads and images that we feel cohere with our sense of social identity and resonate with our individual aspirations and fantasies. Most importantly, this entails creating a sense of otherness towards categories of consumer that are not us. The distinctions between categories of consumer open up the possibility for consumer discretion and choice. In a given TV or poster ad the casting, the set, the scene props and the dialogue are all powerful signifiers of the kind of human who is supposed to favour a given brand.

It is a cliché in advertising that half the budget is wasted, but no one knows which half. The value of segmentation to organizations is that it can make marketing efforts appear more cost-effective by reducing the amount within a marketing budget that is misdirected at undesired consumer groups. Clearly there is a potential drawback to targeting a given segment. If the target group is wrongly identified then there is a risk that the entire marketing budget might be misdirected, instead of only half of it. As we have seen, brand planners might see sales increases as a long-term consequence of a strongly sustained brand personality. An over-emphasis on targeting might neglect to project the brand personality to non-consumers. This could be an important omission given that the brand personality depends as much on the perceptions of non-consumers as of consumers.

Political Advertising

Consumer marketing is not alone in using integrated marketing communication planning. Advertising has been extensively deployed in the case of socially important causes and non-profit organizations such as charities, care organizations and political parties (Peng and Hackley, 2009). For example, DDB London has been involved in many non-profit campaigns and also in political advertising in the UK (Peng and Hackley, 2007). This earned it the title 'Labour's ad agency'[9] in UK media circles. It has been behind many of the campaigns that have persuaded British voters to elect the Labour Party to power in three successive general elections (writing in July 2009). The agency is also proud of its cause-related advertising and has produced a record of many of these campaigns in a hardback book[10] (replete with a quote from the British prime minister, Tony Blair, that 'The examples of work … in this book show how advertising can contribute to social change'). Clients include the charities War on Want and Amnesty International, several unions (the National Union of Teachers and Unison, the public-sector workers' union) and local authorities, as well as the Labour Party itself.

Organizations that promoted causes of social welfare, such as the Labour Party and the trade unions, were historically unsympathetic to advertising because they associated it with a sell-out to capitalism. As a result such organizations were unable to promote themselves effectively. A change of viewpoint eventually emerged, significantly because of the involvement of DDB's chairman at the time, Chris Powell. This change of view about using advertising to promote left-wing politics and issues coincided with the political revival of the Labour Party.

Advertising today is being increasingly used as an arm of government policy. As we have noted, the government's Central Office of Information (COI) is now one of the biggest single buyers of advertising in the UK. One the one hand, it seems entirely proper to use the power of marketing to promote safer driving, more sensible drinking or to discourage fraud in unemployment benefit claims. On the other hand, all advertising that is sponsored by government can be seen as political advertising in a sense, since it promotes that government's values and agenda of the day and makes government action seem more visible and present (see for example, Hackley, 2009b; Hackley et al., 2008b).

Non-profit advertising, including charities, public sector, health services and public safety and information campaigns, have collectively become a significant sector of the advertising business. Campaigns in these areas are subject to the same planning processes as commercial advertising and promotion. The differences lie in the fact that each sector serves different stakeholders and, therefore, has different objectives to fulfil and different expectations to meet. Increasingly, though, non-profit campaigns are being designed to similar criteria as commercial campaigns, adjusted for the differing stakeholder requirements.

Integrated Marketing Communications Planning

The idea of Integrated Marketing Communications or IMC (Schultz, 2003; Schultz and Kitchen, 1997; Schultz et al., 1993), then, reflects the need to take a global view of a brand and to ensure that brand communications across all media are consistent in terms of the brand image, values and personality, and that the media channels used are complementary with regard to segmentation, positioning and targeting. IMC has become more popular because of various factors, notably the fragmentation of media audiences and changes in the media consumption patterns of these audiences in the light of an explosion of **new media** channels and vehicles. Concomitantly, IMC reflects a shift in power from manufacturers to consumers, a shift from mass to niche media channels and vehicles, the emphasis on data-driven marketing, and the move to 24/7 consumption.

Integration of media implies the use of online and offline media channels. Offline media channels could include the traditional 'old media' of television, print (newspapers, magazines), radio, cinema advertising, and also outdoor advertising, direct marketing, public relations, personal selling and sales promotion. Online channels could include dedicated websites, optimization of search engine results, email, banner and click-through advertising, podcasts, blogs and other web-based exposure.

BOX 3.3

Creative Execution: The Role of Art and Dramatic Realism

Ad agencies use imagery and metaphors from classical art and literature to create aesthetically inspiring dramatic portrayals of the product along with 'an account of … the social benefit that the consumer could be expected to derive' (Leiss et al., 1997: 79). Marchand (1985) describes the advertising technique used to accomplish this effect as 'dramatic realism'. For example, an everyday situation such as dirt on clothes might be portrayed as a problem that the model housewife solves, with the help of Daz, Omo or some other branded detergent. The picture accompanying the advertising text would be carefully drawn as graphic art, perhaps with an attractive model in a striking pose, in juxtaposition with the brand logo and packaging. Advertising realized the consumer's need for aesthetic stimulation and symbolic self-expression and bridged the gap between manufacturers and creative artists. In this way the design of American advertising and the products themselves was improved (Leiss et al., 1997: 81). Consumers were treated to advertising that was aesthetically attractive and a product that could express something about the consumer personality and social identity.

Two Dimensions of Integration for Brand Communication: Themes and Channels

It is important to understand the rationale behind the integration of marketing communications. One key issue has been noted above. That is, the primacy of the brand as the concept which drives marketing activity. All marketing activity is designed to support, enhance and reflect the brand as a symbol of certain values and characteristics which differentiate it in the market. Consumers seek out brands, we recognize them and we pay more for the reassurance that quality brands offer. A brand may comprise many tangible things, and consumer preferences may be developed through the direct experience of buying it. But there is also a powerful element of communication involved since the brand image is built up not only through direct personal experience of the brand's utility but also through less tangible attitudes and perceptions which are influenced by the communication we read, hear, see and express about the brand. The management effort to ensure a co-ordinated and coherent approach to integrated brand planning rests on two overlapping and connected dimensions: (1) brand themes; and (2) media channels.

The first, themes, concerns the need to manage the distinctive brand values and personality as they are expressed through all communication, from corporate to product–market communication. This focuses on the visible elements of the brand, including its colours, logo, typeface, and other aspects of the visual representation. So there should be particular themes which reflect and portray the brand positioning that can run through all marketing communication for a given brand to ensure that the brand is recognized and its positioning is distinctive. This is no easy task when campaigns may have many parts, perhaps designed by different sub-contracted agency specialists. Nevertheless, it is the key task of brand planning to ensure that the brand retains its integrity whatever the medium or creative execution may be.

The second dimension concerns channel integration. We live in a world of integrated and interlocking media. If we have a favourite TV show we don't just watch the show. We can read weblogs posted by fans or critics, we can go to the show's website for stories about the characters and the actors or to buy merchandise. We can even download episodes via the internet, to listen to via podcast or on a mobile device. We can buy magazines which carry articles for fans of the show. And so it goes, a given brand, whether it be a car, a watch, or a clothing range of a movie or syndicated TV show, can be exposed on many different media channels. It is therefore incumbent on the brand management to utilize these different media channels in promotion of brand, and to try to manage the brand image through these channels by influencing the editorial. Existing and potential new consumers will form perceptions of a brand from an aggregation of their encounters with it across different media channels.

The Integrated Marketing Communications Plan

There is no definitive formula for planning or implementing IMC. The precise composition of an IMC plan will differ according to the particular market and communication context, and according to the custom and practice of particular organizations. A plan is not a prescription and nor is it a checklist. It is a guide for action. Typically, an IMC plan would have the following general elements.

- Executive summary
- Brand research and competition analysis
- Target audience
- Communication objectives

- Advertising strategy
- Creative approach
- Media plan
- Action plan and tactics
- Budget estimates
- Effectiveness.

Brand Research and Competition Analysis

It is rare for brands to require a radical re-positioning which distances the brand from its earlier manifestations. In most cases, the brand needs some continuity from one campaign to the next to reflect the coherence and stability of the brand personality. This is why it is so important for the agency to research the brand and the client organization in order to try to fully understand its history and values. This includes looking at previous promotional campaigns. In addition, it is important to thoroughly understand the competitive context in which the brand is operating. Brand values and personalities must be understood in the context of alternatives – the reason for the brand is to differentiate the offer from competitors, so it must be understood in relation to those competitors. This differentiation expresses the brand's positioning, and it also reflects the attitudes and values which consumers project onto the brand. So for an integration in brand communication to be achievable, it is a prerequisite that the advertising agency has a deep understanding of that brand.

In many cases, the agency will take two or three weeks over this research and analysis stage. The account team will rely mainly on secondary sources but they may also make use of primary sources in the form of focus groups with consumers and in-depth discussions with the client staff. After all, if a client thinks its brand values are different to those the consumers think it has then there is a fundamental communication problem to address. Advertising agency staff are fond of relating stories about clients who didn't understand their own brand. It is easy to understand that internal organizational values and politics might make it difficult to face reality if, for example, a brand personality has been distorted through negative media coverage. Sometimes a dispassionate agency view can highlight such incoherence between the brand values as envisaged by the client and those as perceived by the consumer. Whether the client can accept such advice is another matter.

Either way, the first element in the process of creating an integrated marketing communications campaign is for the agency to gain a thorough and insightful understanding of the brand, its history and values, and its competitive context.

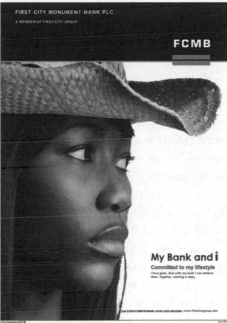

Picture 4   First City Monument Bank of Nigeria have positioned their brand as one which chimes with their customers' dreams and aspirations (see chapter case).

Reproduced by kind permission of FCMB and Centrespread FCB.

(See the colour insert near the middle of this book for a full colour image.)

Target Audience

Advertising agencies need to know to whom the client wants them to speak. This refers to the tasks of **segmentation** and **targeting**. But knowing who the target audience is, is simply not enough. A conscientious agency will also want to understand the lifestyle preferences, consumption habits, media consumption patterns, values, attitudes, drives, aspirations, income, priorities and influential **peer groups** of its target segment. Qualitative research in the form of discussion or focus groups, or surveys, can be of assistance in this stage of the process. Secondary data sources detailing demographic and other information important to segmentation and targeting can also be invaluable.

If the mentality, lifestyle, demographic characteristics and buying preferences of the target group are understood, then this can form the basis for a creative execution which speaks to its members in a way which they will recognize. Defining the target audience is a difficult task with major implications. Once the audience is defined, this will drive the media plan and advertising schedule. It will also heavily influence the advertising strategy and creative execution. Get it wrong, and all the effort is wasted. If the defined audience is too narrow then opportunities for consumer engagement will be lost and the campaign will not yield the desired return on investment. If the target group definition is too wide, then the impact may be lost or the campaign might be scheduled on a medium which the real targets don't use.

Communication Objectives

Building on the above information and insights, the account team will be ready to formulate communication objectives. These will guide the overall approach and should dovetail into the client's marketing plan objectives. Communication objectives are key because they will form the bridge between the marketing plan and the integrated marketing communications campaign. They will clarify how communication can support the marketing objectives.

Life in brand marketing and advertising agencies consists of a lot of meetings at which every step in the planning process is debated and discussed. Each element of the IMC plan will be interrogated for its coherence and viability. The elements of the brand personality and its 'essence' are so difficult to pin down that this kind of process is necessary in order to keep everyone's attention focused on the key brand values and personality and to ensure that these are superimposed throughout all communication channels and mix elements.

Communication objectives might, for example, be to engage the interest of the target audience and inform them about the kinds of problem-solving challenges entailed in active army service, as in the case at the end of Chapter 10. In this case, a campaign designed by the publicity agency for the British Army, called 'Start Thinking Soldier', made use of a computer game to engage the desired target audience, a technique sometimes called 'advergaming'. The target group was young males who were likely to be familiar with war strategy gaming. The overall marketing objective was to achieve army recruitment figures. But it is a given that about half of the target group will simply not consider an army career. However, there may be targets set for the number of online gamers who actually contact the army for a careers information session in relation to the number who go online just to play the game. Clearly, if thousands play the game but hardly any then contact the army for an interview, the campaign will have failed. A further consideration might be the quality of those applicants who do apply. If the campaign generates a lot of inquiries but only a small number actually get accepted for an army career, then again the success of the campaign could be called in to doubt. On the other hand, even before it gets into full swing the campaign has attracted press coverage and blogging comment, so it has already raised general awareness that the British army is seeking recruits with IT and problem-solving skills.

The communication objectives might state a need to position, or re-position the brand in terms of market-leading competitors. It might express a need to create a stronger brand personality, or to access a new, younger market. It might be about raising awareness of a new brand launch in an established market. Whatever the objective is, it should be something that can be achieved through communication and which supports the marketing objectives.

Advertising Strategy

Advertising has to have a purpose in order to succeed. If no one knows what they want to achieve by a campaign, then success is not possible because there will be no yardstick by which to measure it. The **advertising strategy** is important because it guides the creative team and encourages them to produce creative work which can motivate the desired consumers in a way which supports the overall communication objectives. To be effective, the advertising strategy should be expressed in simple terms without jargon, so that creatives (who have no patience with marketing jargon) can understand it.

The advertising strategy should explain what the ad is going to do. For example, should it motivate an immediate response? Does the client want people who engage with the ad to pick up the phone or go on the internet to contact the company? Or is the aim to encourage an emotional response from the viewer in the interest of building a long-term brand equity? Is it to persuade the consumer to trial the product, or to convince them that it is better value/cooler/a higher quality than those of competitors? Is the strategy to change consumer attitudes or buying habits? The advertising strategy will inform the creative brief which is the document the creative team has to work from. It is therefore essential that the advertising strategy, the reason for advertising, is clear, coherent and consistent with the overall brand personality and communication objectives.

Creative Approach and Creative Brief

Once the marketing and communication objectives have been decided and the advertising strategy devised, the most important part of the whole process is undertaken – this is the creative approach. The creative approach can undo all the careful planning and waste the budget, or it can leverage the brand and generate benefits of positive publicity far in excess of expectations. For example, some striking creative approaches capture the public imagination and are talked about in the press and over the internet. As Dichter (1966) noted, the ways in which a creative approach is talked about (or not) are of great importance to the success or failure of a campaign. A campaign which is talked about will receive unsolicited attention which spreads the brand values and reinforces the brand presence. A creative execution which is ignored because it's regarded as boring might lack impact and resonance for the target group. On the other hand, with some campaigns and some brands it is more important to portray the brand values in a clear and coherent way than it is to be creatively striking. As with all other elements of the IMC plan, the precise marketing and communication objectives in the context of the brand's values, positioning and competitive position will inform the creative approach.

The creative approach is decided on with reference to the creative brief. The **creative brief** is an important document which is discussed in more detail in the next chapter. It is the guide from which the creative team will work and it represents an agreement between the agency and the client regarding what the advertising should achieve. The brief disciplines the creative work to ensure that the creativity is not over indulged simply because it looks great or because it's so funny. The aim of advertising is not to win awards for creatives or to gratify their creative urges but to generate business for clients. The creative brief is the document which represents the client and agency interest in the campaign. It is the creative expression of the communication strategy.

The creative team must express the brand values and the advertising strategy in a way which attracts the right kind of attention from the target group. The creative approach also needs to consider practical issues such as the budget, length or size of ad, medium or channel. Most importantly, it needs to be focused according to the particular type(s) of person to whom the advertisement must speak. Creatives will tend to claim that if they know their audience, whatever kind of person that is, they can produce a piece of work which motivates that audience. So the brief has to be based on careful research and clear commercial reasoning. For example, the visual created by Centrespread FCB for First City Monument Bank (see Picture 4, p. 85) encapsulated the campaign strategy and objectives (see Chapter 3 case).

Media Plan

In any advertising campaign there are important decisions to take regarding media, and many issues to consider. Most media buying agencies are now independent of advertising agencies, but media should have been kept in mind from the beginning of the IMC process because media and creative execution are interdependent. How can the target group be reached most efficiently and with the greatest impact? Do media choices have to accommodate a direct response element? Does the budget allow for broadcast media, or does it confine the campaign to local print media?

The media plan (discussed more extensively in Chapter 5) directs the campaign to the right target audience with the maximum impact and reach, at the lowest possible **cost-per-thousand** consumers reached. Some campaigns will burst on to the scene saturating all media channels for a week, and then disappear. Others will be planned to drip feed the communication into consumers' consciousness in short exposures at longer intervals over a protracted period of time. Still others will be focused on seasonal demand issues, such as when chocolate manufacturers spend a large proportion of their advertising budget in the UK over the Christmas period because of the high concentration of chocolate sales at that time. The media schedule depends not only on the budget but also on the brand, the market, the target audience or segment, and the campaign objectives.

BOX 3.4

Tracking the Effectiveness of BT's 'It's Good to Talk' Campaign

One example of effective campaign tracking involved the use of a statistical technique called multivariate analysis to try to establish a strong correlation between a campaign and a change in customer behaviour. A famous UK campaign (called 'It's Good to Talk') conducted for British Telecom (BT) by London agency DDB attempted to change the telephone usage habits of domestic British customers. The advertising agency's consumer research had established that the average length of British domestic telephone conversations was significantly shorter than those in other countries such as the USA, Italy and Germany. It seemed that there was a British mentality that saw talking on the telephone as a cost which should be minimized. In fact the cost was and is small as a proportion of household income. In many other countries domestic telephone users seemed to regard telephone conversation as a necessary expense and spoke for far longer on average on each call. This consumer research insight formed the basis for the campaign. A series of TV ads dramatically portrayed the typically succinct British phone user as someone lacking in empathy and warmth. The message was that it was kinder to talk at greater length, especially when talking to loved ones. The ads also suggested that telephone communication could strengthen bonds of family and friendship if people used it generously. It was claimed that the campaign resulted in a major social change: domestic telephone usage habits in the UK were substantially altered. A near 60 per cent increase in call revenues to BT was claimed. The agency used multivariate analysis to correlate the electronic data on telephone conversation length with the exposure of the TV ads, thus demonstrating the success of the campaign.

Budget and Effectiveness

In reality, in many cases, the budget has been set by the client before the first stage in the IMC planning process has begun. Where the agency does have scope for action is in accounting for the success, or failure, of a campaign. Any campaign can be assessed against the objectives set for it, though doing so is not always a simple task. Calculating the return on investment (ROI) is a difficult but important task in marketing and advertising since it reflects the effectiveness of different kinds of marketing intervention and the implications go straight to the bottom line of profitability. The ROI is also important in deciding for the future what budget to allocate to particular forms of advertising.

Chapter 4 looks at ways in which the effectiveness of advertising is measured. As noted above, well-planned campaigns have clear and achievable objectives precisely so that their achievement (or lack of it) can be judged. For example, if the communication objective of a campaign were to change attitudes towards eating a brand of breakfast cereal so that consumers would start to eat it in the evening as a snack, it would be relatively easy to conduct a street level survey asking respondents when they ate this brand of breakfast cereal before and after the campaign. Before and after surveys of attitudes or behaviours are common methods of measuring campaign effectiveness. Another common approach is to use internal company records to look at sales patterns or new customer inquiries which might be linked in principle to advertising exposures. Many measures of effectiveness rely on long-term data regarding the market share or sales volume, so the true effect of an advertising campaign can often not be fairly judged until many months after that campaign.

Limitations and qualifications to IMC

IMC has made a big splash in academic journals but its resonance for practitioners is variable (Eagle et al., 2007). On the one hand, practitioners tend to agree that integration is a given in contemporary advertising planning. The use of new media is essential if clients are to fully leverage the promotional budget. On the other hand, many professionals dispute whether it is possible or desirable to formalize IMC. This intersects debates within strategy and marketing on the virtues and practical difficulties of planning per se. In many cases, business plans are created through an internal process that focuses minds and helps to disburse resources, but often departs more than somewhat from what actually takes place. Plans tend to rest on assumptions, the full implications of which will only become apparent when the action is underway. This is not to argue that planning is irrelevant in business and administration, it is merely to point out that while planning is a necessary and fundamental part of managerial processes it does have its limitations.

With regard to IMC, many industry professionals ask whether it can ever be more than partially achievable. Media integration is something which depends very much on the circumstances of the brief, on the creativity and lateral thinking of the teams involved, and on the objectives for the campaign. How can there be theories or principles of IMC if each brief is so very different? What is more, from a practical perspective, should there be an assumption that IMC is a necessary virtue for any campaign?

It is by no means clear that integration will benefit every brief. It is a standard part of advertising planning that there will be an evaluation of media channels in terms of segmentation and targeting, audience reach, resonance and cost-per-thousand target consumers. In this regard, some practitioners argue that IMC is nothing new. The media channels have changed and the media vehicles have multiplied, but advertising has always been subject to such changes and has adapted accordingly. It has always been the conventional wisdom in advertising that media channels are used selectively: why use every channel just because they are there?

One reason might be that media consumption patterns have changed in such a way that reaching a target consumer through all possible channels is now feasible, where it wasn't before. But even this is dubious. The ideal of controlling the message via every medium by which the target audience might access brand communication is all very well in principle, but there are many barriers. Firstly, absolute control of brand communication is not possible – there will always be leakage between media, say through media editorial coverage. User-generated content such as blogs and wikis, Twittering, and so forth, occupies much internet space and neither this, nor everyday news stories connecting with the brand, can be controlled. They can be reacted to and incorporated into communication plans, but this is a reactive process largely charged to the media relations function.

Furthermore, absolute control over brand communications on every medium may not even be desirable, even if it were possible. Brands are products of culture. They result from the interactions of consumers in the social context in which they are seen and used. They are not entirely the creation of the brand owner. Most brands, indeed, are building user generated content into their strategies through Web 2.0 applications and consumer engagement initiatives. Arguably, this is less about control and more about opening up the brand to consumer engagement which feeds back into brand and communications planning.

Where there is less argument is around the need for advertising and promotional planning to integrate creative themes across different media platforms. This is dictated by the logic of branding – a brand must represent distinctive values and these are linked with certain conventions of visual and auditory representation. Put more simply, a brand ought to be distinguished by the same colour scheme or signature tune whatever the medium, so that consumers can recognize it as that brand. But many professionals regard this as a given, and no more than professional common sense, rather than a theoretical or formal planning principle. IMC is undoubtedly an area which professionals in communication cannot ignore. It is perhaps not surprising that academic and scholarly research focuses around trying to gather together general principles or theories, while professionals are focused more pragmatically on **client briefs** which can be utterly different from day to day.

Naturally, if academics can generate a theory of IMC which helps practitioners get more out of their clients' budgets then there would be less scepticism and much applause from the industry. But like so much research and theory in business and management, the ambition of IMC scholarship and research has not yet been realized in terms of its relevance and effectiveness for practice. Nonetheless, several factors will ensure that IMC as an idea continues to receive attention from all sides. One factor concerns the possibilities for greater efficiency and accountability opened up by electronic advertising media, especially Web 2.0 applications and the increasing advertising potential of mobiles. While this area may not be accessible to a general theory, it is certainly one in which practitioners will be interested to receive any useful general insights or principles. In particular, the economic recession and the consequent squeeze on promotional budgets will mean that greater attention will be paid to cost-per-thousand and return on investment criteria. These returns can be measured most effectively through new media. Another factor concerns the fragmentation of media audiences and changes in media consumption patterns (see Chapter 5) which mean that advertising and promotional planners often have to deploy integrated campaigns simply in order to reach sufficient numbers of their desired market segment. Finally, the increased attention being paid to consumer engagement with brand communications also pushes planners towards new media which can facilitate such an engagement in far more cost efficient and user-appealing ways than conventional media.

Chapter Summary

Chapter 3 outlined the brand planning and integrated marketing communication process. It explained the distinctions between marketing objectives, communication objectives and advertising strategy. It also discussed the distinctions between marketing strategy and tactics, and noted that advertising and promotion can be strategic as well as tactical. The two main dimensions of integration were explained, these being an integration of the brand theme across channels, and the integration of media channels in advertising campaigns. The chapter then listed the basic stages in a typical IMC plan. Each stage in the plan was outlined in Chapter 3 while many of these are developed in greater detail in other parts of the book. Finally, limitations and caveats around the somewhat fashionable notion of IMC were discussed. While interest in the concept will likely continue, there is so much variation in communication briefs that general theories or principles of IMC will probably be less likely to emerge than fragmented and context-dependent insights. Chapter 4 moves on to discuss the internal processes and roles of advertising agencies engaged in this process.

 ■ Review Questions

1   Collect 10 video, radio or print advertisements and divide them between two groups. Each group should try to ascertain what each of their ads was intended to accomplish. In other words, what was the planning rationale behind the ads? Then the two groups should swap ads and perform the same exercise on the other group of ads. The two groups combined should discuss their respective analysis of each ad and decide which analysis seems the most likely to be accurate. The intention behind the ads should be considered in the light of such issues as: (a) the likely target audience for the brand; (b) other possible stakeholders; (c) the apparent brand positioning indicated by the ad's creative approach; (d) the choice of medium; and (e) other marketing issues concerning this brand.

2   List as many examples as you can of marketing objectives that might be supported with advertising and promotion. Be prepared to justify your choice with examples or reasoning.

3   Is the role of communication in marketing primarily tactical or strategic? Give reasons for your answer.

4   Develop a scenario in which your group has been asked to offer outline creative ideas for the launch of a new brand of chocolate confection called 'Slick'. Focus on the segmentation, targeting (especially media) and positioning issues.

CASE

My Bank and I – First City Monument Bank[11]

In mid-2009, First City Monument Bank[12] of Nigeria wanted a campaign to make them the number one financial services brand in Nigeria in the 'hearts and minds of the customers'. The core proposition of the campaign was to be empowerment of the customer and the campaign should aim to enhance and sharpen the brand positioning and generate organic growth. Research had shown that the bank brand had already generated considerable recall and emotional bonding with its target audience through the 'My Bank and I' campaigns. FCMB enlisted the Lagos (Nigeria) agency Centrespread FCB[13] to extend the campaign with the aim of deepening this bond, extending the brand internationally and developing a strong platform for subsequent product communications.

FCMB were pleased with the impact of the 'My Bank and I' theme but highlighted some challenges which remained. One was to transfer the emotional response and recall into product trials on a greater scale. Campaign tasks included developing an IMC approach over a two-year period through 2010 and ensuring an international standard of creative execution to position FCMB alongside other global bank brands. The ads had to have the right look for a leading national brand with global ambitions.

Campaign objectives included: 'Increase brand visibility and spontaneous awareness; increase brand trial; offer world-class communications which creatively showcase the African origins of the brand; and elevate the proposition to an operational phase which delivers on the brand promise'. The campaign aimed to generate high recall and aspirational, distinctive associations for the brand. The 'My Bank and I' tag line would continue to run through the campaign, as would the FCMB brand colours and icons.

The primary target audience consisted of local customers aged 35–45, **socio-economic groups** C2–C1, with a higher than average education and income and also an urbane, international outlook. A secondary target audience was international businesspeople and entrepreneurs. The communications campaign was to be carried out alongside operational improvements in service delivery to connect the brand message with the consumer experience. The campaign was planned with a 360 degree media approach including television, print and out of home (OOH), radio, and **below-the-line** approaches such as experiential marketing and sales promotion.

The creative theme sought to resonate with warmth by reflecting its customers and their aspirations on a personal level, yet also embodying the brand values of professionalism, ambition, creativity and excellence. Centrespread FCB produced a series of print ads with a similar theme, picturing different individuals with the same copy theme (see Picture 4 for one example which shows an image of aspiration realised in the face of a customer) to underline the proposition that the bank was about its customers.

■ Case Questions

1 The FCMB campaign was grounded in detailed consumer and market research under the planning function. What do you feel the planning function adds to the campaign strategy? NB more detail can be seen on the planning function in Chapter 4.

2 What kinds of research do you feel banks and financial services brands could do to generate relevant consumer insights?

3 As a financial services brand, are there any specific issues FCMB has to address, or do you feel that brand marketing challenges are essentially the same whatever the sector?

■ ■ Further Reading ■

Eagle, L., Kitchen, P.J. and Bulmer, S. (2007) 'Insights into interpreting integrated marketing communications: a two-nation qualitative comparison', *European Journal of Marketing*, 41 (7/8): 956–70.

Holt, D. (2004) *How Brands Become Icons: The Principles of Cultural Branding.* Boston, MA: Harvard Business School Press.

Percy, L. and Elliott, R. (2009) *Strategic Advertising Management*, 3rd edn. Oxford: Oxford University Press.

Pickton, D. and Broderick, A. (2005) *Integrated Marketing Communications*. London: FT Books.

Schultz, D. (2003) *IMC – The Next Generation*. New York: McGraw-Hill.

Schultz, D. and Kitchen, P. (1997) 'Integrated marketing communications in US advertising agencies: an exploratory study', *Journal of Advertising Research*, September/October: 7–18.

Schultz, D., Martin, D. and Brown, W.P. (1987) *Strategic Advertising Campaigns*, 2nd edn. Lincolnwood, PH: NTC Books.

Web-based Resources

Many professional associations offer marketing resources through the web. All the sites below offer useful resources and links illustrating how advertising has addressed marketing and communications planning issues.

Account planning group, a group of professionals in account planning: www.apg.org/uk

A site about creating advertising strategy: www.adcracker.com/strategy/Advertising_Strategy.htm

Advertising Association (UK): www.adassoc.org.uk

The UK Chartered Institute of Marketing resources section: www.cim.co.uk/resources/home.aspx

Advertising creativity site: www.adcritic.com

Advertising Research Foundation (US): www.arfsite.org

American Advertising Agency Association: www.aaaa.org/

American Advertising Federation: www.aaf.org

UK Institute of Practitioners in Advertising: www.ipa.co.uk

World Advertising Research Centre (UK): www.warc.com

American Marketing Association teaching cases: www.marketingpower.com/Community/ARC/Pages/Teaching/Cases/default.aspx

On the Companion Website

These journal articles are freely available on the companion website (www.sagepub.co.uk/hackley).

Business, Advertising, and the Social Control of News
Robert L. Craig
Journal of Communication Inquiry, Jul 2004; vol. 28: pp. 233–252.

Firm-to-Firm and Interpersonal Relationships: Perspectives from Advertising Agency Account Managers
Diana L. Haytko
Journal of the Academy of Marketing Science, Jul 2004; vol. 32: pp. 312–328.

Marketing Dèjá Vu: The Discovery of Integrated Marketing Communications
Harlan E. Spotts, David R. Lambert, and Mary L. Joyce
Journal of Marketing Education, Dec 1998; vol. 20: pp. 210–218.

Notes

1   The traditional four P's model has, of course, been adapted in many cases to include additional Ps such as People (to cover the training and personal service element) and Processes (for business processes covering service, safety or manufacturing quality).
2   www.theenginegroup.com/ (accessed 9 April 2009).
3   www.wcrs.com/ (accessed 9 April 2009).
4   www.theenginegroup.com/what-we-do/ (accessed 9 April 2007).
5   See Naomi Klein, *No Logo* website, or for a sociological critique of branding read George Ritzer (2000), *The McDonaldization of Society.*
6   Countline is a category of confection in the grocery trade in which chocolate is combined with another element, say, wafer, biscuit or nuts. Flake and KitKat were repositioned by their respective manufacturers (Cadbury and Nestlé) to move away from long-standing positioning strategies.
7   Source: Business Week Online website, http://bwnt.businessweek.com/brand/2005/ 'The Top 100 global brands scoreboard', data provided by Interbrand (accessed 20 July 2006).
8   The source for this and some other examples in this chapter is the IPA publication, *It Pays to Advertise*, Advertising Effectiveness Awards, 1996 (published 1997). The IPA awards books are available through www.warc.com
9   Source: feature article in the *Guardian* national newspaper, 'Labour's ad agency told to sell euro entry as "patriotic"', 29 June 2003.
10 *How the Left Learned to Love Advertising: Social and Political Advertising by BMP DDB 1970–2000*, published by DDB London.
11 With thanks to First City Monument Bank and Centrespread FCB of Lagos, Nigeria, for kind permission to adapt this material. Special thanks to Dr Tayo Otunbanjo of Centrespread FCB.
12 www.firstcitygroup.com/newfcmb/index.aspx
13 www.centrespreadfcb.com

4 Advertising Agencies: Creative Work and Management Processes

Chapter Outline

The opening chapter explained that advertising agencies are operating in an uncertain environment. New advertising funding models are being driven by digital and mobile communication and this is having an impact on spot advertising revenues in traditional mass media vehicles. Many agencies are meeting these challenges and adapting to the new environment by mixing new knowledge and techniques with established practice. Chapter 4 offers an overview of the advertising process. It describes how communications campaigns are created, from the client brief to the campaign launch and evaluation. The individual roles in typical agency account teams are examined. The way these roles contribute to communications planning and development is discussed. Particular issues addressed include conflict, creativity and the role of the account planning function in creative development.

Key chapter content

- Advertising agencies as cultural intermediaries

- Advertising agencies and the marketing communication disciplines

- The leading agency brands

- Advertising agency working processes

- The creative advertising development process

- Evaluating advertising effectiveness.

Advertising Agencies as Cultural Intermediaries

Adverting agencies act as cultural intermediaries in the sense that they take elements of culture such as art, language and music, and then use them to make up new forms of communication aimed at a selected audience. Culture in this sense is meant broadly to mean not only high art, classical music and serious literature, though these are certainly part of the advertisers' vocabulary, but also aspects of everyday culture such as current affairs and media news stories, popular fashions, fads and trends, not to mention the everyday practices of consumers. Advertisements take culture and reflect it back at itself, making new meanings some of which become culturally iconic themselves (Holt, 2004). This circular movement of cultural meaning, interwoven with commercial messages, gives a particular resonance to the work of advertising agencies from the point of view of cultural, sociological and media studies (see, e.g. Blake et al., 1996; Cronin, 2008; Deuze, 2007; deWaal Malefyt and Moeran, 2003; Fowles, 1996; Kelly et al., 2005; Leiss et al., 2005; McCracken, 2005; Nixon, 2003; Svensson, 2007).

Operating at the interface of culture and commerce, advertising agencies can be seen to have a powerful ideological role in normalizing social practices as diverse as cigarette smoking, being cheeky to parents, playing computer games, being conscious of the status implications of brands, shouting aggressively at football matches, drinking alcohol and wearing bikinis. Some of these social practices are controversial in some cultures, and this illustrates the difficult position advertising agencies occupy in contemporary culture. Advertising is often a target for criticism because of its putative influence over behaviour and cultural values. But on the other hand, advertising uses culture as its material – it takes what is already out there and combines it with images of consumption in order to gain the attention of its audiences. So the question of whether advertising causes certain things or merely reflects them becomes a circular one because of its role as cultural intermediary, taking language, behaviour, values and trends from everyday culture and transforming them into messages of consumption. Advertising may magnify or even distort social practices, behaviour and values that are already out there, but whether it really exercises the negative influence that some critics assume is open to question. The advertising industry contributes to its own difficulties by, on the one hand, exaggerating the positive effects of advertising, and, on the other, denying responsibility for its perceived negative effects.

Part of the fascination of advertising and promotion for practitioners is that it entails solving problems of communication when the main basis of communication, language, is continually adapting to express new kinds of experience and to accommodate new influences. The English language is especially popular in advertising the world over probably because of its flexibility and global familiarity as the language of business. Of course, advertising's use of imagery and music makes it a richer device of communication than language alone. Indeed, as we have noted, part of advertising's uniqueness as a discourse form derives from its capacity to combine language with music, pictures and substance or medium (Cook, 2001). But language itself carries meaning within its context: there is a medium of transmission (written or aural) and meanings are nuanced through the combination of language with tone, gesture and other aspects of context. Advertising and promotion offer forms of communication that not only set language in any social context with which we are familiar, but also invent new contexts through novel combinations of imagery, words and music. The possibilities for novelty in advertising communication seem limitless. Advertising can be seen as a form of discourse since it is an identifiable form of communication that can be described. As a discourse, advertising is defined by its conventional forms and styles, even though these are constantly changing.

As we have noted, advertising and communication agencies produce cultural texts that portray consumption by drawing on social practices and symbols extant in the wider, non-consumption culture. For example, at the simplest level, a promotion that pictures people riding on a public bus cannot communicate anything unless viewers of the ad are familiar with the cultural practice of riding on a public bus. Riding on a bus is not merely an act: it is a cultural practice because it is subject to agreed rules that are never actually stated. There are ways of paying one's fare, ways of taking one's seat (or not taking one and standing up), ways of disembarking at the correct stop, even ways of speaking to fellow passengers or to the driver. If one tries to take a bus ride in a strange country with an unfamiliar language the importance of these conventions becomes all too apparent and one can look, and feel, socially inept because one does not know them. Advertisements presuppose the consumer's cultural knowledge of local social practices (Thompson et al., 1994). Consequently, it is important for the creators of advertising to share or understand the social milieu of consumers so that the ads they create will be invested with a social significance for viewers (Bakhtin, 1989; Brown et al., 1999; Hackley, 2002, citing Scott, 1994a and b; Iser, 1978).

In portraying everyday activities in rather magnified and glamorized ways, advertising and promotion reveal us to ourselves. The ordinary things we do are portrayed in film and photography, from taking a shower to buying a coffee. No doubt advertising's use of high-quality cinematography and print techniques and elaborate sets, together with its prominence in public spaces, make our everyday activities portrayed in this way seem dramatically compelling and loaded with significance. Taking a shave with a Gillette wet razor, for example, is portrayed as a symbolic statement of social status and material aspiration, and confers a powerful (symbolic) sexual attraction on the shaver. Underlying all advertising communication is the implicit message that it is consumption, and not merely its portrayal in advertising, that can make our experience of life more fulfilling. For this communication to work there has to be a shared cultural vocabulary between the makers and consumers of advertising. Advertising and promotional agencies operate at this cultural interface, continually reprocessing cultural meanings to create this communication between brand marketing organizations and consumers.

Advertising is, of course, a formidable commercial tool as well as a form of hybridized communication art. Mass advertising can be a powerful marketing blunderbuss, browbeating consumers into compliance by conditioning through repetition. It also has the flexibility to support many kinds of marketing and business objectives with tailored specificity. It can reflect and magnify social changes and is an important cultural influence. The ways in which advertising and promotion are produced and consumed are constantly changing, reflecting rapid and far-reaching innovations in technology, media and the organization of agencies. A viable account of advertising practice, then, must be able to accommodate some of this complexity.

Advertising Agencies and the Marketing Communication Disciplines

This chapter will use the traditional, full-service agency as its point of departure for describing the marketing communications business. However, it should be noted that the way agencies are organized and the range of expertise they offer are coming under increasing pressure for change both from clients and from structural changes in the industry. The specialist, above-the-line advertising agency may be in decline, as clients demand **integrated solutions** (as discussed in Chapter 3) and media agencies acquire greater power and importance.

Movies and books (such as Vance Packard's *The Hidden Persuaders*, 1957) have contributed to the slightly sinister image of the advertising profession (see also Deuze, 2007; Hackley, 2007; and Hackley and Kover, 2007). It is probably fair to say that advertising does not enjoy the same kind of professional prestige as, say, medicine or architecture, or perhaps even politics. Yet there is also a certain glamour attached to working in advertising and promotion.

Competition for graduate trainee or creative positions in agencies is intense because careers in the area are so prized. Advertising attracts the attention of caricaturists because it is difficult to categorize and its professional activities are not widely understood. It occupies an industrial sector of its own; it is a service but it is also more than that, it is almost, but not quite, a branch of entertainment. It is a business, but then again, not exactly like other businesses. It is part of the creative industries, but quite unlike a theatre company or publishing house.

The integration of marketing communications has been a recurring theme for consultants and academics in the last decade and-a-half, but the industry of communication management remains largely organized along specialist functional lines. As well as advertising agencies and their traditional emphasis on above-the-line mass media, there are agencies that specialize in below-the-line sales promotions, word-of-mouth and **viral marketing** communications, direct and database marketing, and also public relations, consumer and market research, industrial or business-to-business advertising, new product development, sponsorship, merchandising, strategic brand planning (including those dedicated solely to new brand names), corporate communications and internal marketing, internet-based promotion and interactive communications, media buying and strategy, and so on.

The remaining full-service advertising agencies may offer services to clients that will include any or all of the above activities. Although their primary expertise lies in advertising, their strategic perspective covers communications as a whole and they may buy in specialist talent in other marketing communications areas for help in executing an integrated, **through-the-line** campaign. In fact, agencies have reported increased requests from clients for communications solutions across media channels rather than only advertising, so they have responded by developing a more laterally integrated way of thinking about client problems. Many have developed in-house expertise in other communications disciplines alongside their core advertising expertise.

The Evolution of Advertising Agencies

The activities of advertising agencies can be better understood in the context of their historical evolution. Advertising agencies emerged as space-brokers, simply buying advertising space in the press on behalf of clients. Gradually, they extended their activities to provide more services to clients and to add value to their business. So they provided artists to draw up the ads for clients as an improvement on text alone. They acquired expertise in typography and print technology, graphic art and photography. With the development of broadcast media, some agencies developed their expertise in media planning, script writing and radio production and, later, film production. Many agencies found that because of their location they attracted certain types of business such as retail advertising in the local press or sales promotion. In these cases, many regional agencies developed as specialists in these categories of work. As new communications technology has emerged, many larger agencies have tried to develop in-house expertise in such areas as interactive television, internet marketing and interactive websites, and even mobile telephony-based communications solutions such as text messaging. However, they have often found that it is difficult to maintain specialist expertise in such fast-moving areas and, in many cases, have come to rely instead on a network of independent specialists on whom they can call for help when it is needed.

BOX 4.0

Advertising since 1600

Advertising is a fast-moving field but few of its techniques are entirely new. Examples of advertising have been noted since the origin of writing itself. In fact, writing may have developed to facilitate marketing (Brown and Schau, 2008). Classified advertising has existed since the advent of print technology and newspapers. It is a common mistake to suppose that, because early advertising was limited to the printed word, it was merely informative rather than persuasive. Detailed research has shown that this was not the case (Harbor, 2007; McFall, 2004). It is another mistake to suppose that techniques such as product placement and branding are modern inventions. For example, British pottery entrepreneurs were keen to get their pottery dinner sets into royal portraits in the Victorian era, and they made use of techniques of segmentation and targeting (Quickenden and Kover, 2007). In another example, a British entrepreneur of the 1800s, Thomas Holloway, pioneered the use of advertising and branding to sell his patented medical remedies. Holloway was said to have employed outdoor posters as far away as China to advertise his health tonics. Holloway was ahead of his time in other promotional techniques too. He managed to get references to his brands inserted into the script of some of the popular plays of the time. He is even said to have asked Charles Dickens to insert a reference to a Holloway brand into his classic *Dombey and Son*. Dickens declined. Holloway made a fortune and used it for philanthropic activities. Among them was the building he financed that is now a college of the University of London, called Royal Holloway.

Advertising Agencies as Marketing Experts

The scope of activities that ad agencies became involved with, and the expertise their staff developed in a variety of disciplines and markets, gave them yet another dimension. Their skills in artwork and typesetting became useful to media owners since they were able to produce advertisements of a quality which actually enhanced publications.

In addition to art, design and copywriting skills, agencies developed their expertise in strategy and brand planning. Advertising agencies had to understand consumers in varied markets, and they also had to understand the businesses of their many clients. They understood marketing in a way that was free of the practical constraints that limited the thinking of manufacturing organizations. They had a special understanding of the powerful role communication could play in exciting the interest of consumers. They had, therefore, a special vantage-point from which to offer strategic advice to clients on a general business strategy, product development, brand planning and brand communication, possible new markets to enter, market segmentation issues and so on. This planning function, offering strategic thinking to clients on a variety of topics in many different sectors, has grown in importance over the years. Not only does it add value to advertising agency work, it has also become a consulting industry in its own right, working outside the disciplinary boundaries of advertising and marketing. Many advertising agency account planners (see below) will move 'client side' in their career to manage the brand planning process from inside the client organization. It should be noted, though, that advertising agencies are not regarded as strategic partners by all clients in all regions of the world. Many clients, especially in Asia and America, treat agencies as service providers who are required to deliver creative ideas, not consulting advice or research (Broadbent, 2009).

Advertising Agencies and Media

The media planning task is discussed in detail in Chapter 5. Here we need to note a few initial points. Contemporary agencies supply strategic communication ideas and sometimes production skills. They also normally possess media expertise and have a voice in deciding how ads will be targeted at selected consumers through particular media channels. In practice, media buying is increasingly a specialist activity handled at arm's length from the agency. As noted above, for media owners it is convenient to work with advertising agencies because they can offer the creative expertise and advertisement production values that cohere with the values and standards of press publications, TV programming and so on. The advertising is intimately part of the text that carries it. Advertising can even enhance and reinforce the market positioning of the medium in which it is placed. For example, glossy magazines carry ads that are like fashion photographs; ads in newspapers often fit with the typography, layout, colour and themes of the publication. Television advertising needs to be of a broadcast standard since sub-standard camera work or production values will make the TV channel look cheap. Of course, this is why television advertising is so expensive to produce: it demands the same production values as the programmes themselves.

Media buying has largely become a separate activity divorced from creative services. In many countries, media-buying services are provided by a limited number of companies because of lateral mergers and a high concentration in the media industry. It can be convenient for media owners to sell advertising space to a small number of buyers rather than to thousands of individual clients. However, lateral mergers between communications groups mean that advertisers can be faced with monopoly suppliers in particular media and this places them in a poor bargaining position. For example, in the UK, licences to provide regional television or radio services are sold on a strictly limited basis so that local advertisers will often have only one company to buy from. This, advertisers argue, maintains an artificially high cost for certain kinds of advertising medium.

Although media buying is a specialist activity, agencies need to be experts in the media in which they operate. For example, there are many agencies now positioned as 'interactive' or 'digital' agencies, because of the creative and production expertise they boast in Web 2.0 applications, website design and so on. Other agencies specialize in mobile or SMS text promotions. Generally, these small specialist agencies work to support larger agencies and provide expertise in the extension of creative campaigns across new and mobile media, and thus contributing to integrated communication solutions.

Table 4.0   Top 15 consolidated agency networks

RANK '08	RANK '07	NETWORKS AND AGENCIES	HEADQUARTERS	WORLDWIDE REVENUE 2008	WORLDWIDE REVENUE % CHG
1	2	DDB WORLDWIDE COMMUNICATIONS GROUP [Omnicom]	New York	$2,800	7.4
		DDB Worldwide	New York	1,509	5.4
		Rapp1	New York	657	11.0
		Interbrand	New York	257	7.1
		Tribal DDB	New York	235	20.0
		TracyLocke	Dallas	115	−5.1
1	1	MCCANN WORLDGROUP [Interpublic]	New York	2,800	7.3
		McCann Erickson Worldwide	New York	1,741	4.6
		MRM Worldwide	New York	391	18.5
		Momentum Worldwide	New York	216	23.4
		McCann Healthcare Worldwide	Parsippany, N.J.	159	2.3
3	3	DENTSU [Dentsu]	Tokyo	2,778	12.4
		Dentsu	Tokyo	2,472	13.9
4	5	YOUNG & RUBICAM BRANDS [WPP]	New York	2,560	10.5
		Y&R	New York	1,100	7.9
		Wunderman1	New York	880	8.6
		Landor Associates	San Francisco	166	1.4
		Sudler & Hennessey	New York	137	−5.5
		Enfatico	New York	115	NA
		VML	Kansas City, Mo.	100	8.7
5	4	BBDO WORLDWIDE [Omnicom]	New York	2,533	5.6
		BBDO Worldwide	New York	1,986	4.6
		Proximity Worldwide	New York	347	6.0
		Organic	San Francisco	129	3.0
6	7	TBWA WORLDWIDE [Omnicom]	New York	1,961	4.0
		TBWA Worldwide	New York	1,357	5.1
		Zimmerman Advertising	Fort Lauderdale, Fla.	186	6.0
		Integer Group	Lakewood, Colo.	136	3.5
		TBWA/WorldHealth	New York	101	NA
7	6	OGILVY GROUP [WPP]	New York	1,920	1.5
		OgilvyOne Worldwide1	New York	1,054	3.0
		Ogilvy & Mather Worldwide	New York	771	−1.0
8	8	EURO RSCG WORLDWIDE [Havas]	New York	1,481	6.1
		Euro RSCG Worldwide2	New York	1,170	5.7
		Euro RSCG Life	New York	178	11.5
		Euro RSCG Worldwide PR	Suresnes, France	125	5.3
9	9	JWT [WPP]	New York	1,381	4.0
		JWT	New York	1,157	5.0
		RMG Connect	New York	153	1.6
10	10	PUBLICIS [Publicis]	Paris	1,260	4.9
		Publicis	Paris/New York	1,071	7.0
		Publicis Modem & Dialog	New York	189	6.6
11	11	DRAFTFCB [Interpublic]	Chicago/New York	1,246	4.6
		DraftFCB	Chicago/New York	955	3.2
		R/GA3	New York	130	20.0
		DraftFCB Healthcare	New York	105	5.3
12	12	GREY GROUP [WPP]	New York	1,190	3.0
		Grey	New York	614	0.2
		G2	New York	439	9.1
		GHG	New York	119	−1.6
13	13	LEO BURNETT WORLDWIDE [Publicis]	Chicago	1,161	6.9
		Leo Burnett Worldwide	Chicago	795	7.2
		Arc Worldwide	Chicago	293	6.9
14	14	HAKUHODO [Hakuhodo]	Tokyo	1,063	12.7
15	15	SAATCHI & SAATCHI [Publicis]	New York	936	0.2
		Saatchi & Saatchi	New York	790	0.1

Source: Ad Age DataCenter revenue estimates

Reprinted with permission from the 27 April 2009 issue of *The Advertising Age*. Copyright Crain Communications Inc., 2009.

The Leading Agency Brands

Given the scope, public profile and economic importance of what advertising agencies do, it is perhaps paradoxical that the names of most agencies are virtually unknown to those outside of the marketing or communications fields. Ad agencies do not generally advertise themselves. A few of the world's top agency brands do have a high-profile presence in corporate life (see Table 4.0) but most are not nearly as well known among the general public as their client brands. This is partly because client organizations prefer the consuming public to be unaware of the talented intermediaries producing the creative executions that add lustre to the brand. Agencies have had to learn to be discreet about their abilities: successful advertising must always be about the client, not about the agency. Agency success lies in bringing success to clients. Another reason for their shadowy character in commercial life is that they operate in what is essentially a business-to-business environment where work is gained through word-of-mouth, relationships and reputation among a small community of communications specialists.

BOX 4.1

Types of Advertising Agency

According to the advertising industry website adbrands.net[1] there are three main kinds of advertising agency. Firstly, there are the worldwide networks, such as BBDO, McCann Erickson, Leo Burnett or Saatchi & Saatchi. Many of these agency networks have local offices in many different countries. One dynamic behind the evolution of the international agency networks was the need for global conglomerates to manage campaigns in many different countries for each of their individual brands. The second category consists of smaller networks, usually based on distinctive strengths in creative work. These might have just four to six offices worldwide. Examples, according to adbrands.net, include Bartle Bogle Hegarty, Wieden & Kennedy and M&C Saatchi. The third category is the most typical, these are individual agencies which might be owned by a larger group but operate independently. Some are quite large and offer a full agency service, while others are more specialist 'creative boutiques' with distinctive creative skills, often in a particular medium such as digital or television.

Even though they operate in a somewhat closed culture, agencies do have some interest in self-promotion. If they can enhance their reputation in the industry they are more likely to be invited to pitch for new business. To this end, some agencies will try to build a reputation in the communication and marketing industry by entering case histories of their work to try to win industry awards (publishing them in bound volumes), publicizing their history and their successes in coffee-table books and producing copies of their ads on video 'reels', CD-Roms and other media. Many agencies will adopt particular creative techniques or advertising development styles and then promote their expertise to differentiate their brand to clients. Frequent social events for awards, campaign launches, annual reviews and so on are an essential part of the networking that is integral to the industry. Advertising is a small community and awards shows and other events create a sense of specialness and exclusivity that is important to the industry in order to offset the lack of a wider recognition for advertising expertise and accomplishment. This tendency for advertising professionals to award each other prizes seems important, sociologically, to the industry and it also reflects a self-referential insularity.

Advertising may be an industry under pressure, but the global communication holding groups generate very big business. For example, the London based WPP advertising group posted revenues of $13.6 billion for 2008, just ahead of New York-based group Omnicom on $13.4 billion.[2] Holding groups such as these own many individual agency brands, reflecting the increased industry concentration through mergers and acquisitions. WPP owns such agency networks as Ogilvy and Mather Worldwide, JWT, Young and Rubicam, and Grey. Omnicom own BBDO, DDB, and TBWA.

Some agencies create reputations for creativity, usually based on the creative awards they win[3] (see Table 4.1). One London agency, Mother,[4] has gained a reputation as an ideas-based agency through a number of unorthodox creative outputs. For example, Mother produced a comic novel in the pages of *Time Out* listings magazine. The agency has also allegedly resolved the timeless advertising contradiction between creativity and business by the simple expedient of insisting that everyone at the agency is creative. Other agencies focus on effectiveness rather than creativity, although many practitioners in advertising would argue that creativity and effectiveness in advertising are not mutually exclusive.

Table 4.1 World's top 10 agency networks 2006 by creative awards

Agency
1 BBDO Worldwide
2 DDB Worldwide
3 TBWA Worldwide
4 JWT
5 Leo Burnett
6 Ogilvy and Mather Worldwide
7 Saatchi and Saatchi
8 Lowe Worldwide
9 McCann Erickson
10 Y & R Advertising

Source: *The Gunn Report*'s top agencies in 2006 by international creative awards, in www.adbrands.net/agencies_index_adv.htm (accessed 21 April 2009)

Reproduced with permission.

Advertising Agency Recruitment

As noted in this chapter, advertising is a talent-based business. The most successful agencies are the ones with the best people. But it remains very difficult for young people to get a foothold for a career in advertising, and not just because it is a small industry. There are many exceptions but advertising, at least in the UK, remains a largely white, male, middle-class dominated business (McLeod et al., 2009). The industry understands that not only is this not fair or in keeping with the spirit of legal obligations for unbiased recruitment – it is also a functional weakness in an industry which has to communicate to every group of people on the planet. There have been initiatives, for example by the UK IPA, to widen the ethnic and gendered make-up of advertising professionals. The pace of change, though, is slow. One reason for this might be the small circle of advertising agency work. Agencies recruit from a self-limiting pool. Another is that, for creative professionals, the process of getting a job often requires months or years of working for no pay in order to build up a 'book' or portfolio of work. Creative professionals need this 'book' to get hired, and if you are working for no pay for some time it helps, no doubt, to have middle-class parents. It should be noted that the industry is making laudable attempts to address the gender and ethnic imbalance. It is also important to note that there have always been many exceptions. There are growing numbers of outstanding female professionals, and there are also those who would describe themselves as 'working class' (McLeod, et al., 2009).

Advertising's Poor PR

In spite of the glittering prizes and industry awards that are so much a feature of the advertising business, advertising and promotion agencies have largely failed to promote a greater general understanding of what they do outside their own industry. Considering the level of public and academic interest, there are remarkably few initiatives to promote a better understanding of advertising in schools, universities and elsewhere.[5] Among academic researchers, the problems of gaining access to agencies for information and interviews are legendary. This perceived lack of interest in the wider world creates a smog of ignorance around the industry. In some respects this may be useful: critics of advertising cannot effectively attack an enemy they cannot see and do not understand. On the other hand generally poor PR for the advertising industry means that the skills of its people are often under-recognized and the contribution of advertising to successful business is itself poorly understood – hence the need for professional bodies such as the IPA, AAF and AAA to continually promote the virtues of advertising to the world beyond the agency village. Not only that, but the controversy stirred up by advertising from time to time can be fuelled by naive ideas about how it influences people and of the processes involved in producing an advertising campaign.

Advertising in general, as we shall see in Chapter 8, is often a convenient target for social critics of all kinds precisely because it is so poorly understood.

Advertising Agency Working Processes

Advertising and promotion agencies are slightly mysterious places. They have great (and often under-recognized) importance in capitalist economies. They produce work that is often striking and remarkable, and they attract some of the brightest and best-educated people to work in them. Yet, explaining exactly how this work results from the hive of activity that is an advertising agency is not an easy task. The advertising agency remains an enigmatic place. Relatively few academics have ventured into this area (but see Hackley, 2000; Kelly et al., 2005; Moeran, 2009; Svensson, 2007; as exceptions). Committed and highly skilled advertising professionals themselves are not quite sure how precisely to explain their work. Like much human organization, results can be surprising given the confusion and conflict that often surround the process of managing and producing output. The enigmatic character of ad agencies means that a descriptive account of roles and working procedures may appear glib. A list of the components of a TV set in no way serves as an account of what it produces. Nevertheless, this chapter outlines these roles and processes while acknowledging that there is much flexibility and indeterminacy in these processes. This is the nature of a creative business. The seemingly chaotic character of agency life may be seen as a reflection of the high intellects and professionalism of advertising folk. Some clients take a different view and regard communications agencies as poorly managed, un-businesslike places that need close direction and cannot be trusted to be prudent with clients' money. The account that follows is organized where possible around the sequence of activities that agencies must undertake in the course of acquiring and executing business. The first step, therefore, will be to look at the nature of the agency as a business brand and how this might influence its pitches for business.

'Pitching' for Business

There are over 700 advertising agencies in the UK all told; many of the major ones are subsidiaries of international advertising agency groups. Agencies get invited to pitch for business by reputation and contacts so a brand presence in the industry can be an advantage. Pickton and Broderick (2000, 2005) state that the process of pitching may be preceded by an invited credentials presentation in which selected agencies will try to persuade the client that they are a credible and professional organization. Track records of successful accounts are important here, as are the reputations of the star personnel. If the agency is already a leading brand then so much the better. The client no doubt has an advertising department and public relations office of its own and needs to be reassured that the agency can add a specialist expertise which it cannot provide for itself. More recently, agencies have begun to add more and more content to their websites and often contribute to industry blogs. The agency website is a shop window and blogs can also be important in generating comment and presence in the industry. Such presence might lead to an invitation to pitch for business.

The client then issues a client brief to the agencies it deems worthy enough to pitch for the business, which outlines the tasks that the client wants undertaken or the objectives they wish to achieve. This contains the background information the client feels is essential to the task, such as the brand name and the nature of the product, the company, the desired market and segmentation strategy, the price, the distribution channel and, most importantly, the budget. The selected agencies then take the brief, decide how they might solve the client's problem and present their ideas in a sales pitch.

BOX 4.2

The Client Brief[6]

The client brief is an important document which sets out what the client wants the agency to do. A written brief facilitates communication and helps each party understand the requirements of the other. The UK Advertising Association publishes a guide on writing a client brief which suggests that essential items of content should include: situation analysis (expressed as 'Where are we now?'); objectives ('Where do we want to be?') and marketing and communications strategy ('How do we get there?'). Other essential topics include consumer segmentation and targeting ('Who do we need to talk to?'); effectiveness measurement ('How will we know when we've arrived?') and practical issues. The entire project should be managed with clear lines of communication and individual accountability, and not left as an informal, *ad hoc* or implicit arrangement. Following these principles reduces the risk that the client–agency relationship may become unsatisfactory or unsuccessful.

The outcome of the pitch may just as well be that a new or a small agency gets the business rather than the huge multinational agency group. The nature of the brief may also influence the kind of agency that is chosen. Some clients will want a full strategic communications service, in which case a larger full-service agency is more likely to be chosen. Other clients may be more interested in getting help with specific activities such as creative, production or media strategy and so might choose a smaller agency. A client who, for example, wishes to advertise a brand launch across international boundaries may have more confidence in an agency group that is already operating internationally. The rise of the big communication conglomerates has been driven by the need for major multinationals like P&G and Unilever to manage campaigns in scores of different countries.

Pitching for business is an everyday activity for advertising agencies. The impact of the presentation is everything; appearances are important and presentational poise and social skills are to the fore. Although it is rare for creative staff to be involved in the pitch itself (London agency Mother claims to be an exception in this) the agency will be judged partly on the creative flair of its ideas, as well as on the strategic planning and professionalism of the pitch. It is the responsibility of **account managers** and account planners to make sure their pitch presentation is highly professional so that the creative work and strategic thinking are seen in the best light by the client. If the client does not like the work, the account person who presented it may be accused by creative staff of not trying hard enough or of failing to do justice to the quality of the work. In some cases agencies may toil for two or three weeks on a pitch only to see the business given to another agency. Even worse, it is not unknown for ideas to be stolen, and used without attributing their source. The agency may charge the client for the work they put into the pitch but ultimately will do this work in hope of winning the business rather than with any realistic expectation of a profit from the pitch itself. Exceptionally, an agency might refuse to divulge creative ideas in a pitch: Ogilvy, for example, are known for this.

BOX 4.3

Client-agency Relationships

The UK advertising agency professional body, ISBA[7] posts detailed information about client–agency relationships on its website, reflecting the importance of the topic to the industry. Many industry professionals argue that effective work results from strong relationships and clear lines of communication between the client and the agency (see, e.g. West and Paliwoda, 1996). Continuity in these relationships gives each the time to understand the other and the business. Agencies claim that a foundation of success is longevity and mutual trust in client relationships, and would prefer reliable clients and repeat business to 'promiscuous' clients.[8] To foster this, agencies claim not to operate a 'star' system but to run a meritocracy based on talent which sustains client relationships. Agencies post news of their campaigns on their websites to publicize their success with prominent clients. For example, the Ogilvy group listed cases with their clients Motorola, Ford, Chivas Brothers, British Gas and IBM on their website in April 2009.[9] Agencies that succeed in retaining clients over long periods have a much better chance of developing the kind of work that will get them noticed, because the best creativity entails risk, and risk is only possible where there is trust in the client–agency relationship.

The Client and the Agency

The client is effectively the invisible member of the account team. The client's wishes and aims are represented in the client brief. Surprisingly often, client briefs require a lot of work by the agency because the client may not have a very clear rationale for communication. It is often up to the agencies to research the client brief in order to understand fully the nature of the client's business, markets and brands. Even if the client is well prepared, agencies will often want to research the client brief on their own terms. Client briefs can come couched in a marketing jargon that communication professionals will find obscure and misleading. Marketing directors tend to compartmentalize marketing management functions. This leads to elements like pricing strategy, product design, distribution and promotion being considered separately without reference to each other. But advertising professionals have the benefit of a more dispassionate perspective on the marketing process and they recognize that the elements of marketing management and strategy are interdependent.

Brand name, price, product design, packaging, distribution and so on are all equally important strategically because each has important communications implications for the brand. Advertising that is able to portray a coherent brand strategy which makes sense to the right consumers has a far greater chance of success than advertising that is trying to use creativity to make up for an ill-conceived marketing strategy. If the account manager can act as a consulting partner to a client and gain in-depth knowledge of the marketing function, this will help the agency devise a coherent and successful campaign.

It is axiomatic that agencies regard advertising as the answer to every marketing problem. If a client is dismayed at falling sales and allocates a large advertising budget to address the problem, the agency commissioned should concede that advertising may not be the answer to the client's problem – it may be that, say, poor customer service, flawed distribution or poor product design are the cause of the client's problems. Account managers will understandably feel under pressure not to turn business away but if a campaign cannot succeed because it addresses the wrong problem then it is wise to advise the client rather than risk the ignominy of a failed campaign. But clients do have to be handled sensitively. Some will not accept that they have misunderstood the nature of their own business and will not be protected from their folly. The decision to allocate an advertising budget and appoint an agency is a highly political one for client organizations. And, as we saw in Chapter 3, advertising can support many different marketing, business and communication objectives. Client relations are always a sensitive area for agencies and demand astute management skills from account managers. In most cases a compromise can be reached so that the client's budget is put to good use even if the client organization has other underlying problems.

The senior board-level account director will be responsible, along with other agency heads, for deciding whether to accept a client brief. There may be reasons for declining it at the client brief stage, if, for example, the agency's research reveals that communication is not the client's problem. More plausibly, the agency will need to decide if a new client will fit with existing clients. Agencies need to try to ensure that they are not open to conflicts of interest when, say, representing two clients who compete in the same market. Agencies will also have to decide if a client is suitable for ethical or political reasons. The client brief may be translated into a communications brief in some agencies. This is where the marketing jargon of the client brief is transformed into a more metaphorically colourful document that tries to convey the emotionality of the client's brand and its relationship with consumers. Assuming that the agency heads give the account manager the go-ahead for an account, the next stage is to devise a strategy for advertising (see p. 121).

Table 4.2   Top 10 UK advertising agencies

Rank 2008	Rank 2007	Agency	Billings 2008 (£m)	Billings 2007 (£m)	Year-on-year % change	Top-spending clients
1	1	Abbott Mead Vickers BBDO	363.2	396.4	−8.37	Sainsbury's, BT, Camelot Group, Homebase, Mercedes-Benz
2	2	McCann Erickson	265.6	288.1	−7.81	L'Oreal Paris, Nestlé, Microsoft, Aldi, Co-operative Group (CWS)
3	3	JWT	246.3	265.4	−7.21	Kellogg's, B&Q, HSBC, Nestlé, Kimberly-Clark
4	4	Bartle Bogle Hegarty	236.5	260.5	−9.21	Unilever (UK), Vodafone, Barclays, Kentucky Fried Chicken (GB), Audi (UK)
5	8	Euro RSCG	222.8	232.7	−4.24	Reckitt Benckiser (UK), Peugeot, Citroën (UK), News International, Hutchison 3G (UK)

Table 4.2

Rank 2008	Rank 2007	Agency	Billings 2008 (£m)	Billings 2007 (£m)	Year-on-year % change	Top-spending clients
6	7	Rainey Kelly Campbell Roalfe/ Y&R	214.5	247	−13.16	Marks & Spencer, Lloyds TSB, Danone Holdings (UK), LG Electronics (UK), Land Rover (UK)
7	5	M&C Saatchi	208.7	251.4	−16.98	Direct Line, Currys Group, PC World, NatWest, Halfords
8	6	WCRS	195.4	248.5	−21.38	BSkyB, Churchill Insurance, Abbey, BMW (UK), Littlewoods
9	10	Ogilvy Advertising	187.5	188.7	−0.64	Ford, Unilever (UK), Mattel (UK), easyJet, Nutricia
10	14	Delaney Lund Knox Warren & Partners	185.6	174.2	6.57	WM Morrison, Halifax, Vauxhall, COI, WH Smith

Source: *Campaign* report 'Top 100 Agencies', www.campaignlive.co.uk/news/wide/886782/ (accessed 29 April 2009)

Reproduced from *Campaign* magazine with the permission of the copyright owner, Haymarket Business Publications Limited.

The pitching system is open to misuse, as noted earlier. It is not unknown for clients to ask a number of agencies to pitch to a brief, then appoint none of those agencies and have the work conducted in-house. This obviously raises the suspicion that the client only wanted free consultancy. On the rare occasions when this happens it results in much bitterness and even litigation. If the pitch goes well, then the agency will be awarded the client's advertising business, called 'the account'.

Account Team Roles and Responsibilities

Work in advertising, media and marketing services agencies is normally organized through account teams. These are the vortex of the advertising development process. The account team roles reflect different yet often overlapping areas of responsibility. The major account team roles are those of account management, planning/research, and creative. These are explained below. In addition, there are ancillary roles. These include media planning and buying. The media function is integral to effective advertising campaigns but it is increasingly an area handled outside the agency account team by an independent media agency. Media planning is discussed in more detail in Chapter 6. The **media planner** must ensure the campaign's effectiveness by placing the promotion before the maximum possible number of targeted consumers within the allocated budget. He or she must also try to ensure that the media chosen have the kind of impact that is appropriate to the brand and its market segment.

Another essential ancillary role is that of **traffic controller**, whose responsibility is to allocate work, monitor progress and ensure that tasks are co-ordinated to the deadline. The traffic controller also ensures that there is a paper trail showing the continuous progress of all the component parts of development. If, for example, the production of a TV ad requires a script to be finished, artwork to be completed and a research brief to be fulfilled before the production company can be given the go-ahead, it will be the traffic controller's job to monitor progress and chase up the staff responsible in order to meet deadlines. Other staff may be engaged in art or TV production. They are required because creative teams are there for the ideas and creative craft they can supply; they do not necessarily have production skills. Staff with expertise in graphic art and computer-aided art production, animation and animatronics, website design and other production activities can be very useful for agencies to have in-house because they can realize the creative ideas.

The Account Manager

If an agency is appointed by a client then the account manager (sometimes called 'account executive' or 'account director', or simply 'account man' regardless of gender) will be the client's first point of contact in the agency. The account manager is essentially the business manager for the accounts held by that account team. He or she is responsible for liaison between the client and the other account team members to ensure that the campaign is planned, developed and produced on time, on brief and on budget. The account manager is often regarded as the business person or, less respectfully, as 'the suit' (Hackley, 2000, 2003f). He or she has to manage the various personalities and tasks to ensure that the work generates revenue for the agency. Consequently he or she requires skills in relationship management, project management, planning and co-ordination. Account managers will normally have a good working knowledge of the whole advertising development process. On one rare occasion an account man (at DDB London, when it was called BMP DDB) actually created a TV ad. It turned out that of all the creative ideas offered in a planning meeting, his was considered the best. In most cases, though, the account person will leave the creative work to the specialists.

What are Consumers Like? How Do We Communicate With Them?

Kover (1995) and Hackley (2003d) have each in different ways highlighted the implicit thinking that guides creative work in agencies. Kover (1995) found that creative staff hold differing implicit theories of communication while Hackley (2003d) found that account team members work to differing implicit models of the consumer. Agency working practices entail lengthy meetings and considerable communication. These two research studies illustrated how difficult it can be for agencies to articulate all the implicit assumptions that guide professional communications practice. The three main account team roles of account management, creative and planning often approach marketing communications problems from intellectually incompatible perspectives. While this is a strength of the team approach it is also a source of conflict because the differing perspectives are not well understood. As noted in Chapter 2, there is no one, agreed theory of how advertising 'works' or of what motivates consumers, so practice is driven by intuition and experience.

The account manager is normally closer to the client than any other person in the agency. In most agencies he or she will have primary responsibility for client liaison and may speak to the client daily. In some agencies it is common for the account person to be the only contact point between agency and client. The account manager is consequently regarded as the voice of the client in the agency since he or she acquires a strong sense of what the client wants and will accept. This can present conflicts of interest when the creative staff want the account manager to argue strongly in favour of a creative execution that the client may not want to accept. Account managers will sometimes admit that there are occasions when they do not fight as strongly for their creatives' idea as they might, simply because they know that it is not what the client wants.

The specific tasks account managers undertake during the creative development of advertising vary from agency to agency, and from account to account. In many cases, they will take the lead in interpreting the initial client brief and developing and presenting the pitch for business. Once the account is won they will convene the various planning and progress meetings to discuss and agree strategy. Either alone or with the account planner they will discuss, research and write the creative brief. In many agencies account managers, rather than account planners, commission consumer and advertising research and interpret the findings at various points in the creative advertising development process. The account manager ultimately holds the responsibility of ensuring that an account is, firstly won, and then retained for as long as possible.

Along with the account planner (see below), the account manager will often have responsibility for measuring the effectiveness of the campaign against the objectives that were set for it.

Account Planning

Traditionally, advertising and promotional agencies have been organized hierarchically, with the account manager leading the account team. However, a new discipline called account planning evolved which gave the account planner equal status with the account manager. The account planning role was initiated in the 1960s in London at JWT and BMP (now DDB London) and adapted in the US by New York agency Chiat Day (Feldwick, 2007: Pickton and Crosier, 2003). The account planner was charged with generating consumer insights through research and with ensuring that these insights were integrated into every stage of the creative advertising development process. Originally conceived as the 'voice of the consumer' within the agency, the account planner's role has broadened with the rise of brand marketing. He or she is now often seen as the brand custodian charged with ensuring that the brand's core values and personality are maintained through all associated marketing communications. Account planners are often assumed to have a wide range of analytical, linguistic and advocacy skills which enable them to articulate the strategic thinking for brands that contributes to the longer-term management and development of the brand vision.

Before the development of the account planning role, account managers would obtain the consumer and market research they needed through the services of a researcher who normally held no management responsibility. The account manager would commission and interpret consumer and advertising research and decide whether the findings were relevant to creative advertising development. This traditional arrangement, where the account manager is the undisputed leader, still persists in many advertising agencies. The account planning role and its implications for agency hierarchies have been widely though unevenly accepted in the UK and US advertising industries for some 40 years now. Nevertheless, there remains much confusion and no little controversy as to what it entails and what it can add to advertising development (Hackley, 2003f and g). Those agencies that promote and espouse the account planning philosophy and function are convinced of its value; some are almost evangelical about the account planning ethos and the benefits it brings to the agency. Others in the industry are hugely sceptical about the claims made for account planning.

The account planner is the expert in marketing and consumer research. He or she is responsible for all research connected with an account and is a full member of the account team with management status and responsibility. In many agencies the creative brief will be written by the account planner. The conceptual and analytical skills associated with this role often mean that planning personnel have social science educational backgrounds, whereas account managers may often have a more formal business education such as an MBA. Planners conduct and interpret qualitative and quantitative research that feeds into the creative development of advertising. They are also responsible for market research and competitive analysis that informs the planning of the account, pre-testing creative executions and, after the campaign has been launched, tracking the effectiveness of the advertising.

Difficulties of the Account Planning Role

There have been three persistent problems facing the account planning discipline, which proves unfortunate when, in the words of one account planner, they see their own role as 'helping creatives and making the work better'. One problem is the hostility of many creative staff towards research (Hackley and Kover, 2007). When the researcher was a lowly backroom person, there was less threat, but when research is a responsibility of the account planner, it has a voice with management status. The account planner is a soft target for the angst of creative staff who feel that judging their work against research findings misses the point of what makes advertising appeal to consumers (Kover, 1996).

Secondly, not only do account planners find themselves at odds with creative staff, they may also be at odds with account managers who feel that their status is undermined. Account planners do many of the tasks that were formerly the sole responsibility of the account manager, such as deciding what research to conduct, liaising with the client and writing the creative brief. In agencies implementing the account planning philosophy there often results a three-way power struggle as creatives and account management, comfortable in their mutual contempt, find common ground in their hatred of account planners.

As if these problems were not enough, thirdly, account planners have a credibility problem in the industry as a whole. Just as those agencies that espouse the account planning ethos are convinced of its positive value, those that are not, will argue their point of view with vigour. Account planners are vulnerable to the charge that they cannot easily answer the question of what craft skills they bring to the advertising development process. Many are expert researchers with substantial educational attainments. Others are not, but have found their way into the post through a facility with words and ideas and a sense of curiosity about people. While creative staff have creative skills, and account management have business skills, account planners are sometimes unfairly seen to have no particular skills that justify their status and power on account teams.

Because of these difficulties, account planners require skills of tact and sensitivity in order simply to do their job. As researchers they require a sensitivity to consumers' attitudes, predispositions and preferences, and an ability to work these out from carefully gathered qualitative and **quantitative** research data.

Creative Teams

Advertising agencies produce and sell ideas. The quality of their creative output is the benchmark of their standing as an agency. The creative team is responsible for this output, and in many agencies the creative work is organized into teams of two people. There may be one creative person who specializes in words (copywriting, script writing, music jingles) and another who deals in images, and undertakes, for example, visualizations of story boards for TV ads, press ad layouts, poster design, typography, and so on. Sometimes, these roles are referred to respectively as 'art director' and 'copywriter'. In US agencies it has been traditional for the term 'copywriter' to be used to refer to the originator of any creative input, the assumption being that a copywriter without visualization (that is, drawing) skills would simply instruct a graphic artist to put his or her ideas into visual form. Quite often these two members in a creative team will have interchangeable skills. In some cases, however, creatives will prefer to work alone (see McLeod et al., 2009).

BOX 4.5

Creative Stars and Agency Culture

Creative professionals in advertising need to have a big ego. It is a career which demands considerable personal drive and confidence. However, where a creative becomes so successful that he or she (most commonly it is a he) comes to dominate the agency with their personality it can destabilize the working process and serve to undermine the objective-driven creative advertising development process. Creatives live and die by peer recognition, marked by the awards they win (Hackley and Kover, 2007), but clients are more interested in their marketing objectives than in creative awards. In some creative-dominated agencies clients' briefs may go straight to the creative star without any initial planning or research taking place. This can be fruitful when the creative person's intuition about the market and its consumers results in an effective creative execution. However, it is a high-risk approach since there is no clearly researched basis for creative work and no carefully thought-through strategy. In such a situation, clear criteria for assessing campaign effectiveness might also be disregarded, to the potential detriment of the clients' interests. The creative brief and the layers of account management and planning which buffer the creative from the client are intended to prevent

---

this happening. The creative brief in particular is supposed to discipline the creative work so that it serves the clients' marketing objectives rather than the fetid imagination of the award-hungry creative. In most cases, clients would wish advertising to be based on a more transparent footing, with a business-like approach to planning and accountability. Generally speaking, agencies that allow the strong personality of a creative star to subvert their management systems will find that there is eventually a price to pay in terms of lost business.

In many agencies, creative teams operate at arm's length from account management. They often occupy their own sub-cultural space in the agency (Hackley, 2000; McLeod et al., 2009). Creative staff often feel disempowered by the advertising development process since the worth of their ideas is judged by other, non-creative people (Kover and Goldberg, 1995). However, creatives who win awards for their work can quickly acquire a star reputation that brings them (and their agency) considerable prestige. In some cases, star creatives can come to dominate an agency.

Creative staff are not normally brought in to work on the account until the initial market and consumer research and strategic planning have taken place. They are then presented with a brief and asked to offer creative executions that will satisfy the requirements of the brief. This brief is an important document that should inspire creative staff and excite them about the creative possibilities for an account, while also providing them with parameters to work within which are derived from the research and strategic thinking that have gone into developing the strategy for advertising. This should ensure that the creative execution will support the desired marketing objectives of the client (Kelly et al., 2005).

When creative work has been approved internally by the agency team (usually by the internal director of creativity) it is presented to the client by the account manager. If the client likes it and agrees that it fulfils the criteria set out in the brief, then the work will be produced and offered for public consumption. Creative staff enjoy a privileged existence within agencies. They must have the discipline to produce ideas to a deadline, starting with a blank piece of paper. While younger creative staff are often very good on ideas, the task of the creative professional requires both experience and resilience, the former of which is necessary in order to know what will work as an execution in different media. Creative work requires strong craft skills aligned to a knowledge of different media and their properties, along with an intuitive sense of the excitement that consumption generates. Creative staff have to be resilient because, in the words of one experienced creative interviewed by the author, 'of every 10 ideas, only one will get made'. Creative staff must accept that the great majority of the ideas they come up with will be rejected as unsuitable for a huge variety of reasons unrelated to whether the ideas are good or not. Getting to be an advertising creative professional and keeping that role for the duration of a career require great perseverance, personal robustness and drive (Hackley and Kover, 2007). Finally, the best creative staff must also have a good understanding of marketing so that they can see the wider implications of their work for clients.

The Creative Advertising Development Process

The creative development process differs in detail in each advertising agency. While these differences are important, it is also true that every agency around the world does broadly similar things in broadly similar ways (Hackley and Tiwsakul, 2008). The differences in management processes between agencies are normally marked by differences of emphasis and tone rather than by more fundamental issues. What follows is a necessarily general but representative outline of the major elements of the process of developing an advertisement.

In most agencies, campaign planning is conducted through lengthy meetings. From the initial meetings (sometimes called 'plans board' meetings) through to strategy development meetings, views will be heard from all major parties, including the client, creative and board-level account management. These meetings are at the heart of advertising development; promotional campaigns evolve through a process of debate and argument. Although creative work can sometimes be the inspiration of one individual, in an important sense all creative development is a joint effort because of the way ideas develop and reach a certain point through intense discussion. This discussion, which sometimes can seem endless, is given direction by the use of documents.

In all agencies there are written documents that perform several functions. They provide a template for practice and thereby act as a tool for management control. Life in agencies is chaotic enough: without pro forma documents the chaos would be total. Documents provide a paper trail of accountability and a basis for contractual agreement. Client and agency have a permanent record of what, exactly, was agreed. Documents also act as stimulus tools for directing thinking along predetermined lines. They are handrails for advertising development.

The advertising development process in any major agency entails a limited number of broadly defined tasks. These are listed in Table 4.3. There is strategy development, then creative planning, pre-testing and ad production, campaign exposure and finally evaluation. The evaluation should then feed back into the strategy development process for monitoring and/or reappraisal. In many agencies, particularly those which espouse the account planning philosophy, every stage of the process is informed by the consumer and market insights generated from research by the account planner (Hackley, 2003f).

Table 4.3 Basic stages in the creative advertising development process

1	Developing the advertising strategy
2	Developing the creative ideas
3	Pre-testing creative executions
4	Creative production
5	Campaign execution
6	Campaign evaluation

The Advertising Strategy

As we noted in the previous chapter, the advertising strategy is all-important. There has to be a clear marketing rationale for advertising and communication. In many agencies, the communication objective represents a more general issue, while the advertising strategy represents a more specific matter. For example, a communication objective might be to re-position the brand to a new market segment, while the advertising strategy might be to persuade this new segment to change their consuming behaviour. However, the distinction between the communication objective and the advertising strategy may be merely semantic in some cases – the two clearly overlap. The main case for having both is that a communication objective actively links the purpose of the advertising to the client's marketing strategy. Fundamentally, an advertising strategy disciplines the account team to think of an advertisement not just in terms of their own personal response to it but also in terms of the behavioural or attitudinal outcomes it is designed to achieve. Advertising has to do something for the client's brand. The strategy expresses just what it is that advertising and promotion should do for the brand in order to support the client's marketing objectives. The strategy document, as with all the other documents in the promotional development process, normally poses a series of questions which the account team members, assisted by other interested parties such as the client, are required to address. These usually include:

- What does the client expect the campaign to achieve? (For example, an increased market share, raised brand profile, changed brand identity.)
- To whom is the advertisement to speak? That is, who is the desired target audience? (For example, motor-car drivers between 25 and 69 years of age using **ACORN** or other segmentation systems.)
- What is the key consumer or market insight which gives consumers a reason to believe the claim made in the advertisement? (For example, that the brand advertised is more reliable/inexpensive/exciting than rival brands.)
- What is the desired reaction the campaign must produce in consumers? (For example, in terms of beliefs, memory, attitudes to the brand and purchase behaviour.)

The advertising strategy is seldom expressed in marketing jargon. Agencies usually insist on jargon-free, simple and even monosyllabic expressions of strategy. The rationale for the advertising must be clearly expressed, agreed by all the relevant parties, commercially coherent and easily communicable to everyone involved. As communication professionals, advertising people strive for clarity and simplicity in their own internal communications. This clarity does not preclude a certain flakiness: phrases such as 'inject a dose of adrenalin into the brand' or make the brand 'compulsory equipment' are not uncommon. These were, in fact, phrases used in the advertising strategy for one of the most successful campaigns of all, for Levi 501s (see p. 214). The value of such phrasing is that it resonates with advertising people who feel that they know just what is meant.

The strategy for advertising will be the measure of the campaign's success or failure. The advertising strategy will form the basis for the creative brief. We should note that just as there may be some overlap between the communication objectives and the advertising strategy, there may also be some overlap in the issues noted in the advertising strategy and in the creative brief. This reflects the inter-dependence of the steps in the creative advertising development process.

The Creative Brief

Each agency has its own pro forma documents for strategy and creative briefs. Of these, the creative brief is very important because it is agreed between the client's representative (often the marketing or advertising director) and the agency account management and planning team. Once it is agreed to and signed by both client and agency it is given to the creative team as the basis for the creative execution. It must be clear, carefully thought through and motivating. Each agency will have slightly different conventions for the brief, though the aims will be similar. Like strategy documents, the brief poses questions that the account team are required to answer. In many agencies the account planner will research and write the creative brief in consultation with the client and account management.

Questions found in a typical creative brief are as follows:

1 Why advertise?
2 Who is the audience?
3 What must this communication do?
4 What must the advertising say?
5 Why must the audience believe it?
6 What is the tone of the advertising to be?
7 What practical considerations are there?

Question no. 1, 'Why advertise?', invites the account planner to state the rationale for advertising, probably drawing on the strategy document. It is obvious that without a clear reason or opportunity for advertising there is little chance of a successful campaign. There must be an opportunity for communication to accomplish an outcome that will support and enhance the brand's marketing strategy. Question no. 2 asks for the target audience or market to be carefully defined. Question no. 3 again refers to the strategy to ask what the outcome of the advertising should be in terms of consumer attitude or behavioural change. It is slightly different from question no. 1 because it focuses on the outcome (for example, to make people feel more positive about the brand) as opposed to the reason for advertising (for example, sales are suffering because people feel less positive about this brand than they did five years ago). Question no. 4, refers to the bottom-line message of the ad that the client wishes the consumer to get from exposure to the ad. This is sometimes called the 'proposition' or the 'take-out' (for example, this brand is the leader in its class).

Picture 5   The Samsung Tocco 'please touch' campaign (see chapter case).
Reproduced with kind permission of Samsung Mobile UK and Cheil Worldwide.
(See the colour insert near the middle of this book for a full colour image.)

Question no. 5 asks the account team to provide evidence to support the promotional claim. For example, much motor-car brand advertising tries to reassure the consumer that the brand is mechanically reliable and technologically advanced. In the case of German car brands this is not too difficult because in many countries German engineering and technology have an excellent reputation. This attitude can be symbolized economically in TV or print ads, with visual images of working engine parts or a cutaway image of an engine interior. The consumer, primed with cultural knowledge about the quality of German motor engineering, understands the inference implicitly. In another example, the iconic BBH Levi 501 ads of the 1980s, the ads were designed to say that Levi jeans were icons of American culture, bound up with mythical American values since Independence. The creative execution helped consumers believe this by filling the ads with period American artefacts like 1950s motor-cars, clothes and, of course, the famous launderette, familiar to many baby-boomers from American movies, featuring actors like James Dean and Marlon Brando. The visual cue was understood by consumers who liked the glamour of American movies and literature from the 1950s. Tellingly, the American provenance theme began to fail in the 1990s because young consumers were no longer familiar with that genre of movies. They no longer understood, believed or valued the association between Levis and the mythical 1950s America of Hollywood movies.

Question no. 6, 'What is the tone of the advertising to be?', refers to the way that brand values are reflected in the creative and production values of the ad. For example, in the creative brief for the Levi 501's ad mentioned above the tone of the ad was described as 'heroic, but period' in its creative brief. Tone can also refer to other stylistic aspects of advertising production, as well as the set, music and narrative. Techniques of cinematography can give an exaggerated realism to the ad. Some ads are shot in black and white, for example those which are trying for an art-house feel. The tone of the ad carries implied values for the brand.

Finally, in terms of practical considerations (question no. 7), ads may have features insisted upon by the advertiser. For example, for many years BMW ads featured no human beings. The focus was to be on the engineering and the aesthetics of the car. The 1980s Levi 501's ad 'Laundrette' featured a soundtrack but no dialogue. The client wanted the ad to feature in many different countries. The only linguistic sign in the ad is the word 'Levis' and the producers were instructed to feature many shots of the jeans themselves and their distinctive rivets. Some ads have contact telephone numbers as mandatory inclusions, website addresses, particular straplines and so on. The creative brief must carry all the instructions the creative team needs to exercise their craft in ways which will fit with the advertising strategy and the brand personality.

The creative brief sets the parameters for the creative work without which advertising cannot be distinctive and memorable. The extensive work that is put into researching and writing this brief in many agencies is a measure of the importance placed on making distinctive advertising.

Tracking Campaign Effectiveness

Once ads have been produced and the campaign has been launched in selected media (discussed in more detail in Chapter 5), it is important for the campaign's effectiveness to be ascertained. This task is a perennial problem in the industry (Cook and Kover, 1997). Clients need to be persuaded that campaigns are effective if they are to continue to pay high costs and keep agencies solvent. Much research is directed at this problem and Chapter 9 discusses some of the theoretical issues in more detail. Some of the main problems and issues are as follows.

The effectiveness of a campaign should, logically, be assessed against the objectives set for it, since the relationship between advertising and sales is subject to many uncontrollable intervening variables in the consumer/market environment. For example, a rise in sales or in measured levels of brand awareness can always be attributed to other, non-advertising causes such as seasonality, changes in income, press coverage of consumer issues or simply inevitable random fluctuations in demand.

Agencies do try to strengthen their argument (and their pitches for business) by writing up case histories of successful campaigns. For example, UK agencies submit case studies of advertising effectiveness to the annual IPA awards.[11] In order to be accepted, these cases have to offer substantial, rigorous evidence supporting the success of the campaign. Direct causal relationships between advertising and other variables can never be proven beyond doubt, of course, but compelling circumstantial evidence can be gathered.

Tracking campaign effectiveness, then, can be a complex undertaking. Finding a statistically significant correlation between two variables is, of course, no indication of a causal relationship. Nevertheless, a correlation can contribute to circumstantial evidence about campaign effectiveness. More typically, campaigns are evaluated by using surveys to see if their communication objectives have been met. In one London-based campaign for the British Diabetic Association (BDA), public awareness of the symptoms of diabetes was tested by street surveys. Some weeks after the campaign (posters placed in underground tube stations), the awareness levels were significantly higher. The BDA's desired objective was to raise awareness of the symptoms of type-1 diabetes without alarming people, stigmatizing sufferers or filling surgeries with hypochondriacs. They simply wanted more people who suspected they might be suffering from the disease to get a proper diagnosis and treatment. The campaign was a success since the awareness of symptoms increased significantly after it, according to street interviews, and doctors reported an increase in the number of people asking for a diagnosis. The fact that a high proportion of these people did in fact have the disease was, if no consolation for the sufferers, an indication that the creative executions had struck exactly the right note.

Prompted and Unprompted Awareness Surveys

Trade press publications conduct weekly or monthly consumer surveys to gauge the impact of various advertising campaigns. There are unprompted awareness surveys in which the participant is asked 'Which TV/press/ radio/outdoor ads do you recall seeing this week?'. To simplify the explanation, if half the consumers surveyed recall seeing a particular campaign it gets a score of 50 per cent awareness. The results are then tabled, with the highest percentage awareness attaining first place in the table for that week. Prompted awareness surveys involve the researcher reading through a list of ads or brands and asking whether the participant remembers seeing an ad for each in that week. Prompted awareness scores tend to be higher, of course, than those for unprompted awareness.

Awareness surveys, like most measures of advertising effectiveness, do not actually measure the effectiveness of the advertising or promotion at all. They measure the consumer's awareness of the advertising or of the brand, which is quite a different thing. Of course, awareness may be a necessary condition for effectiveness, but it is not a sufficient condition. Awareness surveys make the implicit assumption that awareness is an intermediary state in a sequence of mental states that lead to purchase. The hierarchy-of-effect model of persuasion discussed in Chapter 2 is implicitly referred to when intermediate variables such as awareness are assumed to offer some indication of the effectiveness of a campaign. This may not be the case, because awareness does not always result in a purchase.

Awareness is a major concern for advertising agencies. Their principal challenge is to get consumers to notice their work amid the clutter and noise of the consumer environment. It makes sense to measure it, though it can be a mistake to read too much into awareness surveys. The quality of that awareness is far more important in informing consumer behaviour and this is something that is harder to measure.

Attitude Scales and Copy-testing

Although recall or awareness is easily measured from a dichotomous question (aware/not aware), liking is usually measured with attitude scales. Scaled responses (often called **Likert scales** after their originator) form the answers to questions asking the respondent to rate his/her attitude to an item, on a five-point scale. For example, a statement such as 'How much do you like this ad?' is answered by ticking a box next to a range of categories, for example, 'Don't like at all/like a little/indifferent/like/really like'. These scales are frequently used in advertising. **Copy-testing**, in particular, uses this sort of scale. Copy-testing is the term used by agencies to measure consumers' attitudes to an ad or parts of an ad before a campaign launch. It is extensively used in the US advertising industry, less so in Britain. In the USA a negative copy-test can result in an entire campaign being returned to the drawing board. The use of copy-testing is discussed in more detail in Chapter 9.

Split-run Testing and Regional Tests

The effectiveness of individual ads or that of components of ads such as the copy or visual can be tested by running two variants of the ad in differing regions or with differing consumer groups **(split-run studies)**. As is usual with effectiveness tests, a change in sales, awareness or attitude measures cannot necessarily be attributed to the variation in advertising exposure or creative execution. Some agencies have attempted control studies in which a given ad is exposed only to a controlled TV region. Unfortunately, such studies are always subject to particular market conditions which make it difficult to draw more general conclusions. In addition it is hard to isolate communications effects demographically or regionally. The development of many regional and special interest media facilitates studies of this kind.

BOX 4.6

Direct Response Promotion and Effectiveness

There are a number of communications techniques that can be used to facilitate the measurement of advertising effectiveness. A direct response element to advertising can be useful if the objective is substantive, as it was for example when the British Army recruitment campaign wanted to increase the quality of potential recruits. The free telephone number on the TV and press ads gave the reader a direct response route (Direct Response Television – **DRTV**). The campaign was integrated through press and direct marketing and these media deployed cut-out and post coupons and reply forms. Internet and interactive TV have a powerful potential for immediate consumer response. Where an easily measured response, such as sales or enquiries, is required, the effectiveness of such advertising can be easily evaluated through a direct response element. Direct response measures form a powerful argument for advertising effectiveness but they cannot capture the contribution the ad made to the brand's long-term equity.

It is just as important to know why a campaign has not been successful as it is to know why it is successful. Agencies and clients learn from their mistakes and a failed campaign may result in a new consumer insight that might form the foundation for a new and better campaign. Advertising effectiveness is continually assessed by advertising agencies and increasingly sophisticated techniques are adopted. The holy grail of advertising research is to establish cause–effect relationships between advertising and communications objectives such as awareness or even sales. The industry however continues to pursue this grail with more vigour than success.

Web 2.0, Convergence and Advertising Effectiveness

As Box 4.6 above suggests, many clients find that direct and contiguous responses to advertising are the most convincing measure of effectiveness. This is why direct mail and direct response advertising are so popular – an ad can be targeted at a defined sales prospect, and the response can be measured and tracked. But as we noted in Chapter 2, one school of advertising holds that it is indeed, mediated salesmanship. In that case, a sale after exposure to the ad is the acid test of success. However, there is also an argument that advertising for brands can operate in a 'weaker' or more 'soft sell' way, contributing to the presence of the brand in the market and building values around it which will feed into its long-term market share. Direct response ignores this 'weaker' model of advertising effect.

Clearly, the rising significance of Web 2.0, mobile and internet-linked television creates new opportunities for the instant measurement of consumer response to advertising. On the face of it, counting click-throughs or traffic figures for a website or web-based advertisement is not difficult. However, measuring brand engagement online is a more complex affair and many minds in the business are trying to understand the ways in which multi-channel media might influence brands. One concept used in this context refers to consumer 'touchpoints' as points on any medium where consumers can engage with the brand. For example, consumer and market research organization Millward Brown has developed a process for agencies to measure the way their clients' brands are exposed in multi-channel consumer touchpoints.[12]

Chapter Summary

Chapter 4 has explained how advertising campaigns are typically created in advertising agencies. It set the culture and working practices of advertising agencies in a wider context by outlining their evolution from space brokers into full-service providers of advertising, research and strategy. It explored the role of agencies as cultural intermediaries, taking material from culture and re-inserting it in hybridized form with a brand association. The chapter also touched on the current state of the industry with its many kinds of agency and layered agency networks. It went on to discuss the main roles, responsibilities and processes typically entailed in creative advertising development and mentioned some of the key difficulties and controversies. The following chapter will explore the key issues in the media planning process.

 ## ■ Review Questions

1 List the main functional roles in a typical full-service advertising agency. How does each of these roles contribute to the creation of an advertising campaign?

2 Form account team groups, one person each taking the role of creative, account manager and account planner. Draft an outline communications plan for the launch of a new brand of long-grain rice. Then each account team should compose a pitch for the business based on their initial ideas. The pitches should cover the likely target market, the major marketing issues, the possible media plan and creative ideas.

3 List, explain and discuss some of the major problems of management and control in advertising agencies. How have agencies tried to resolve these problems?

4 Describe the process by which an advertising agency creates an advertisement. Discuss the concepts of creativity and accountability as related to this process.

CASE

Integrated Campaign Planning for the Samsung F480 Tocco[13]

Samsung Electronics is a global market leader in high-tech electronics manufacturing and digital media. Cheil Worldwide, also part of the Samsung group of companies, handles the advertising and communications for many of Samsung's electronics brands and works as their in-house advertising and communication agency. Cheil is a big company in its own right with more than $2 billion worth of billings in 2007. It supports Samsung advertising campaigns with the considerable resources and skills at its disposal, from its base in Korea to its global agency network.

The Samsung Tocco (product name F480) is a touchscreen mobile phone created to compete with the most advanced handsets in the market in terms of functionality, usability and aesthetics. Its key feature is the camera; it is one of the slimmest full touchscreen 5 megapixel camera phones in the world.

For its launch in the UK the positioning was expressed in the campaign brief as 'Sophisticated, stylish, technological and very high end'. The target market was 'people that are looking for style and cool features – 60 % male, 40 % female', and seeking 'the real touchscreen experience' with a style akin to the Samsung Armani F700 and F490. These people would be peer group leaders and trend-setters who were discerning mobile consumers and heavy users of multimedia.

The advertising objectives were to 'position the Samsung Tocco as a designed and technologically advanced product; to make the F480 the hero product in the style category; and to continue to support Samsung's corporate strategy as a leader and premium brand in the UK mobile market'.

'Tone of voice' for the campaign was to emphasize style, sophistication, high fashion and (creative) intelligence. The campaign was to be supported with consumer-led insights around touch screen functionality in relation to its competitors. The media plan emphasized the camera as the USP and dovetailed into Samsung's sponsorship of the Beijing Olympics 2008. Public relations coverage was also important for the product to be clearly differentiated from direct competitors such as the iPhone. Finally, there was a need for experiential marketing initiatives to engage consumers directly with the touchscreen functionality. Research had shown that the opportunity to actually use the product was important in exciting interest and confidence in handling the functionality.

The launch plan emphasized the sophistication and aesthetics of the phone, reflected in its name: 'tocco' is Italian for 'touch'. The advertising and promotion had to use touch as a clear but understated connecting theme with elements of 'art, beauty, mystery and intrigue' to create a clear and distinctive differential brand positioning in a crowded market. The communication strategy aimed to 'increase unaided awareness, brand preference and emotional appeal', and the 'key thought' was 'unique touch'.

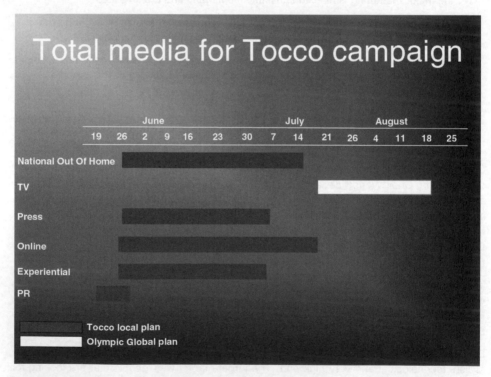

Picture 6   Samsung Tocco outline media plan for UK launch.

Reproduced with kind permission of Samsung Mobile UK and Cheil Worldwide.

The Samsung Tocco was launched in the UK in May 2008 with a 'Please Touch' exhibition held for invited journalists and VIP customers at the Azam Gallery in London. A Dali exhibition was being held in adjacent rooms, reinforcing the theme of the Tocco as an art object as well as a technological product. The cultural capital to be gained from an association with the art world was being leveraged into the mobile phone market. Considerable PR activity was generated around and after the launch event with press coverage and 'advertorials' in style magazines which quickly reached over 25 million unique users. Supporting activity included 'celebrity seeding', giving free product to people who would then receive media coverage with the product. This focused on a 'goody bag' given to attendees at the 'Glamour Women of the Year' awards in London, an event which had generated several million pounds worth of media coverage the previous year.

The creative work carried across print, TV, online and out of home media (see Picture 6), with supporting public relations and experiential marketing initiatives. A print ad depicting the phone as an art object on display subverted the typical art gallery instruction not to touch the exhibits with the slogan 'Please touch' (see Picture 5). The creative theme of the art object that you are allowed to touch was continued in online micro-websites and even specified for in-store product displays. Experiential activities coinciding with the launch included consumer competitions held in major shopping centres and based around a touchscreen *Minority Report* style game, building on the consumer insight that confidence in touchscreen usability was often based on direct experience.

The crowning advertising event was the global Olympic television ad with a DJ using his Samsung Tocco to co-ordinate a music composition made from sampled sounds from Olympic sporting events.

Product campaigns for Samsung Mobile are also supported by regular corporate promotions and experiential initiatives in partnership with other brands. These have included ongoing sponsorship and joint promotions arrangements with Chelsea FC and a partnership with the movie *27 Dresses*.[14]

The Samsung Tocco was the number one pay monthly handset in the UK in 2008.[15] Samsung plan to build on this success with the Ultra edition, launched in early 2009.

■ Case Questions

1 List and explain the elements of media and creative integration you can see in this campaign. How did these elements create synergy for the campaign?

2 Reflecting on your own experience as a mobile user, what do you feel were the key communication problems the company faced in launching the Samsung Tocco and positioning it as a prestige brand in a technology-focused market?

3 Create a campaign plan and advertising plan for a new brand of touchscreen mobile phone positioned at the high tech, high end of the market. What could you learn from the Samsung Tocco campaign, and what additional or different ideas would you bring to the new brand launch?

Deuze, M. (2007) *Media Work.* Cambridge: Polity Press.

Hackley, C. and Kover, A. (2007) 'The trouble with creatives: negotiating creative identity in advertising agencies', *International Journal of Advertising,* 26(1): 63–78.

Jones, J.P. (1999) *The Advertising Business.* Thousand Oaks, CA: Sage.

Packard, V. (1957) *The Hidden Persuaders.* New York: McKay.

Pollitt, S. (1979) 'How I started account planning in agencies', *Campaign,* 20 April: 29–30.

Steel, J. (1998) *Truth, Lies and Advertising: The Art of Account Planning.* New York: John Wiley and Sons.

On the Companion Website

These journal articles are freely available on the companion website (www. sagepub.co.uk/hackley).

The Organization of Creativity in Japanese Advertising Production
Brian Moeran
Human Relations, Jul 2009; vol. 62: pp. 963–985.

The Elephant in the Room? Class and Creative Careers in British Advertising Agencies
Charlotte McLeod, Stephanie O'Donohoe, and Barbara Townley
Human Relations, Jul 2009; vol. 62: pp. 1011–1039.

Gender Relations and Identity at Work: A Case Study of Masculinities and Femininities in an Advertising Agency
Mats Alvesson
Human Relations, Aug 1998; vol. 51: pp. 969–1005.

Notes

1 www.adbrands.net/agencies_index_basics.htm (accessed 21 April 2009).
2 www.wpp.com/wpp/press/interviews/wpp-pips-omnicom.htm (accessed 21 April 2009).
3 For example, in the UK, the IPA Advertising Effectiveness Awards; in the USA, the ADDY creative awards; in Thailand the TACT awards, and so on in practically every country that has advertising.
4 www.motherlondon.com

5 The UK-based initiative 'Adsmart' is one exception, funded by the industry and aiming to help children develop a more sophisticated understanding of advertising.

6 A guide to client briefing is one of several joint industry guides available, from finding an agency, to communication strategy, to judging creative work, agency remuneration and evaluation, produced by the CAF (www.cafonline.org.uk), the IPA (www.ipa.co.uk), the ISBA (www.isba.org.uk), the PRCA (www.prca.org.uk), the MCCA (www.mcca.org.uk) and the UK Advertising Association (www.adasscoc.co.uk).

7 www.isba.org.uk/isba/enhancing/consultancy-services/client-agency-relationships (accessed 22 April 2009).

8 Reported in *Advertising Age*, special report, 14 January 2002.

9 www.ogilvy.co.uk/index.php/our-work (accessed 22 April 2009).

10 A Classification of Residential Neighbourhoods.

11 See, for example, the Advertising Works series of case study compilations, published by the World Advertising Research Centre (WARC), Henley, UK.

12 www.millwardbrown.com/Sites/MillwardBrown/Content/Services/ConsumerTouchpoint Selection.aspx (accessed 23 April 2009).

13 My thanks to Samsung Mobile UK and Cheil Worldwide for their kind permission to reproduce this material.

14 Details at http://uk.samsungmobile.com/promotion/index.do (accessed 29 April 2009).

15 Source: independent GfK analysis, http://uk.samsungmobile.com/products/tocco/showroom/index.do (accessed 28 April 2009).

5 Promotional Media in the Digital Age

Chapter Outline

The media infrastructure for advertising and promotion has changed radically over the last 20 years and continues to do so. This chapter discusses the implications for media strategy and planning. The medium on which promotional communication is conveyed informs the consumer's interpretation of the message. In other words, the 'medium is the message' (McLuhan, 1964), and this chapter describes the qualities of each medium. It also indicates the many categories of advertising and promotion that can be carried on differing mediums, and it identifies the key problems and possibilities that the contemporary media environment raises for advertising.

Key chapter content:

- **The media planning task**

- **The changing media infrastructure for advertising**

- **Media strategy, targeting and audience segmentation**

- **The media mix – channel characteristics and strategy decisions.**

The Media Planning Task

Advertising media consist of 'any means by which sales messages can be conveyed' to audiences (Jefkins, 2000: 74). Communication is usually said to be mediated (that is, carried on a medium) when there is some intervening vehicle between the source and the receiver, such as a newspaper or poster site. Advertising messages can be carried on radio waves, static outdoor billboards, paper and ink, ceramic mugs and ballpoint pens, dynamic outdoor sites such as motor vehicles and public transport; even air balloons and loud hailers can carry promotional messages. The media planner should, in principle, be au fait with all media, though this is a lot to ask. What is more, while there are media professionals specializing in, say, TV or radio, there is increasingly a requirement for them to facilitate campaigns across all media. As Dawson (2009: 28) points out, 'Integration is now so much the norm that the term itself seems almost obsolete, with "new" and "old" media rapidly blurring into a single communications armory... Interruption and engagement channels are complementary tools rather than "old" pitted against "new" media'.

By 'interruption' Dawson is referring to advertising media which disrupt the audience's media engagement, such as where the TV shows are interrupted to show the ads. 'Engagement' advertising media is a term used to describe advertising which is woven into the media consumption experience, as with, for example, product placement (discussed in Chapter 6) or internet advertising (discussed in Chapter 10). What this means is that now it is incumbent on media planners to think not only in terms of advertising exposure but also in terms of brand contact touchpoints, that is, all the points across all media at which the consumer has contact with the brand. Hairong Li[1] suggests that

> Brand contact is any planned and unplanned form of exposure to and interaction with a product or service. For example, when you see an ad for *VW* on TV, hear a *Mazda*'s 'zoom zoom' slogan on the radio, are told by a friend that her *iPod* is the greatest invention, or sample a new flavor of *Piranha* energy drink at the grocery store, you are having a brand contact. Television commercials, radio ads, and product sampling are planned forms of brand contact.

Word of mouth is also an example of brand contact. It is more difficult to plan for, but has always been an important hidden element of advertising success (Dichter, 1966).

The media planning and buying tasks are of key importance in advertising. As Manning (2009: 11) points out, media is where the bulk of the money is spent. Typically, a TV campaign can cost £300,000 to make but £3,000,000 to show. The cost of mass media exposure means that getting the media mix right

Table 5.0 Basic elements of the media planning task

1 Set media objectives (with reference to campaign objectives and advertising strategy)
2 Select target audience (also with reference to campaign plan)
3 Select media channels
4 Schedule media exposures (the media plan)
5 Buy media
6 Assess media effectiveness

is every bit as important to the success of a promotional campaign as getting the creativity right. However, according to commentators such as Manning (2009) and Binet (2009), many advertising agencies remain relatively poor at accurately calculating the return on investment of advertising spend on digital media. There is some science in media planning, but it also remains something of an art.

The basic media planning task (see Table 5.0) is to achieve optimum levels of exposure for the campaign, utilizing the most cost-effective and appropriate combinations of medium possible. The media planner negotiates and buys the space on which the advertisements will be shown, whether TV or radio airtime, outdoor sites, print ads in press publications, click-through or banner ads on internet sites, or whatever. The media planner seeks to expose the creative execution to a relevant audience defined by segmentation criteria such as age, sex, demographic, socio-economic or lifestyle/ **psychographic** characteristics. They try to achieve the greatest possible reach and **penetration**. Reach refers to the proportion of the target audience reached by an exposure. Penetration refers to the accumulated reach over time, including repeated exposures. Timing is important, since the advertisements must be exposed at times when they will achieve the highest impact. Media planners will schedule advertisements according to the campaign objectives, perhaps in a short burst of intensive exposure (called a 'blitz'), or alternatively in a stepped exposure of, say, one week on, one week off, over several months (called 'pulsing'). Issues of seasonality of demand also need to be considered. The cost effectiveness of the exposure is often assessed by the cost-per-thousand members of the target audience reached criterion, though calculating the advertising return on an investment by media channel is a very difficult task.

Media Planning Terms and Concepts

In an era of integrated marketing communications the terms above-the-line and below-the-line are heard less often in the industry than was once the case. Their rationale, which was based on the now largely outdated commission model for agency remuneration, is now redundant as most agencies today charge by each labour hour. The terms still have resonance though. Above-the-line refers to mass media advertising, television, cinema, press and commercial radio. Once, ad agencies were paid through the commission they gained from buying spot advertising on these media. Below-the-line refers to everything else, from direct mail and database marketing, sponsorship, product placement and celebrity endorsement to sales promotion and merchandising. The term through-the-line is often heard referring to media planning which deploys both mass advertising media and non-advertising promotion.

Another term which has become popular in media planning for advertising is **media-neutral planning**. Media-neutral planning refers to the way the agency agenda has been broadened from merely advertising to brand communications of all kinds. In the past, advertising agencies were notorious for their attitude that mass media advertising was the default solution for any clients' communication problem. This was driven by the fact that agencies, especially in the UK, used to earn income from the media space they bought for spot advertising, as noted previously. Today, agencies tend to be paid by the hour. There is also more pressure for them to provide integrated communication solutions. The media-neutral planning attitude holds that the solution to the client's communication problem might lie in any medium, or in any combination of media, even if none of these include mass media advertising.

Other important concepts in media planning include the Gross Rating Point (GRP) which is a measure of the proportion of households who are exposed to an advertisement. Reach refers to unique audience members, while GRP refers to the accumulated figure as a result of repeated airings of the ad. Frequency refers to the number of opportunities a member of the audience has to see the ad. These concepts can be used in setting media objectives. For example, a campaign might be planned to reach 75 per cent of the target audience.

There are different views about the usefulness of repeat exposures. Some commentators feel that many repeated exposures can serve a purpose, while others feel that there is little point to any beyond the first exposure. However, as always, it depends on the nature of the communication problem being addressed, the market, the competitive context and the target audience characteristics, all of which influence the advertising and the media objectives.

Media Planning and Media Strategy

Clever and thorough media planning is indispensable to the success of advertising. A promotional campaign cannot be effective if it is not seen by a sufficient number of relevant consumers. Broadly, media planning refers to the task of placing finished ads in appropriate media channels for maximum target group exposure, while media strategy usually refers to the judgements made concerning the fit between media channels, creative executions and the brand personality. The media strategy has to ensure that there is coherence between media, brand and creative execution. The two terms, media planning and media strategy, are often used interchangeably, given the imprecision of the business.

The media planning task tends to be quantitatively driven by the cost-per-thousand and number of exposures, as noted above, but it is a mistake to suppose that it is just about procurement. Judgement is required to decide which combination of media (known as the media mix) will provide the maximum impact for a given advertisement. Questions such as 'What are the viewing/reading/listening habits of the target audience'? and 'How might they be reached'? have to be answered. Also, 'What interval frequency of advertising exposure will best support the campaign objectives?' 'Can the campaign creative executions be integrated across differing media so that consumers' view of the brand is reinforced from a number of sources?' A significant constraint, of course, is the budget. This might constrain attempts to shout as loud as competitors. The term 'share of voice' refers to the proportion of advertising spend by one brand in relation to the total over a period of time for that particular category. Share of voice is an important aspect of competitive advertising activity, since a declining share of voice can often coincide with a declining market share.

One important consideration concerns the distinction between **media channel** and media vehicle. The media channels could be TV, radio, press or outdoor. The media vehicle is the specific TV show, radio show, newspaper or magazine chosen to air the advertisement. Different media vehicles will have very different audiences and audience characteristics which will have relevance for targeting.

International Campaigns and the Media Infrastructure

Campaigns which cross international boundaries present more planning and scheduling problems for the media planner, in addition to the creative problems of cross-national advertising (see Chapter 7). The media infrastructure varies enormously region by region and country by country, and this variation accounts for major differences in the character of advertising and promotion in different national and international contexts. In the developed North there is a complex communications infrastructure that reaches most of the population through thousands of press publications, radio and TV shows and other media. In the developing South there is a far less well-developed communications infrastructure, and also lower levels of TV ownership, internet access and adult literacy. Audiences are, in general, more difficult to reach where the communications infrastructure is less developed. However, the global reach of digital communication is also having a striking effect on the tone, type and cost structures of advertising in all its forms, not to mention its effect on audience reach.

The tasks of media strategy and planning have never been simple, and they have become more complex because of the rapid changes in the global media infrastructure during the last 15 years. These changes need to be examined before discussing the particular qualities of each available medium.

The Changing Media Infrastructure for Advertising

The media buying scene is today characterized by the media independents, agencies that specialize in media planning, scheduling and buying. In a sense, the evolution of advertising agencies has turned full circle, since advertising agencies began as media brokers before developing in-house functions of copywriting, artwork, strategy and research as well. Over time, media broking and research have been farmed out to become independent agencies. One such is Zenith Optimedia, owned by Publicis and part of the world's biggest media services group.[2] Many advertising agencies that formerly bought media through in-house operations now buy their media space through independent media brokers which have been devolved into a separate business, such as OMD UK.[3]

Lateral mergers and takeovers have increased the industrial concentration in the media industry over the last decade, resulting in fewer sellers and fewer buyers. This means that media costs have been driven up, and advertisers usually have to go through the big media buyers to get the best economies of scale. The rise of the independents has partly been a response to the increasing media buying costs, as well as to technological advances including digital media. The rise in the cost of advertising media, partly resulting from the monopoly position of many regional media owners, has not been well received by agencies. Media buyers therefore needed more buying power to generate economies of buying scale. As a consequence there has been increased industrial concentration among media buyers parallel with that among media owners.

While media planning decisions should be uppermost at every stage of the creative advertising development process, the increased complexity of market conditions for media planning and buying necessitates specialist agencies with the expertise and buying power to perform this function effectively.

UK Media Adspend and the Rise of Digital

In the UK in 2007 more than £19 billion was spent on advertising. Most of this went on display advertising in all media, the remainder on classified (small) ads, recruitment and business press advertising, and company announcements. Expenditure on internet advertising in the UK rose by 38 per cent from 2006 to 2007, reaching £2.8 billion.[4] According to the *Internet Advertising Bureau* (IAB), internet advertising took a 16 per cent share of total UK advertising expenditure ('adspend') in April 2008. TV advertising remains the biggest media advertising expenditure category but online advertising spend is set to overtake it by late 2009. There are three commercial terrestrial television channels serving the UK, made up of 15 programme companies (not counting cable and satellite channels). In all there are about 400 television channels carrying advertising. The UK allows up to seven and a half minutes advertising per hour on terrestrial channels, and up to nine minutes per hour on satellite and cable channels. Organizations also spend significant additional sums on other forms of communication, such as exhibitions, sponsorship, sales promotion and mail order. In the UK, there are well over 10,000 printed publications serving all types of readership, though at the time of writing in 2009 newspapers globally are suffering from a sharp downturn in advertising revenue which threatens the continued existence of some long established news titles. The 10 major daily national newspapers in the UK sell in excess of 14 million copies per day in total. Also serving the UK are over 240 commercial radio stations, plus outdoor sites, cinema advertising and many other media.

In some cases, the media tail is even beginning to wag the advertising dog. Media agencies are offering strategic planning services and creative work is being outsourced to specialist creative boutiques. This appears logically sound when one remembers how ad agencies evolved. As media become increasingly integral to the creative development of advertising, there may well be a major challenge ahead facing advertising agencies that want to retain their current structures and working methods. In the USA, media agencies are even beginning to produce TV shows as vehicles for advertisers, so that advertisers have maximum control over the exposure their brand receives. Like most things in marketing, this is not new – the phrase 'soap opera' comes from the shows created for US TV and radio by Lever Brothers and Proctor and Gamble in the 1950s to promote their products. But for some years this went out of fashion.

Audience Fragmentation and Media Vehicle Reach

The reduction in press production costs because of digital technology has resulted in many new newspaper and magazine titles coming onto the market, plus free newspapers, special sections in the press and a burgeoning number of specialist magazines. However, circulations, especially of the national daily newspapers and major magazines, are considerably lower than they were in the 1980s and early 1990s. For example, the national daily papers in the UK lost on average 4 per cent of their circulation between 2007 and 2008.[5]

The general trend to lower readerships and viewing figures holds, with few exceptions, across all traditional media all over the world. In some cases, established newspapers in the UK and the USA are facing bankruptcy at the time of writing because of shrinking circulations and advertising revenue. The key problem is that audiences have so many more opportunities to access news, comment and entertainment than ever before, especially online but also through new print media vehicles such as free newspapers. There are more media vehicles than ever before, but each is competing for a small share of the audience. Hence, audiences are 'fragmenting' across the spectrum of the media mix. Many more special-interest publications allow ever more precise targeting of advertising, but to smaller groups. For media planners, the implication of this trend to audience fragmentation is that targeting to specialist interest groups is easier and more precise, but it requires more media vehicles and a wider media mix to achieve the required audience reach.

This trend is true also for outdoor (known as out of home or OOH) media. There is a global trend towards more public space in urban and non-urban settings being given over to advertising. Between 1996 and 1998 there were over 100,000 more outdoor sites in Europe. In the USA there was a similar increase. It may be that changing geopolitical trends have undermined resistance to advertising in public social spaces. In a post-communist world the economic imperative of wealth generation has superseded other social values. The increase in **ambient media** advertising assimilated into traditionally non-promotional social contexts such as bus or underground stations, pubs and bars and even schools has exploited this lowered resistance. In general, advertising and promotion inserted into otherwise non-commercialized social settings has become much more common. Walls, floors and signage in public spaces all carry advertising, and the backs of theatre programmes, bus and car-park tickets are now rarely without sponsored messages.

Digital telecommunications technology has lowered start-up costs and made possible not only many new magazine and newspaper titles but also many new TV and radio stations. In the UK in 1988 there were four TV channels. Today there are some 400 including digital and cable channels. As with magazines and newspapers, most TV channels carry lower viewing figures than they did when there was less consumer choice. In the UK in the 1980s it was not uncommon for the most popular TV shows to attract viewing figures of over 25 million. Today, it is exceptional for a show or televised event to attract more than 12 million viewers. In contrast, in the USA the Superbowl American

Football final can reach 100 million viewers, and advertising time during the Superbowl is the most expensive money can buy. But this is an exception. Top-rated US TV shows today typically achieve audience figures of around 10 million. Having said that, many syndicated TV shows reach an aggregated audience of many millions when the effect of re-runs, DVD sales and internet exposures are factored in. The problem with this aggregated measure for the channels is that it is good for product placement but doesn't help spot advertising reach.

In radio a similar picture is emerging since new digital radio stations have made major inroads into the audience share of older stations. In the UK, the popular non-commercial BBC radio stations once attracted larger audiences, just like television. Today they have competition in the form of commercial, digital radio stations such as Classic FM, Heart FM and TalkSport, three stations that vie for the largest slice of advertising revenue.

These changes in the media landscape have major repercussions for advertisers. Conventional wisdom about the strategic importance of a particular medium and also about targeting, audience segmentation and cost-effectiveness has been challenged. Media strategy and advertising strategy increasingly have to be understood as two dimensions of the same thing. Most importantly, account people and media planners can no longer easily categorize their target audience by external indicators like social class, age, income or sex. Instead they have to think in terms of the lifestyle choices of brand consumption communities and the implications of these choices for media planning.

Media Strategy, Targeting and Audience Segmentation

The increase in the number of media channels and vehicles, and the consequent fragmentation of media audiences, mean that target groups of consumers are both easier and more difficult to reach. They are easier to reach in the sense that audiences have fragmented into narrow interest groups that are served by hundreds of special-interest magazines and TV channels. If an advertiser wants to reach, say, trout fishermen, sports-car enthusiasts or TV soap opera fans, there are specialist publications and TV shows that are ideal vehicles for targeting such narrowly defined audiences. But consumer groups are also more difficult to reach because agencies have great difficulty in categorizing audiences into target groups that are sufficiently large to be viable for general advertisers. Being able to target trout fishermen is useful if you are selling fishing tackle, but not for general fmcg (fast moving consumer goods) sales which require varied target groups. While trout fishermen probably have other consumer interests too, media vehicles that cater for one hobby are of limited use to most advertisers.

Each commercial medium that is funded by advertising has a research-based reader/listener/viewer profile which provides an idea of the typical person who consumes their medium. This information is important for selling advertising space or time to advertisers who need to know the age, sex, income and economic behaviour of the typical consumer. It is not difficult for media owners to construct this kind of profile. Never before have there existed more data sets on consumer habits, behaviour and attitudes. Electronic communications and transactions mean that it is possible to construct and cross-reference massive databases of consumer information. The difficulty brand organizations have is how best to use all these data to focus on the key characteristics of their typical consumer.

BOX 5.1

The UK National Daily Press Circulations

The UK has a population of about 61 million. Newspaper readership, though declining, remains relatively high. The *Sun* is the most popular national daily newspaper with around 3 million sales daily. Its figures have held up well at a time when most UK national newspapers are losing sales. Other leading titles include the *Daily Mail* with a circulation of 2.2 million, the *Daily Mirror* at 1.45 million and the *Daily Star* at 0.75 million. Among the 'quality' dailies, the London *Times* sells 600,000, the *Daily Telegraph* 860,000, and the *Guardian* 330,000 (figures at September 2008 from *Guardian Media*).[6]

The *Sun* is an expensive publication in which to buy advertising space not only because its readership is large but also because its reader profile is relatively young and consumes many kinds of product or service. In terms of socio-economic groupings (see Figure 5.0) the *Sun* can deliver to advertisers around 3 million B, C1 and C2 readers daily. Given that many copies of the newspaper are read in workplaces or households, the actual number of readers may be double the sales figure. These consumers are in the market for many kinds of fmcg and services. Many advertisers want to reach young consumers because they are at that stage of life in which consumption is very important and they have disposable income. *The Times* newspaper in the UK may be more internationally famous than the *Sun* but with daily sales of less than a third of the *Sun*'s it cannot deliver the same volume of consumers to advertisers. Furthermore, *The Times*'s reader profile is somewhat different from that of the *Sun,* being slightly older, with higher average income and greater average educational attainment. *The Times,* therefore, is attractive to different advertisers. For example, *The Sunday Times* carries many pages of classified advertising for elite brands of motor-car such as Porsche and Mercedes-Benz. The *Sun* is probably a better advertising vehicle for many kinds of household durable item.

Demographic Segmentation and Consumer Heterogeneity

The problem for advertisers is that although they may need to reach large numbers of consumers in order for advertising expenditure to be recovered in

The socio-economic grouping system was devised by the British Civil Service in the late 1940s. It classified citizens according to the occupation of the 'head' (male) of the household because this criterion was a reliable indicator of all the household members' level of education, income, professional class and leisure habits. Today the socio-economic classification system is still used in British media, but its limitations are widely acknowledged. The categories are as follows.

A   Higher managerial, administrative and professional (3% of the UK population)
B   Intermediate managerial, administrative and professional (20.4%)
C1 Supervisory or clerical and junior managerial, admin and prof (27.2%)
C2 Skilled manual (21.8%)
D   Semi-skilled and unskilled manual (17.4%)
E   State pensioners, casual workers or unemployed (10.2%)

Figure 5.0   Socio-economic groupings in the UK

increased sales, the behaviour of these large groups is heterogeneous. Specialist media, then, facilitate more closely specified targeting than mass media, but they tend to serve audience numbers that are much lower than those formerly served by mass market media. The mass media channels of TV, radio and press were once easy access routes to large, relatively homogeneous, audience groups. Today, mass audiences display far more heterogeneity in their consumption patterns and behaviour than they used to. Increased income levels and social and geographical mobility in many countries mean that a person's social status no longer reliably indicates his or her consumption behaviour or lifestyle.

Demographic and social changes have rendered the old socio-economic groups of A, B, C1, C2, D and E increasingly redundant (see Figure 5.0). No longer can household members be easily classified and their consumer behaviour predicted on the basis of the occupation of the (male) 'head' of the household. In Western developed economies rising rates of divorce, increasing numbers of females involved in the professions, greater social mobility and increases in the number of single-person households have changed the composition of media audiences. For example, the greater social mobility today in the West means that it is no longer so unusual for the children of a manual or unskilled worker to go to university and acquire a profession. In the past, it was more likely that a person's social status, education level and employment would be the same as their father's, hence the profile of the father was a more reliable indicator of the status of the rest of the family.

There are, as noted, several problems with the contemporary relevance of the socio-economic groups classification system. Another one is that the classification of manual or non-manual occupation no longer necessarily indicates income levels in Western developed economies. Many non-manual workers earn less than skilled manual workers. Plumbers or builders can earn more than teachers or junior civil servants, and they may be just as likely to take holidays abroad and drive an expensive car.

All these factors have changed the presuppositions that media planners bring to their task of targeting promotional messages to relevant audiences. Advertising agencies have tried to keep track of the changing currents of consumer groupings by conducting their own segmentation research. For example, 'psychographic' profiles (discussed below) categorize consumers based on surveys of their lifestyle behaviours and attitudes. Consumer groups are no longer segmented only by demographic criteria such as age, sex and income. Brand marketing organizations often refer to brand 'communities' of consumers that are linked only by their consumption of a given brand. Brand consumption may be all that these people share, but advertisers assume that there is some common behavioural, psychological or social denominator underlying the motivation to consume this brand.

Brand Communities

The UK soccer club Manchester United, for example, is marketed as a brand and has the largest supporter base of any soccer club in the world. These supporters, united in their love for football and enthusiasm for Manchester United, are hugely diverse in terms of their nationality, age, sex, income, occupation and social class. But for many of these people, Manchester United is more than a consumption opportunity – it is an obsession. They spend large amounts of money on team shirts, scarves and countless other items carrying the club crest, they invest in satellite TV to watch the matches, they pay fees to join supporters' clubs and receive regular newsletters and offers, and they engage socially with other supporters through meetings, website chatrooms and so on.

Brand communities can cut across categories of age, sex, geography and social class (Parsons and Maclaran, 2009). The group may be radically hetero-geneous, except for the commonality that motivates their interest in the brand. This may be quite nebulous, defined in terms of abstract values and intangible aspirations. The attention advertising agencies now pay to brand communities amounts to an admission that they have only the vaguest notion of what consumers are about. When age, sex, income, geographical location, educational attainment, professional and social status no longer have any relevance for brand communities such as the global group of Manchester United supporters, advertising agencies have nothing to unite the group other than by saying that this is a brand community united by a shared love of the brand. Consumers have become so eclectic in their choices and behaviour that only highly abstract notions seem able to capture the phenomenon that is occurring (see also Cova et al., 2007).

Psychographics and Segmentation

Advertising agencies and brand managers clearly have an interest in appearing to understand consumers. Since the 1970s advertising agencies have tried to formally monitor and track the changing currents of consumer groupings. One attempt has involved commissioning research to delve into consumer lifestyles and behaviour in order to form new classification systems that can capture the intangibles that evade systems based on demographic data alone. Some of the lifestyle categories generated by a pseudo-science called psychographics became part of popular vocabulary in the UK. Consumers were classified as Yuppies (Young, Upwardly Mobile Professionals), Dinkies (Dual Income, No Kids) and many other irreverent, acronymic soubriquets. The agencies' objective was to persuade clients that in spite of the breakdown of traditional mass audience characteristics, they still understood the motivations and behaviour of discrete consumer groups. They could, therefore, claim that they had a proprietary knowledge and insight that enabled them to reach exactly the kinds of consumer their clients wished to reach.

Proponents of psychographics drew on psychological principles to make the approach seem intellectually more robust. Abraham Maslow's[7] theories of human motivation have proved particularly useful for marketing practitioners and academics seeking to lend credibility to their claim that they have special knowledge about consumer behaviour. It should be said, though, that the use of Maslow's theories by marketers, especially his 'hierarchy of needs', does not do justice to them. Maslow was a pioneer of the humanistic psychology movement which was partly a reaction against the behavioural and experimental psychology that reduced humans to entities that behaved according to rules. Maslow wanted psychology to help people find a higher and happier state through personal growth and development. Advertising agencies (and marketing academics) have used his theories to support their contention that humans can be categorized according to their consumption needs. These are said to evolve from biological essentials such as warmth and food, to the need for safety and social company, and then to progress to more egocentric needs such as esteem and self-actualization. Proponents suggested that psychographics-based segmentation systems were useful for predicting consumption from a person's position on the hierarchy of needs. While this application of the theory has some explanatory value, it does not hold any predictive capacity. In any case, the theory was not conceived with advertising in mind and is based on assumptions that do not cohere with the thinking of advertising professionals. For Maslow, the highest state of self-actualization occurred when humans rejected selfish (including material) values and instead gave back to their fellow humans in some way. One could hardly think of a less appropriate model for advertising or marketing (see Hackley, 2007, for discussion).

Generation 'X' and Elusive Consumer Groups

One important feature of brand communities for marketing communications professionals is that they may resist influence from conventional mediated promotion. In developed economies, consumers are often sceptical of advertising claims and over-familiar with advertising techniques, and many young consumers fall outside the reach of mass media because they do not regularly watch national television or read national newspapers.

People aged 18–25 form an important group of active consumers for brand marketers and will become more important as their incomes rise and consumption needs increase. In the UK, this group was notably difficult for advertisers to reach because they had opted out of mainstream media and took part only in their own exclusive sub-cultures. They didn't watch much terrestrial TV and didn't buy a daily newspaper. They were labelled 'Generation X' and many agencies tried to devise tailored targeting schemes to deliver this group to brand advertisers. This trend, part of the more general fragmentation of media audiences, is yet another factor in the increased complexity of media planning.

Some advertisers claimed that they could reach Generation X by placing 'shock' advertising in cinemas. It was assumed that while Generation X would not read newspapers or watch TV they would go to the cinema and notice ads that subverted advertising conventions. Ads featuring unusually graphic violence or sex were popular for a time in the UK because agencies were trying to reach Generation-X consumers. Their success was difficult to assess. Some commentators argued that Generation X was an agency myth and that, in fact, these consumers were no more difficult to reach than other groups who shifted their viewing, listening and reading habits on a regular basis.

More important for advertisers are those consumer groups who actively resist marketing itself. There have been many news items about anti-globalization protesters at World Trade Organization (WTO) meetings. Such groups tend to be against many of the manifestations of global marketing, especially the dominance of internationally marketed brands and the power that brand organizations wield to influence international economic policy. Other groups (perhaps with some commonality of membership) have reacted against specific brands for a variety of reasons and called for consumer boycotts. The McDonald's restaurant brand has received considerable critical attention, especially in France where good cuisine and national culture are greatly prized; the corporatism and culinary vulgarity that McDonald's represents for such consumers make it an obvious target. Authors such as Eric Schlosser *(Fast Food Nation)*, Naomi Klein *(No Logo)* and George Ritzer *(The McDonaldization of Society)*[9] have written pungent critiques of brand corporatism that have been received enthusiastically by many thousands. Naturally, this groundswell of consumer resistance to brand marketing and global corporatism has created a new consumer segment that is being exploited by book marketing organizations. Even anti-brand positioning can be conceived as a brand by marketers. Nevertheless, consumer boycotts and other forms of active resistance to brand marking create more problems for advertising agencies trying to categorize consumers on the basis of their receptivity to marketing activity.

Even in this scenario of flux in the media world for advertising, some aspects of the media planning task remain unchanged. Media planners have to find suitable media with which to target relevant consumer segments with advertising campaigns that will be effective in that particular context. A prerequisite for this task is a general understanding of the kinds of media channel available and their qualities and characteristics.

The Media Mix – Channel Characteristics and Strategy Decisions

Sales promotion, TV advertising, press, SMS text messaging, direct mail, radio, outdoor billboards, point-of-sale promotion and merchandising, cinema advertising, product placement and sponsorship, trade conference and exhibition stands, some types of public relations, internet and interactive TV, CD-Roms and DVDs, even product packaging and non-mediated channels such as viral marketing, personal selling and word-of-mouth campaigns can all be understood broadly as advertising that uses different channels to reach and influence its audience. These different channels are increasingly used in combination in integrated and through-the-line campaigns.

The way that major companies approach communications planning is changing to reflect the blurring of media channels and marketing disciplines. Media planning is becoming more clever and more creative. Choices of media channel continue to be made on a relatively subjective basis, often relying on conventional wisdom concerning the aura that different media channels bestow on the advertising message and, concomitantly, on the brand personality. Some media agencies have developed tools based on their research that can assist planning for particular kinds of campaign. Nevertheless, rules of thumb and experience remain the most commonly used criteria. Clearly, advertising strategy is central to media channel decisions: the choices made must take account of the particular objectives that are desired for a given campaign. This is where it is important to have an informed view on the strengths and weaknesses of each medium from the brand's perspective.

The choice of media channel is often based on criteria such as the following:

- Coverage of the target audience
- The type of engagement that consumers have with that medium with respect to the brand personality

- The communication context that the medium provides for the brand
- The cost in relation to the promotional budget.

These issues have to be considered in the light of specific campaign objectives. A campaign to raise awareness for a new brand launch demands a different kind of engagement with the consumer, and possibly a different medium, from a campaign requiring a direct response from consumers. Audiences engage differently with different media. The mood of a TV viewer is likely to be relaxed, relatively passive and open to suggestion. A newspaper reader may be more critically engaged with the medium, actively reading and thinking about the content. A radio listener may be preoccupied with other tasks and may use radio as a form of minor distraction. A cinema audience may pay greater attention to pre-show ads than, say, a TV audience. Media channels are often considered by professionals to have particular strengths and weaknesses. For example, conventional media wisdom holds that TV is good for raising brand awareness but poor for stimulating trial and purchase, and vice versa for sales promotion (see examples in Table 5.1).

Table 5.1   Communication Channels: Main Strengths and Weaknesses[10]

Medium	Strengths	Weaknesses
TV	Dramatic audio visual impact Large mass audience reach Can demonstrate products Prestige	High production cost Low attention Short exposure Long lead time
Newspapers	Source credibility Immediacy Regular exposure	Cost can be high Short exposure Uneven audience reach
Magazines	Special interest targeting Long life in household	Lower circulations High cost
Radio	Regular, repeated exposure Lifestyle targeting Immediacy Low cost	Low attention Low prestige Short-lived
Out Of Home (OOH)	Prominent in busy settings High local visibility Repeated exposure for commuters Creative possibilities (electronic, 3D)	High cost Geographically limited
e-marketing communication	Engagement Direct response Measurability for ROI Personal targeting	Constant monitoring Sensitivity to PR Crowded arena Technically complex
Direct marketing	Personal communication Tailored message Sales trigger	Resistance Database currency Low response rates

Picture 1   Advertising is a communication medium visible in most social spaces, as in this example of outdoor advertising in New York's Times Square. (*See also page 18.*)

Picture 2   Front Cover: The picture on the front cover of this book is a still from the 2007 Sony 'Bunnies' ad, created by London agency Fallon in their striking campaign for the Sony Bravia TV, and following on from their equally celebrated ads 'Paint' and 'Balls'. In 'Bunnies', 200 Play-doh rabbits rampage through New York in a riot of colour, a vivid entertainment in itself as well as a promotion for the colour reproduction qualities of the TV set.

Picture 3   Strand cigarette advertisement. Miscommunication in advertising.

The 'You're never alone with a Strand' strapline acquired legendary status in the ad industry because consumers interpreted it to mean that only the friendless smoked Strand cigarettes. The ads were photographed in a film noir style around London and Brighton in 1960, with actor Terence Brook, dressed in a white raincoat and trilby, defiantly lighting up a Strand. On the face of it, the iconic, rugged individualism of the Strand character could be seen as a British counterpart to the enduring Marlboro cowboy. But even though the public loved the ads, and they made the soundtrack a chart hit, the cigarette brand was soon taken off the market.

Image courtesy of The Advertising Archives.

Picture 4   This billboard ad by AMV BBDO inverted the well know aphorism 'great minds think alike' to wittily suggest that *The Economist* is a magazine for readers who like to be intellectually challenged.

Reproduced with kind permission of *The Economist* and AMV BBDO.
(*See also page 49.*)

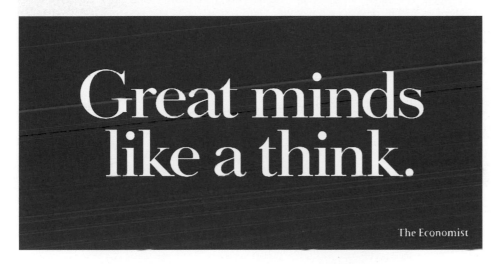

Picture 5   This print ad by AMV BBDO asks readers whether they can afford not to keep abreast of current events in economics and management by reading *The Economist*.

Reproduced with kind permission of *The Economist* and AMV BBDO.
(*See also page 49.*)

Pictures 6 & 7   Screen shots from the Guinness Surfer with White Horses advert.
The Guinness brand is associated with some of the most memorable creative executions in
the history of advertising. Surfer, which was voted best ad of all time in a poll by UK TV
Channel 4 in 2002[1], was created in 1994 by London agency AMV BBDO. Like many
Guinness beer ads it celebrates the time it takes for a carefully poured draught Guinness
beer to settle. The surfers wait too, until the ultimate wave arrives. One story claimed that
the Hawaiian surfers, who were not actors, were actually quite alarmed to be riding such a
huge wave. The Guinness brand strapline 'Good things come to those who wait' applied to
the ad as well as to the drink – it took nine days to film, and longer in post production to
add the horses.

Surfers

'Good things come to those who …'

[1] http://www.channel4.com/entertainment/tv/microsites/G/greatest/tv_ads/results.html **accessed October 6th 2009.**

Picture 8   First City Monument Bank of Nigeria have positioned their brand as the one which chimes with their customers' dreams and aspirations (see Chapter 3 case).

Reproduced by kind permission of FCMB and Centrespread FCB.
(*See also page 85.*)

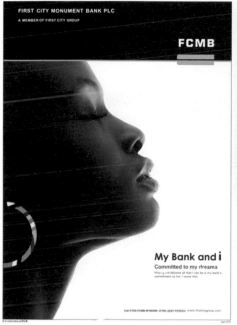 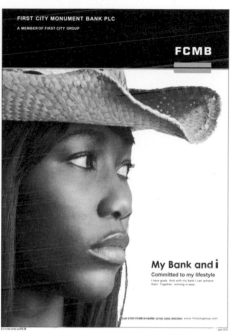

Picture 9   The Samsung Tocco 'please touch' campaign (see Chapter 4 case).
Reproduced with kind permission of Samsung Mobile UK and Cheil Worldwide.
(*See also page 123.*)

Picture 10   Out Of Home (OOH) advertising has become a familiar part of the urban environment.
(*See also page 155.*)

Picture 11   This ad forms part of the Dove 'Campaign for Real Beauty' that is linked with the Dove Self-Esteem Foundation, a funded charity concerned with activities and education designed to boost the self-esteem of girls and young women.

Reproduced with kind permission of Ogilvy UK and Unilever.
(*See also page 281.*)

Wishes she were blonde.

Picture 12   Ogilvy and Mather's Real Women ad for Dove beauty products in 2004 resulted in a reputed 700% sales increase of Dove firming creams for manufacturer Lever-Faberge.[2]

Reproduced with kind permission of Ogilvy UK and Unilever.

[2] Stephen brook, Real Women ads do Wonders for Dove Figures, The Guardian, July 24th 2009 http://www.guardian.co.uk/media/2004/jul/29/marketingandpr.advertising1 accessed October 6th 2009.

Table 5.1

Medium	Strengths	Weaknesses
POS and merchandising	Close to purchase Persuasiveness	Limited reach (in-store) Low coverage
Sales promotion	Sales generator Local impact	Creatively limited Limited coverage
Conferences and exhibitions	Source credibility B2B capability	High cost per event Time intensive

Television

TV advertising remains the most visible and prestigious form of advertising and the most convenient way to reach an audience of millions. It can be an expensive medium. As noted above, 15 commercial television programme makers serve the whole UK population through the ITV network. The BBC does not carry advertising on any of its stations. A single 30-second weekday exposure during the commercial break of a popular TV show on commercial television can cost more than £30,000. In television regions with fewer viewers the price can be considerably less, depending on the time of day the ad is aired. In the UK, advertising in the commercial break of a show such as Granada TV's soap drama *Coronation Street* is usually the most expensive because of the show's regular viewing figures of over 10 million. In the USA, as also noted earlier, buying advertising time during the commercial breaks of the Superbowl American football final is possibly the most expensive television advertising decision in the world. In the UK, all TV sets that receive BBC stations must have a television licence. The money from these 23 million licences goes to the BBC for its programme funding and administration. Although the BBC does not carry advertising, its existence gives UK TV a distinctive character and influences the programming of the commercial stations.

TV may be ubiquitous in developed and also in developing economies, but it is a recent social innovation. TV has such a dramatic impact that it will often dominate a room, demanding attention even if the people present are not particularly interested. Appearing on TV bestows prestige on a brand that ripples outward to impress not only consumers but also employees, suppliers and other stakeholders such as shareholders. A TV ad sends a message about the aspirations of the brand and places it in juxtaposition with the most prestigious brands. TV is the media vehicle that most powerfully reflects and projects audience aspirations and fantasies. It is therefore the perfect medium for portraying brands as accessories to these aspirations.

In addition to TV channels, there are over 1,500 independent production companies making TV programmes. Most of the new stations are commercial, funded by advertising and sponsorship revenues. Audience fragmentation into **consumer communities** and lifestyle groupings has made selected audiences more accessible through lifestyle and special-interest TV channels. Millions round the world now have access to satellite TV channels that cross international borders.

TV has an extraordinary power to convey values and to communicate norms across cultures, where the ways it is consumed show a striking similarity. TV is viewed in a relaxed mood, often in the home and in the company of other people. It can be a social occasion as well as a leisure pursuit and a source of relaxation. TV gives advertisers access to domestic settings. What is of interest to advertisers is that TV's assimilation into social settings means that people are suggestible when they are watching. TV advertising reaches those who are looking for entertainment, information and ideas about new ways of living and consuming.

Even in an environment of falling TV advertising revenues, TV retains its importance in the media mix because of its potential to create a huge dramatic impact for a brand. The creative possibilities are vast for televisual portrayals of a brand in lifestyle settings. The global reach and prestige of TV advertising, still, surpass any other medium. For many brand clients, though, TV advertising is problematic because of its lack of calculable cost efficiency. Get it right and it can create a powerful sales impetus for brands. Get it wrong and a lot of money disappears very quickly. As noted above, production costs for a modest TV ad are often a mere tenth of the cost of airing the ad a few times on prime time. Such ads can take many months from storyboard to airtime exposure. They last only a few seconds and usually date very quickly. Furthermore, the individuals watching TV ads may be highly inattentive and some studies have even suggested that TV viewers do not watch the ads at all, though they are conscious of the TV ad at some level in their awareness (see Heath and Feldwick, 2008). Typically, television channel advertising cost structures equate TV show viewing figures with the figures viewing the ads shown in the commercial break. Of course there is likely to be a considerable difference. For brand clients, a TV campaign represents something of a leap of faith. The potential benefits are great but these come at a potentially crippling financial cost.

Newspapers and Magazines

As Table 5.2 indicates, the UK has a wide coverage of daily national newspapers. The extent of press coverage varies widely throughout the world.[11] Press coverage attracted 40 per cent of UK adspend in 2008/09, keeping its place as the biggest single category of adspend in spite of the fact that it shrank almost 2 per cent on the year before.[12] There are many kinds of print publication,

Table 5.2   UK advertising expenditure 2007, % share

Press	39.8
Television	24.1
Internet	15.6
Direct mail	11.2
Outdoor & Transport	5.5
Radio	2.8
Cinema	1.1
TOTAL	**100**

Note: These figures are inclusive of production costs.

Source: Advertising Association's *Advertising Statistics Yearbook 2008*, WARC[8]

including national and local daily newspapers, local free-of-charge newspapers, local and national general-interest magazines and special-interest magazines. Conventional media wisdom holds that newspaper and magazine readers may be more critical and more attentive than TV viewers when consuming advertising. Press advertising might, therefore, be well-advised to use more rational content and offer greater product detail, while TV advertising should rely on the simple message with a big impact. Press advertising, especially daily newspaper advertising, has a quality of immediacy that TV does not. That is, press advertising can respond to current events in a day, whereas TV advertising requires months of production and planning. The readers of particular newspapers, while heterogeneous in their consumer behaviour, will often share particular demographic characteristics of age, social status and income, which render specific newspapers useful media vehicles for particular brand advertisements.

Regional and free newspapers offer opportunities for advertisers to reach local consumers within the context of local news and events. This too is an opportunity to present the brand in a setting that makes it more accessible for potential consumers. In many regions of the world reading the newspaper is a symbolic social ritual, engaged in daily, often at the same time every day, perhaps in the same place, in the same company and accompanied by the same refreshments. Newspapers consumed as intimate parts of social normality are powerful vehicles for promoting other types of consumption, since the context of the advertisement implies that the products and services portrayed are also a normal everyday part of the social fabric.

Radio

In the UK there are now over 240 commercial radio stations serving all regions. Radio has been regarded as a poor relation to TV for advertisers, but in recent years it has acquired greater credibility among advertisers for its reach and impact, and has even been used as the main medium for new brand awareness campaigns. Its increasing credibility has raised the price of radio ads, though at about £150 per 30-second slot for regional radio and £600–£1000 for national commercial radio it still represents a cheaper alternative to TV (figures current at the time of publication). Radio has the quality of immediacy, since many radio ads can be produced in a few hours and broadcast that very day.

Unlike TV or print media, radio is seen as a medium which occupies the periphery of people's attention. It is often background music in workplaces, motor-cars or households and listeners are generally doing other things while the radio plays. However, radio ads can generate momentary listener attention if they are striking enough and with the radio on for long periods of time there is plenty of opportunity for a listener to hear and recognize a given ad. Furthermore, radio may play an intimate part in listeners' lives if they forge a relationship with a particular show or announcer that they listen to at the same time each day. Most consumers listen to the radio at some time during the week, so the medium has extensive reach to many kinds of consumer segment.

Radio's immediacy can be a major advantage. Advertising revenues at the TalkSport commercial radio in the UK increased 38 per cent in November 2003, the month England's rugby team won the rugby world cup. This increase is apparently part of a trend of increased advertising revenue for a large number of UK commercial radio stations. This may be a result of changes in the UK TV advertising scene, an upturn in general advertising revenues, or a change in the way radio audiences are measured. In spite of this rise in revenue, radio accounted for less than 4 per cent of total UK adspend in 2001. It lacks the perceived glamour and profile of TV as an advertising medium, but growth in revenues and an increase in the share of listeners to commercial stations suggest that more advertisers regard it as an important medium.

Outdoor or Out Of Home (OOH) Advertising

Like radio, outdoor advertising has undergone a renaissance in recent years as advertisers have realized that it has greater impact and reach than previously thought. New approaches have developed outdoor poster sites that appear to move as the viewer goes by in a car, sites that are three-dimensional with large items (sometimes motor-cars) stuck on to the site for added effect, and laser-beam projected promotional images on the sides of large buildings. There are more than 118,000 static poster sites in the UK, most near or in large centres of population, especially by roads with a large traffic volume. There are also numerous non-static, outdoor advertising sites. For example, many vehicles such as London taxis and public bus companies sell their advertising space. There are companies specializing in providing advertising space on air balloons or airships for exposure at large, open-air public events or simply in the sky above towns and cities.

Picture 7   As indicated in this picture, Out Of Home advertising has become a taken-for-granted part of the urban environment.

(See the colour insert near the middle of this book for a full colour image.)

Digital outdoor has taken off in a big way with video outdoor sites showing a range of ads in strategic urban settings.

BOX 5.2

Outdoor Promotion

Outdoor promotion specialists (such as CBS Outdoor)[13] offer packages that include (in the UK) advertising on trams, tube trains and buses: according to the Target Group Index (TGI), 29 million people in the UK see an ad on a bus each week. Entire buses can be painted (wrapped) with the advertisement to maximize impact. Lenticular designs allow advertisers to use moving images, making a 3-D effect on bus sides. Bus advertising can be used regionally to coincide with TV campaigns. The London Underground is a fertile site for outdoor advertising since commuters using the underground are predominantly young (49 per cent are between 15 and 34 years old) and in the ABC1 socio-economic category. Outdoor specialists offer custom paint and design services to convert virtually any visible object in the urban environment into an advertising medium.

Posters can be used on either static or mobile sites. Of course, car drivers are supposed to be focusing only on the road, but posters situated on other vehicles or at the roadside may be a welcome diversion from the monotonous landscape which faces the urban motorist. Agencies specializing in outdoor advertising know that static and mobile poster sites are noticed by high volumes of consumers who may see them every day over long periods of time. While national coverage is difficult to achieve and targeted audiences cannot be well-defined, outdoor advertising can be a powerful medium for generating localized pockets of high awareness.

Integrating the Brand Image with the Media Mix

We have already seen how the media context is important in the meaning of an ad. The medium in which an ad appears is very significant in the reader's construct of the brand advertising itself. Press publications, TV and radio shows, even internet sites, all have a sense of their own brand identity. They seek advertisers whose brands will fit with the brand personality of the medium.

Newspapers and magazines each offer opportunities for advertisers to display ads for particular brands within a coherent context set by the editorial and advertising content and tone of the publication. A press publication is a brand in its own right and seeks to convey sets of values and ideas that will resonate with the values and aspirations of its particular readership. For example, in the USA the brand positioning of the *Washington Times* is very different from that of *USA Today*. In the UK, the biggest selling Sunday newspaper is the *News of the World*, which is positioned differently to the *The Sunday Times*. Advertisers are very keen to place their brand in a setting that complements the brand values and projects the brand personality. A given advertisement is interpreted in the broader context of the publication in which it is set. The brand can be portrayed as part of an ensemble of brands that are fitting accessories to the lifestyle aspirations of the reader of a particular publication. Placing advertising for a brand in a publication that is strongly disliked by the brand's target market is a serious marketing error. The advertiser has to act as a *de facto* custodian of the brand and needs to be aware of any negative connotations that might emanate from the wrong media vehicle.

Chapter Summary

Chapter 5 has reviewed key issues in media strategy and planning. It described the tasks and terminology of advertising media planning and outlined the ongoing changes which are taking place in the global media infrastructure.

Chief among these are changes in the cost structures of media, changes in the relative reach and impact of media channels, and changes in audience media consumption patterns. The main driving force behind many of these changes is the digital communications revolution which is opening up the internet and mobile to many new advertising and business models. This has implications for media mix integration, and this part of the discussion is continued in Chapter 10. At the same time as these profound changes in the media environment for advertising, traditional media retain their capacity for impact in certain circumstances and maintain their place at the core of most, though certainly not all, major advertising campaigns.

 ■ Review Questions ▬▬▬▬▬▬▬▬▬▬▬

1 Devise a media plan to support the launch of a new model of motor car. The creative executions include a 20-second TV ad, national daily press ads and direct-mail shots to current owners of cars in that class. How would you plan your targeting? Which media vehicles might you use? Explain the timings of this exposure. What are the main problems and difficulties of this task?

2 Discuss the axiom 'The medium is the message'. What does it imply? Offer examples to support your suggestions.

3 Discuss ways in which media impact might be reconciled with segmentation and targeting issues. Is there an economic trade-off between impact and targeting?

4 List the main changes in the global media infrastructure over the last 15 years. What new problems and solutions have these changes generated for media planning and strategy?

5 Imagine that you are part of an account team devising a campaign for the launch of a new chocolate snack called 'Sleek'. It is to be positioned to a largely female market as a sensuous indulgence. What suggestions would you have for media planning?

▬▬▬▬▬▬▬▬▬▬▬▬▬ CASE ▬▬▬▬▬

Leveraging the Internet for TV Advertising Revenue – Media Funding Models in the Digital Age

ITV is the biggest commercial broadcaster on UK television.[14] ITV operates as a network, linking 15 regional television producers. It commissions, markets and schedules programmes for its main channel, ITV1, and its four digital channels. It is funded by selling the advertising on ITV1, but its responsibility is not only to shareholders. Under the UK television licensing system, ITV is heavily regulated by the UK office of communication, Ofcom,[15] and also has to provide a number of public services. For example, it is obliged to offer regional news coverage and other non-commercial programming through its regional franchises. ITV remains a significant force in the UK media infrastructure with a huge budget and some of the most watched shows in the country. However, it was facing difficult times in April 2009 with shrinking advertising revenues and a share price crunch which left the company valued at barely one-third of its market value a year before. ITV's Chairman, Sir Michael Grade, announced on 23 April 2009 that he would relinquish day-to-day control of the company and step back to a non-executive position. Sir Michael had restored ITV's share of audience but was unable to forestall the biggest drop in advertising revenue ever seen in the industry.

Just when ITV seemed to be at its darkest hour, up stepped unemployed 47-year-old Scottish singer, Susan Boyle.[16] Ms Boyle, an unmarried part-time church worker, decided to audition for the ITV show *Britain's Got Talent*.[17] The suggestion to audition had come from her mother, with whom Ms Boyle had lived until her death a year before. *Britain's Got Talent (BGT)* is a flagship ITV show, generating healthy viewing figures of more than 10 million, over half the UK's total TV viewing audience at that time slot. This volume of viewers, in turn, provides a good platform for 'interruptive' spot advertising during the show's commercial breaks. This spot advertising represents ITV's revenue and a return on the considerable costs of the producing and airing shows, along with the costs of producing non-commercial regional programming and paying the UK government for the broadcasting franchise.

Susan Boyle's performance on the show is now the stuff of legend. In just a week, Ms Boyle's act was viewed in total by some 100 million people on *YouTube*. She belied her un-star-like appearance and demeanor by singing a moving ballad from *Les Miserables* with perfect pitch and a rich, pleasing vocal style. The studio audience were on their feet applauding and she has won legions of fans around the world. Ms Boyle has since been feted on top US TV shows such as the NBC *Today Show* and *Good Morning America,* and she has been invited to appear on *The Oprah Winfrey Show*. But ITV, which foots an estimated bill of some £1 million per hour to make BGT, made the clip for *YouTube* and they earned nothing from Boyle's fame and the 100 million views. And, what is more, neither has *YouTube*. Ms Boyle's clip is one of many featuring former BGT contestants which together have been viewed many millions of times on *YouTube*, and several million times on ITV.com, ITV's own website. No doubt, *BGT* fans are grateful for this free service which builds on and enhances the popularity of the show and broadens the popularity of the performers. But how can a broadcaster in dire need of revenue benefit from the huge digital traffic the show creates?

YouTube is a runaway success as a video-sharing website and a cultural phenomenon. It was bought by *Google* for $1.65 billion in October 2006. But *YouTube* doesn't make any money, and it is costing *Google* an estimated £1 billion per day to run it. The reasons why *Google* bought *YouTube* are a matter for speculation. They could try to get viewers to accept more banner advertising, but other social networking websites have tried this and their viewers didn't like it. There could be a less obvious and more farsighted rationale behind *Google*'s investment. If more television shows are viewed over the internet, *YouTube* might be in a position to provide a platform for TV content which the TV channels would pay for. Indeed, the TV production company that makes *BGT*, Freemantle Media, was reported to have done a deal with *YouTube* to show Susan Boyle's and other *BGT* clips to which Freemantle owns the overseas digital rights on a dedicated *YouTube* channel. It is negotiating to find a sponsor and plans to sell advertising around the clips. ITV and Freemantle would share some of the revenue from international viewers of *YouTube's BGT* channel and ITV.com. There is to date no deal in place, though, with *YouTube* UK, according to press reports.[18]

The benefits of this to the TV companies themselves are hard to see, besides potential but probably small shares of advertising revenue. For TV companies in countries where they are allowed to receive payment for brands placed in the script or a scene of the show, a technique known as product placement, airing over the internet would leverage massive internet traffic and justify high prices for the placements. UK TV companies, though, would not benefit because they are not currently allowed to receive payment for brands placed in shows. However, the UK Government recently announced that this could change, reversing an earlier decision (see Hackley, 2009c and also Chapter 6). Another question is, would *YouTube* viewers have watched the clips so many times if they had had to go to a specific channel and put up with advertisements at the beginning of each clip?

Media funding models are evolving because of the internet but the problem of how to monetize internet traffic is proving intractable. For some commentators, a revenue model based on 'eyeballs', that is, the number of viewers, lacks subtlety. They feel that the new media environment of Web 2.0 demands more complex and lucrative funding models. For example there is much talk in digital marketing about calculating 'online brand engagement',[19] and figuring out the complex relationship between digital encounters with a brand and long-term profitability.

 ■ **Case Questions**

1   Brainstorm ideas about how ITV and *YouTube* might monetize digital viewing traffic. What are the advantages and disadvantages of each?

2   Individual performers can be understood as brands (see Schroeder, 2005) and many artists leverage the internet to enhance their appeal and broaden their fan base. Internet websites provide a platform for this service, but how might a TV show brand benefit from the exposure?

3   What does the case of Susan Boyle and *BGT* tell us about the dynamics of integrated media in the digital age and what are the implications for typical brands?

■ ■ Further Reading ■

Croft, R. (1999) 'Audience and environment: measurement and media', in P.J. Kitchen (ed.), *Marketing Communications: Principles and Practice* London: Thomson Learning. pp. 111–34.

Jenkins, H. (2008) *Convergence Culture: Where Old and New Media Collide.* New York: New York University Press.

Katz, H. (2006) *The Media Handbook: A Complete Guide to Advertising Media Selection, Planning, Research and Buying.* Mahwah, NJ: Lawrence Erlbaum Associates.

Kelley, L.D. and Jugenheimer, D.W. (2008) *Advertising Media Planning; A Brand Management Approach*, 2nd edn. Armonk, NY: M.E. Sharpe.

On the Companion Website

These journal articles are freely available on the companion website (www.sagepub.co.uk/hackley).

The Last Gasp: Cigarette Advertising on Billboards in the 1990s
James E. Marlow
Journal of Communication Inquiry, Jan 2001; vol. 25: pp. 38–54.

Advertising Agencies, Media and Consumer Market: The Changing Quality of TV Advertising in Japan
Nobuko Kawashima
Media, Culture & Society, May 2006; vol. 28: pp. 393–410.

Are we measuring the same attitude? Understanding media effects on attitude towards advertising
Soo Jiuan Tan and Lily Chia
Marketing Theory, Dec 2007; vol. 7: pp. 353–377.

Notes

1 'Advertising media planning – a primer' (2007) by Hairon Li, Michigan State University www.admedia.org/ (accessed 24 April 2009).
2 www.zenithoptimedia.com/about/ (accessed 24 April 2009).
3 ukgroup.omd.com/omduk/ (accessed 24 April 2009).
4 www.iabuk.net/en/1/pwcadspendstudy080408.mxs (accessed 23 April 2009).
5 Roy Greenslade, *Guardian Media* www.guardian.co.uk/media/greenslade/2008/sep/05/twoyearcomparisontellsreal (accessed April 25 2009).
6 www.guardian.co.uk/media/table/2008/sep/05/abcs.pressandpublishing (accessed 25 April 2009).
7 See www.maslow.com for a list of publications currently in print.
8 As on www.brandrepublic.com/News/815284/UK-ad-spend-reaches-194bn/ (accessed 25 April 2009).
9 Eric Schlosser (2001) *Fast Food Nation: The Dark Side of the All-American Meal*, HarperCollins; www.nologo.org; George Ritzer (2004) *The McDonaldization of Society*, New Century edn. Thousand Oaks, CA: Pine Forge Press and Sage, website at www.pineforge.com
10 For the first edition of this book Table 5.1 was adapted with permission from Admap, November 2003, p. 11. This version is somewhat changed, and similar to many such tables in other texts, but the Admap version is still worth a look.
11 For print media circulation figures of international press see www.printadvertising.com/circulation_figures.html (accessed 25 April 2009).
12 Source www.brandrepublic.com/News/815284/UK-ad-spend-reaches-194bn/ (accessed 25 April 2009).
13 www.cbsoutdoor.co.uk/
14 www.itv.com/aboutitv/ (accessed 25 April 2009).
15 www.ofcom.org.uk/ (accessed 25 April 2006).
16 www.youtube.com/watch?v=9lpOIWv8QZY (accessed 24 April 2009).
17 'Can Susan Boyle be the Saviour of ITV?' By Neil Midgely, 21 April 2009, *Telegraph*, www.telegraph.co.uk/culture/tvandradio/5172435/Can-Susan-Boyle-be-the-saviour-of-ITV.html (accessed 24 April 2009).
18 'Susan Boyle YouTube deal', *Business Digest, The Sunday Times Business Section*, 26 April 2009, p. 2.
19 See comment on online media engagement on media blog http://joeadamfry.com/ (accessed 24 April 2009).

6 Non-Advertising Promotion in Integrated Marketing Communication

Chapter Outline

The categories of marketing communication are blurring and changing in response to new techniques, trends and technologies. While consumers treat all promotional communication as advertising, in one form or another, it is also important to recognize that there are differences between promotional techniques and these influence communication planning and consumer reception in different ways. Chapter 6 reviews a number of the most popular non-advertising promotional techniques focusing mainly on below-the-line approaches, and sets these within the broader context of increasing integration.

Key chapter content:

- Non-advertising techniques in the promotional mix
- Sponsorship
- Product placement
- Corporate communication and public relations
- Other elements of the promotion mix.

Non-Advertising Techniques in the Promotional Mix

One of the main themes of this book is that advertising is evolving new forms in concert with developments in digital communications and the thrust for integrated communications planning. These new forms challenge traditional classifications of the promotional mix. As a general category, non-advertising promotion has assumed greater importance in the media mix in the last 10 years. Brand clients want to see the brand values portrayed across several platforms simultaneously in 'through-the-line' or 'integrated' campaigns. As we have noted previously in the book, traditional advertising has had to face a number of challenges. Spot advertising on television, classified or display ads in print media, outdoor/out of home advertising, commercial radio and cinema advertising spots before the main feature all retain their importance because of the profile and presence they offer. But alongside these traditional methods there are two things which distinguish non-advertising approaches. One concerns the rise in importance and share of adspend of techniques such as direct marketing, product placement, embedded and entertainment marketing, sponsorship, public relations and celebrity endorsement, and internet and mobile advertising. Changes in media consumption patterns and developments in consumer segmentation have driven the increased attention paid to these non-advertising approaches.

Alongside these developments are new ways of doing traditional advertising, especially where traditional categories of marketing communication are blurred by integration between old and new media. So, for example, internet sites carry banner advertising but also include click-through links and pop-ups; outoor billboards carry traditional posters but can also be adapted to carry electronic images or images which change depending on the angle from which they are viewed; a celebrity might appear as an actor, without speaking directly to camera, in a traditional TV ad; and television advertisements may have a website address listed for further information. In ways such as these, traditional advertising takes on a hybrid character as it merges with non-advertising techniques such as using the internet and Web 2.0, static advertising merges with moving advertising, and traditional TV advertising merges with celebrity endorsement.

Marketing communication is in a state of flux as new techniques evolve and old ones take on a new importance because of new technology and new consumer trends. Advertising agencies have tried to reflect this by adopting a media-neutral planning approach which looks at a communication problem across all media platforms rather than privileging advertising over other forms of promotion. Agency planners are expected to consider non-advertising promotion on an equal basis with advertising in campaign planning.

The Coca-Cola Brand

Coca-Cola is the 'biggest-selling soft drink in history, and the best-known product in the world'.[1] It was created in Atlanta, USA, in 1886, by Dr John S. Pemberton. Brought to the UK in 1900, it was sold widely in London throughout the 1920s. Coca-Cola advertising campaigns are among the most iconic in advertising history – one is widely credited with popularizing the image of Father Christmas or Santa Claus in the Western world as a rotund, cheerful man with a white beard and always dressed in red. The company also makes use of extensive non-advertising promotion, for example through its websites which promote its sponsorship of music and football and offer fans free stuff and other ways of engaging with the brand and its sponsored activities experientially. The Coca-Cola Championship, the second tier of UK football after the Premiership, is now the fourth most watched football league in Europe with over 16 million paying fans watching the live games In 2008/09. Of European professional football leagues, only the UK Premiership itself, Spain's La Liga and Germany's Bundesliga attract more fans to live games.[2] Add television coverage and this means a powerful number of eyeballs for sponsors from this platform.

Sponsorship

One particularly powerful dimension of the trend for integration is the way that entertainment, marketing and advertising have merged in important respects under various kinds of sponsorship arrangement. For example, the Guinness brand sponsors rugby and features rugby in some of its print ad campaigns. Global growth in sponsorship expenditure slowed but remained positive in the economic downturn of 2009.[3] Sponsorship takes a modest but still significant proportion of some companies' overall promotion budget. Growth in sponsorship has been rapid over the past three decades. The sum spent on sponsorship in the UK rose from £105 million in 1982 to £781 million in 2001. The growth has continued.

In some cases, brand marketing organizations have been forced to move to sponsorship by factors beyond their control. For example, many governments have legislated against mass media tobacco and alcohol advertising, forcing brand owners in these industries to seek other promotional methods. Another factor pushing advertisers toward sponsorship is the increase in cost of mass media advertising relative to other channels. Still another factor has been the growth of affluence which, for the fortunate, has seen increasing leisure time for sport and TV viewing. Consequently, TV programme makers naturally looked to new spectator events that could provide cheap TV. Many sports events now receive blanket media coverage and constitute a highly attractive vehicle for brand marketing organizations (Amis et al., 1999; Meenaghan, 1991; Meenaghan and Shipley, 1999). For example, in the UK, entrepreneurial sports agents have introduced sponsors to unlikely spectator sports such as snooker and darts as their popularity and media profile have grown. In the 1980s, snooker became, for the first time, a televised sport in the UK. A minority sport became a global television phenomenon because of the charisma and publicity-generating acumen of stars such as Alex 'Hurricane' Higgins.[4] Cigarette and alcohol companies realized that the sport needed funds for promotion and prize money, and they faced increasing controls on their mainstream advertising. Sponsorship of televised sports offered a new way of getting their brand into mainstream media. Sports sponsorship offered the perfect alignment of need and opportunity.

BOX 6.1

Nike Takes Sponsorship to New Places

Not only cigarette and alcohol brands use sports sponsorship. Nike has taken sports sponsorship to unforeseen lengths since Phil Knight, Nike's founder, persuaded the US middle-distance athlete Steve Prefontaine to wear his running shoes. Since then Nike has targeted countless sports personalities who gain international fame so that each post-performance TV or press interview is accompanied by an image of the hero of the hour wearing the ubiquitous Nike logo on his or her clothing or cap. This is celebrity endorsement, but the endorsement is implicit, making it sponsorship. The suggestive sub-textual power of sponsorship is telling; no explicit celebrity statement is required. The unspoken message is that Nike is cool by association. Sponsorship taps into the sub-text of mediated communication by juxtaposing brands with images of success and objects of desire. The message is covert and all the more powerful for its subtlety.

Sponsorship is essentially a mutually beneficial business arrangement with defined outcomes between two or more parties (for definitions see Fill, 2002, 2009; Head, 1981). Sponsorship was originally seen as a part of public relations since it offers a support medium to mainstream advertising and is not necessarily as explicit as advertising. Television sponsorship has a high profile and it has been common in the USA from the beginning of the television era in the 1950s. Figures for total sponsorship expenditure are difficult to verify since sponsorship has so many levels of activity. In the UK, Mintel reported that television sponsorship was worth £183 million in 2001, and it is growing annually. Estimates of the total value of sponsorship expenditure in the UK in 2009 arrived at a total figure of about £1 billion. As noted, figures for sponsorship expenditure have to aggregate many different forms of the technique, and precise figures are difficult to ascertain.

The *Economist* Intelligence Unit defined sponsorship in the following way.

> The essential elements of the term sponsorship as it is used in the UK today are: (i) a sponsor makes a contribution in cash or kind – which may or may not include service and expertise – to an activity which is in some measure a leisure pursuit, either sport or within the broad definition of the arts; (ii) the sponsored activity does not form part of the main commercial function of the sponsoring body (otherwise it becomes straightforward promotion, rather than sponsorship); (iii) the sponsor expects a return in terms of publicity. (quoted in Head, 1981: 4)

Such a definition, while helpful in categorizing sponsorship activities, does not necessarily capture the subtlety and intertextual character of much contemporary sponsorship. Very often, sponsorship is used as one part of an integrated communications approach in which the sponsored element raises and reinforces brand awareness and positioning in tandem with mainstream advertising.

BOX 6.2

Sports Sponsorship

In the UK, the Barclays Premiership is the major soccer league (sponsored by Barclays Bank), while the car brand Volvo sponsored the World Match Play golf championship in 2009. Motor-racing teams raise huge revenues from the sponsorship of many brand organizations which pay to have their logo or brand name appear on the driver's racing suit and on the car itself. AIG and Manchester United football club have the biggest shirt sponsorship deal in football, worth some £56 million over four years.[5] All these brand marketing organizations are well aware that the TV and press coverage ensure that their brand is seen in households in the context of an ostensibly non-promotional entertainment experience. Creating promotion that appears to be something else, such as entertainment, is a particularly persuasive technique since we experience the communication without any critical resistance. The brand is merely a part of the entertainment scene. Sponsorship of highly popular broadcast events achieves the dual purpose of a far-reaching exposure for the brand and an implicit link between it and the event. Most importantly of all, the brand is produced as a normal everyday part of social life. It is on the way to being taken for granted by consumers and this is, in fact, a powerful position for a brand to exploit.

Sponsorship of the Arts and Good Causes

Sports events sponsorship is very popular among brand organizations because of the extensive media coverage, large audiences and positive connotations of sport. Sponsors also make use of the arts. A brand name seen in association with a book award or theatre production has high-brow connotations that may resonate with the target group of consumers. Such prestigious promotion can also have a positive influence on the perceptions of other interested groups such as shareholders, local government authorities or the press. Arts sponsorship provides funds for traditionally under-funded arts organizations and so there are social benefits which can generate general goodwill towards the brand organization (Chong, 2009). Gaining publicity for the sponsorship among a wider audience may depend heavily on whether the sponsored organization can gain media coverage.

Sponsorship of good causes is also popular for the positive values which attach to the sponsoring organization. In a variation on the theme, Barnardo's, the children's homes charity, engages in cause-related marketing with sponsoring companies who finance particular initiatives to help children.[6] Sponsorship links between commercial and non-profit or charitable companies are based on mutual benefit: goodwill and publicity for the commercial organization, revenue for the charity.

Sponsorship Evaluation

Sponsorship is an intuitively appealing communications technique because of the potentially high profile it can generate through public relations and press coverage, the targeted audiences it can reach and the positive connotations it can generate around the brand. Its drawback is that it is a promotional technique the precise effectiveness of which is far from easy to measure.

Large sums are spent on research studies that look at brand recall, awareness, liking and purchase intention as a result of sponsorship. Sales and inquiry patterns are, of course, also carefully tracked. But, generally speaking, sponsorship is regarded as a long-term brand-building tool rather than as a short-term sales or customer generator. Sponsorship, like other forms of marketing communication, may exert a powerful influence on sales through a long-term publicity effect. However, like many measures of effectiveness in advertising, it is possible to gather evidence that can, with careful interpretation, provide insights into the impact of a campaign.

Measures of audience viewing habits and purchasing behaviour deriving from **panel data** provide some data-driven insights into the effects of sponsorship, which, like advertising, needs to be used in a given marketing context. Its effectiveness is invariably contingent on the objectives that were conceived for it. Measures of awareness may be irrelevant in comparison with the way that the meaning of the brand is reinforced and consumers are reassured through the sponsored link. The outcome can only be conclusively assessed in terms of long-term brand profitability. Sponsorship, like advertising, works to normalize a set of contrived brand values by juxtaposing the sponsoring brand with a separate brand in another field, for example where the bank RBS engages in sponsorship with Barnardo's children's charity. This kind of exposure can be seen to be extremely powerful, since it operates at the sub-textual level of suggestion.

BOX 6.3

Broadband TV Stations Looking for Sponsors

Established and emerging TV channels, both terrestrial and digital, are always looking for sponsorship deals to contribute much-needed revenue. A website calling itself the UK Sponsorship database[7] lists stations looking for such deals. Listed stations include broadband TV channels such as Green TV, an environmental channel, and Zoom TV, an interactive music channel. More established channels include Bravo, Channel Four, the History Channel and Discovery Channel. Some channels are looking for general sponsors while others are offering specific opportunities based around particular shows. The sponsorship database also lists news of non-broadcasting sponsorship deals, from international brands like Barclaycard to local community brands such as the Fox and Hounds Football club.[8] Benefits from sponsorship can cut both ways. A major sponsorship deal will attract editorial coverage in general and business media, as well as reaching the customers of the sponsored brand.

Product Placement

Product placement (also called brand placement) refers to the brands featured as scene props or script references in entertainment vehicles such as movies, TV shows, pop songs, novels, radio broadcasts, computer games or stage plays (Lehu, 2007; Tiwsakul et al., 2005). In movies, in particular, it has become common for brands to feature as part of a commercial arrangement, generating a contribution to production costs for the movie production company, and getting valuable exposure in a glamorous setting for the brand. For example, General Motors (GM) provided 67 cars for the movie *Transformers: Revenge of the Fallen*. GM did not charge a fee for the cars but enjoyed huge sales of the Camaro model as a result of its role in the movie.[9] There are a number of advantages to product placement as a promotional technique. One is that, as with sponsorship, the link between the entertainment vehicle and the placed brand is implicit rather than explicit. This means that the consumer is left to read the association in the entertainment text. Leaving the consumer to complete the Gestalt, as it were, can be powerfully persuasive. What is more, product and brand placement offers brand organizations a way of circumventing consumer resistance to or cynicism towards, conventional advertising. Its ambivalent status as a marketing communication in the context of dramatic entertainment makes it powerful for marketers, but problematic for some consumer groups. In addition to the dramatic force and implicit persuasion entailed when a brand features in a popular mediated entertainment vehicle, there are cost advantages. The brand owner pays once for a placement but there may be multiple re-runs, DVD sales and internet clips, not to mention the leverage to be gained if a movie or TV show becomes a big hit winning huge audiences. On the other hand, the brand owner paying for the placement takes the risk that the movie might bomb, making the brand placement poor value for money. Generally, while costs of placements vary widely, they compare favourably with the costs of producing a TV advertisement and paying for airtime.

BOX 6.4

Brands Star in Hollywood Movies

Since exposure in *ET: The Extraterrestrial* sent sales of Rees's Pieces up by 65 per cent (according to the confectionery firm Hershey), brands have been keen for parts in major entertainment projects. Received wisdom among Hollywood marketing agents is that just 'showing the can' is no longer enough (Hackley, 2003a). Brand owners want to project the brand personality, so they need full creative access to projects. If the right deal can be struck, that is what they get. Recent product placement deals in movies include *Star Trek* (Budweiser, Corvette, Jack Daniels, Nokia),[10] *X-Men Origins: Wolverine* (Caterpillar, Chevrolet, Ford) and *Gran Torino* (Coca-Cola, Honda, Reebok, Toyota and many others).

But brands have become so ubiquitous in movies that there is a movement against excessive movie product placement deals. Movies can have scores of placement deals (listed on the brandchannel[11] website). In order for brand placement in entertainment communication to be effective for both parties brand owners are expected to accommodate the needs of the script and negotiate with costume and set designers. In this way it can be ensured that the brand's appearance does not seem contrived or incongruent with the themes and tone of the entertainment product. For example, Airwark designed the footwear for the *Matrix* movie productions because they were willing to make a product that fitted the movie concept. Brand agents who expect the actors to be mere models for a mass-produced product will get short shrift from studio costume designers. But if they are prepared to work with the movie-makers they can get invaluable exposure. To leverage synergy most effectively the branded item has to be woven into the plot so that it tells a story. The brand's presence may not require a physical presence: the reference can be very subtle indeed. However, the pressure on costs, and the fact that brand placements in movies are more and more common and accepted, have meant that some movie production studios are tempted to accept placement deals which have nothing to do with the plot or script. As a result, some movie fans have been critical of this tendency since they feel that it impairs the creative integrity of the movie (see, for example, a list of the top 10 worst movies for product placement).[12]

Categories of Product and Brand Placement

There are broadly three categories of product placement. D'Astous and Seguin (1999) defined these as: implicit product placement; integrated explicit product placement; and non-integrated explicit product placement. Implicit product placement, as the label suggests, is not formally referred to in the context of the show or movie. For example, in the US TV series *Friends*, an episode in which Rachel flew to Ross's wedding in London took place on board a Virgin plane. The Virgin logo was clearly visible in the scene and Sir Richard Branson made a cameo appearance in the episode, but no explicit mention was made of the Virgin brand.

Integrated explicit product placement is when a brand not only appears in a show but is also formally expressed in some way so that its attributes are explicitly demonstrated. For example, Tom Cruise drinks Guinness in the film *Minority Report*. In the movie *Love Actually* one character goes into a bar in Milwaukee and asks for a 'Budweiser please, king of beers'.

Finally, non-integrated explicit product placement is close to sponsorship in that the brand will be formally expressed in the context of the show but not in the actual scene or script, for example, '*Sex and the City* is sponsored by Bailey's' or 'A Mini drama with *Cold Feet*' (see Tiwsakul and Hackley, 2006).

These three categories of product placement can be supplemented by a further three that express different dimensions of the practice. Russell (1998) discussed screen placement, script placement and plot placement. Branded products can be used as props in a scene; the brand name can be spoken by actors; or the brand can form a central aspect of the plot itself, almost taking a dramatic role in the narrative. One Hollywood release, a high-tech re-make of the 1960s classic *The Italian Job*, starred the BMW Mini Cooper in numerous chase scenes. Within a week of the movie's release stocks of Minis were sold out in Los Angeles. These techniques of product and brand placement hint at increasing subtlety in the field and form the basis for a new marketing communications paradigm, that of embedded marketing (Hackley and Tiwsakul, 2006).

'**Embedded marketing**' is used to refer to certain forms of product placement and sponsorship. The term captures something of the convergence of sponsorship and product and brand placement techniques in entertainment-driven media. Just as movies themselves are now regarded as brands and marketed as such, studios and producers are increasingly willing to talk to brand marketers about mutually beneficial integration. Each can gain from the synergy of linking product and service brands with entertainment. Today in many instances the brand communication and entertainment product have been assimilated into each other. This is most common in Hollywood movies and TV shows, but is far from unheard of in magazine features or radio shows. The marketing logic is the same as for sponsorship or brand placement but the formal (and contractual) relationship between brand owner and entertainment producers differs. The end result for consumers is that, as entertainment audiences, they do not necessarily know when a brand reference in an entertainment product has been contrived for mutual advantage. For example, television drama shows need brands as props and directors will often use brands for convenience rather than because there is a contractual agreement with the brand owner.

Product Dis-placement

The need entertainment vehicles have for large numbers of brands as scene props can lead to problems where the brand owner did not want the exposure. Product dis-placement refers to incidents where brands in shows are deleted at the brand owner's insistence.[13] For example, the Oscar-winning movie *Slumdog Millionaire* featured a Mercedes-Benz car in a scene in the slums of Mumbai. The manufacturer decided that the brand logo had to be deleted from the movie. Subsequently, the movie won multiple Oscar nominations and widespread acclaim. It was reported that Coca-Cola also refused permission for their brand to appear in *Slumdog*. The movie was set in the poorest districts of India, so hardly a glamorous backdrop for brand placements. Yet some brand planners would see such exposure in a positive light. Placement strategy is a matter of creative judgement.

Entertainment Marketing and the Entertainment Industry

The appearance of brands in movies or other entertainment projects such as computer games is widely accepted by consumers, especially by younger ones, because of the ubiquity of brands in everyday life (Hackley and Tiwsakul, 2006; Lehu, 2007). Movies, books and computer games often tap into the genre of dramatic realism and try to reflect the social settings that we live in, in order to seem more realistic and therefore more dramatically resonant. Brands in movies enhance realism and communicate values. If an actor smokes Marlboro cigarettes you do not have to smoke to understand the sub-textual message. The brand is a part of our cultural vocabulary and we know we are being told that the character is a tough yet lovable maverick. Brands can act as a symbolic reference in movies to signify values, attitudes or behaviours that cohere with the narrative.

What is more, advertising and movie-making have become parts of the same industry complex, and entertainment producers have become more amenable to the needs of brand marketers. There has been a change of culture in Hollywood: as studios have become more marketing-orientated in their own activities they have recognized the power of brands to resonate with consumers and enhance the storyline of shows and movies (Hackley, 2003a). The people working in entertainment and advertising have skills and social circles in common, which helps foster this mutual accommodation. Several noted British movie directors (for example, Ridley Scott, *Gladiator*; Peter Jackson, *Lord of The Rings*; and Alan Parker, *Fame, Mississippi Burning, Evita*) learned their skills in the advertising industry. Expertise also moves in the other direction. US movie directors such as David Fincher *(Panic Room, Fight Club)* have also directed commercials. The industries may be different, but they talk to each other and each recognizes the value of high-quality movie direction. Advertising agencies understand that good production values and striking creativity get ads noticed. Techniques of cinematography are interchangeable between the advertising and entertainment industries.

Movie-makers have been influenced by advertising techniques. The powerful cinematography and concise storytelling of advertising have been adopted by movies and TV shows. Brand references fit neatly into this style and enhance dramatic realism. Few doubt that consumers buy into brand personalities at some level. Movie audiences have always adored stars, who are marketed as if they were brands. The insight of the entertainment economy is that consumers treat stars and brands in the same way. We project personalities on to brands and we derive brand benefits from our affinity with movie stars (Tiwsakul, 2008). In embedded marketing brands, are seen being actively used in an attractive lifestyle context. The brand association exists at a subtextual level, beneath the narrative. Seeing a star actively use or refer to a brand creates a more powerful message for consumers than having that star feature in an explicit (and patently insincere) product endorsement.

Another culture change in Hollywood that has helped embedded marketing to develop is a shift in attitude by artists towards brands. Artists are now happy to develop their own market presence through an association with brands. Celebrities can reposition their personal brand and find new audiences by lending their image to an advertising campaign (Schroeder, 2005). Singing star Celine Dion and actor Paul Newman are two figures who have sold their services for brand endorsement in paid-for advertising. The actress Uma Thurman was pursued for years by the fragrance brand Lancôme before she finally agreed to feature in their ads. It is no longer uncool for serious artists to do advertising campaigns.

Musical Placements

Even the background music that brings brands to life in ads can make stars of the artists. For example, the Dandy Warhols gained valuable exposure by licensing their music for ads. More established artists like Lenny Kravitz have used ads to pre-launch a new single, bypassing the radio playlist route to get exposure to millions for nothing. Artists such as Lady Gaga and Irish band The Script have entered into a deal with *Clikthrough* to feature product information on their pop videos shown via computer.[14]

The realization that an association with brands can enhance the prestige of artists, and not just the other way round, has softened Hollywood's attitude to an involvement with IMC initiatives. People in the advertising business recognize that the right music makes the targeted audience pay attention. In some cases, a campaign provides an opportunity to showcase a new artist. There have been cases of artists being paid by brands to mention them in the lyrics. Since brands became cool, their presence in popular songs can enhance the street credibility of both song and artist – something inconceivable just a few years ago when being seen to be 'selling out' to commerce would leave an artist's credibility shot to pieces.

Brand exposure, then, provides leverage for the entertainment property, making stars out of the artists providing the soundtrack. Music publishing companies such as BMG can license classics from artists from Iggy Pop and Frank Sinatra to Christina Aguilera and Coldplay to provide a musical hook to a broadcast advertisement. The track guarantees the attention of a particular audience. The advertiser who wants to use an original track to give the ad extra impact has to buy rights to both the CD master and to the published sheet music which will often be owned by different music-licensing houses. They have to get the agreement of the original artists as well. In some cases the stars as well their music become vehicles to gain the attention of the desired target audience: Iggy Pop featured, in person, in a series of 2009 advertisements for an insurance company.

Another aspect of embedded marketing is the intertextuality (see Chapter 2) of our mediated experience. The tendency of differing media to draw on shared symbols and reference points can instantly convey particular values in association with a brand. We listen to music for our own entertainment, if we hear the same track in an entertainment vehicle such as a movie this provides a bridge between the world of entertainment and our personal lives. Music, in particular, is a deeply personal choice, bound up with our sense of identity (Shankar, 2000). It can reach out with an emotional hook to segmented audiences. The presence of a brand in an entertainment setting carries a dual marketing benefit. On the one hand, it makes that brand taken for granted because we see it in an everyday context which is important to us in our daily consumption of mediated entertainment. On the other hand, the brand has the benefit of exposure in a setting that is much more glamorous than our everyday existence, so it becomes an object of desire in our aspirational consumption field. Embedded marketing in movies and sporting event settings can achieve these two apparently contradictory objectives in one exposure.

Product Placement and Embedded Marketing Implications

Product placement or embedded marketing reflects the merging interests and priorities of the entertainment, communication, advertising and brand marketing industries. It should be noted that, as with all marketing techniques, embedded marketing is difficult to execute and financially risky. A brand organization might engage in a contractual agreement with an entertainment studio only for any one of many things to potentially go wrong: the movie may not be a success, the brand's scene may be cut during the editing process, the producer may have taken out side-deals with other brands that do not fit well with each other.

Brand managers and communications directors need to understand exactly what IMC developments in Hollywood can and cannot deliver. Movie audiences are self-selecting target groups for marketers. They are influential and active consumers. Furthermore, the influence of movies spreads beyond the theatre in the form of press editorial, broadcast media coverage, word of mouth, outdoor, associated websites (with retail interfaces) and franchised product links. Integrated marketing communications can become a web of influence around the brand, with numerous threads emanating from the same source.

Movies and other broadcast entertainment products such as sports coverage and TV drama provide a huge potential for powerfully synergistic marketing links. Even when sophisticated audiences are aware of such commercial arrangements, the power of the link is undiminished because embedded marketing acts at a sub-textual level. The streets are full of people wearing branded clothing and carrying branded holdalls; we have become culturally primed for the appearance of a brand symbol in almost any social context. It is inevitable, and even natural, that movie and broadcast entertainment scenes reflect this cultural reality. Embedded marketing represents the logical convergence of communications media within the cultural-entertainment-marketing complex.

Product Placement Regulation

Product placement is subject to different regulations around the world. For example, in the UK, as in a number of other European countries, product placement was not permitted in television programmes until very recently. There are some anomalies with that position,[15] since the free prop supply system which places brands in television drama shows is open to manipulation. What was more disconcerting for the TV channels was the fact that they were showing American dramas which were full of placed brands. The American programme makers take fees for placing brands in the shows, and their brand clients know that the brands will gain extra exposure in the UK, but the UK channels were not allowed to take any fee for this. So UK television was effectively a free advertising medium for brands placed in American or other imported shows (Hackley, 2009c). In 2009, the European Union Audio Visual Media Services Directive allowed member states to create their own rules on product placement. The UK government decided to retain the current ban, to the amazement of most observers. In late September 2009 the UK government announced that they would reverse this decision and allow paid-for product placement in certain categories of commercial programming, but not on the BBC. This major change of policy apparently reflected a realisation that by insisting on a total ban the UK government was making it harder for its own television industry to compete internationally. In many other countries, of course, placements have been allowed for decades. In some cases they tend to be so obvious and clumsy that they interfere with the viewers' enjoyment of the show (Hackley et al., 2008a). Nevertheless, many viewers still prefer this to having their favourite shows interrupted by spot advertising. On the other hand, American producers make some of the most popular television drama and comedy in the world and placements in these shows are rarely commented upon by viewers in the UK. This indicates that brands can be placed in shows in ways which fit with the plot, scene and characterization and do not therefore detract from the dramatic integrity of a show.

Even in countries which allow placement there are usually rules governing controversial products such as prescription drugs, weapons or alcohol. Programme makers face a dilemma. They need real settings and props for their scenes. Dramatic realism is the most popular genre for television drama and verisimilitude is necessary – viewers won't believe the drama if the sets don't look real. If, say, you have a drama portraying a violent bank robbery, the director has to have a getaway car, and the robbers have to have weapons. Many brands seen on TV are there coincidentally and not as contracted deals. In many other cases the quid quo pro is simply that the brand owner lets the makers have free product, as in the *Transformers* movies which were provided with cars by GM. There is mutual benefit to this since the creative entertainment vehicle (such as a movie, TV show or computer game) can gain additional publicity and credibility through its association with a well-known brand. The brand, of course, gets valuable exposure, especially if the show is a hit and is watched by millions of viewers. What is more, brand placements in broadcast entertainment have a half-life of decades through re-runs on TV and, increasingly, over the internet, and DVD sales (both legal and pirated).

The key issue in product placement regulation in the UK is the principle of a separation of editorial from advertising, which has underpinned broadcasting regulation since television began. It is enshrined in the regulator Ofcom's rules. It is highly questionable, though, whether this principle remains relevant in today's interlocking and commercially-driven media environment. The era of a monolithic broadcasting industry and patriarchal regulation in the UK has long past, and audiences today decide for themselves whether they trust programme integrity regardless of what the regulator tells them. The default position for media audiences is cynicism; they typically assume that media content is spun to favour certain interests. All they are interested in is whether they like the show or not. Clearly, not every genre of programming is suitable for placements, but in allowing programme makers to receive some revenue for brands in popular shows which air to large audiences the UK government is finally allowing UK television to compete on a fair basis with international programme makers. The UK rules on product placement on television are scheduled for a fundamental overhaul in 2011.[16]

Symbolic Consumption and the Entertainment Economy

The expression 'the entertainment economy' (Wolf, 1999) draws attention to some notable features of post-industrial economies. Of course, marketing activity is not all about entertainment; it is also about innovation, materials sourcing, design, organization, manufacture, logistics and more. But important features of marketing are converging in the entertainment and communications areas. In post-industrial economies, increased affluence and leisure opportunities have created a huge demand for entertainment. Furthermore, the emergence of the internet and digital communication technologies has created opportunities for consumption itself to become an arm of the entertainment industry. Technology has driven a boom in this area, as demand has grown for the individual consumption of movies, magazines, music and anything that can be covered on TV such as sports and popular shows. Electronic audiovisual goods are a derived demand since they are required because of the initial demand for MP3 music, DVD and video-format home movies and so on. The entertainment industry is driving the technological development of new entertainment media.

Many consumers now use the internet to research and buy all kinds of consumer products from houses to holidays. Indeed, the availability of information and purchase opportunities on communications media has shifted consumption itself into the entertainment arena. Many people shop for pleasure, whatever the goods or services on offer. Cable TV stations like The Shopping Channel, QVC and The Auction Channel are entirely devoted to consumption as entertainment. People watch and shop purely for pleasure. Most consumption categories have special-interest websites and magazines through which people can research and communicate their interests, whether it is cosmetic surgery, haute cuisine or body-building. Shopping is in itself a consumption practice laden with symbolism and rich in meaning.

The boom in demand for entertainment and the movement of consumption into the entertainment arena have many implications for marketing. Entertainment and consumption have become so closely associated that they are at times inseparable. Watching a movie exposes the viewer to product placement and advertising. Consuming mobile phones, DVD players and other electronic goods is functional, but also fun. As consumer affluence in developed economies has shifted the emphasis of promotion away from utilitarian values towards symbolic values, even purchases such as shoes, cars and detergent are portrayed through brand advertising as lifestyle choices that will enhance the user's sense of status and social identity. Many researchers have alluded to this symbolic aspect of consumption (Elliott and Wattanasuwan, 1998; Holbrook and Hirschman, 1982).

Consumption of virtually anything, then, can tap into symbolic values of social status and identity. We view ads or product placements while we are being entertained by movies, TV shows and radio shows, or while we are reading magazines and newspapers. Frequently, direct-response ads, interactive TV or websites mean that we can engage with a retail interface almost instantly. The insertion of images of consumption in entertainment and news media powerfully signifies the central importance of consumption to economies and lifestyles. The symbiotic relationship of entertainment, communication and marketing represents an ideologically powerful mix that promotes the consumption of brands as it promotes the consumption of communicated entertainment itself. The culture industry, written about by Horkheimer and Adorno (1944), has come to pass in the sense that entertainment, marketing and news media are now intimately linked in the promotion of corporate interests. The absence of an explicit sales message in much embedded marketing communication does not impair the promotional effect: humans are interpreting creatures, we seek to impose meaning and coherence by making sense of our experience. We actively make the connections between brands and values that are left implicit in embedded marketing initiatives. The implications of marketing as an ideological force are explored in critical perspectives on the subject (Hackley, 2003c; 2009a, b).

Corporate Communication and Public Relations

Corporate communications, like corporate identity and public relations, are distinct fields of study and practice. While a detailed consideration of each is beyond the scope of this book, it is nonetheless important to touch on pertinent issues, since each discipline converges with advertising in significant respects and each is part of the greater convergence of marketing communications generally. As Marchand (1998) has shown in his historical studies of corporate America, big business combined public relations, advertising and corporate communication to manufacture a sense of legitimacy for the great corporations at the beginning of the twentieth century. They used corporate advertising to give a human identity to corporations and portray them in a caring, responsible light. They also used PR techniques, including well-publicized corporate philanthropy, sponsorship of good causes and better customer relations.

BOX 6.5

Unilever Recognizes the Power of Family Branding[17]

For many years Unilever has not featured its corporate brand in product advertising. In 2004 it spent a reported £10 million with consultancy Wolf Olins redesigning its logo in a new 'open and friendly' style to feature on the packaging of many of its brands.[17] Unilever hoped that its new design would epitomize its ethos of 'adding vitality to life by meeting everyday needs'. From March 2009 it will extend its family branding policy into the UK for the first time, following what it has done across other regions of the world. Unilever claims that its research has shown it that consumers have a relatively low awareness of the corporate brand. But if they buy one Unilever brand, they are more likely to buy another. The company plans to make more of the Unilever family brand, reflecting recent trends toward a higher profile for corporate-level marketing communications.

Brand advertising and marketing reflects on the 'family' brand of the manufacturer. If, say, Cadbury promotes a new chocolate bar successfully it may be attributed partly to good product design, packaging and advertising. If the product turns out to be seriously harmful to health because of a lapse in quality control it constitutes a PR setback for the whole firm. Cadbury has engaged in a number of corporate level branding exercises, including sponsorship of popular TV shows and a controversial sponsorship of the UK 2012 Olympics.[18] Some people have suggested that a chocolate company is an inappropriate sports sponsor, given the current publicity surrounding national levels of obesity. Then again, Cadbury has one of the finest records of corporate philanthropy in the history of UK business. Other corporate sponsors for the 2012 Olympics include Adidas, British Airways, BP, BT, EDF Energy, Lloyds TSB, Nortel, Deloitte, McDonald's, Coca-Cola and Samsung. Sponsoring the biggest global sporting event of all should generate high profile exposure for the brands concerned in association with the Olympic values of fair play, competition and health. Arguably, those values have been superceded by more contemporary ones linking sport with glamour, success and showbusiness, but nonetheless the Olympics offers a major opportunity for brands with the resources to pay upwards of £20 million for the privilege.

Corporate communication (Melewar, 2003; Melewar and Wooldridge, 2001) intersects marketing and branding at product and market levels in the sense that it offers an overarching set of values and imagery which should, ideally, dovetail with those of brands at other levels of the corporation. In many cases, the corporate brand is the most highly visible, as with Coca-Cola, Nike and Ryanair. In other cases brands at the product/market level may have a higher profile than the corporate brand. As noted earlier, Unilever has taken a decision to feature its corporate brand more strongly, which represents a change of policy because for many years it was almost anonymous while the brands themselves were highlighted without the corporate brand.

Public Relations

The Institute of Public Relations (IPR), the main professional body for the discipline in the UK, defines public relations as 'the planned and sustained effort to establish and maintain goodwill and understanding between an organisation and its publics' (Harrison, 1995: 2) The Public Relations Society of America (PRSA) emphasizes PR's task of helping an organization to interact, communicate with, and win the co-operation of, its public.

PR is a function where the aim is to create goodwill towards the brand or the corporation, to deflect criticism, or to foster a generally positive view of the corporation or brand among stakeholders and the general public. It encompasses the dark art of 'spinning', much used and criticized in politics. 'Spinning' means putting a positive interpretation on information or news that might be interpreted negatively. Public relations in this sense is in essence a rhetorical skill, often practised by people with media relations expertise. The aim is to put out a positive and coherent public message.

BOX 6.6

Corporate PR and Ethical Brands

There are some key brand communication issues that cannot be managed purely by advertising. The public relations dimension of a corporate image can be perceived as a powerful statement of brand values. For example, when Innocent Smoothies accepted a £30 million

---

buy-in from the Coca-Cola company,[18] for some customers, this represented a collision of corporate values and they have not been slow to express their concern in internet blogs and chatrooms as well as in the press. Innocent has been positioned as an ethical company promoting good health and good causes – it donates 10 per cent of its income to these good causes. For some consumers, Coca-Cola is the antithesis of such values with its sugar-heavy drinks and global record on environmental standards, water extraction and employee rights. Coca-Cola, on the other hand, attracts criticism as the world's biggest brand so it can be difficult to assess the merit of such charges. But where major corporations have taken over or bought into a partial control of niche brands they have usually managed to preserve the integrity of the original brand. Examples include Ben and Jerry's (bought by Unilever), Pret a Manger (McDonald's, before a private equity company stepped in), Green & Black's (organic chocolate brand bought by Cadbury) and The Body Shop (sold to L'Oreal). In each case the smaller company needed a new injection of funds and access to wider distribution networks to continue expanding. Public opinion is an important consideration in the design of corporate communications plans and in the light of mergers.

PR practitioners will also try to influence the media by, for example, issuing press releases of stories they would like to be published as editorial. They will also engage in an informal dialogue with journalists to promote their own versions of events, perhaps by taking journalists to dinner, and, in some cases, they will hire lobbying firms to promote a company's views and interests among influential people and organizations. Most organizations like to tell 'good news' stories as often and as loudly as possible. PR specialists (often former journalists) will solicit stories, write them up as press releases and use their journalist contacts to get coverage for them. Sometimes, press releases are printed in their entirety as editorial, with a house journalist taking the by-line. Sometimes they are adapted and used in part, and very often they are ignored. PR specialists need to have a journalist's nose for what will seem like a good story to practising journalists.

The PR function in an organization can have a great impact on a corporate image. The discipline of corporate identity is often concerned with the visual aspects of corporate presentation (but see Melewar, 2003, for a general review). Brochures, letterheads, vehicles and all the physical manifestations of the corporation contribute to the corporate identity. In order to manage an identity programme, a corporation has to introduce a cross-functional role that co-ordinates all aspects of public presentation. Like PR, the corporate identity function seeks to manage and control the corporation's public image. All organizations have problems with the management, co-ordination and control of activities. The separation of overlapping organizational functions comes about because of the need to co-ordinate multiple activities undertaken by many people who are often spread over wide geographical areas and numerous, separate businesses.

Publicity for Academic Studies

The value of publicity has reached well beyond the commercial world into politics, the non-profit and charitable sectors and even into the academic world. For example, a research team made up of academics from the Universities of Bath and Birmingham, and Royal Holloway University of London, conducted a major study into alcohol and young people funded by the Economic and Social Research Council (ESRC). The team wrote a press release highlighting one of the main findings and the PR was covered worldwide on the internet and in the UK national media. The respective universities, and the ESRC, were no doubt pleased with the outcome which generated television coverage as well as radio and press. The academics who conducted the interviews found that it was not an easy process and wondered if their message was really getting across.[19] It was difficult to tease out the complexities of research methods and findings in radio or television debates (see Hackley, 2008). The media coverage, though, was regarded as hugely valuable in building the brand equity of the universities featured.

Customer Relationship Management (CRM) through Communications

PR can take many forms, often using the advertising media as noted above in attempts to influence public opinion favourably towards a brand, whether that brand is a product, an artist, a movie or a corporation. Much communication with customers essentially fulfils the PR purpose of creating goodwill among existing consumers. For example, registered BMW car owners in the UK will receive a copy of *BMW Magazine*. The magazine contains many advertisements for prestige products and services in addition to BMWs, since the BMW driver would form part of the desired target segment for such products. One of these, an ad for Fairline ocean-going motor-yachts, pictured a luxurious yacht moored off a grand riverside house. The house and garden are bathed in light as if a lavish party were underway. The strapline says 'Let there be no doubt. You've arrived'. Fairline assume that BMW drivers are attracted to quality with panache. The luxury and prestige of the yacht offer a step up in symbolic status from the BMW car. The copy plays on the literal meaning of 'arriving' and also on the colloquial use of the word to refer to someone who has 'arrived' in the big time or achieved fame and success. *BMW Magazine* and other forms of customer relationship building through communication are attempts to develop goodwill with consumers in ways which can leverage the interests and aspirations of those consumers.

Other Elements of the Promotion Mix

Direct Mail

Direct mail (incorporating many forms of database marketing) continues to be popular for its accountability. Of all media, only TV attracts a higher proportion of advertising revenue, although the internet is closing the gap. The attraction of direct-mail advertising over broadcast media is that each mailshot can be directed at a named person who may have a personal interest in the products or services being offered. As any householder knows, the belief of advertisers that direct mail is good value is highly suspect; much of it ends up unread in the trash, and a lot is misdirected because the customer databases driving direct mail campaigns are notoriously difficult to compile and maintain accurately. Databases have to cleaned regularly otherwise they date rapidly as addresses and phone numbers change for an increasingly mobile population. In spite of these difficulties, direct and database marketing continue to grow in importance. The advent of **database mining software** such as Viper[20] enables marketers quickly and accurately to segment their databases in many ways in order to generate new possibilities for direct mail.

BOX 6.8

Charities Marketing Through Direct Mail

The Institute of Direct Marketing (IDM)[21] in the UK produces case studies of direct marketing successes to promote the medium. In one such case a charity based in Ireland called Concern achieved its marketing objectives through an integrated promotional campaign which relied heavily on direct communication. The case illustrated the flexibility of a direct and database-driven approach. The charity specialized in channelling aid to alleviate human disasters as they occurred. It began in response to the plight of people in Afghanistan, whose economy and infrastructure had been devastated by years of war. The charities sector in general has been subject to increasing competition as more charities compete for a limited well of public donations. Concern found that they were unable to pursue the aid projects they wished to because of a wildly fluctuating donation income. They realized, as other charities had, that a marketing-driven approach was needed and hired marketing staff with experience in the commercial fmcg sector.

   Approaches included setting up and maintaining an accurate up-to-date database of donors. The administrative structure of the organization was improved so that it could set up appeals and channel donations within 48 hours of news of a disaster breaking on news media. The database was used to target donors with carefully redesigned direct-mail shots asking them if they would become long-term donors by setting up standing orders from their bank accounts.

(Cont'd)

If successful this initiative would offer a long-term income stream and enable long-term planning to be undertaken. Email targeting was set up so that all past donors could be targeted within two hours of a disaster. Concern knew that speed was essential in generating donor income from disasters covered in the news media. They had to get in first before other charities. Radio and direct-response TV ads were set up in addition to email and website initiatives. The results were startling: all revenue targets were exceeded, and awareness of Concern as a charity brand increased significantly both in Ireland and mainland Britain.

Internet and Not-so New Media

An increased pressure for cost-effectiveness in media buying has resulted in greater attention being paid to non-traditional media, especially digital and mobile. 'New media' is still a term used in the business although most forms of new media are no longer new at all. It is now common for brand advertisers to set up a dedicated website, to offer a web-based retail interface, to target consumers with SMS text or multi-media messaging or to produce CD-Roms, DVDs or videos for publicity purposes in through-the-line, integrated campaigns which can operate across the media mix. Interactive television is another new medium with great marketing potential, but one that has so far proved less popular among TV viewers than the industry expected. It took TV 13 years to get 50 million users; it took the internet five. The potential for marketing communications with mass coverage and targeted themes is clearly attractive to advertisers. New agencies specializing in SMS text messaging or other aspects of digital communications are emerging, chasing the popularity of mobile phones and their ability to target consumer groups using tailored messages with direct-response potential. The growth of new media opportunities is compounded by a similar rise in ambient media opportunities to insert promotional messages into non-advertising spaces in the consumer environment (Shankar and Horton, 1999). Issues of e-marketing communication are developed in greater detail in Chapter 10.

Sales Promotion

Sales promotion refers to a vast range of novelty items that can carry promotional messages or a visual representation of the brand. Often these items, such as coffee mugs, pens, bags, T-shirts or other things, are given away, so the element of goodwill is bound up with the brand when they are used by a consumer. Of course in recent years brands have become so cool that it is now rare to see paid-for clothing or accessories that are not overtly branded. Brands have realized that they can have consumers pay to wear sales promotional items such as FCUK tops, Gucci bags, and so on.

Sales promotion also refers to in-store promotions such as two-for-the-price-of-one, 10 per cent off, free gifts, redeemable coupons, competitions or money-back for returning so many bottle-tops or labels (the latter technique is called the self-liquidating premium). Conventional marketing wisdom holds that the major strength of sales promotions is that they can persuade people to try the brand. It can also be argued that some brands use perpetual sales promotions to encourage repeat purchases and brand loyalty. McDonald's hamburgers often have a promotional offer of free toys with children's meals, usually thematically tied in with a movie release. This device encourages not just trial but also long-term, repeat purchases. Some sales promotional techniques converge with customer relationship management (CRM) approaches in that they seek to reward, and thereby encourage, brand loyalty.

Airlines and credit cards try to reward repeated use with air-miles for free travel and points or money-back. Mortgage providers in the UK have found that if they offer low promotional interest rates for new customers but do not offer the same for existing customers, the existing customers may take their business elsewhere. Banks rely on customer inertia: many consumers are reluctant to go to the trouble of changing their bank account or mortgage provider. But this policy can result in lost business, as more financial services consumers are prepared to consume actively and exercise their choice by switching providers. Credit card companies often offer good rates to new customers for loan servicing (switching negative balances from another provider), but the promotional rate reverts to the existing customer rate after six months or a year. Many consumers now switch credit cards more readily to take advantage of promotional interest rates.

Some retailers have abandoned the conventional wisdom of the sales promotion inducing trial and have opted instead for continuous sales promotion to solicit bargain-conscious consumers. In Europe, Aldi and Netto supermarket brands are positioned as cheap, no-frills providers, in the airline market there has been a rapid growth in low-cost air travel, with firms such as Easyjet and Ryanair, and many hotel chains have developed low-cost, no-frills rooms such as the French chain Formula 1 and the Holiday Inn Express chain of budget hotels. Sales promotion, of course, implies a tactical manoeuvre which is short-term, while low-cost as a marketing strategy is a rather different approach. Nevertheless, low-cost marketing strategies simply extend the logic of sales promotion, because many cost-conscious consumers are not brand-loyal as such but shop around for bargains all the time. Most sales promotion campaigns will have a temporary effect: when UK daily newspapers compete in periodic price-cutting wars, sales rise then gradually return to a stable level once the old price is restored.

Trade Conferences and Exhibitions

The UK Advertising Association has estimated that around £1 billion is spent annually in the UK on exhibitions. Many of these are trade exhibitions for business-to-business promotion but some also include consumers, such as trade exhibitions for motor vehicles, home furnishings and leisure crafts. Higher education providers, for example, make extensive use of exhibitions for recruiting international students to their courses. Exhibitions can generate a massive throughput of actual and potential consumers while also acting as a presence in the market in general. Many UK universities employ teams of international officers who man stands at British Council and other educational exhibitions around the world to field enquiries and take applications for UK university courses. Universities from around the world have a presence at MBA exhibitions as they compete for the best students. The advantage of trade exhibitions is that audiences are pre-segmented. The disadvantage is cost and time, but a well-attended conference and a well-organized stall can generate considerable business.

BOX 6.9

Email Marketing by Virgin

When Virgin Atlantic airlines created a new standard of upper-class air travel with lie-down beds and personal service in their new upper-class cabins they sent email alerts to air travellers (targeted using their Flying Club membership database) with a hypertext link to the Virgin Atlantic website. On the website customers could take a virtual tour of the new cabins, check routes and buy flight tickets electronically. Perhaps more upper-class passengers would be attracted to paying the premium fare by the sense of exclusivity and comfort in the new cabins.

Virgin's integrated communications make use of a membership scheme with benefits, a web presence with a retail interface, and service extras such as VIP lounges that enhance the brand and increase customer happiness.

Ambient, Viral and Guerrilla Marketing

Guerrilla marketing, ambient and viral marketing use various media. Viral marketing originally only referred to internet-based forms of marketing communication modelled on the establishment and growth of Hotmail. Now, the term tends to be used more broadly to refer to spontaneous eruptions of consumer interest that spread through personal and/or mediated communion. The categories are often linked; for example both viral and guerrilla marketing initiatives are usually designed to create a groundswell of WOM interest in a brand. Some also seek to generate a media 'buzz' and editorial coverage and hence fall into the area of publicity or PR.

Ambient media (discussed, for example, in Shankar and Horton, 1999) consist of promotional messages inserted into the consumer (usually urban) environment, frequently in novel and often unexpected ways. Ambient media come in many forms and can cross into other categories such as outdoor, packaging, sales promotion or direct mail. The key element is how the promotional message has been inserted into the consumer's environment. For example, ambient promotion has a longstanding, in-store tradition in retailing: supermarkets will pipe the smell of baking bread into the shop to create a relaxed and pleasing ambience that is conducive to uncritical purchasing. They will also play lift-music that relaxes shoppers so that they put more goods into their basket than they really came in for. There are countless examples of ambient advertising, such as promotional messages on the backs of bus, theatre, and car-park tickets, and messages on beer mats in bars. In the USA some telephone companies will pay for 'free' local calls by making callers listen to recorded advertising that interrupts their own telephone conversation. Many landowners in the UK receive income from mobile trailers on sites near major roads carrying advertising hoardings to catch the attention of passing drivers.

Ambient media sometimes cross into viral marketing and Word-of-Mouth (WOM) communication strategies. Although WOM is not strictly a mediated communication channel advertisers are aware of the power of consumers talking (positively) about a brand. Many advertisers have responded to the increased difficulty of targeting particular consumer segments by creating campaigns which seek to contrive an apparently spontaneous groundswell of public interest in a brand. There are many examples of advertisers using viral, guerrilla and similar techniques to try to reach audiences that are sceptical of mainstream advertising and do not consume conventional TV and press. To some extent such techniques are similar to those of classic propaganda in that the motive and source of the message are often hidden. If people are hired to sit in bars and drink a particular brand, then engage other drinkers in conversation about the virtues of that branded drink, this is not conventional marketing communication at all but has a marketing motive. Sometimes PR stunts are deployed to try to generate popular and (perhaps) media interest in a given topic. Marketers will even pose as discussants in web chatrooms to contribute positive views of a brand and thereby influence general opinion. Guerrilla marketing, WOM and many other publicity tactics are ethically problematic because the financial motives of the information source are not necessarily revealed. Hiding the financial motives of the communication sender can, incidentally, be useful in generating consumer insights, though ethically problematic. For example, students are sometimes enlisted as 'brand ambassadors' to make use of their insider access to students as a consumer market. In Box 9.10 a student passes around a questionnaire to classmates and they fill it in even though they don't really know what it's about, because it would seem rude to refuse a friend, though he is generating valuable data for his brand employer. When marketing advertising and consumer research techniques are not apparent for what they really are, this raises questions about ideological influence and ethics (Hackley, 2002; Hackley et al., 2008a).

| BOX 6.10

Illegal Guerrilla Marketing

In some areas of the UK spray-painted graffiti appears on the walls of derelict buildings. The graffiti depicts a website address, as if a member of the public has spontaneously committed this act of public vandalism so delighted were they with the website. Of course, the organization concerned has paid people to spray-paint public property with their web address and take the risk of being caught and prosecuted. The effect is striking: the spray-painted message is antithetical to glossy, mainstream advertising and carries connotations of an underground, people-driven movement. The messages are huge, painted on walls which thousands of cars pass every day. Illegal fly-posting has also long been a common advertising technique in the music business to promote new bands or local performances. Spray-painting the message as if it is graffiti is a neat, attention-grabbing (and usually indelible) twist on this technique.

Point of Sale and Merchandising

POS advertising is a context rather than technique, but it is nevertheless an important promotional area because of its influence over merchandising at the point of purchase. Merchandising is normally a term used in a broad sense to refer to the whole retail setting for purchase, particularly including the way the product is displayed and promoted in the retail store. POS is the point at which the sale takes place and while advertising and sales promotion might get a consumer into the store the sale still has to be made. POS promotion may entail a sales person offering free samples, or a cardboard model of the product featuring prominently on display to put the brand foremost in consumers' minds at the point of sale. The term can also be used more broadly to refer to any in-store promotion such as liquid crystal TV screens placed in-store showing continuous ads for a brand sold there, or other promotional structures such as 'tubes' – printed with promotional images of brands – which customers have to walk through.

Advertising and promotion at the POS are intended to create a persuasive ambience in the space where the consumer makes a decision and hands over their cash. POS should give a cutting edge to the broader merchandising activities that are common in retail marketing. In the small TCN shops (tobacco, confectionery, newspapers) that are common in much of the UK and Europe, brand marketers know that the position their branded item occupies is crucial to its sales performance. The 'golden arc' consists of an arm's length radiating from the cashier's position on each side. This is where leading brands of tobacco and confectionery will insist they are located in the shop for easy viewing and access. In larger retail stores brand marketers know that the volume of shelf space occupied is a powerful generator of sales and they will use all the bargaining power they can to get retail managers to devote as much of this volume as possible to their brand. In the frozen ice-cream business Walls gained a near monopoly in the UK by cleverly supplying retailers with freezers for stock. Rivals were reduced to the undignified practice of going into shops and surreptitiously moving their product to the top of the freezer while burying rival brands in the depths.

Personal Communication

Personal communication can be mediated, for instance when an entrepreneurial business person offers his or her personal endorsement for the brand in a piece of corporate advertising (perhaps more accurately described as quasi-personal communication). Indeed, advertising was once defined as salesmanship in print (see Chapter 2). Much early advertising did conform to the conventions of sales encounters with copy that pre-empted and answered consumers' 'objections' to purchase and emphasized the rational reasons to buy. Of course, much contemporary advertising eschews the rational appeal and develops a nebulous brand personality through vivid imagery and a compelling narrative.

Personal communication is useful to organizations in many respects. As a non-mediated communication channel, personal selling is particularly valuable for instilling confidence in consumers or potential consumers, for responding to questions and for persuading sales prospects to buy. Personal communication clearly has flexibility, the potential to attract and keep attention, and an emotional dimension and credibility that mediated communication forms lack. A skilled employee can create a lasting impression for the brand organization by appearing sincere, engaged in the consumer's life and needs, and empathetic to the consumer's experience in ways that mediated communication can never achieve. Ads, however funny or lovable, are merely impersonal communications not subject to the social rules of listening, responding and believing. Neither can they instil confidence in the listener in the way that a personal encounter might.

Personal communication at some level is unavoidable for most forms of brand marketing business. It is also very expensive in terms of possible coverage. A brand marketing organization can reach, say, a potential audience of millions with a national newspaper ad. For a similar cost, say £50,000, the organization could keep one sales person on the road for a year with a modest car and no expense account, possibly managing sales encounters with 500 potential consumers per year. The economics are quite clear: communication that is mediated is far more cost-effective.

Chapter Summary

Chapter 6 has reviewed a number of non-advertising promotional techniques. Beginning with sponsorship, then moving on to product placement and embedded marketing, the discussion looked at techniques for placing the brand within mediated entertainment. This approach is growing in popularity because of its cost effectiveness and its ability to circumvent consumers' natural scepticism towards conventional advertising. There is also a cultural change whereby brands are such a ubiquitous presence in the everyday lives of consumers that we expect to see them in our entertainment and new media for realism. This creates a marriage of convenience whereby entertainment shows can generate revenue streams from the brands placed in them. This practice is not universal, as noted, since it is not permitted on television in some European countries (see p. 174). There are brands on UK television, but they are usually placed there through props agencies rather than by an arrangement between the programme maker and the brand owner. The chapter went on to discuss direct marketing and direct mail, a sector of the promotional mix which comprises some 12 per cent of total promotional spend in the UK. Finally, personal communication was discussed and viral marketing outlined.

Review Questions

1 Video an evening's TV viewing on commercial channels. Play back the video and list the number of sponsorship and product placement events. Categorize these using the categories explained in this chapter. What do the results tell you about the changing practices of sponsorship and brand placement on broadcast entertainment? What impact do you feel such events have in comparison with conventional TV advertising? Has the character of TV advertising changed to reflect the growth in sponsorship and its variants?

2 How can sponsorship of TV shows generate tangible benefits for brand organizations?

3   Imagine that you are the public relations officer of a soccer club, a university or a retail organization. Think of six ways in which you could draw on other communications disciplines to promote a positive public perception of your organization.

4   What is meant by the phrase 'the entertainment economy'? What are the major features of the entertainment economy? Form two groups to debate the social implications of the entertainment economy and the economic benefits.

CASE

The Global Appeal of the UK Premier League and Stoke City FC

Premiership football clubs in the UK like Manchester United, Chelsea, Liverpool and Arsenal have a global fan base. The clubs are marketed as brands to exploit their international appeal. Televised matches from the Premiership which are aired on cable channels internationally achieve significant viewing figures, and high fees for the clubs. This helps develop the brand and deepens the loyalty of international fans towards particular teams. The top teams travel to Asia and the Middle East for pre-season tournaments and friendly matches because this engages with their fan base. These matches attract large paying crowds, making the tours highly profitable. The engagement with fans abroad also sells merchandise, club shirts and other services such as mobile alerts and streamed match highlights, generating additional revenue streams. The biggest clubs pay close attention to their relationships with fans by, for example, maintaining a database of fans and sending them regular updates, news and offers.

But the less famous teams in the Premiership cannot access such a large international fan base, and its revenues, in the same way. Teams like Stoke City, Hull City and Wigan Athletic don't tour beyond Europe pre-season because they can't draw the crowds to make it worthwhile. An idea was mooted that all Premiership clubs should play a 39th game each season in another country. This was intended to broaden the international market appeal of the Premiership itself as well as the appeal of the lesser known clubs, but UK fans and clubs alike rejected the idea that they would have to travel abroad to watch their club in a normal league game.[22]

The problem remains that there is a massive gap between the revenue that the top four clubs can generate from their fan base abroad, and the rest. This of course means that the other clubs will never be able to catch up because they cannot afford to bid for the best players. How could Stoke City, for example, increase their international appeal to open up a market for pre-season exhibition games in Asia or the Middle East? The club is based in Stoke-on-Trent, Staffordshire, a city of 250,000 people which is world famous for its pottery and ceramics industry. This industry is in decline but brand names like Wedgwood, Spode and Royal Winton retain their prestige, while thousands of tourists visit Stoke each year, attracted by its cultural heritage. Stoke also has a rich tradition as a football city. Stoke City FC was founded in 1863, making it the oldest club in the Premier League and the second oldest professional football club in the world. It has won few trophies in that time but has boasted some fine players, including the legendary Stanley Matthews, England's World Cup winning goalkeeper Gordon Banks and England internationals of the 1970s including Alan Hudson, Peter Shilton, Jimmy Greenhoff, Alan Dodd, Geoff Hurst and Mike Pejic. True, these names don't spark much recognition from modern football fans but they were players who distinguished the club and also the England national team at a time when Stoke City were equal to anything Manchester United or Arsenal could offer on the pitch some 35 years ago. The recent era had been less illustrious for the club until its return to the Premier League in 2008, bankrolled by local entrepreneur and club chairman Peter Coates.

As a Premier League club, Stoke City attracts sponsorship from international companies such as Barclays Bank, Seat and Carslberg.[23] Most home games are sell-outs with 27,500 of the loudest fans in football shouting their team on. But generating the revenue to keep up with the bigger teams is an ongoing job for the club's commercial team. The website stokecityfc.com offers various services for fans including mobile and internet updates, merchandise and information, while the club has begun a partnership initiative with a US team, Austin Aztecs, to raise the club's profile among American 'soccer' fans. But the club could really leverage paid-for services such as these, and perhaps even play exhibition matches in other continents, if it could broaden its fan base globally and especially across Asia, Africa and the Middle East.

■ Case Questions

1 Using the internet, try to ascertain the main elements of communication in football club marketing.

2 What are the strengths, weaknesses, opportunities and threats facing the Stoke City FC brand on the global stage?

3 Design an integrated marketing communications plan to help Stoke City FC increase its brand profile and fan base across one of the following regions: Southeast Asia, China, India and the Middle East.

4 In what ways could Stoke City FC generate new revenue streams through initiatives based around Web 2.0, mobile, direct mail or other marketing communication channels?

■ ■ Further Reading ■

Hackley, C. (2003) 'IMC and Hollywood – what brand managers need to know', *Admap*, November: 44–7.

Tiwsakul, R., Hackley, C. and Szmigin, I. (2005) 'Explicit, non-integrated product placement in British television programmes', *International Journal of Advertising*, 24 (1): 95–111

Varey, R.J. (2000) *Corporate Communication Management: A Relationship Perspective*. London: Routledge.

On the Companion Website

These journal articles are freely available on the companion website (www.sagepub.co.uk/hackley).

Advertising and the Consumer Information Environment Online
Ronald J. Faber, Mira Lee, and Xiaoli Nan
American Behavioral Scientist, Dec 2004; vol. 48: pp. 447–466.

Advertising and Publicity: Suggested New Applications for Tourism Marketers
Marsha D. Loda, William Norman, and Kenneth F. Backman
Journal of Travel Research, Feb 2007; vol. 45: pp. 259–265.

The History of Outdoor Advertising Regulation in the United States
Charles R. Taylor and Weih Chang
Journal of Macromarketing, Mar 1995; vol. 15: pp. 47–59.

Notes

1 www.coca-cola.co.uk/ourbrands/ (accessed 18 May 2009).
2 'Coca Cola Championship is now the fourth most watched in Europe www.daily mail.co.uk/sport/football/article-566567/Coca-Cola-Championship-fourth-watched-League-Europe.html (accessed 18 May 2009).
3 www.sponsormap.com/global-sponsorship-spend-remains-positive-for-2009/ (accessed 18 May 2009).
4 See comment in C. Hackley (2006) 'I write marketing texts but i'm really a swill guy', Chapter 15 in Stephen Brown (Ed.) *Consuming Books: The Marketing and Consumption of Literature.* London: Routledge, pp. 175–82.
5 www.manutd.co.uk/default.sps?pagegid=%7B235041B8-C516-4517-8D04-AEEBB5882B8A%7D&sponsors=aig (accessed 19 May 2009).
6 www.barnardos.org.uk/get_involved/corporate/company_corporate_supporters.htm (accessed 19 May 2009).
7 www.uksponsorship.com/tv3.htm (accessed 29 April 2009).
8 This website does not make it clear whether brands looking for sponsorship are clients of the website or have merely been listed without their permission.
9 'Transforming the future of advertising', by Neil Merrett, *Melbourne Age*, 21 July 2009, www. the age.com..au/business/transforming-the-future-of-advertising-20090720dqu 7. html?page=-1
10 www.brandchannel.com/brandcameo_films.asp (accessed 19 May 2009).
11 www.brandchannel.com/brandcameo_films.asp?movie_year=2009#movie_list
12 www.theshiznit.co.uk/feature/top-10-worst-movies-for-product-placement.php (accessed 19 May 2009).
13 Examples can be seen at http://tvtropes.org/pmwiki/pmwiki.php/Main/Product Displacement (accessed 19 May 2009).
14 www.clikthrough.com/theater/video/13 (accessed 9 July 2009).
15 'Is Andy Burnham right to ban product placement on television?', by Chris Hackley, Royal Holloway University of London, and featured on www.utalkmarketing.com/pages/Article.aspx?ArticleID=13378&title=Is%20Andy%20Burnham%20Right%20to%20Ban%20Product%20Placement%20On%20UK%20Television (accessed 26 May 2009).
16 'Is Andy Burnham right to ban product placement on UK television?', by Chris Hackley, www.utalkmarketing.com/pages/Article.aspx?ArticleID=13378&title=Is%20Andy%

20Burnham%20Right%20to%20Ban%20Product%20Placement%20On%20UK%20Television

17 www.unilever.co.uk/ourcompany/newsandmedia/pressreleases/2009/ubrand.asp (accessed 4 May 2009).

18 Source: WARC Newsletter 14 May 2004.

19 'Olympic 2012 chief insists Cadbury is an appropriate sponsor', by Mark Sweney, *Guardian Media* (accessed 26 May 2009) www.guardian.co.uk/media/2008/oct/20/olympicsandthemedia-advertising

20 'Smoothie operators sell out to coke', by Martin Hickman, *The Independent*, Tuesday 7 April 2009, pp. 12–13.

21 Coverage on BBC News http://news.bbc.co.uk/1/hi/health/7132749.stm; in *The Sun* www.thesun.co.uk/sol/homepage/news/article563837.ece, *The Times* www.timesonline.co.uk/tol/news/uk/article3025862.ece. See also a piece in the *International Journal of Market Research* reflecting on the process of media coverage for academic studies www.mrs.org.uk/publications/ijmr_viewpoints/hackley.htm, and another piece in *The Times Higher Education* magazine on the pros and cons of media exposure for academics, www.timeshighereducation.co.uk/story.asp?sectioncode=26&storycode=405999

22 www.smartfocus.com/

23 www.theidm.com/ 'Premier League's voyages of plunder reveal rationale behind 39th game', by Sam Wallace, *The Independent*, Monday 27 April 2009.

24 www.stokecityfc.com/page/Home/ (accessed 28 April 2009).

7 International Advertising

Chapter Outline

Brand marketing is now conducted in an international space which crosses national and cultural boundaries. Standardizing brand marketing communication across the globe is attractive to organizations because of the potential savings and control over the brand image. However, communicating one message to different national cultures raises many difficulties. This chapter discusses some of the managerial opportunities and problems of promoting brands internationally, and explores some of the wider implications of the globalization of the marketing environment. The chapter ends with a case study illustrating an internationally standardized advertising campaign.

Key chapter content:

- The specificity of cultural practices of communication
- Internationalization of marketing
- Standardization and localization of marketing communication
- The economic case for a standardization of marketing and advertising
- Protests and controversies surrounding global marketing
- The allure of foreignness and country-of-origin effects
- Advertising in Asian economies.

The Specificity of Cultural Practices of Communication

Advertising is inherently a cultural product. The managerial problems of advertising internationally cannot be reduced simply to a matter of accurately translating the message. Different cultures interpret advertising communication through quite different systems of value and symbolism. In a general sense, all advertising communicates exactly the same message. It tries to persuade us to buy stuff. Advertising represents a global value system, the value system of capitalism and the consumer lifestyle, from a predominantly Western perspective representing the historical economic dominance of the West. Therefore, advertising holds a unique place in contemporary discourse, it permeates culture at a global level, carrying a consumer ideology which is then set within local cultural meaning systems.

The task of designing an advertising communication for international consumption can be thought of in terms of two extremes. On the one hand, an advertisement which is shown the world over must tap into meanings which are common to different cultures in order to be understood. The possibilities for this are rare and difficult to execute, but there have been some notable successes. On the other hand, advertising which is recreated anew in every local culture must carry some commonality in order to preserve the sense of brand identity. For example, McDonald's advertising is different in many different countries, but it is also always instantly recognizable as McDonald's. Advertising executions for global brands which cross cultural borders have to achieve this dialectical balancing act, so that the sense of the brand is preserved in a persuasive way but articulated through local cultural communication codes.

Exacerbating the problem further, people will take different meanings from a promotional communication even if they happen to have the same cultural background. Where cultural backgrounds differ, there is even more scope for consumers to take different meanings from the same advertisement. The elements of cultural background which might influence interpretation include ethnicity, language, locality, religion, family, sub-culture, peer group, education and any other influences which have featured in individuals' formative environments. Clearly, the potential for consumers to decode communication in ways which were not anticipated presents a challenge for marketing communications professionals. Making the communication as simple as possible is not necessarily a solution, since simplicity in communication is itself a cultural construction. Like the stereotypical British tourist who tries to make himself understood in a foreign land by shouting louder in English, some advertising campaigns which no doubt seemed direct and clear to their creators fare poorly with another language dubbed over the visual.

It may seem self-evident to draw attention to differences in cultural and meaning systems and the challenges these present for advertisers. After all, these differences may not always be particularly significant for globally recognized brands which, in some senses, seem to transcend cultural boundaries. Nevertheless, it is important to understand that all of us can fall into conventional, culturally-bound ways of seeing the world which can impede our understanding of other-ness. We constantly interpret visual and linguistic signs whose meanings, as we easily forget, are highly specific to our own culture. International advertising offers examples of cultural differences in communication which can consistently surprise because cultural communication tends to be so very localized and taken-for-granted.

Gesture and Communication

As a useful exemplar of the quirkiness of communication practices it may be instructive to look briefly at the communication codes of physical gestures. In many countries, similar gestures can carry quite different meanings, illustrating the varied communicative practices of cultures. This self-evident feature of cultures carries profound implications for international marketing communication. Non-verbal communication is an integral feature of many visual promotions. Insults tend to be particularly fertile ground for gesture analysis. In Britain, raising the first and second fingers to another person in a V-shape is normally considered an insult, unless the palm is facing outward in which case the V is taken to stand for 'victory'. Other cultures have their own insulting gestures, such as the fingers scraped outwards under the chin in an Italian gesture of contempt, or the hand thrust outward, fingers separated and palm outermost, in Greece. Soccer players in continental Europe seem quite accustomed to spitting at each other in moments of anger, but if the object of the bile is a British player the British media become very excited, regarding spitting at someone else as an especially contemptible insult.

Gestures are important not only in insults but also in benign social exchanges. For example, crossing one's legs while sitting is commonplace in many countries. But in Thailand, if the sole of the foot is exposed in the direction of another person, it is considered a serious breach of social etiquette, although an allowance is made for foreigners. Beyond physical gestures, other non-verbal social practices of communication can be important. For example, the giving of gifts to business associates is relatively rare in the West but common practice, and sometimes compulsory, in the East where gift-giving is an important part of the complex practices signifying relative social status and relationships. In the UK, a long-running series of HSBC (formerly known as the Honk Kong Shanghai Bank) advertisements entertainingly depicted many of these cultural differences of gesture and behaviour. The message was that an international organization such as HSBC was well placed to understand the cultural differences that can hinder attempts to do business in foreign cultures.

BOX 7.0

National Stereotypes in Promotion

In Europe, there are stereotypical beliefs that the best policemen are British, the best chefs French, the best mechanics German, the best lovers Italian and the best organizers the Swiss. As the old joke goes, 'Hell is where the police are German, the chefs are British, the mechanics French, the lovers Swiss and it is all organized by the Italians'. Such stereotypes can be exploited in promotions that humorously draw attention to them while also using them to illustrate a serious point. Advertisements for HSBC and VW Passat have been successful in drawing attention to cultural differences. Clearly, there is also the potential to offend or disparage audiences if the communication is not handled sensitively. The British have a reputation for being able to laugh at themselves, but their advertising creatives and television script writers have persistently forced this virtue on every other nationality, so useful can national stereotypes be for the hard-pressed creative who is up against a deadline.

Using national stereotypes in creative executions (see Box 7.0) can work both for and against advertisers. If they are invoked to represent a positive and enduring stereotype then they can support the brand. A creative execution for the DDB London Volkswagen Passat campaign in the UK used the stereotypical British belief that Germans are good at motor engineering to present the Passat as the best of German engineering. The scenarios gently mocked Germans while also admiring the personal dedication of VW engineers ('A car born of obsession' went one strapline). However sophisticated and international in outlook consumers and marketers become, the trusty national stereotype still often seems to be a ready solution. This might be a bit lazy creatively but it reflects the sheer difficulty of finding communication codes which cross geography and time for large numbers of people.

Context and Communication

As Cook (2001) points out, communication always has a context that informs the meaning of a message. Viewing ads in the company of people from countries and cultures other than one's own can be a salutary reminder of this truism. A university class of international students asked to explain a particular ad will usually illustrate this vividly with widely diverging interpretations. Advertisers therefore need to be especially sensitive to the use of gestures in a TV commercial script or press ad, in case meanings are construed that do not reflect well on the brand. The international marketing world is awash with stories of brand names, packaging designs or ads that failed because they were interpreted to mean something inappropriate or outrageous in some regions. This generally results because the brand planners did not think outside their own cultural **frame of reference**. This is a communications lesson that even domestic advertisers and marketers must learn. It is a fundamental precept of brand planning that the cultural beliefs and practices of the target consumers have to be thoroughly understood by creative teams and brand planners who do not share that culture, if communications are to be designed that resonate with meaning for the intended target audience. Communication always has a context (see Chapter 2), and the sensitivity of meaning to context is especially problematic in cross-national advertising and promotion.

Before we look further at international advertising and promotion, it is worth examining briefly some of the practical management issues and problems behind the internationalization of marketing activity.

Internationalization of Marketing

Global marketing entails risk, but there remain sound and pressing reasons why brand marketing organizations want to operate on a global scale. In fact, given the increase in access to television and the internet, it can be difficult for brands to remain local. A website, for example, is intrinsically a global presence, at least in the sense that it can in principle be accessed by anyone, anywhere. Information and advertising cross cultural boundaries increase consumer choices and raise consumers' lifestyle expectations. The scenes of affluence portrayed in brand advertising or in movies viewed around the world on satellite TV or the internet have a powerful effect. This helps to stimulate the latent demand for brands and in so doing helps to wear away cultural and political resistance to controls on the movement of labour, goods, services and capital. This creates potential foreign markets for domestic producers. When domestic demand reaches a point of slow growth because of increased competition or saturated local demand, foreign markets offer a means of continued organic growth. In addition, domestic competition drives up labour costs and foreign countries seeking inward investment can offer global brand corporations cheaper labour and production costs, adding momentum to the cycle of internationalization.

BOX 7.1

The International Appeal of the BMW Mini[1]

BMC (British Motor Corporation), formed from the merger of the UK car brands Austin and Morris, launched the Mini in 1959. The car, owned by Rover, ceased production in the UK in October 2000 after over 5 million had been manufactured. The revolutionary front-wheel drive design of Sir Alec Issigonis created a car with great appeal, but sales were falling sharply by the late 1950s. BMW bought the brand in 2001 and Frank Stephenson redesigned the car, keeping the sense of fun and style but producing a vehicle that is contemporary in substance and performance. The promotions for the new Mini positioned it as a pan-global small car. Brand communications utilized conventional (though quirky) mass media advertising, web-based communications, sponsorship of TV shows, brand placement in movies, numerous publicity stunts, outdoor promotions and extensive PR coverage (both solicited and unsolicited). The BMW Mini has been a resounding commercial and critical success across the world, even selling heavily in the large-car-dominated US market. Its international success reflects a conscious effort on the part of BMW to position the car internationally rather than over-exploiting its British heritage. Many new consumers of the Mini are unaware that it is an icon of 1960s' Britain. This connotation of the car, while arguably an important part of its appeal, was not an explicit feature of the marketing communications for the new BMW Mini. However, the original Mini did feature prominently in the original *Italian Job* movie, while the new BMW Mini was also a major feature of the 2003 re-make of *The Italian Job*.

The impetus for global marketing may often derive from competitive activity. If brand X is active in a particular foreign market, then brand Y will want to be there too in case it loses ground against the competition by not having a presence in that market. Another factor in the globalization of markets is the relative ease of technology transfer. National boundaries no longer hinder the transfer of production capability to low-wage economies. The competitive need for international expansion, the ease of access to new consumer markets and low-wage labour markets, and the cross-cultural communication driving an ideology of brand consumption are, taken together, important drivers of the globalization of corporate activity.

So, while global markets are far from homogeneous (see Levitt, 1983) there are considerable opportunities for international brand marketing activity given the relative ease of capital transfer and cross-border transportation, the internationalization of financial payments, and the latent demand for many brands created by the international reach of, and increasing access to, cable television, movies and the internet.

Managerial Problems of Marketing Internationally

Marketing in non-domestic markets presents a number of managerial problems that may be less acute when dealing with domestic markets alone. For example, the marketing and communications infrastructure may differ widely between regions. In advanced economies well-developed road, rail and air transport links, the presence of wholesale distribution facilities and easy access to local retail or other sales outlets facilitate marketing by domestic or non-domestic firms. In less developed economies the absence of a well-established communications and marketing infrastructure may present real difficulties. Logistics can be a problem: while densely populated cities may have good communication links, vast numbers of people live in areas with poor communications and few retail outlets. Rates of literacy and access to TV and telephones differ widely from region to region. Factors such as these clearly have major implications for the design of marketing initiatives.

In addition to practical and managerial problems of marketing internationally there is the self-evident difficulty of communication across linguistic, cultural and ethnic boundaries. These difficulties encompass not only advertising but also personal communication and relationship management. As Hackley and Tiwsakul (2008) point out, advertising management is culture-bound. On the one hand, ad agencies the world over operate in ways which have strong similarities. On the other, they are dealing in culturally specific linguistic and social practices and this local knowledge is indispensible to coherent and resonant promotional communication.

Advertising agency management is subject to much the same kinds of cultural variation as advertising itself. A great many international agencies are organized along similar operational lines with account management, account planning or research, creative and media roles in account teams. There are, nevertheless, differences in approach that reflect broader cultural differences. West (1993) refers to apparent differences in approaches to creativity in advertising in different regions, and Hackley (2003a) has indicated some differences in approaches to consumer research in major UK and US agencies. To take another example, while the Thai advertising industry has evolved under Western influence (Punyapiroje et al., 2002), it has also developed a distinctive style reflecting the particular cultural mores and traditions of Thailand.

A further managerial difficulty of advertising internationally is the fact that codes of advertising practice, media law and consumer marketing regulation can differ greatly from country to country. In France, for example, no alcohol advertising is permitted. In Italy, the use of children as models in advertising is restricted, while in some countries such as Greece it is forbidden to advertise children's toys on television before 9pm. In the UK, advertising cigarettes in mass media is forbidden. The differences in international advertising regulation present a further problem for standardization in international advertising campaigns.

Business Behaviour and Cultural Difference

There are many differences in the cultural practices of international business. For example, the difficulty of getting distribution agreements for Western brands in Japanese markets is legendary. This is at least partly because the Asian tradition of building mutually advantageous business relationships carefully over long periods of time is difficult for the Western business mentality, which is based on instant rapport, agreements of convenience and instrumental relationships. A further difficulty is that the language and dialect used in neighbouring regions may have nuances that can only be understood by local people, creating highly local and specific trading and communicating conditions.

Communicating and doing business may be very difficult for foreigners who do not have a deep knowledge of the local culture, language and business practices. Systems of business regulation and attitudes to communication can differ widely from culture to culture. For example, what is acceptable in advertising in one country may not be allowed in another. In Muslim countries, for example, the portrayal of females in advertising must adhere to the public standards of dress and conduct expected. Portraying sexuality and nudity in advertising is often more liberal in Europe than in the USA and the UK. Specific rules about the advertising of particular goods can differ. For example, in Sweden no TV advertising directed at children under 12 is permitted. Marketing internationally encounters numerous differences in regulation, infrastructure and consumer culture.

BOX 7.2

Germany and New Zealand United in a Co-branding Promotion[2]

The German sportswear manufacturer Adidas won a contract to supply kit to the famous New Zealand All Blacks rugby team. This was more than a promotional agreement, it was a cross-national, co-branding initiative. The association of a German sportswear brand and the New Zealand rugby team might seem incongruous on the face of it. Thus initially it met with resistance from the New Zealand media. New Zealand people are passionate about the All Blacks and the team represents the national identity in an emotionally powerful way. Many people felt that a local sponsorship deal was more appropriate. Saatchi and Saatchi developed creative executions for advertising that played on the reverence New Zealanders feel for All Black players and reflected the proud winning tradition of the team.

In one TV commercial execution a film of the famous Haka Maori war dance that All Black players perform before matches ended with a simple 'Adidas'. In another, a plaintive song about heroes accompanied a gathering of All Black players pulling on their jerseys. Again, the Adidas name was an understated presence at the end of the ad, tapping into the passion for sport felt by New Zealanders and seeking to legitimize the Adidas brand in this highly charged emotional context. The incongruence of the respective national cultures (rugby has few followers and little tradition in Germany) seemed overridden in this case by the linked connotations of the respective brands.

Standardization and Localization of Marketing Communication

An important question facing brand organizations is to what degree they ought to try to standardize their marketing communications throughout the world. We have already seen that the meaning of advertising narratives is often unstable and open to a variety of interpretations, even within relatively homogeneous consumer communities. How much more difficult must it be to control the interpretation of brand communications across different cultural and language communities?

In spite of the difficulty of standardizing meaning across cultures, advertising and marketing communications have been at the forefront of the globalization of corporate activity in recent years. Many markets have grown beyond national boundaries and media and telecommunications developments have created opportunities for brand marketers to reach global audiences. Indeed, while globalization itself can be seen as a nebulous, even a mythical notion, the global manifestations of advertising are clearly apparent. Consumers the world over are often aware of global brands because they have encountered branded goods, brand ads, logos, sponsored sports events on satellite TV, branded computer games and movies. Marketing communication is a significant thread in the globalization debate. Certain brands have global recognition because advertising has been created that resonates with consumers of every origin. As brand organizations compete to internationalize their brands they face the decision of how best to do this in a way that minimizes costs.

Converging Cultures – a Redundant Debate?

The standardize or localize question arose partly because the communications infrastructure evolved to make standardized global advertising possible.

Hollywood movies have been popular the world over for many years. The emergence of video technology, satellite TV, the internet and international travel allowed this popularity to gain full expression through the global consumption of entertainment products. Another factor in the debate was the tendency of academic and consulting business writers to cast it in the rhetoric of dichotomy: an either-or choice, to standardize globally or to adapt locally. In an article in the *Harvard Business Review*, Professor Ted Levitt[3] raised the question of whether heterogeneous cultures around the globe are converging in attitudes, aspirations, tastes and beliefs. The main site of this apparent convergence was consumption. The logic of the argument was simple. If you can see Nike trainers and McDonald's hamburger joints in practically every capital city in the world then is this not evidence that consumers the world over are essentially the same in their needs and wants?

The suggestion that the aspirations and values of differing cultures have united under the ethos of consumerism seems far-fetched nearly 30 years after Levitt wrote his article. The values of economic neo-liberalism have swept across the world in some respects (Hackely, 2009b) but there remain powerful and often strident voices articulating alternative visions. At the very least we can say that Levitt's article understated the robustness and uniqueness of local cultural values. However, it also seems that this in some regards adds another dimension to the internationalization of marketing since the produce, values and lifestyles of different regions and cultures are themselves marketed as unique brands.

It is important to specify just what might converge in differing cultures and what cannot. Indeed, the notion of converging cultures makes little sense since cultures are defined by enduring and powerful differences. In important regards, what is of a particular culture can only be understood in terms of its difference from other cultures. But in the smaller world of advertising it is still worth posing the question because of the evident commonalities between cultures that make global consumer brands possible. One might also view this from a critical perspective in terms of the power of marketing to transcend, or perhaps to suppress, cultural difference. This latter viewpoint is the one that most attracts the opposition of anti-brand and anti-marketing voices which argue that marketing in particular and economic neo-liberalism in general tend to obliterate local cultures. One of the reasons why the question gained credence among the academic and consulting circles of management was the appeal of the idea of global standardization for brand marketing organizations. Not only does having a global reach appeal to the adventurism of brand marketing organizations, it also makes business sense.

BOX 7.3

Western Celebs Reap Dividends in Japanese Advertising Roles

Japan has been a particularly lucrative source of extra income for Western celebrities prepared to appear in brand advertising. Movie and TV stars such as Leonardo DiCaprio (Orico credit card), Matt Le Blanc (cosmetics), Arnold Schwarzenegger (energy drinks) and Brad Pitt (Edwin jeans) have all appeared in advertising in Japan, as have pop singers Maria Carey (Nescafé) and Jennifer Lopez (Subaru). The British soccer player David Beckham and his wife Victoria promoted Tokyo Beauty Centre salons. In spite of well-developed Asian movie and sports industries, Western stars remain potent symbols of glamour and affluence for many Asian consumers. The association with Western celebrity remains powerfully prestigious for brands seeking a point of differential advantage in their advertising, even though Asian economic strength is growing rapidly.

The Economic Case for a Standardization of Marketing and Advertising

The appeal of standardized international marketing lies in economy and control. As regards cost, it is expensive for a brand organization to appoint a local advertising agency to create bespoke campaigns for the same brand in each country. All production and media costs are multiplied by the number of different campaigns that are needed. Economies can result from standardization because of using just one ad agency and one media-buying agency to produce one standardized ad campaign for the whole region. Costs are kept relatively low in relation to the scale of the advertising operation.

Cost minimization is one issue, while control over the way the brand is represented is another. Control results from keeping creative executions under a central command rather than having to co-ordinate the work of local agencies, so that brand values and the brand personality are portrayed in exactly the desired way in every region. International brand organizations take a great deal of time and trouble to develop the ideas of their brand's values and personality, and to plan how these values might be portrayed in advertising and promotion. Giving control of advertising away to an agency in another country is a risk for major brand organizations because they know how costly mistakes in communication can be. Local agencies will invariably employ a culturally-specific interpretation of the brand values, which may not always be the interpretation that the brand organization conceived of in its strategic planning.

In practice, the question of whether to standardize or localize marketing communications is not a straight choice between alternatives but a question of degree. Most international organizations will reach an accommodation between the need for localized communications strategies driven by culture-specific knowledge, and a need for control over costs and creative executions.

'Glocalization' as a Response to Difficulties in International Marketing Communication

Most international brand marketing organizations have found that neither localization nor global standardization will serve their purpose. What they require instead is a policy that reconciles the need for a consistency in presentation of the brand in all communications across the world on the one hand, and the need for advertising to resonate with culturally-specific consumer groups on the other. To achieve the specificity required, the brand values and personality have to be portrayed in terms of the local language, priorities and practices. The broader marketing mix activities, in addition to the advertising, have to reflect local realities and practices.

The term '**glocalization**' refers to the local adaptation of globally oriented marketing. Global brand marketing organizations will often seek to impose control over the presentation of their brand at a certain level, allowing local marketing agencies some licence to portray the brand in ways that will cohere with local cultural meaning systems. So, for example, the brand logo and colour scheme might be mandatory inclusions specified in the creative brief, and perhaps the strapline and music, even if the creative execution in other respects is generated by the agency to match local consumer interpretive frames.

A glocalization policy in international advertising is often pragmatically the best course. The attractions of international markets and the appeal of brands that cross national boundaries have to be understood in terms of local cultural meaning systems. Local agencies can place the brand in an appropriate localized context while preserving some aspects of a generic brand personality. If a brand is known to have a global presence this in itself adds appeal to the brand personality.

A relatively small number of brands have been able to standardize advertising cross-culturally when their ad agency has found a common denominator of meaning that transcends cultures. They have to exploit this common meaning by devising ingenious creative executions. Finally, even brands with a global presence are subject to the forces of change. No communications solution is effective indefinitely and brands must remain connected to the ebb and flow of consumer cultures if they are to retain vitality and relevance in the marketplace.

BOX 7.4

De Beers Gem Diamonds' Standardized Campaign[4]

One interesting example of a standardized campaign was that of De Beers Gem Diamonds. De Beers is a South African diamond producing and cutting organization. In 1996, in response to competition from West African diamonds, De Beers commissioned JWT to create a campaign which would stimulate wealthy consumers to trade up to a higher quality. JWT's consumer research found that one common factor linked the meaning of diamonds across all cultures – diamonds meant love. This theme was adapted into the differing diamond-giving practices in different countries in creative executions designed to resonate with local consumers. So, for example, the UK version of the ad showed a man giving a woman a ring to signify a marriage proposal, while the Middle Eastern version showed an altogether more lavish scale of diamond giving signifying extravagant family wealth. In many countries, gold or pearls are traditionally preferred to diamonds as gifts of love. The campaign, called 'Shadows', used the same cinematic technique in all the ads with local variations of music, copy and narrative, and a local voiceover. Each ad was made to be culturally relevant to a wide but connected geographic region. Significant sales increases were reported and the campaign was reputed to have helped change the cultural meaning of diamonds by encouraging their use in cultures not traditionally predisposed to diamond-giving. In Japan, for example, it was said that there was no word for diamond before the 1960s but the term *diamondo* became widely understood after the De Beers campaign.

Crossing, Transcending or Colonizing Local Cultures?

One can argue that many globally recognized brands represent something that does not *cross* cultures at all. The fact that many global brands are American in origin cannot be a coincidence: US-based brands have a global exposure through Hollywood movies. Of the most widely recognized global brands, most are US in origin. Only two of the top 10 brands listed in Box 3.2 are not American in origin: Nokia and Toyota. In the Western economic boom of the 1950s, US products gained a reputation for representing luxury, affluence and high-quality production standards. American provenance is no longer a guarantee of prestige. Economic times have changed, Asian economies are advancing at speed. At the time of writing, General Motors, once the world's largest company, was going into administration. Goods of US origin have long lost their technological advantage over Asian-produced goods, but nevertheless a fragment of the chewing gum, silk stockings, Hollywood movies and Coca-Cola of the American dream remains in the cultural consciousness, and of course the USA is still the world's pre-eminent geopolitical superpower. The point here is that the spread of brand consciousness and consumer culture across borders and cultures may be regarded as a form of Western cultural imperialism, or as a sign of progressive economic and political liberalization, depending on one's point of view.

As the world's major economic, political and military power, the USA is a brand in its own right. Perhaps branded consumer items that are known to originate from the US have the advantage of this cross-over effect (sometimes called the country-of-origin effect). Certainly, in many economically disadvantaged countries, products known to be of Western origin are powerful symbols of an affluent consumer culture. Brands of Asian origin are making headway but it remains the case that Western brands often have the advantage in prestige. Prestige consumer brands are a particularly interesting case for the insights their popularity offers into the cultural construction of power, social identity and social status. Why do ladies from South East Asia, for example, spend such huge sums of money on a bag made by Gucci or Prada (Chada and Husband, 2006)? Is it because these brands have created subtle and penetrating marketing strategies which somehow passed under the cultural radar to appear equally appealing in different countries the world over? Or is it simply that some affluent consumers in some countries seek out cultural signifiers which have a meaning which they find empowering? Or could it be that their sense of aesthetic discernment is fired up by these particular products and not by locally produced ones?

Sometimes cultural changes in meaning are neither caused by nor reflected in advertising. Cultural change occurs and leaves advertising looking out of date. The cultural meaning of signs and practices is not stable indefinitely, as we will note in the Levis case below.

As the ideological sharp end of capitalism, advertising has a crucial role in promoting consumption itself by teaching new approaches. Consumption becomes much more fun if we attach abstract ideas to material goods. Advertising and promotion show us an array of states of mind, ways of being and relating, and forms of enjoyment, all of which are orientated to consumption. Most of us seem more than happy to be offered these choices, which we take according to the preferences that we are taught through our exposure to marketing. Globally successful ad campaigns, then, might be seen not as triumphs of cross-cultural communication but simply as examples of creative brand advertising that transcend cultural borders.

Whatever the case, the country of origin of some brands in particular markets seems to give them a striking competitive advantage. The question of whether marketing campaigns ought to be standardized or localized, or indeed glocalised, has to be addressed managerially in the brands' particular cultural context (see Holt, 2004).

Protests and Controversies Surrounding Global Brand Marketing

In spite of the global popularity of many brands, especially Western ones, there has been notable resistance to globalized, and standardized, brand marketing. In France, for example, there have been popular movements against the establishment of Walt Disney attractions and McDonald's restaurants. Of course, France has a powerful and well-developed economy in its own right. These movements are a reflection not merely of resentment against the symbolic power of richer nation-states, but also of concerns that these US brand icons represent a kind of cultural imperialism in which the massive financial power of huge US corporations allows them to establish brands that obliterate the local culture. But there have also been more specific concerns about the way that global brands represent corporate interests against the interests and needs of local consumer communities. The McDonald's ethos of fast and simple food is anathema to French cuisine, but the restaurants remain popular in France as elsewhere. McDonald's has also attracted criticism for its effect on agriculture. In the USA, the brand has created a supply chain establishment that has apparently changed the structure and culture of the farming and cattle processing industries (Schlosser, 2002). French farmers have been worried that the same thing might happen in France. The protests against the Walt Disney theme parks may have an element of cultural prejudice, however they were not built to serve the expressed leisure needs of local people, but rather to attract international tourists.

Nike was the subject of considerable adverse press coverage because of media stories that they manufactured products in low-wage economies where labour laws were either inadequate to protect children or were not applied. Even mainly US-produced brands such as Levi Strauss attracted bad press coverage because of the way they tried to save production costs by shutting down a factory. Global brands make excellent copy for media editors, and hostile stories make better copy than favourable versions. It is right that global brand corporations should be subject to close scrutiny regarding their social and environmental responsibility. But there can be little doubt that global brands have become convenient weapons in media circulation and political contests. Arguments over whether they are applying the same standards of labour protection, environmental management and pay in their licensed overseas manufacturing plants as in their domestic plants are difficult to resolve and cut across political and competitive issues as well as environmental and labour process issues. Few global brands have entirely escaped controversies over their manufacturing practices abroad, and recent press stories have covered BP, Shell and Coca-Cola.

The activities and consequences of global brand corporations operating in local cultures is an important area of debate and investigation. It is the global profile itself that makes the corporation both more powerful and more vulnerable to criticism. Our concern here is not with the wider issue of the corporate social responsibility of big corporations, however the general values of the organization will influence the perceived values of their brands. Global brand corporations have certain resources and media, especially advertising, under their direct control. They have influence rather than control over others, such as public image. News stories, from whatever source, that are connected to global brands wield important influence over them. Global corporations are well aware of the importance of public perception. Consumer movements that turn attention away from consumption of the brand and towards the activities of the producer can be powerful influences on corporate behaviour.

Given the sensitivities over the activities of (mainly Western) brand corporations, communications assume great importance in managing or responding to consumer and activist attitudes and expectations.

The Allure of 'Foreignness' and Country-of-Origin Effects

Foreignness can be a marketing virtue. Country-of-origin effects can bestow a halo of prestige on brands emanating from particular countries. For example, in the UK, German motor-car design and engineering, Japanese technology, Swiss watches, French food and wine, Italian fashion, Colombian coffee, Indian tea, Belgian beer and holidays in Thailand are all thought to have special qualities. In many Asian consumer markets brands with a European connotation are often thought to have special glamour or prestige. UK press ads for an executive Volvo model featured an elegant woman of east Asian origin, whereas the Japanese ads for the same car showed a blond Caucasian woman. Each ad had a symbol of desire that might appeal to the domestic business executive who might be a typical sales prospect for that particular model of car.

The French Renault Clio car ad for the UK featured an attractive woman with an amused look in her eyes and the strapline 'The New 16 Valve Clio. Size matters'. Japanese press ads for a very similar Renault model showed a new French-sounding name (the 'Lutécia') and a circus trapeze scenario, suggesting fun and excitement but safety too. The differential advertising signifies different positioning and targeting strategies in each country, as well as an adaptation to various cultural norms of advertising. Japanese advertising would be most unlikely to use an image of a woman with a humorous double-entendre, although such themes are common in the British tradition. The Publicis agency created the famous 'Papa, Nicole' TV campaign for the Clio that became a huge and popular success in the UK. The campaign traded on French elegance and sexual sophistication to position the Clio as a car for independent young females not afraid to shock older people in the cause of having fun.

Other country-of-origin effects may be based on cost. Taiwan and China have become associated with mass-produced, low-cost, low-quality goods. It has been estimated that 70 per cent of the toys and games British children play with are produced in China and Asia. India is still seen as a relatively low-cost country in which to establish manufacturing or service operations for global brands. But this may be changing slowly, as China and India are rapidly advancing in economic size and status. In general, consumer acceptance of foreign culture has proved remarkably flexible and the appeal of particular brands often seems to transcend historical or geo-political issues. The economic status of particular countries is not immutable – for example, Britain, once the cradle of the Industrial Revolution, has become a post-industrial economy. The UK is still the fifth largest economy in the world but it has ceded much of its domestic manufactured goods markets to other countries.

It is very human to feel a desire for the unattainable or the unfamiliar. No doubt there is something of human nature in the country-of-origin effect. National or regional reputations, myths and symbols that resonate with consumer aspirations are powerful drivers of consumption. It can be a strong lever for advertising and marketing internationally. And, as we have seen, there can be an adverse effect for brand marketing corporations if they happen to be closely associated with a country that acquires negative press coverage and receives international disapproval for whatever reason.

Advertising in Asian Economies

Some examples of advertising in Asia might serve here to illustrate issues of cross-cultural communication in advertising. Even where an economy is developing, this does not mean that there are not large and sophisticated consumer markets in the urban centres. In developing countries the cultural juxtaposition of Western-influenced consumer advertising and local cultural and economic norms can seem particularly discordant.

The economic and cultural influence of advertising in Asian economies is difficult for a Westerner to appraise. There is a well-established link between advertising activity and economic growth. Advertising is a powerful driver of consumption. In countries in which poverty is the greatest enemy of social progress, advertising does not always attract the critical scrutiny that it does in more affluent countries. Nevertheless, developing countries should not have to turn themselves into servants of the global corporations, providing both cheap manufacturing and large consumer markets for global brands. They need to develop wealth on a model that fits with their culture, traditions and particular needs. Consumption itself might be said to be a practice that unites differing cultures, but the particular context for consumption differs from culture to culture.

Advertising in Malaysia

In Malaysia, for example, many magazine ads seem to locate Western consumer values in an Islamic cultural context. Malaysia is a culturally complex country, with three main ethnic groups, Indian, Chinese and Malay. Each has a separate language and many differing traditions, but there is also a great deal of commonality. There are also groups of Thais, Filipinos, Taiwanese and Indonesians. Advertising in such a context has to be distinctively Asian and must conform to local sensitivities. Approval for ads is often given directly by government officials. There are detailed codes of practice for the advertising of different products and services.

BOX 7.5

Muslim Values in Western-style Advertising

A Bahasa fashion magazine has many examples of 'glocal' advertising portraying Western products with Western values but in a creative execution that is adapted to be acceptable to Muslim readers. One product, Johnson's pH5.5 cooling body wash, is intended to be used in the shower. However, it would not be allowed to show a photograph of a female in the shower, so the ad shows a woman with naked shoulders in a sensuous pose while a graphic, water-like abstract design fills the background. The model's hair is fixed in place so that she might even be wearing a headscarf. The ad's suggestion of a female in the shower is clear, but the advertisers can claim that it does not show a naked female.

The art of adhering to advertising codes and regulations literally while going beyond them is symbolically a mark of advertising under advanced capitalism. Ads such as the one described in Box 7.5 illustrate the ideological force of advertising, which promotes the values of consumption while subtly circumventing other cultural values. Clearly, capitalism and the ideology of consumption have had to chip away at religious and other values in Western countries as well as Eastern ones. Advertising does this precisely because it is seen as trivial and benign. It is also the case that the imperative for wealth creation means that advertising is usually seen as a lesser evil than poverty.

Other Malaysian ads portray females in a way that offers a compromise between the traditional values of home-making and husband-nurturing and the less traditional values of female independence. One ad for a 'Pewani' savings account offered by Bank Islam (in a daily newspaper) promotes a savings account for women with the strapline 'Nurturing success for today's women'. The visual shows a woman in a traditional headscarf with her husband and children and promotes the idea of the account as a gift to her family. Presumably, the ad has become necessary because more Muslim women in Malaysia are going out to earn money independent from their husbands.

BOX 7.6

International Influences in Thai TV Advertising

Many ads on Thai TV reflect an interest in non-Thai culture and global brands, for example, those that mix Japanese with the Thai language and culture. An ad for a Japanese snack food Bun Bun carries Thai-language subtitles; other brands such as Lays seaweed-flavour crisps, Pote snack food and Giffarine facial cream (a local brand) combine Japanese and Thai influences in their advertising. Thais are also very interested in international brands such as L'Oréal, McDonald's (the 'I'm lovin' it' jingle is sung in Thai) and Scott's toilet tissue (showing the same ad as in the UK). Sony, Samsung and Orange all create Thai advertising executions for the Thai market. Chinese culture influences Thai TV ads for Choice soup mix, Mistine powder for oily skin and Pond's facial foam. The leading Thai brand of cooling powder, St Luke's Prickly Heat, was established in Thailand by a British entrepreneur.

Japanese Ads and Consumer Individualism

Japan is a very different economic, religious and ethnic proposition for brand advertising from Malaysia. Even so, advertisers have to use symbolism to suggest meanings that they hope will prove persuasive to consumers. Indeed, symbolism, particularly erotic symbolism in advertising, seems to be a mark of the state of development of the consumer markets it serves and reflects. Tanaka (1994) (see also Chapter 2) employed a distinction between covert and ostensive meaning in advertisements. The use of covert meaning, in which meanings are suggested but in such a way that the intention or identity of the speaker is not made clear, allows ads to suggest associations which would be considered outrageous or forbidden were they made in an ostensive, explicit way.

In one pair of examples (in Tanaka, 1994: 46–51) two ads for a miniature TV set were shown, each of which appeared in the risqué publication *Fookasu* in 1985. In one, the TV set was pictured in a scene with two girls and a man in a sensuous setting. The innuendo is supported by the advertising copy which claims that the satisfaction of curiosity is the key to mankind's development. It goes on 'Can't do this, can't do that ... there are many things forbidden in this world. What's the point of living unless we can at least watch what we want to when we want to ...'. The other ad shows the TV in a scene with two girls embracing over a piano. Sexuality is generally not a subject for public discourse in Asian countries. The magazine or ad agency could easily deflect accusations that they were promoting either in a literal sense. But, as we saw in Chapter 2, much of the power of advertising lies in its ability to suggest meanings which are not accessible unless read by the audience, thus imputing the meaning to audience interpretation rather than to the artifice of the advertiser. The ads were in tune with the risqué editorial tone of the publication in which they appeared. They allowed a mundane item to be portrayed in a way that made it seem, perhaps, far more interesting to some readers.

While these ads are not typical of Japanese advertising as a whole, they do illustrate how advertising can be devised which undermines, or at least evades, local cultural taboos and norms. Consumption can therefore be made to appear an act of symbolic self-realization that reinforces individual identity because it (symbolically) transgresses social conventions. This individualistic dimension of consumption is often taken for granted in the West, but in the more collective social culture of the East such implicit individualism may promote and also reflect a far-reaching cultural change.

Advertising in Thailand

Thailand is one Asian country that shows intriguing examples of sophisticated advertising in a developing economy with sharply contrasting centres of urban development and rural poverty. The Thai advertising industry is a mixture of locally owned agencies and branches of global communications conglomerates such as Saatchi and Saatchi, JWT, Publicis, Dentsu and many others (Tiwsakul, 2008). It leads many other Southeast Asian countries in advertising expenditures[5] (Punyapiroje et al., 2002). Production standards are as high as in any developed country, as are standards of creativity, and advertising content tends to be liberal. A predominantly Buddhist country, Thailand is not subject to specific broadcasting rules concerning behaviour, dress, eating and other practices. Thai advertising tends to be soft-sell and replete with scenes of humour, fun and love, reflecting the easy-going and creative character of Thai consumers (Supharp, 1993). Typical advertising is often very visual, reflecting low literacy rates among the rural population and indicating the subtleties of tone, image and gesture in visual communication to which

Asian consumers are attuned. Thai consumers love freedom and novelty and this is reflected in brand-switching behaviour (Sherer, 1995). Thai ads are often sensuous although Thailand is, in fact, a socially conservative country in which good manners and proper behaviour are regarded as essential, and respect for elders is especially valued.

According to Punyapiroje et al. (2002), the Thai advertising industry draws heavily on Western influences modified to suit Thai culture. However, there is at least one major difference between Thai and Western ways of doing advertising business. Advertising consumer research using questionnaire surveys and experiments in which respondents are asked to answer questions is common in Western advertising, but according to Hoy et al. (2000) Thai social etiquette demands acquiescence and people do not like to offer views that might offend by contradicting their interlocutor (Mulder, 1996). Thai advertising professionals will combine research results with their intuition, emotion and creativity (Tiwsakul and Hackley, 2008). Incidentally, as we shall see in Chapter 9, some in Western advertising hold the view that the Thai approach to consumer insight is best because of doubts about the integrity of questionnaire-based and quasi-experimental consumer research data.

Thailand is one of the Asian economies that has demonstrated enormous potential for further economic development. Ownership of Western goods once signified membership of a social elite (Tirakhunkovit, 1980). Today, Thailand is a developing country with very uneven distributions of wealth and educational attainment. In Thailand, as in many other Asian countries, the ownership and display of branded goods have assumed a key importance in signifying the social status of the owner, as these have in the West (Chada and Husband, 2006). Economic development in Asia is uneven but seems set on a long-term upward trajectory. Thailand represents the cutting edge of advertising practice in the region and will continue to be a fertile source of creative advertising and new brand markets. The role of advertising in this context is particularly powerful in promoting a brand-conscious mentality and in encouraging consumption as a lifestyle. The extent to which this influence may be seen to be complementary to local traditions and values or merely exploitative of them will offer valuable insights into the cultural influence of advertising in other regions too.

Chapter Summary

Chapter 7 has reviewed issues of international advertising, focusing mainly on the managerial perspective. The discussion revolved around the dichotomy of standardized versus localized advertising, taking in issues such as differing local advertising regulations and codes of marketing practice, differences in language and culture, and resistance and protest towards brand 'imperialism'. Another issue touched upon was the cultural role of advertising as a carrier of (Western) consumer ideology, and the tensions this can create where it conflicts with traditional values in particular countries. The chapter concluded with some comments about advertising in Southeast Asia and a short case study of a legendary standardized international advertising campaign.

■ Review Questions

1   In groups, decide upon a local brand that you feel has the potential to be marketed internationally. Decide on the core brand values that may be communicated. Devise an outline communications plan with creative themes using integrated media channels. How will you ensure that the brand values are interpreted appropriately? What are the major difficulties of promoting this brand internationally?

2   Choose six print or TV advertisements that promote internationally marketed brands. Discuss the need for globally marketed brands to accommodate cultural differences in their advertising. Use specific examples of cultural differences of behaviour, attitude or social practice to inform your discussion.

3   Try to find examples of advertisements for the same brand in different countries. Compare and contrast the respective ads and try to work out the possible differences in local segmentation and positioning and communication issues.

4   What is glocalization? In what ways is the concept relevant to advertising internationally? Offer examples to illustrate your points.

5   Try to think of potential international co-branding opportunities. To explore the coherence of the respective brands, you will need to list all the possible connotations of each brand and discuss their various merits both singly and in conjunction with the co-brand. What opportunities do you think might arise from such co-branding initiatives?

CASE

Levi 501s and the Changing Cultural Meaning of Denim Jeans

Bartle Bogle Hegarty's legendary 1980s TV campaign for Levi 501s caught the imagination of denim jean wearers the world over. The original ad (called 'Laundrette' because it was set in one) was produced to be shown all over the world. There was no copy or voice-over, so there were no language problems to overcome. There were lots of shots of the jeans, along with many images suggesting their American provenance, many of them evocative of the style that actors such as Marlon Brando and James Dean brought to 1950s Hollywood movies. The ad was played to a classic music track ('I Heard It Through the Grapevine' by Marvin Gaye).

The campaign targeted male jeans wearers aged 15–19 as an influential style leading group, but it also appealed to other age groups of both sexes because of the wit of the narrative and sex appeal of the actor. A young man enters a laundrette, takes his clothes off down to his boxer shorts and washes them in a machine, then puts them back on. The astonished reactions of the other customers are nicely contrasted by his laconic style. The male jeans wearer is cast in the same light as Brando or Dean, rebellious, sexy and heroic, a universal symbol of teenage rebellion and timeless cool. The denim market had been in recession and the Laundrette ad began a revival that saw denim jean sales leap by a reputed 800 per cent across all brands.

The stunning success of the 'American hero' style of Levis' ads lasted for a decade until the allure of American provenance faded. The research organization NOP World has reported[6] that there is 'diminishing respect for American culture' with a subsequent 'domino effect on US brands'. The research, conducted among 30,000 respondents in 30 countries, highlights a change in reports of general perceptions of the USA among non-US consumers. Country-of-origin effects are well known in marketing, meaning that certain countries confer prestige on certain brand perceptions. This research appears to show that the prestige of the USA as a source of brands may be suffering a general decline, although whether this translates as downturns in specific sales or market share remains to be seen.

The World Advertising Research Centre (WARC) reported[7] that the DDB Worldwide chairman, Keith Reinhard, conceived a 'Business for Diplomatic Action (BDA)' plan in 2004 to promote US brands internationally. BDA planned to raise $1 million to fund work countering the declining global prestige of America and American brands. The initiative gained urgency because of the NOP World survey finding that trust in American brands had fallen dramatically, noted above.

The jeans market as a whole eventually lost sales and fragmented into niches, each with a somewhat younger profile and different style values. The Levi 501 campaign was right for its time and struck a chord in many cultures. Its values seemed to transcend the cultural particularities of the countries in which it was shown; it shamelessly played on Hollywood iconography to confer a powerful sense of style to clothing that was merely everyday workwear in the USA. But by the early 1990s the cultural meaning of denim jeans had changed. For young people who had never heard of Brando and Dean and never seen movies like *Rebel Without a Cause* the American hero ad style meant nothing. Jeans simply meant comfort and informality. They no longer represented rebellion or any distinctively adolescent virtue: how could they when your Dad was wearing them?

Later Levis' Campaigns

Levis changed its approach to cater for niche markets and ended its long successful series of hero ads. One later campaign was, however, international and made a huge impact. A campaign for Levis' Sta-Prest range by the UK agency BBH achieved highly successful results by featuring a hand puppet called Flat Eric from an art student's short film. The character generated huge popular interest and media coverage. The levi.com website received more than 1.1 million hits around the time of the campaign. The research company Millward Brown found it was one of the most popular ads they had tracked in the UK for Levis. Sta-prest volume sales increased by a factor of 21 in the UK in four months, and the sound track to the ad achieved 2.5 million sales across Europe.[8] The contemporary and youthful feel was continued with a campaign for 'Twisted' Levis. In 2003 a UK TV campaign produced for Levis by TBWA/Chiat Day/San Francisco used a similar creative theme to 'Twisted'. The 'Flyweight Jeans' ad showed a Hispanic youth walking through a teeming urban scene with a quirky post-production twist to his gait.[9]

■ Case Questions

1 Ask four of your colleagues under 25 years old to list all the associations they can when they think of denim jeans. Now ask four people over 40 years of age to do the same thing. Are the responses different? If so, why do you think this is? Could it be that the two groups are interpreting denim jeans from differing cultural frames of reference?

2 Levis developed integrated campaigns for some of their products by creating websites that featured the characters in the ad. How can websites add value to marketing communications campaigns? Why does it matter for the brand that the website achieved a million hits in a few weeks? What other ways can you think of which might add value through the use of additional media?

3 What problems of cross-cultural promotional communication did the 1980s Levis' campaign solve and how did it do this? In a group, draw up an outline global campaign plan for a well-known brand of your choice. What particular difficulties arise when conceiving of a cross-cultural communication for this particular brand?

■ ■ Further Reading ■

Banister, L. (1997) 'Global brands, local contexts', *Admap*, October: 28–30.

De Mooij, M. (2005) *Global Marketing and Advertising: Understanding Cultural Paradoxes*. London: Sage.

De Pelsmacker, P., Geuens, M. and Van den Bergh, J. (2004) *Marketing Communications: A European Perspective*, 2nd edn. London: Financial Times/Prentice-Hall.

Forceville, C. (1996) *Pictorial Metaphor in Advertising*. London: Routledge.

Tanaka, K. (1994) *Advertising Language: A Pragmatic Approach to Advertisements in Britain and Japan*. London: Routledge.

Usunier, J.-C. (2009) *Marketing Across Cultures*. London: Financial Times/Prentice-Hall.

On the Companion Website

These journal articles are freely available on the companion website (www.sagepub.co.uk/hackley).

English and American Culture Appeal in Russian Advertising
Irina P. Ustinova
Journal of Creative Communications, Mar 2008; vol. 3: pp. 77–98.

Glocalization and English Mixing in Advertising in Taiwan: Its Discourse Domains, Linguistic Patterns, Cultural Constraints, Localized Creativity, and Socio-psychological Effects
Hsu Jia-Ling
Journal of Creative Communications, May 2008; vol. 3: pp. 155–83.

Advertising in the Global Age: Transnational Campaigns and Pan-European Television Channels
Jean K. Chalaby
Global Media and Communication, Aug 2008; vol. 4: pp. 139–156.

Notes

1   Source: www.mini35.co.uk/history
2   Case described in J. Motion, S. Leitch and R. Brodie (2003) 'Equity in co-branded identity – the case of Adidas and the All Blacks', *European Journal of Marketing*, 37(7/8): 1080–94.
3   T. Levitt (1983) 'The globalization of markets', *Harvard Business Review*, April/May: 92–107.
4   This case was featured in the IPA awards 1996.
5   Global adspend trends: Asian adspend, a review of its development and future prospects', *International Journal of Advertising* (1998) 17(2): 255–63.
6   Source: WARC newsletter, 10 May 2004, citing www.adge.com as it's source for figures. Original story in *Thunderbird Magazine*, Spring 2005: 'Brand America: how to restore its tarnished image in an angry word' www.thunderbird.edu/wwwfiles/pdf/about_thunderbird/publications/magazine/OS-spring.pdf (accessed 12 September 2009).
7   Source: WARC newsletter, 14 May 2004. Original story in *Brand Republic* www.brandrepublic.com
8   Source: presentation by Martin Smith, Deputy Chairman of BBH, to the Advertising and Academia marketing educator's form, IPA, Belgrave Square, London, September 1999.
9   Source: http://ad-rag.com/749.php

8 Advertising: Ethics and Regulation

Chapter Outline

Advertising and promotion, as we have seen, occupy a particular cultural space. Promotional messages perform an economic function but they are also part of the free flow of communication and ideas. As such, they can elicit great controversy and disagreement among different audiences. Advertisements can generate a sense of 'giving offence' on a scale and with an intensity that even the most controversial works of art, drama or literature would find hard to match. The chapter outlines some of the major issues of advertising ethics and regulation, and introduces some concepts of moral philosophy which can be of assistance in understanding the ethical dimensions of advertising.

Key chapter content:

- Advertising and marketing ethics

- Advertising's ideological role promoting consumption and corporatism

- Ethics and controversy over advertising

- International Advertising Regulation

- The UK codes of advertising practice

- Ethics and alcohol advertising in the UK

- Advertising to children

- Applied ethics and advertising regulation

- Ethics and contemporary advertising.

Advertising and Marketing Ethics

Ethics refers to what is right, good or consistent with virtue. The study of ethics is often concerned with abstract principles, and the study of morals is seen as an applied field that focuses on personal behaviour in specific situations. However, the terms are also linked and sometimes used interchangeably, as in 'applied ethics'. Marketing in general offers a variety of ethical issues for consideration, many of them mobilized through advertising (Hackley et al., 2008a). For example, is it right to advertise to children using the same techniques that are used when advertising to adults? Is it right to advertise toys which are not necessarily good for children's development? Should advertising be permitted to use imagery and words that shock, offend or insult particular groups? Should advertising intrude on such a large number of social spaces such as roadside billboards, posters and even in-school advertising? Indeed, is advertising intrinsically a medium of exaggeration, mendaciousness and illusion? Should it be permitted at all?

Advertising communications commit many acts of dubious ethics in their attempts to seduce us into buying. Some are listed here.

- Overselling
- Exploitation of vulnerable groups
- Deception
- Misuse of lists
- Intruding on privacy
- Promoting racial or sexual stereotypes
- Promoting prejudice against certain vulnerable groups
- Promoting socially or personally harmful values or behaviours
- Offending public taste
- Vulgarity
- Exploiting base motives of greed and envy.

Ethical issues in product or service marketing can be relatively clear-cut in the sense that if, say, a car explodes when shunted from the rear because of a rear-mounted petrol tank, this is clearly a dangerous manufacturing practice. If a product or service is injurious to health such as cigarettes or alcohol, again this is subject to public view and can be handled accordingly. We can probably all agree that things which might harm anyone's health are generally bad. The problem with advertising, as we can see straightaway, is that ethical judgments in general are predicated on certain values and interests that are not universally agreed upon. People cannot agree on matters of secular civil governance that are, on the face of it, quite concrete and substantial, like the right penalties for particular crimes or the right way to fund education. How much more difficult is it to agree on the ethical status of an advertisement, especially since all too often, as we saw in Chapter 2, it is far from easy to agree on exactly what the ad means?

Advertising's Publics

For some people, business is business and one should always be sceptical, even cynical, in assessing commercial claims. *Caveat emptor*, or 'buyer beware' is a maxim which could apply here. Another way of putting this is to say don't be a sucker or you deserve to be ripped off. Advertising is just trying to sell us stuff so perhaps we should not be surprised if it sometimes crosses boundaries of hyperbole applied to other forms of public communication. But just because someone wants to sell you something can they be excused from any ethical standards? Is making money more important than other values? It is all very well to say that buyers in a marketplace have a responsibility to look out for themselves, but should they not also be protected from unscrupulous or mendacious sellers? Furthermore, advertising is a profoundly symbolic communication form which is often very hard to define in black-and-white terms of truth or lies, right or wrong. It serves many disparate interests: consumers, manufacturers, media owners, government agencies, charities, the economy as a whole, employers, employees, and so on and so forth. Consequently, deciding whether an ad is ethically acceptable by agreed standards, or unacceptable, can be a complex matter because of the different interests advertising must serve. Finally, are all these groups equally able to look out for themselves when it comes to assessing advertising claims? What about children, the elderly, the less educated, the poor? Should not vulnerable groups have some degree of protection from the wiles of advertising?

BOX 8.0

Interpreting the Meaning of Offensive Ads

Advertising regulation tends to hinge on debates about the meaning of ads, which often assumes that they carry distinct meanings, as with legal or scientific material. As we have seen, much advertising carries both ostensive and covert communication which, in combination, leave the precise intended meaning of the ad open to interpretation. Cook (2001) uses the example of a British TV ad for a Cadbury's Flake chocolate bar to illustrate that ads, like any discourse, have connotations that are subtle and personal. The classic Flake campaign was open to a Freudian interpretation.[1] Some UK viewers find the Cadbury's Flake ad an amusing and sexually risqué visual metaphor. However, drawing attention to this feature of the ad risks

(Cont'd)

the response that such an interpretation says more about the viewer than it does about the ad. As Cook (2001: 51) states: 'This kind of dispute, with its assumption that meaning resides in the text quite independently of group or individual perceptions, is depressingly common in discussions of advertising'. Of course, the fact that certain individuals, perhaps even large numbers of individuals, might read such a connotation into the ad may well be a stratagem of the advertiser. Such indeterminacy makes ads a more intriguing and more compelling communication. Ads are frequently accused of using sexual suggestiveness and symbolism; they are able to do this without risk of official censure by locating a sexual connotation within the covert dimension of the ad, where its presence cannot be proven nor agreed upon.

The publics which advertising serves are many and include legislators, consumers, citizens, parents, children, politicians, business and industry, media organizations, and public health bodies. Some of these have an interest in advertising from the point of view of the way it portrays particular groups or popularizes particular consumption practices. Advertising has a cultural role in that it can illustrate the social norms and conventional values of its time. Advertising, in the broadest sense, is a historical document detailing changing tastes, fashions, norms and attitudes. It reflects current standards of public taste and decency and modes of public discourse. By implication, from an ethical perspective, we get the advertising we (as in the silent majority) want and deserve. Of course, the 'we' in question are a heterogeneous group with the sharply differing views and values of the communities in which they live. Controversies about advertising, then, can serve a social function as a public forum for revealing fundamental differences between social groups.

Less abstract issues are also inflected by advertising, such as public health and alcohol, obesity, or lung disease and cigarette advertising, not to mention issues around guns, drugs or environmentally damaging products. All can elicit protests from lobby groups promoting a particular cause.

Advertising's Economic Role

All these potentially problematic issues cannot obscure that fact that advertising exists for a very important reason. It creates wealth, for individuals, for companies and for economies. The regulations surrounding advertising must take account not only of ethical issues but also of the economic functions advertising fulfils. Advertising performs the indispensable economic function for capitalist economies of communicating offers to consumers. Through advertising producers are able to:

- Expand their markets and thereby take advantage of economies of scale to reduce unit production costs
- Sell the large stocks they produce and stimulate demand for new offers
- Make consumers aware of far more choices than they would be without it
- Increase the total market size and reduce unit costs by communicating offers and stimulating competition.

In terms of whole economies, there is a strong correlation between advertising expenditure growth and growth in gross domestic product (GDP). Growth in advertising expenditure reflects general economic confidence and feeds through to increased demand. So, advertising is indispensible to economic growth, wealth and job creation. Without it, competition would be blunted since consumers would not be aware of the rival offers and product features available. Manufacturers could not communicate offers and local monopolies would thrive. Companies would have no incentive to be more efficient or to improve their offer. Advertising is the price we pay for wealth creation. For some people, poverty is the greatest evil and if advertising can help reduce it by creating demand, jobs and income then it should not be subject to regulation at all. But for others, advertising is too important not to be regulated since uncontrolled advertising could not only discriminate against minorities and offend public decency, it could also undermine public trust in marketing by making exaggerated or untrue claims. The expression 'public trust in marketing' might have brought a smile to some readers' lips but the role of trust in economic growth should not be underestimated. At a basic level, we need to believe that if we pay for something, we will receive the product we saw in the advertisement. It helps too if we can feel pretty confident that the things an advertisement says about a product or service are substantially true. Trust, in this sense, is a fundamental requirement of commercial communication.

Advertising's Ideological Role Promoting Consumption and Corporatism

In order to understand our reactions to advertising it is important to appreciate that it has always been a contested area. Even 400 years ago there was public concern at advertising's presence as a form of 'social pollution' (Hackley and Kitchen, 1999) in London streets (McFall, 2004). Even in the USA, advertising was not always welcomed with enthusiasm. In particular, early advertising was associated with the large corporations. The activities of these corporations were met with great suspicion, and even open hostility, in the USA at the turn of the century. These corporations needed some help to create the public acceptance of mass marketing and mass retailing that they required: it was to advertising agencies that they turned for that help.

The historian Roland Marchand (1985, 1998) has described how the rise of big business in the USA was facilitated by advertising and communication. At the turn of the twentieth century, there were many mergers and acquisitions in US business. As a result there were fewer, bigger corporations. Many Americans regretted the demise of the local high-street store and the rise of vast, 'soulless' corporations. As corporations grew, many feared that they posed a threat to American values and institutions such as the church, the family and the local community. Serious questions were asked at a presidential level about the activities of these leviathans and their influence over American cultural life. The entrepreneurs who created great corporations such as AT&T, GM, GE, Ford Motors and US Steel were acutely aware of the need to legitimize their activities and manufacture a 'soul' for the new corporatism. Over the following decades a profound transformation took place in the public image of corporations. From being perceived as potential threats to American values, they became the very epitome of those values and a legitimate part of American life.

Marchand (1998: 2) points out that this new legitimacy flew in the face of classical economic theory which held that the nature of competitive businesses is that they cannot rise above self-interest or the dictates of the market. As these companies attained extraordinary size and power it became clear that they were no mere slaves to market forces but exercised considerable monopolistic power. Not only did they have to persuade the public of their right to play a part in American life, they also had to create an identity in order to anthropomorphize and therefore soften their soulless image. The corporations addressed this pressing problem partly through welfare capitalism and patriarchal initiatives to improve the workforce through education and training. They also used grand (and grandiose) architecture to impress their status and power on the skyline, such as the gothic spectacle of the Woolworth building in New York City and the massive factories of manufacturers such as the Jell-O company and Pillsbury's.

Corporate advertising and public relations also played a significant part in creating a soul for corporate America. Their advertising agencies produced a stream of imagery and copy on postcards, posters, in magazines and press editorial and, later, on radio portraying the corporations in terms of such values as integrity, service to the community, localism, tradition and moral uprightness. This corporate advertising also served a more pragmatic purpose in helping to produce an internal sense of corporate identity (and a sense of collective purpose) for thousands of employees.

In legitimizing capitalist corporatism and selling consumption to citizens as a lifestyle, advertising was central to the development of the marketing ideal of consumer orientation. Consumers were taught, through advertising, that manufactured products reflected their discernment and met their requirements. Through responses (or non-responses) to advertising, consumers could play a part in the market mechanism and cast a vote in favour of their own personal consumer vision. Consumers' collective sense of self-interest is fired by the drama of consumption played out in advertising. Clearly, in affluent economies most categories of consumer need are not fundamental and absolute but derivative and relative. Consumer goods are not created by advertising, but the social status of the attributes of goods is (Leiss et al., 1997: 299). Advertising teaches us that the social status of brand attributes is scarce and carries a premium cost.

In this important historical sense, advertising has been central to the development of the idea of consumer marketing. The consumer orientation preached by marketing management textbooks can be seen as a continuation of the ideology of the early American corporations. In spite of the practical limits to consumer orientation in large manufacturing organizations, marketing texts nevertheless deploy the rhetoric of consumer orientation to promote a sense of connection between the little consumer and the big corporation. The rhetorical force and apparent popularity of marketing rhetoric (satisfying consumer needs, being customer-focused) might reflect a continuing need for capitalist corporatism to claim legitimacy (Hackley, 2003g) amid a contemporary crisis of confidence in the activities and motives of global business corporations. Advertising's success in setting the preconditions for a consumer society has been striking even while organized resistance to global capitalism is evident in the form of sporadic but numerous consumer protests and boycotts (see, for example, Klein, 2000).

Advertising's Collective Effect

On a wider scale, it can be argued that advertising and other forms of promotional communication collectively create the cultural preconditions that lead to consumers' acceptance of marketing and the consumer society (Wernick, 1991). Of course, marketing communications managers and brand managers are interested only in the efficacy of advertising for their particular brands. However, in order to fully understand advertising's specific effects it is necessary to also appreciate its collective influence. It is a form of communication which consumers have to learn. There is a level of cultural understanding that is a precondition for interpreting ads (Scott, 1994a, cited in Hackley, 2002). Once we are acculturated to reading advertising texts, experiencing new forms of advertising modifies our understanding of subsequent ads. Advertising and promotion within promotional culture constitute a self-generating system of signs that frames our experience as consumers and places our sense of social identity and economic relations within a consumption-based sign system. By being exposed to different kinds of advertising text over time, consumers are educated to understand advertising in all its complexity and variety, which masks the fact that at one level all advertising promotes the same thing – consumption.

Taking one further aspect of advertising's collective influence, there is a sense in which advertisers who fund a successful high-profile campaign can be said to be subsidizing their competitors. A creatively striking TV ad for, say, the Ford convertible Street Ka may do much for the brand. However, it cannot help but glamorize driving and car ownership in general. Ads for branded goods and services always carry the sub-text that consumption as an end in itself is exciting, fun and important. Furthermore, if one TV ad in 10 is creatively striking, it will act as an incentive to viewers to sit and watch the other nine less interesting ads just in case a good one follows. In a sense, perhaps the great ads create space in consumers' minds for the majority of less inspired ones.

Ethics and Controversy over Advertising

The subjectivity of ethical judgments means that questions of ethics in advertising are clouded in a fog of contrasting opinions, which are often held very strongly indeed. Particular ads or campaigns occasionally become topics of controversy, that is, they attract widely diverging opinions that are expressed in public forums such as newspapers' letter pages, editorials, TV documentaries and even in political debates. Of course, not all controversy over advertising is based on questions of ethics. But many disagreements emerge from differing ethical standpoints. Promotional campaigns for brands such as Benetton, Calvin Klein, French Connection UK, 'Opium' fragrance and even for charities such as Dr Barnardo's in the UK have generated much editorial coverage in the media because of the numbers of people who felt that they ought not to have been allowed. Often, the media stories are given their narrative hook by strongly held opinions about whether an ad or campaign should or should not be permitted. In many cases, the brands are grateful for this coverage since, even though it is critical, it publicizes the brand to a far greater extent than the advertisement alone could have done.

BOX 8.1

'Opium' Fragrance

Many complaints are received from the public or from special interest groups on the grounds that specific ads are more sexualized than (some people feel is) appropriate and therefore give offence. In 2001 an ad for Yves Saint Laurent 'Opium' fragrance that featured the model Sophie Dahl apparently naked attracted around 1,000 complaints to the UK print advertising regulatory authority the Advertising Standards Authority (ASA), considerably more complaints than any other ad that year.[2] In comparison, the most contentious print ad of 2002 attracted some 315 representations to the ASA. Many of the complaints about the 'Opium' ad were from young women. The ad had attracted little attention when it was displayed in the pages of fashion magazines where portrayals of sexuality are the norm. The complaints poured in when the ad was made into a poster and displayed on street billboards. As we have seen in other examples, one important factor in interpreting the meaning of ads is the context in which they appear. The 'Opium' ad was regarded as normal in the context of a fashion magazine but inappropriately sexual on a billboard. Billboards are viewed by a far wider social group. The complaints were upheld and the ad returned to its magazine setting. The public reaction to the 'Opium' ad seems curious given that advertising has become far more sexualized in the last decade. It is now commonplace to see forthright sexual encounters posed by beautifully photographed models on TV, billboards and of course in magazines. Often these are for brands of fragrance or clothing (and even ice-cream, as in the case of Häagen-Dazs).

Controversy as a Public Relations Tool

In some cases, controversy over advertising is nothing more than a marketing technique which leverages extended public relations coverage by generating media chatter. Brand owners with a youthful and edgy positioning for their brand know that if they can succeed in antagonizing groups other than their own target market there are likely to be useful side-effects, such as free editorial publicity and a stronger brand identity. The letters pages of national newspapers and weblogs can act as forums for strongly held feelings about advertising campaigns which are perceived as being offensive, dishonest or irresponsible. If there seems to be a rising tide of popular opinion, editorial comment starts to appear in the form of feature articles and opinion pieces in the press and on 'magazine' TV shows. Pretty soon, the brand is all over the media, earning sales and a brand presence because of all the free publicity.

For example, sales of Calvin Klein clothing ranges reportedly rose considerably even as child protection groups in the USA and elsewhere were campaigning against the use of apparently very young models in (arguably) sexualized poses in CK ads. In another example, the Benetton brand of clothing (see chapter case) became the second most-recognized brand in the world for a time because its advertising campaigns generated huge amounts of public and official protest. In this case, the ethical sensibilities of citizens were, it seems, being exploited for commercial advantage. As a principle, it seems that if the brand personality has a rebellious and anti-establishment aspect, then creating promotions that irritate social authorities is an astute way of endearing the brand to its young target audience.

It should also be remembered that controversy over advertising can sometimes be used as a platform to gain publicity for other interests. Advertising is a soft and highly visible target for all manner of complaints and if lobby groups can generate publicity for their cause by complaining about a particular advertisement, they often will.

To some extent, the considerable media coverage of advertising in the form of magazine articles and talk on chat shows, dedicated websites and compilation TV shows, reflects advertising's status as a part of the media complex. It is unsurprising that advertising is often used in the editorial content of the popular press and TV shows, given the symbiotic relationship between advertising and other media such as the press, movies and TV entertainment. Substantial sections of the media are funded entirely by advertising revenue. The interests of media vehicles such as TV shows, newspapers or magazines are economically locked into those of brand marketing corporations and other sponsors of advertising. In developing countries, advertising is part of the effort to generate increased economic growth. It is therefore bound up with the interests of state officials and governing political parties.

Interest in advertising is not new. There are, for example, letters to London magazines expressing disquiet over advertising dating back over 200 years (McFall, 2004). Controversy over the quantity of advertising, over its styles of representation and over the ways in which it seems to wield its influence has not been confined to the post war era. Advertising has, though, grown in volume and now reaches us on many new media technologies. With so many ads competing for our attention, advertisers push the boundaries of content and try more striking kinds of appeal in an effort to get consumers' attention. As noted in Chapter 1, public interest in advertising has also grown in a positive sense. It fascinates people. It often seems as if TV ads are more entertaining than the actual TV shows. But advertising's high profile also makes it an easy target of blame for all manner of social evils. Advertising has evolved into this high-profile hybrid of the entertainment, media and publicity industries because of its economic importance.

BOX 8.2

Iggy Pop and Insurance Ads

Iconic 1960's rock star Iggy Pop was enlisted by an insurance company to feature in television and press ads. Pop brought his unique performing style to the ads, and his credibility as an artist who never sold out his artistic integrity for commercial gain. Some fans felt that Pop's appearance in the ads undermined his unconventional image, but the ads nevertheless were met with a positive reception until it emerged that not only was Pop not insured by the company, they had a policy of never insuring drivers who worked in the entertainment industry,[3] and this policy was stated on their company website. The UK regulator the ASA subsequently banned the ads because in the script Pop said that he was insured with the company. Generally, people do not expect celebrity endorsers to necessarily use the products they endorse, and the company stated that he had been employed as an actor for the ads. But the news that Pop's profession was considered too risky to insure deeply undermined the campaign. It was later reported that, in an attempt to minimize the damage, the company stated that it would change its policy of denying insurance cover to musicians.[4]

Advertising Controversial Products

Some controversies over advertising relate to the nature of the product rather than just to the advertising. Advertising for alcohol, drugs, guns and cigarettes all tends to attract close critical scrutiny because of the intrinsically difficult ethical problems surrounding the marketing of those products. In the UK, for example, direct-to-consumer (DTC) advertising of pharmaceutical drugs is not allowed at all, though in the USA and many other countries it is common. Advertising for cigarettes has been banned in the UK for some years as evidence of the damage of cigarette smoking to health mounted, but it is allowed in many other countries. The World Health Organization (WHO) has called for a worldwide ban on all cigarette advertising.[5] It argues that where partial bans have been instituted in many countries, the benefits in terms of lower smoking rates and reduced lung cancers and other diseases are significant. The problem for health authorities is that cigarette companies simply shift resources to different media when necessary. So, for example, when cigarette advertising was banned in the UK, cigarette manufacturers shifted resources to sports sponsorship and out of home advertising.[6] On the other side of the debate, pro-smoking campaigners argue that tobacco companies are promoting a legal pursuit which mature individuals have the right to indulge in without interference from the state. The tobacco industry generates large revenues for shareholders and large tax revenues for governments, while also sustaining many jobs. In one region of China, the economic downturn has apparently encouraged an unusual campaign promoting local industry. According to Western media reports[7] the Gong'an regional government in Hubei province has given state employees targets to smoke more cigarettes in order to support local brands and generate tax revenues.[8] China has high rates of cigarette smoking and central government has been trying to discourage take-up of the habit among doctors in order to set a better example. The conflict between public health issues and economic imperatives is strikingly illustrated in the matter of cigarette marketing and advertising.

International Advertising Regulation

It is to be expected that attitudes towards advertising vary in different countries, reflecting differing public standards of propriety and levels of tolerance. Consequently, approaches to advertising regulation differ widely. In some countries there are systems of industry regulation which overlap with legal constraints. In others, advertising is part of a censored broadcasting communication system which is directly overseen by state agencies which have to approve every promotional communication. In many countries there are widely differing standards applied to advertising as regards, for example, the veracity and level of proof required for product claims, the timings and placing of advertising on broadcast and print media, and the portrayals of consumption and language used in advertising content.

The following list outlines some issues of advertising regulation in different countries:

- In France TV advertising for movies, alcohol, tobacco and medicines is not permitted. The ban on advertising books and newspapers has recently been changed to allow limited advertising.[8]
- In France there are restrictions on the advertising of mobile phones to children.
- In Eastern Europe, alcohol advertising is heavily restricted.
- In Sweden, TV advertising for toys cannot be directed at children under 12.
- In the UK, tobacco advertising is banned.
- In Argentina, all advertising was banned on subscription cable-TV channels in January 2004.[10]
- In Austria and Finland, the use of children in ads is heavily restricted. Italy also banned the use of children in advertising in 2003.
- In many predominantly Muslim nations, women in advertising must be fully clothed and wearing headscarves, and the advertising of non-halal food products is not allowed.
- In Hungary, it is prohibited 'to use erotic and sexual elements in advertising for purposes not justified by the object and substance of advertising' and no advertisement 'may be such as to reduce the reputation of the advertising profession or undermine public confidence in the advertising activity'.[11]
- In the UK, alcohol advertisements cannot use actors who appear to be under the age of 18 and they cannot show people drinking quickly; they must sip their drinks.
- In Greece, TV advertising of toys to children is banned between 7 pm and 10 pm.

Regulations such as these do tend to change as different lobbies win attention for a particular cause, or as conditions change. Some of the above regulations may no longer be in force, but new ones may have been substituted. Other issues are governed not by regulation but by conventional practice. For example, UK television advertising tends to be quite conservative as regards nudity or sexual references when compared to advertising in some other European countries such as Sweden, Denmark, France and Germany, but it is quite liberal in this respect when compared to advertising on American television. It is enough for many issues simply to apply a general rule of thumb. For example, the UK Advertising Standards Authority (ASA), an independent, industry-funded body responsible to the government communications regulator Ofcom, applies a rule that advertising must be 'Legal, Decent, Honest and Truthful'.

The UK Codes of Advertising Practice

It is rare for advertising in the UK to fall foul of the law since this is well known and most agencies and advertising media have legal advisers to check ads before publication. There is, though, another level of regulation that governs advertising. Advertising agencies and the sellers of advertising space agree to be bound by the rulings of the Advertising Standards Authority (ASA), even though there is no legal requirement for them to do so. The ASA is part of Ofcom, the UK media regulator. The ASA applies the codes of advertising practice that are created by the Broadcast Committee of Advertising Practice (BCAP). Its remit covers press and print advertising, email and SMS text message advertising, broadcast advertising and also internet advertising where this originates from an identifiable UK-based source. The ASA rulings may not have the force of law but they do offer a quicker, more flexible and more efficient regulatory system than the law could provide.

BOX 8.3

Advertising Law and Industry Regulation

Each country has its own regulatory codes for ads. In some countries government ministers will sometimes rule directly on whether particular advertisements should be banned or not. In the UK, advertising is covered by law to some extent, just as all commercial transactions must conform to Acts of Parliament such as the Trades Descriptions and Sales of Goods Acts. So, advertisements must not falsely describe the goods that are for sale, and the goods or services advertised must do what is claimed for them. In addition, specific categories of advertising must conform to the relevant laws. For example, recruitment advertising in the UK must not contravene the Equal Opportunities or Sex Discrimination Acts otherwise they may be subject to legal action on grounds of unfair recruitment as regards sex, race or disability.

(Cont'd)

Other laws have an indirect effect on advertising because they rule on matters such as product safety. Advertising must be careful about claims regarding the efficacy of products or services, offers of prizes or guarantees. Advertisements cannot make factual claims which they are unable to prove. For example, one famous pet food ad strapline claims that '8 out of 10 cats prefer Whiskas'. If the manufacturer is to continue using that line they must be prepared to set up an experiment which representatives from the ASA can watch to verify the claim. Another famous strapline used for many years by British Airways claimed that the UK carrier was 'The World's Favourite Airline'. This was mere hyperbole and the ASA finally ordered the ads to stop making this claim. The legal requirements for advertisements represent one tier of regulation in the UK – the ASA and BCAP codes of practice represent another. It is relatively rare for ads to contravene the legal rules because these are well known.

Advertising regulatory bodies have general rules that they will try to apply in specific cases through codes of practice for particular circumstances. As noted above, the UK's, ASA publicizes its ruling maxim as being to ensure that all (printed) ads are 'Legal, Decent, Honest and Truthful'. The Hungarian code of advertising ethics uses the principles 'Lawful, fair and true'. The ways in which such principles are applied differ in various regulatory systems. In the UK, for example, TV ads are viewed by the Broadcast Advertising Clearance Centre (BACC) before their campaign launch to ensure that they conform to the BCAP guidelines. The BACC can tell an agency to make substantial (and costly) changes to an ad if it deems these necessary to ensure that the BCAP code of practice is satisfied. There is no pre-vetting procedure for poster or print ads and in the opinion of some commentators this is the reason why some occasionally seem to be more cavalier about offending the public than TV ads. The ASA sometimes require advertisers who have complaints upheld to have future ads vetted before exposure. FCUK poster ads, for example, were required to do so after some serious transgressions of ASA rulings.

BOX 8.4

The ASA Cracks Down on Loan Advertisements[11]

Television advertisements for loans became familiar to UK viewers since the de-regulation of financial services in the 1980s. The loan business was worth some £95 billion per year and these advertisements often portrayed people as seeming happy and carefree, presumably because they had taken out a large loan which 'combines all existing debts into one easy monthly payment' in the words of a typical advertisement. What the advertisements did not say was that many of these loans were secured on the house of the person taking out the loan, so if they defaulted on the loan they lost their home. While house values were rising this didn't matter but as the economic downturn hit home in 2009, the UK Advertising Standards Authority decided that it was time to regulate loan advertisements more strictly. Lord Chris Smith, the Chairman of the ASA, announced that the ASA would henceforth invoke a social responsibility clause to regulate loan advertisements which would ban many of the current advertisements. Complaints to the ASA have been rising with a record number of over 24,000 in 2007. The complaints were levelled at a record number of advertisements, more than 14,000.[12] The ASA investigates every complaint to see if its guidelines have been adhered to but the great majority of complaints do not result in a ban. None of the top 10 most complained-about ads in 2008/09 was banned.[13]

Public Complaints about Advertising

The UK's regulatory bodies are useful to the advertising industry since they act as a mechanism for gauging the limits of public tolerance towards advertising content. If members of the public object to an ad for any reason they can make a complaint to the ASA. Their complaint will then be investigated by a panel who will judge it according to their interpretation of the codes of practice. If the complaint is upheld, the regulatory body may tell the agency concerned to take the ad out of circulation and in some cases may censure the agency or the brand commissioning the advertising. The system is reactive because regulatory agencies merely respond to public complaints (and, as noted above, posters are not normally even reviewed before public exposure). All the judgements of the ASA are published on their website.[14]

BOX 8.5

Cultural Attitudes to Vulgar Language in Advertising

A long-running campaign for French Connection UK by London agency TBWA became notorious for flouting ASA rulings in the UK. In Singapore, FCUK posters on public buses were greeted with outrage and the strength of public opinion forced the bus company to demand changes.[15] In the UK, in contrast, the use of language once considered unacceptable is now common on television. This has perhaps softened attitudes and made this kind of campaign possible. FCUK saw its profits rise by 84 per cent in the first half of 2000, the year it launched

(Cont'd)

its campaign in the UK. Thanks to advertising designed by TBWA's Trevor Beattie, French Connection's advertisers are acutely aware of the power of the acronym to get attention. A High Court judge in the UK commented that the campaign was 'obnoxious and offensive'.[15] The French Connection legal representative is quoted as replying that while she and His Lordship might find it offensive, young people who buy French Connection clothing 'find it amusing'.[17] The key point from a brand marketing point of view is that the use of the logo enables the brand to appear cool and anti-establishment in the eyes of some of the young people who are the targeted market segment for FCUK clothes. The more the logo irritates authorities such as High Court judges, the cooler it appears to its own consumers.

A complaint to the ASA about an email campaign for FCUK was upheld on the grounds that it 'might cause serious or widespread offence'. FCUK responded with a poster which declaimed 'FCUK the Advertising Standards Authority'.[18] The ASA upheld a complaint about this poster.

The FCUK campaigns may have seemed like a piece of wit to the agency and its target market, and it certainly was in tune with the trend in UK media for more liberal attitudes to swearing. To critics, though, it reflected the weaknesses of a self-regulatory system which can only advise and cannot compel compliance. The FCUK campaign was successful for a time, but also incurred the acute disapproval of many in the advertising business. FCUK sales fell away sharply in mid-2005 and the brand has since toned down its outrageous advertising.

The advertising industry was once concerned to promote and legitimize mass consumption by representing brand marketing corporations in a paternalistic and socially responsible light. Today, corporate social responsibility (CSR) is a major field of consulting, academic and policy research, but some advertisers seem keen to represent brand corporations as a subversive social influence. This, perhaps, illustrates the wider acceptance of advertising, as well as differing cultural attitudes to controversial language in the UK and elsewhere.

Reading ASA judgements offers a useful insight into how the voluntary regulatory system works. The complaints also reflect current public tastes and trends. What was acceptable in advertising in 1950 or 1960 may not be considered acceptable today, and of course, the reverse would also be said to be true – much advertising today would seem excessively vulgar or sexualized to a 1960s' audience. Alcohol advertising is a particularly powerful indicator of changing social roles, especially with regard to gender relations. Ads that are taken for granted today might well have provoked heated complaints 10 or 20 years ago, and many ads from earlier times now provoke amusement or astonishment in modern viewers.

Ethics and Alcohol Advertising in the UK

In many countries, alcohol advertising is a source of ethical sensitivity. In Muslim countries it is forbidden, as is alcohol consumption, while in many other countries there are limits placed on the type and extent of alcohol promotion. Alcohol advertising has become an area of considerable controversy in the UK because of possible links with increases in alcohol-related diseases such as cirrhosis of the liver, especially in young British females. The World Health Organization made alcohol advertising control a key priority in its anti-alcohol campaigns (WHO, 1988, in Nelson and Young, 2001). The sexualization of alcohol advertising and its role in constructions of gender have been linked with increased alcohol consumption among young people and the promotion of a binge drinking mentality[19] (Szmigin et al., 2008). The website of the ASA (www.asa.org.uk) carries many case reports of complaints made against advertisements of this type. The British Medical Association (BMA) has repeatedly called for an outright ban on alcohol advertising.

As cigarette advertising since the 1950s has changed the historical view of femininity and promoted cigarette smoking as a normal social practice of the liberated and independent woman (Williamson, 1978), alcohol advertising is seen to be playing a similar role in locating alcohol brands as discursive resources for the construction of female (and male) social identity (Griffin et al., 2009; Lemle and Mishkind, 1989; Young, 1995). Young people are often thought to be particularly vulnerable to this form of marketing (Calfee and Scherage, 1994), which associates drinking with social and sexual success.

The extent of official disapproval reached such a pitch that the ASA and BCAP were forced to re-write the code of practice on alcohol advertising[20] to try to ensure that it did not link alcohol with social or sexual success or overtly promoted drinking to young people. TV campaigns such as those for rum, vodka and other drinks have attracted complaints that their scenes of wild partying so glamorize alcohol consumption that they may implicitly promote high-risk sexual behaviour in both sexes. The ASA responded to the increased sensitivity around alcohol advertising by banning a number of ads and insisting that the codes of practice were to be strictly adhered to. The alcohol industry has representation on the ASA committee and lobbies in favour of the industry, arguing that it promotes responsible drinking and constitutes an important economic sector. Nevertheless, there is much evidence that regularly drinking in order to get drunk has become a normal activity for many young people in the UK, and it is also true that marketing activity around drinking has multiplied in the last two decades in terms of the number of branded drinks offered and also in terms of the amount spent on promotion by the alcohol industry (Griffin et al., 2009; Measham, 2004a, b; 2006).

BOX 8.6

Promotion and Patterns of Alcohol Consumption in the UK

Although very high levels of alcohol consumption per head are not characteristic of the UK, according to recent measures, patterns of alcohol consumption in the UK are unusual. There is, apparently, a culture of drinking alcohol at a young age as a rite of passage and of drinking very large quantities in each session, both dangerous to health. Alcohol brand marketing techniques, especially advertising, that target segmented consumer groups differentiated by age, ethnicity, affluence and attitude to risk-taking have raised particular disquiet. Alcohol-related groups (for example Alcohol Concern)[21] have expressed concern over the role of advertising in these trends. Advertising researchers (Ambler, 1996) have tried to ascertain the influence of advertising in excess alcohol consumption, but results have been unclear. What is beyond doubt is that the quantity of branded alcohol drinks and the volume of promotional activity surrounding them have increased significantly over the past 10 years (Szmigin et al., 2008). This has coincided with rapid rises in alcohol-related ill-health, hospital admissions and social problems, especially among younger age groups (Hackley et al., 2008b).

Gender and Alcohol

The representation of gender in UK alcohol TV advertising has turned full circle over the last 30 years. In the 1980s ads for Hofmeister lager featured a man in a bear suit who was the centre of an admiring crowd of young men and women. The ads featuring the lager drinker as a cool, streetwise and charismatic male character allowed females only to be the grateful objects of male lust. These ads, created by legendary advertising man John Webster (see Box 8.7) replaced those that portrayed females only as domestic drudges. In later campaigns for Archer's, Lambrini and other alcoholic drinks targeted at females it is female drinkers who are portrayed as independent, quick-witted and rebellious. The men portrayed are mere accessories. Such advertising would have been unthinkable in 1960s' Britain. One might argue that these ads represent a step forward in gender representation, placing women on an equal footing with men, at least when it comes to drinking. Others would take a different view.

BOX 8.7

Trends in UK Alcohol Advertising

The agency DDB London held the Courage beers account for some 25 years. When the account moved elsewhere the agency produced a compilation video which is a revealing document of social history. The tape runs from the 1970s ads with elderly Northern English men enacting scenes of conspiratorial male congeniality in ads for John Smith's Yorkshire Bitter. In these ads stereotypes abound, with men portrayed as children whose main aim in life is to escape the 'nagging' wife. In the 1980s the trend turns to light beers drunk by younger 'Jack the lad' heroes in watershed advertising moments such as John Webster's Hofmeister bear ads. Webster created many iconic campaigns of that time and was particularly fond of dressing actors up in bear suits – he also created the Sugar Puffs Honey Monster character. Subsequent campaigns for Foster's and Castlemaine XXXX, which ended with surreal scenes of *Mad Max* post-nuclear destruction, self-deprecation and ironic humour, continued the youth-oriented thrust through the 1990s and beyond. The young drinkers who are displaying strikingly increased rates of liver and other alcohol-related disease today are the first generation who were toddlers when alcohol advertising on TV started to use imagery previously only seen in pre-school TV.

The UK's Hofmeister beer ads were a turning-point in alcohol advertising not only because they contributed to a major shift in UK beer drinking habits from dark to light beer. They also used imagery attractive to children to advertise adult products. The bear in the ads was a character that children enjoyed and understood. Previously, a man dressed in a hairy bear suit would only have been seen at a children's entertainment aimed at pre-schools. The ads took a cultural sign that denoted kids' entertainment and placed it in an adult context in connection with an adult pastime, beer consumption. While the product was not targeted at children, the advertising had become very attractive and memorable to them.

Advertising and Children

The ASA code of practice today forbids alcohol ads that use imagery attractive to children, but much alcohol advertising seems to be designed to do exactly that. The use of imagery in adult advertising that a short time ago one would only associate with children's shows has become commonplace. Many ads on UK TV use animated cartoon characters but are ostensibly directed at adults to sell, for example, branded chocolate, tea and gas central heating.

This trend towards infantilism in advertising reflects the relentless pursuit of novelty in the industry but also springs from an increasing awareness by brand marketers that children are very important to the advertisers of adult products. Children enjoy advertising, they remember it and they discuss it. The attention of a child brings a brand into the household and it then becomes a brand that is considered in household buying decisions. Innocent viewing of children's TV shows, such as *Recess* on the Cartoon Network cable station, is frequently interrupted by ads for personal loans even though one has to be over 18 and in employment to qualify for such loans in the UK. Not only do children influence the household budget, they learn about and become conscious of brands at a very early age. Market researchers showing logos for adult brands to kindergarten children find very high rates of recognition for these as well as children's brands.

In recent years there has been rising concern about the influence of advertising over children worldwide. Entering the words 'advertising to children' on the *Google* internet search engine produced 4,760,000 results when the first edition of this book was written in 2005. Today, in June 2009, it returned 107 million. The debate is intense and hinges on several factors . These include the age at which children become aware of the commercial motives of advertising, the duty of care society and in particular television ought to exercise over children's moral development, and the form this care should take. Is it more responsible to protect children from advertising, or to encourage them to engage with it so they become more aware consumers? The UK's ASA has its own code of practice on advertising to children.[22]

Arguably, many children under 10 are often unaware that when they are watching TV advertising what they are watching is in fact an offer to buy. They have not yet grasped the nuances of commerce-tinged communication. They are, therefore, defenceless against the sophisticated techniques of persuasion used by advertisers. Some advertising industry lobbyists claim that in fact children are very commercially aware and are capable of critically evaluating advertising.[23] But the concern about certain topics, for example the rise in child-onset obesity in the UK, has caused the government to be involved. In general, there has been a tide of opinion turning against food and beverage advertising that promotes high-sugar, high-fat, high-calorie and low-protein products in ways that are attractive to children.

One general area of ethical concern is the tendency of ads to promote acquisition as a virtue. Adults are in a position to understand that other values are more important to health, happiness and relationships, but children view advertising from a much less well-developed frame of moral reference. In the absence of moderating influences on their development, advertising shows children a world in which you are what you own, and if what you own is not a desirable brand, you are not worth very much at all. At least, that is one possible construction that can be placed on much children's advertising.

As noted above, there is a total ban on TV advertising directed at children under 12 years old in Sweden, and there are strict limits on TV advertising of toys in Greece. Young children make demands on parents if they want a product that they see advertised. These demands are not necessarily well informed by an understanding either of the nature of commercial messages or of the economic implications for parents.

An opposing point of view to the Swedish one is that early exposure to advertising enables children to develop a critical commercial awareness. However, this view presupposes that the social context children occupy when engaging with commerce is supported by adult attention and counsel. Where this context is lacking, for example when children engage in consumer activities such as watching TV unsupervised, there is no guarantee that they will develop a sophisticated understanding of commerce. Children may not become more critical consumers by watching ads if their domestic circumstances are not conducive to their moral and intellectual development in other ways.

Brand Recognition and Children

The act of recognition seems to carry emotional significance for both children and adults. It is psychologically reassuring to recognize a feature of one's environment. Brands play on this psychological need. An adult recognizing a brand in a shop will often feel enough reassurance about the quality of the product to buy it, even though similar, non-branded products may be just as good. Of course, many brands really do get their quality control right and the reassurance consumers feel is well founded. But children do not have the opportunity or experience to critically appraise brands. They simply enjoy recognizing them because it gives them a sense of power over their environment and can signify their knowledge of the world of adults to other children. They keenly shout out the names of brands such as Pepsi, Coca-Cola and children's products when the logos are held up for them to look at. In fact most children, when asked about their favourite ad, will cite an adult brand.

Children's recognition of adult brands takes place in the absence of actual brand usage or purchase. The marketing industry in the UK is aware of the tendency for children and adolescents to use advertised brands as symbols of social and group identity. This gives brands a powerful social presence that is quite independent of the product or service associated with it. For brands on sale to children this awareness gives sales an extra leverage because children may pester their parents to buy them. The influence goes beyond advertising when sponsorship, product placement or other communications channels are used to insert brands into the daily mediated experience of audiences. When a chocolate brand sponsors a TV soap opera or where condom and cigarette brands sponsor televised sports events, the brand gains exposure to children of all ages.

Children as Objects of Advertising

Children in advertising can be a subject of controversy as well as children as targets of advertising. In Italy, for example, the use of cute kids as models to sell anything reached such a pitch that the industry was forced to limit its use of children as advertising models. Ads for children's causes can also generate controversy. In the UK, ads for the children's charity Barnardo's have featured a striking image of a baby apparently injecting itself. Another campaign showed a baby with a cockroach forced into its mouth. The images are unpleasant but are shown ostensibly in the interests of children: charities know that shocking ads generate increased donations and gentle ads are ignored. The ASA allows ads for charities and government public service campaigns such as AIDS awareness or public safety more licence to shock than brand advertising, on the grounds that the cause is good. The Barnardo's ads generated complaints both from the public and from other charities,[24] who felt that the ads misrepresented the lives and attitudes of the poor and the socially disadvantaged. Nevertheless, the complaints were not upheld – in the UK, shock advertising seems immune from censure by the regulatory authorities, provided it is for a good cause.

Advertising industry groups lobby to maintain the freedom of advertisers to target children with responsible advertising (for example, in the USA, the Children's Advertising Review Unit). Other groups try to raise awareness of the potentially damaging effects to children of unrestricted advertising. For example, one website for teachers carries an 'Adsmart' resource that points out that a million children start smoking cigarettes each year and that many children aged 3–6 are able to recognize the Joe Camel cartoon character and link it to the cigarette brand.[25] Other sites address internet advertising to children and the special issues of influence and control that this topic raises.[26] The lobbyists on both sides have strongly-held views about the effects of advertising on children's social, cognitive and moral development. One important feature of advertising sometimes raised in these debates is the notion that advertising is viewed as a matter of choice and it can be avoided. However, this assumption seems increasingly unrealistic when one considers the volume of advertising and the extent to which children can access mobile media over which even vigilant parents can exercise little control.

Children and Obesity

There are now concerns about the effects of advertising for fast food on growing rates of child (and adult) obesity in the UK, USA, and increasingly in other countries too. There is evidence that where fast food outlets have become established in Asian countries, obesity among children is becoming an issue there too. In the UK, advertising for foods high in fat, salt and sugar (HFSS) was banned during programming watched by a majority of under-16s. This seems to date to have had a sharp effect on commercial television advertising revenues but not on rates of childhood obesity, which continue to rise.

Clearly, the existence of codes of practice and voluntary regulatory regimes does not reassure these groups that the brand marketing and advertising industries are exercising proper social responsibility. Debates about advertising's influence on social issues are invariably clouded in supposition, since there is no proven and direct causal link between advertising and behaviour. Yet, while textbooks have regarded this lack of a causal theory of advertising as a problem, the industry itself has managed very well.

In this book there are examples of advertising campaigns for which compelling circumstantial evidence has been gathered showing that they did indeed influence consumer thought and behaviour. Even if this point is accepted, the idea of stricter advertising regulation jars with the freedom of choice that advertising represents. Certain individuals and groups have always been quite favourably disposed towards lifestyles which might be regarded by some as unwise or unhealthy. Advertising presents a smorgasbord of options and consumers have the right to exercise their choices as they see fit. Then again, in some regards advertisers have far more power than individual consumers, especially young or poor ones. The ability of consumers, and especially children, to exercise truly individual choice may be sharply circumscribed where there is an acutely asymmetrical power sharing between consumers and brand marketing corporations. For all the marketing textbook rhetoric about consumer sovereignty, consumers clearly do not have multi-million dollar budgets to spread their point of view all over the media.

Applied Ethics and Advertising Regulation

Advertising regulation has a connection to ethics since it is concerned with values. It is inspired by an idea of what is good in the applied context of social policy. But there is also a significant difference: by its very nature public policy regulation is political and pragmatic, while ethics in its pure sense is the study of value in itself. Advertising regulation is a political process in that it acts under the influence of complex interests. The values that influence advertising policy are not always those of what is good but those of what is possible in the circumstances. They may also cohere with the values of commerce irrespective of what is good, but there is an assumption that the values of commerce are themselves good in that they promote wealth creation and freedom of expression, and therefore benefit individuals. While ethical study is concerned with principles of value, it also embraces the study of morals: it asks how ethical principles might be applied by individuals in practical situations.

Advertising regulation presupposes that advertising itself is legitimate because it reflects the interests not only of the public but also of advertisers and brand marketing organizations. Politically, bodies such as Ofcom, the UK Office of Communication, exist as much to protect advertisers from the wrath of the public as to protect the public from the excesses of advertisers. As we have seen a mechanism exists through which regulation is seen to act in response to public concerns. Simply having this mechanism serves the important political purpose of superficially democratizing advertising policy, almost regardless of the adjudications that are actually taken. The presence of regulatory systems reassures the public even though they know very well that regulators represent interests that are, in the end, far more powerful than those of any consumers. Nevertheless, there is an implicit ethical dimension to advertising codes of practice. However obscured advertising regulation may be beneath complex webs of interest, its rationale at some level is to make life better or more acceptable in some way than it would otherwise be without regulation.

Advertisers know that many individuals will complain about ads which are not offensive or inappropriate for the majority. The regulators have to try to represent views which are neither unreasonable nor extreme. They also have to preserve the economic benefits of advertising, so in a sense they are also there to protect the advertisers from the public. In many cases, the regulatory system may leave many individuals feeling disempowered and unhappy. One of the ASA's most complained about ads featured people singing while their mouths were stuffed with burger. The complaints were that it was rude to sing (or speak) with one's mouth full of food. These were not upheld. Voluntary regulation does have the virtue of being efficient and, within its limits, responsive. In many cases the UK regulators will take ads out of circulation after complaints by as few as a dozen individuals, and sometimes from just one (who may well be a rival competitor). As a reactive system it depends on public feedback. In a typical year the ASA receives only about 12,000 complaints from individuals or groups about print advertising. If vast numbers of the public do not complain about ads the industry can only assume that people are, in general, happy with the state of advertising.

Value Ethics, Advertising and the Good Life

If we are to analyse the role of ethics in advertising regulation we need to have some ethical concepts to work with. Ethics is broadly concerned with asking questions about the best or most correct way to live, but using terms such as 'better' carries implicit value judgements that complicate ethical debates. The study of ethics has its roots in ancient religious and philosophical systems. It entails thinking about which particular acts, thoughts or practices are consistent with living the good life. The good life is one of virtue according to given standards. For many followers of formal religious systems, living the good life means living in accordance with particular moral precepts and codes of behaviour that have been set down by religious authorities. The great world religions all place great importance on these codes and compliance is considered compulsory. Observation of the codes is therefore a matter invested with both individual as well as collective significance. But secular ethical systems deny the need for prescribed codes of behaviour or belief and aver that reason and experience, not religious authority, are an appropriate basis for all moral decisions. Humanism, for example, denies the need for either the fixed codes of morality or the eschatology (doctrine of last things) and moral judgement of formal religions.

Moral precepts are, of course, culturally bound and informed by religious traditions. For example, one could make a crude distinction between the Judao-Islamic-Christian traditions on the one hand, and the eastern religions such as Hinduism and the versions of Buddhism found in Japan, China and parts of Southeast Asia on the other. Both groups of religious traditions promote an adherence to abstract moral principles such as honesty, compassion, sobriety, piety, non-violence, and so on. These abstract principles are supplemented by specific rules about clothing, eating and food preparation, sexual conduct and so forth. For example, head coverings for females, not eating meat on Fridays, not consuming alcohol or pork, abstaining from sexual relations outside marriage and attending a designated place of worship one day a week are all features of traditional religions. However, the specific rulings on behaviour as manifestations of wider moral principles are often subject to cultural variations. As noted in Chapter 7, what is morally or ethically acceptable or unacceptable in advertising can be subject to cultural variation. Advertising has to negotiate religious sensibilities in regions where religion is the chief authority. In the West, where secular values predominate, the religious point of view, while still important, becomes one among many.

Advertising and Philosophy

We might seek some clues as to the ethical status of advertising by looking at the works of ancient and modern philosophers (Hackley and Kitchen, 1999). Advertising is far from new – evidence of promotional communication has been found in the ancient civilizations of Greece and Egypt. Modern advertising has been seen since the development of print media in the West some 400 years ago (although printing itself was first developed in China long before). In general, though, advertising, as an aspect of commerce, escaped the specific attention of ancient philosophers. The conduct of business in the twenty-first century creates many situations which are impossible to predict and difficult to assess according to ancient ethical codes. The great moral and religious thinkers of the past two millennia did not offer thoughts on the ethical status of fragrance advertisements. But many people would not take this omission to indicate that advertising is too trivial to enter ethical discussion. Indeed, religious groups are often among the most active lobbyists about advertising standards. It might be possible to draw an ethical parallel between advertising and the literature ancient philosophers discussed in their works on ethics.

In many cultures the social elite regarded commerce as a necessary evil and its exponents as trivial, sinister or both. Traders and shopkeepers were seldom lionized like poets, kings and soldiers in ancient literature. Commerce was not normally considered an occupation worthy of the educated upper classes until the modern era. While advertising may be a part of commerce, it is also a part of literature because it entails the creation of public texts. Advertising might be regarded in the same light as the street-corner storyteller in that it recounts the myths and legends of its time. Of course on another level it is also analogous to the street hawker, and perhaps sometimes to the bar-room comedian.

Advertising in its modern forms is like literature, because it panders to popular sensibility, is seen on a wide scale, and excites and alters the emotional states and values of those to whom it is directed. The poetry of Homer and the plays of Aeschylus were written to produce a similar effect. In *The Republic* Ancient Greek philosopher Plato specifically mentioned Homer's poetry as a candidate for censorship because of its morally degrading influence on young people. There are those today who would take a similarly stringent view of the influence of advertising.

One might infer that Plato would not appreciate advertising, though as a member of the elite social class he had no need to respect the imperatives of commerce. But Aristotle, another famous Greek philosopher, eschewed social engineering in his *Nicomachean Ethics*, written for his son Nicomachus. He seemed to have little paternalistic interest in the improvement of the plebs but rather adopted the view that individuals should take a balanced approach to personal ethics based on their own predispositions and needs.

Aristotle's view of advertising might be liberal, in the sense that advertising would be seen as but one of the challenges individuals must face in the world. By coming to a moderate accommodation with advertising one reaches an ethical standard that is personal to oneself. Aristotle saw the world as a place full of potential deceit, indulgence and temptation that one must learn to live with ethically. He took no account of the need for vulnerable groups to have some degree of protection from the wiles of the powerful.

Another, more contemporary liberal view came from John Stuart Mill, whose book *On Freedom* famously argued that free and unfettered expression and behaviour were necessary prerequisites for a progressive society in which individuals were free to develop according to their needs and imagination. Advertising, it is often claimed, is one form of free expression that should not be regulated. But Mill was aware that some popular voices could drown out those of others and he warned against a 'tyranny of the majority'. In other words, free expression that allowed the loudest and most populist voice to dominate public discourse was not consistent with genuine freedom. Perhaps Mill would have regarded advertising as a tyranny of the majority, because it takes the ordinary person's experience of daily life and reflects it back bathed in the warm glow of consumption. The voice of commerce dominates public discourse and makes alternative (not consumption-oriented) ways of thinking, being and behaving difficult to express amid the hectoring insistence of advertising.

Ethical Concepts for Judging Advertisements: Deontology and Consequentialism

The ethical status of an act may be judged according to whether it is regarded as intrinsically good or bad (Hackley et al., 2008b). Such judgements can be said to apply a **deontological** principle because they assume that acts in themselves may have an ethical status. For example, if an ad promotes condoms, some people judge this to be ethically inappropriate because their religious beliefs forbid the use of birth control. If an ad uses vulgarity or swearwords it may be judged unethical on those grounds alone if the person making the judgement regards either of these to be unacceptable in public.

Deontological judgements, then, rely on preconceived moral values. In some cases there would be wide agreement on the ethical status of an ad if, say, it promoted something that was illegal. In matters which do not in themselves have legal status, like eating, everyday social interaction or drinking, a deontological judgement would depend on a person's individual sense of right and wrong. Clearly, deontological judgements regarding the ethical status of advertisements have limited use where there is a wide divergence of views on what is intrinsically good or bad.

Consequentialist approaches may come into play where people cannot agree whether an ad is intrinsically good or bad in itself but may be able to agree on its ethical status by evaluating whether the consequences of showing the ad are likely to be good or bad. Good or bad in this case may be concerned with positive or negative social effects. For example, an ad promoting the use of condoms in safe sexual behaviour might be shocking to someone who feels that the public depiction of sexual relations in any context is indecent and therefore wrong. However, if the consequences of the ad were that fewer members of the general public became infected with sexually transmitted diseases then the consequences of the ad might be good, at least from the public health point of view.

Utilitarianism, the doctrine that acts should be judged on the criterion of the greatest good for the greatest number, is a consequentialist doctrine. Advertising that has socially good or benign consequences would be permissible when judged according to a consequentialist ethical approach. Of course, we still have the problem that deontological and consequentialist approaches entail implicit value judgements about what is a bad act in itself or what is a good consequence. But it is perhaps helpful to refer to ethical concepts such as these in an effort to clarify the intractable questions of advertising and ethics.

Ethics and Contemporary Advertising

Even after a decade has passed the famous (and infamous) Benetton campaigns are perhaps the most fruitful source of material for examining the cultural status of advertising with particular reference to the ethical dilemmas of advertising communications. The case at the end of this chapter outlines the circumstances through which Benetton's advertising earned such notoriety. Benetton ads have probably generated more high-profile public controversy across the world than any other campaign in brand advertising. But they are very different from, say, the Calvin Klein, Yves St Laurent 'Opium' or French Connection FCUK ads discussed above.

The Benetton ads which generated most complaints (for example, the kissing nun and priest, the images of men condemned to death under the American penal system, the dying AIDs victim and his family, the black woman breast-feeding a white baby, the black and white hands handcuffed together) did so on a wide variety of grounds. Some generated outrage and offence, though in most cases the outrage was expressed by relatively small groups who interpreted the advertising in terms of their own particular political beliefs. For many complainants the use of certain imagery in the ads was wrong *per se:* in a deontological sense it offended their code of moral decency, although the use of similar images in other contexts such as news programmes would probably not have been seen in the same light.

Few had complaints on explicitly consequentialist grounds, although some might say that were such images allowed it could lead to adverse social consequences. For example, the theme of racial integration implied in some ads was seen as a bad social consequence by racist consumers. And it should be remembered that the great majority of people who viewed the ads saw no reason to complain at all, although reading a default position into non-complaints is problematic. Inertia may prevent offended people actively registering their disapproval, so advertising regulation has to assume that complaints received reflect a larger body of opinion.

Some people felt that the Benetton ads were exploiting vulnerable groups rather than raising awareness of their plight, although permission had been given for the more intrusive ads such as the scene of a man dying of AIDS with his grief-stricken family. Other ads were misinterpreted, for example the black-skinned hand photographed handcuffed to a white hand. The ad does not necessarily imply that the white hand belonged to a police officer. That implication was, revealingly, read into the ad by some British viewers. Other ads revealed the prejudices of consumers, such as where posters of a breast-feeding woman were greeted with complaints. The fact that the breasts were black-skinned and the baby white exacerbated the effect for the racially sensitive. Nevertheless, as Oliviero Toscani pointed out, there seems no intrinsic reason why such images of life should be regarded as objectionable. Of course, as we have seen in this book, the interpretation of the meaning of a cultural sign as in the case of an ad is highly influenced by the context. It may not have been these images in themselves that generated the complaints; it may have been seeing the images as advertising that was the difficult thing for people to understand.

Whose Ethics?

Toscani's final campaign, the death row series of ads, was commercially ill-advised and insensitive to those whose lives were damaged by crime. It did, however, have an ethical position at its core, the case against capital punishment. Capital punishment is a legitimate topic for public debate. What Toscani did that was new was to frame the issue in a commercially loaded context. However strong the views people hold on the topic, they can accept debate about it in the context of late-night TV talk shows or Sunday-morning radio shows. Many people could not reconcile the topic with its context when it was seen as an advertisement. The fact that the matter was directly personalized in a way that it rarely is in current affairs debates clearly made a difference, in addition to the context. The (alleged) perpetrator was photographed and the family of the victim knew his identity.

But the negative reaction to this campaign, seen most strongly in the USA, raises another paradox. People often complain about advertising's triviality, but when Toscani raised non-trivial matters in advertising the reaction was very mixed. His ads were sometimes accused of using serious topics such as crime, racism and AIDS to sell sweaters. It was almost as if people felt that advertising had stepped beyond its cultural remit. Ads that address serious or unpleasant matters for good causes sometimes generate uneasy reactions, such as the Barnardo's charity campaigns described above. But such ads are generally accepted because they are in a good cause. Toscani claimed that his Benetton campaigns were not about selling knitwear but about raising the profile of social issues. He enjoyed the power of having every high street and magazine in the world display his photographs of the social world he saw around himself. His claims about the awareness-raising motives for Benetton advertising were greeted with cynicism. It is clear, though, that the campaigns met both objectives to some extent. They generated a powerful brand image for Benetton in association with social values, and they simultaneously placed the social issues they raised high on the public agenda.

Whether they did so in a way that was constructive is another question. Toscani argued that images of war, starvation and AIDS had become banal and clichéd when seen in the conventional news media. As advertisements they had a fresh impact. Toscani's justification for the advertising could be seen as somewhat disingenuous given his expert knowledge of the cultural role of mediated communications. Images of human suffering have arguably become news media clichés but is not their use in advertising simply drawing attention to the cliché and not to the suffering involved?

The Ethical Status of Benetton Campaigns

What, then, of the ethical status of Benetton ads? Many of the most controversial print and poster ads did not seem to contravene formal advertising codes of practice. The creative themes evaded regulatory codes by being so novel. Perhaps it had simply not occurred to the people who devise advertising regulations that anyone would want to publish photographs of copulating horses, newborn babies or breast-feeding mothers in the name of brand advertising. The regulations did, of course, cover consumers' feelings of offence or disgust in response to ads, but reactions to the Benetton ads were very mixed. Some newspapers refused to publish certain ads because of the sensitivities of their readers. In fact, in some cases it seemed as if the ads raised more objections from corporate interests, ostensibly fearful of a consumer backlash, than they did from consumers themselves. It seemed clear, though, that the negative reaction to the Benetton death row ads was serious and sincere. Of course, the notion of taking offence is culturally relative. In June 2009 an ad for ice cream which featured a nun and priest about to kiss was banned by the UK's ASA who received 10 complaints that it was offensive to those of a religious sensibility.[27] Benetton's ad featuring a nun and priest kissing, published a decade earlier, won creative awards in some countries.

All the ads were contrived to be difficult to categorize in terms of codes of practice or ethics. They crossed boundaries by using images of social reality in a brand advertising context. In some cases they seemed to reveal the prejudices of the people who complained about them with regard to racial stereotypes or public (and cross-racial) breast-feeding. They do illustrate the deeply provisional nature of social agreement on advertising as it is expressed through codes of practice and tacit agreements between advertisers, media owners and the public. The Benetton campaigns seemed to open up some of these tacit agreements to scrutiny and this made for uncomfortable viewing. They mocked the notion of ethics in advertising by questioning and challenging advertising's cultural role and status.

Advertising is normally a purely commercial text that links images of health, happiness and success with the consumption of marketed brands. Images of social reality are normally confined to news media or government-sponsored campaigns. Toscani's advertising created a new form of cultural communication but one that generated discomfort. Advertising as a whole is a powerfully ideological medium, perhaps the 'super-ideology' of the age (Elliott and Ritson, 1997). It expropriates values and signs from non-commercial human culture and assimilates them into a text that promotes consumption above all else. Toscani's work simultaneously revealed and undermined advertising's ideological character and this created a frisson of unease that, perhaps, revealed the profound cultural significance of advertising. The tacit agreements and interpretive consensus that surround the public face of advertising were fractured. Ethical judgements applied to advertising were seen in themselves to be based on highly provisional and culturally sensitive notions of value.

Chapter Summary

This chapter has explored advertising's considerable capacity for generating intense controversy. The chapter discussed why such controversy sometimes comes about and what different countries try to do to forestall such debates and to preserve essential confidence in the integrity of advertising in particular and the media in general. Some examples of differing regulatory regimes were noted in different countries, and more detail was offered on the UK's voluntary system of advertising regulation through the regulatory body, the ASA. The chapter then turned to outline some concepts of ethical philosophy which may help in analysing the ethical status of particular advertisements and campaigns. Deontology and Consequentialism were invoked to draw the distinction between ads which are deemed unethical in themselves and ads which are deemed unethical on the grounds of their consequences. Finally, the chapter used examples from the successful but now notorious Benetton campaigns of the 1990s to illustrate some of the complex issues of advertising ethics.

 ■ **Review Questions**

1   How is advertising regulated in the UK? Illustrate how it is applied with examples from the ASA website.

2   Discuss the ethical status, as you see it, of three specific print or TV ads. What ethical concepts might you employ to bring some intellectual clarity to the debate? In your view, do these concepts bring clarity to the debate?

3   Using the ASA website, print off five recent adjudications on ads for which you can obtain printed copies. Ask a group of your peers for their views on the ethical status of each of these ads. Discuss the views expressed and compare them with the ASA adjudications. What do the various opinions reveal about the people who hold them?

4   Is advertising ethical? How can ethical principles be applied fairly with integrity in a diverse, market-driven society? Use practical examples and theoretical concepts to discuss your response to this question.

5   Examine the arguments for and against advertising regulation. What might be the result if advertising were not subject to any regulation at all?

■■■■■■■■■■■■■■■■■■■■■■■■■■■■■■ **CASE** ■■■■■■■■■■■■■■■■■■■■■■■■■■■■■■

Benetton[28]

Oliviero Toscani, one of Italy's top advertising photographers, was given sole control over Benetton's advertising by Luciano Benetton in the early 1980s. He decided to change the focus of Benetton advertising from product to lifestyle. Toscani's work turned Benetton from a quality, local clothing company into one of the world's most recognized brands. From 1984 the creative executions increasingly carried Toscani's personal agenda of social injustice into the commercial world. The 1984 campaign featured teenagers of different races together with the slogan 'All the Colors of the World'. The print and billboard campaign was distributed by JWT in 14 countries and generated complaints from racists in South Africa and also in the USA and the UK. Toscani, suitably encouraged, continued with the United Colors of Benetton theme for subsequent campaigns. From 1989 Benetton took all its advertising production in-house to give it complete independence and control. The ads were consciously provocative to racial sensibilities. They outraged many consumers while continuing to give a massive profile to the Benetton brand. One poster, as described earlier in Chapter 8, featuring a black woman holding a white baby to her naked breast generated such protest in the USA that it was withdrawn. For some consumers it evinced an era of slavery. For others, public breast-feeding itself was offensive. The ad also received more praise than any other Benetton visual and won awards in five European countries. Other ads continued the theme of racial juxtaposition. One featured a black hand handcuffed to a white hand. It generated complaints in Britain where it was assumed that the white hand belonged to a police officer. London Transport refused to display the poster.

Other themes of social injustice attracted Toscani's attention. Ads featured brightly coloured condoms and a dying HIV-positive man surrounded by his grieving family. They also featured a wide variety of striking images, including a kissing priest and nun, copulating horses, a newborn baby with its umbilical cord still attached and HIV-positive people with an HIV stamp on their naked bodies. Some newspapers refused to publish particular ads, afraid of the backlash from irate customers or other advertisers. Reaction to the ads was mixed. The French advertising regulation body, the Bureau de Vérification de la Publicité (BVP) recommended the withdrawal of the poster showing the kissing priest and nun. The same poster won an award in the UK. In the UK the newborn baby ad (titled Giusy) generated 800 complaints to the ASA and was withdrawn. It was also banned in most other European countries, but it won an award in Switzerland.

The Turning Point for Toscani

The controversial themes continued and were often greeted with (by now predictable) outrage from various parties. Toscani's last campaign for Benetton was in 2000. As Benetton had gained a bigger reputation for provocative advertising, sales had begun to suffer in some markets. Occasionally, Benetton retailers themselves had suffered; some shops were even vandalized. Several hundred Benetton shops were closed down in the USA. In an attempt to recover lost ground there, Benetton entered into an agreement with Sears to put Benetton outlets in their stores across the country.

Toscani, meanwhile, decided to raise awareness of the plight of the thousands of young black men on death row in America's jails. He gained entry to a prison, took photographs of some of the prisoners and used them in a poster campaign. Although the permission of the prisoners and their families had been obtained, Toscani had neglected to tell the prison authorities what he was planning. This oversight added to the furore when the campaign was launched. Families of the victims of the murderers pictured in the campaign waged a passionate protest against Benetton and picketed the Sears stores. The campaign against Benetton gained pace in the USA and Sears cancelled their agreement. Toscani left Benetton three months later, after 18 years in charge of their advertising.

 ■ **Case Questions**

1 The Benetton campaigns illustrated that advertising discourse, while loose and flexible as a category, also has limits to which audiences are sensitive. In other words, some people felt that certain Benetton ads had violated the rules of advertising discourse by raising issues and using images that were not suitable in the contexts used but were appropriate only for news and documentary media. Discuss the limits that seemed evident from the reactions to three different Benetton ads.

2 The Benetton ads created controversial reactions because they did not obviously contravene existing regulatory codes. Discuss the question of whether this reveals weakness in the current codes of advertising practice in various countries. Are codes of practice ultimately impotent against creativity? If so, how can societies defend themselves against advertising?

3 Arguably, Benetton dispensed with its controversial advertising themes when the commercial consequences became clearly adverse. What do you feel this reveals, if anything, about advertising discourse and its relationship with ethics?

Hackley, C. (1999) 'The meanings of ethics in and of advertising', *Business Ethics: A European Review*, 8(1): 37–42.

Hackley, C. and Kitchen, P.J. (1999) 'Ethical perspectives on the postmodern communications leviathan', *Journal of Business Ethics*, 20(1): 15–26.

Macklin, M.C. and Carlson, L. (eds) (1999) *Advertising to Children: Concepts and Controversies*. Thousand Oaks, CA: Sage.

Manchanda, R.V., Dahl, D.W. and Frankenberger, K.D. (2003) 'Does it pay to shock? Reactions to shocking and nonshocking advertising content among university students', *Journal of Advertising Research*, 43(3): 268–79.

Pollay, R.W. (1986) 'The distorted mirror – reflections on the unintended consequences of advertising', *Journal of Marketing*, 50(April): 18–36.

Web-based Resources

Advertising Association list of websites dealing with advertising regulation and education: www.adassoc.org.uk/html/uk_websites.html

On the Companion Website

These journal articles are freely available on the companion website (www.sagepub.co.uk/hackley).

Transnational Advertising and International Relations: US Press Discourses on the Benetton 'We on Death Row' Campaign
Marwan M. Kraidy and Tamara Goeddertz
Media, Culture & Society, Mar 2003; vol. 25: pp. 147–165.

Exorcising the Ghost of Cigarette Advertising Past: Collusion, Regulation, and Fear Advertising
John L. Solow
Journal of Macromarketing, Dec 2001; vol. 21: pp. 135–145.

Dear Santa: The Effects of Television Advertising on Young Children
Karen J. Pine and Avril Nash
International Journal of Behavioral Development, Nov 2002; vol. 26: pp. 529–539.

Notes

1 You can view this ad and many other UK TV ads on this link www.classictvads.co.uk/ctv2.html

2 Reported on *Guardian Unlimited* website, 'Naked Sophie is most offensive advert of 2000', http://media.guardian.co.uk/advertising/story/0,7492,477315,00.html

3 www.telegraph.co.uk/finance/personalfinance/insurance/motorinsurance/5236374/Iggy-Pop-advert-banned-because-rock-star-would-not-be-covered.html (accessed 10 May 2009).

4 www.brandrepublic.com/News/901639/Swiftcover-insure-musicians-Iggy-Pop-ad-banned-watchdog/ (accessed 10 May 2009).

5 news.bbc.co.uk/2/hi/in_depth/7428976.stm (accessed 4 May 2009).

6 www.independent.co.uk/news/uk/politics/cigarette-firms-smoke-out-ways-to-beat-ad-ban-597558.html (accessed 4 May 2009).

7 Yahoo news published the story from the AFP news agency on Monday 5 May (link in note below) and the next day the UK *Independent* newspaper published it under a correspondent's by-line. The link to the *Independent* story is here www.independent.co.uk/news/world/asia/have-a-smoke-and-help-save-the-economy-china-tells-party-officials-1679006.html (accessed 6 May 2009).

8 http://uk.news.yahoo.com/18/20090504/thl-no-butts-china-orders-officials-to-s-aa1aa08.html (accessed 4 May 2001).

9 After a 35-year ban, books and newspapers were allowed to advertise on cable and satellite TV in France from 1 January 2004. Source: *The Times*, 26 December 2003: 15, 'Burrell's book in historic TV advert'.

10 Source: WARC email newsletter, 3 January 2004. With a penetration of 50% of Argentinian households the cable-TV advertising market was the biggest in South America. COMFER (Comité Fédéral de Radiodefusion) the Argentinian regulatory body, argued that too much time was being given over to advertising during movies which subscribers had paid to see.

11 The Hungarian code of advertising ethics, www.mrsz.hu/eng_ethics.html

12 "The Advertising Standards Authority (ASA) Annual Report 2007, published today, reveals that a record number of advertisements (2, 458) were changed or withdrawn last year. The number of advertisements complained about reached an all-time high of 14,080 – an increase of 9.6 per cent on the year before. The total number of complaints received was 24,192 – an increase of 7.9 per cent on 2006." Source: ASA Annual Report 2007 www.asa.org.uk/asa/news/news/2008/ASA+Annual+Report+2007.htm (accessed 14 September 2009).

13 'TV adverts for personal loans face ban', by Martin Hickman, *The Independent*, Wednesday 29 April 2009, p. 9.

14 www.asa.org.uk. ASA adjudications are published on www.asa.org.uk/adjudications

15 BBC news website for Asia-Pacific region at http://news.bbc.co.uk/1/hi/world/asia-pacific

16 According to a report on the BBC News website homepage dated Friday, 3 December 1999.

17 http://news.bbc.co.uk/1/hi/uk/548249.stm

18 Source: BBC News online web pages.

19 See H. Cristol (2002) 'Teen drinking on the rise', *The Futurist*, Washington, 36(4): 14. and UK *Sunday Times*, 17 August 2003: 'Alcohol lads' ads to be sexed down'.

20 www.asa.org.uk/cap/news_events/news/2004/Ad+industry+to+consult+on+new+alcohol+rules.htm

21 www.alcoholconcern.org.uk

22 www.asa.org.uk/asa/landing_pages/google/Children+and+Advertising?gclid=CP7Eg8POopsCFZgU4wodE08_Aw

23 www.toy-tma.com/industry/publications/fbcurrent/advertising.htm

24 'Barnardo's ad provokes storm of protest', feature by social affairs editor, John Carvel, 13 November 2003, on *Guardian Unlimited* website at http://society.guardian.co.uk

25 http://scienceu.fsu.edu/content/adsmart/docs/tobaccolist.html

26 http://www.mediafamily.org/facts/facts_internetads.shtml

27 'Offensive' ice cream ad is banned', UK MSN news 1 July 2009, http://news.uk.msn.com/odd-news/article.aspx?cp-documentid=148278031

28 Further information see, 'Benetton campaign causes controversy', *Daily Mirror*, www.dedham.k12.ma.us/dhs/mirror/February2000/Benetton.htm, and for a detailed case study on Benetton see the INSEAD-CEDEP 'United Colors of Benetton' case, 1996, available through the European Case Clearing House, Cranfield, Surrey.

9 Advertising Research

Chapter Outline

Agencies act as intermediaries between consumers and brand marketing organizations. In order to fulfil this role they need to have research craft skills to generate actionable consumer and marketing insights. The aims, methods, purpose and relevance of research are all matters for intense debate both within agencies and between agencies and clients. This chapter outlines the main research techniques used in the field and sets this within a discussion of the major debates about the methods and the uses of research in advertising and promotional communication.

Key chapter content:

- Research in advertising: role, issues and origins

- Uses of advertising research

- Types of research in advertising

- Quantitative and qualitative advertising research

- The account planning role and research

- Debate and dissent around research in advertising

- Research ethics.

Research in Advertising: Role, Issues and Origins

Research is the foundation of effective advertising. Effective promotional campaigns of all kinds are based on knowledge of who the target segment is, where they are, what they do, what they're like and how they think and behave. There is also a need to understand the market in which the brand operates, the competition and the wider economic conditions. Finally, research is needed to pre-test advertising executions and post-test campaign effectiveness against agreed objectives.

Broadly, research in marketing tends to operate around five main stages:

1 Defining the research problem
2 Setting research objectives
3 Deciding on a research method
4 Collecting data and analysing results
5 Presenting the findings.

Malhotra and Birks (2003) note that ESOMAR[1] suggest two main reasons for carrying out a research study in marketing. One is to 'identify opportunities and problems', the other is to 'generate and refine marketing actions' (p. 7). Research in advertising is no different and these two broad issues tend to cover the scope of most studies, with an emphasis on the practical matters raised by the second point. Research in advertising is typically undertaken to improve the effectiveness of communication or to generate ideas for strategy. There are, of course, also pragmatic considerations in the choice of research method, in terms of cost and timescale.

It must be admitted that many creative professionals in advertising would deny that research has a useful role. They often see research as no more than a reason not to use their work (Hackley and Kover, 2007). Many creative professionals would argue that their intuitive sense of what will resonate with consumers, motivate and inspire them is informed by an artistic sensibility which is not accessible to scientific methods of research. But, even though this may sometimes be true, there is a political need for research to justify the courses of action the agency wishes to take. The need for an evidence-base for decisions in the creative advertising development process is driven by the client marketing directors, board and shareholders, all of whom need some reassurance that their investment in promotion is reasonably likely to reap a good return.

There are many successful case examples in advertising in which a research-inspired consumer or market insight provided the hook of reality around which turned the fantasy of advertising. On the other hand, there are also cases where an inspired piece of creative imagination apparently did not need a research base. The advertising industry is both similar and different across the world. It is similar in that it does pretty much the same thing everywhere, and in superficially much the same way. It is different in that each agency has an individual style and difference of emphasis which manifests in its working practices and style of work (Hackley and Tiwsakul, 2008). So there is room in a creative industry such as advertising for a range of different approaches. Nonetheless, the role of research has been and continues to be a major one in influencing the kinds of advertising we see.

There are widely diverging opinions about the role and methods of research in advertising. In agencies, knowledge, about the market and the consumer, about communication, and about the brand, is a hotly contested area. The winners get their decisions actioned in a campaign. As we noted in Chapter 4, different agency disciplines often carry quite different implicit assumptions into their work. Advertising agencies are not known as places where a meeting of minds is the daily norm. More often, the relevance and implications of research findings for the creative development of a campaign are a matter of passionate debate. Some commentators feel that the field would benefit from a stronger sense of clarity and direction. For example, Hedges (1997: ii), writing on the uses of research in advertising, maintained that 'What we need urgently in this field is a better and clearer understanding of what we are about – a longer and broader perspective will lead to a reordering of priorities'. Today, some commentators still make the same call. There is a view among some practitioners that research in advertising is often used in the same way that a drunk uses a lamp-post, for support rather than illumination. Clarity about the aims, limits and purpose of research can help to focus the illumination it can offer.

This may all seem simple, or perhaps obvious, but it becomes very complex when two other fundamental questions are asked. These are, what do we mean by research, and how do we know what research is telling us? Research findings are often invoked as if they are beyond dispute because they are scientific. But research in all fields is a highly contested area and advertising and marketing are no different. There is a welter of different opinion on what research methods are best suited to particular purposes. In advertising, there is a body of opinion which doubts the usefulness of research at all. But clients are most unlikely to accept the agency's strategic advice unless it is backed up with evidence from research findings. In this chapter we will try to negotiate a route through this complex area to outline the most commonly used research approaches in advertising and promotional communication. We will also examine the key areas of contest and debate around the uses of research in the field.

Syndicated Panel Data

Advertising agencies do not always commission or carry out their own survey research in every case. They also buy the use of secondary data which are produced by commercial research organizations. Major research companies such as A.C. Neilson and Taylor Nelson AGB publish syndicated panel data based on continuous surveys of consumers. Studies may investigate trends in, for example, household brand shopping and usage, TV viewing, radio listening or internet usage. For example, Taylor Nelson AGB compile a 'European Toiletries and Cosmetics database' in which 14,000 consumers across Europe are paid to keep daily diaries of their purchase and use of cosmetics and toiletries products (described in Malhotra and Birks, 2003: 9). The general information contained in these surveys can be useful for advertising professionals to understand the underlying trends and behaviours that are typical in a given product or service category. Neilson Media Research, for example, publish the viewing figures for the top US TV shows. In June 2009 the top 10 included *NCIS*, *The Mentalist*, *Two-and-a-Half Men*, *CSI*, and *60 Minutes*, all with over 8 million viewers. In a nation of some 200 million people, it seems clear that, while television retains a high profile, there is a need for promotional campaigns to utilize media other than, and in addition to, television. Statistics such as these help brand clients on decisions such as advertising strategy and targeting.

Origins of Advertising Research

Advertising research has a long history (see Hackley, 2010, for an overview). Agencies need to know as much as possible about the client's business, the market sector and the relevant consumers before devising an advertising strategy. The advertising legend David Ogilvy (1983) points this out emphatically. He refers to the need for advertisers to 'do their homework', in other words, to find out as much about the client's problems as they can before trying to devise solutions. According to Richards et al. (2000: 20), JWT began to commission research in 1916 to acquire a greater understanding of the social and demographic trends and structures that formed consumer groups. Universities were called upon to add methodological sophistication. For example, the behavioural psychologist John B. Watson was diverted from his university career to become an advertising man for JWT. Behavioural psychology aspired to provide a unified theory of human learning and behaviour. If the behaviourists were right, then ads could be conceived as teaching devices, changing human behaviour through **operant conditioning** and behavioural reinforcement. Many other university social science research methods have been tapped into by advertisers to add sophistication to their strategic approach. Over the years this has generated some mistrust among the public. At the extreme, advertising agencies have been accused of a sinister manipulation of consumer behaviour (most famously by Vance Packard, 1957; see also Hackley, 2007, for a discussion).

Agencies eventually established their own research departments. The distinct fields of audience, attitude and mass communications research were used as sources for advertising research approaches. In time, many advertising agency research departments grew to become successful businesses in their own right. Many of today's leading market and consumer research agencies were originally advertising agency research departments.

The Exchange of Ideas Between Academic and Practitioner Research

Professional advertising research has turned to the social and statistical sciences for legitimacy. Some advertising practitioners feel that the contribution to the field from academic empirical social science has been negligible (Hedges, 1997: 86). Entire volumes on advertising research have drawn attention to the difference in mentality that divides academics and practitioners on the topic (see Wells, 1997). Cook and Kover (1998) feel that this divide is based on language. They draw on work by Wittgenstein to suggest that the two professional fields of academic and practitioner research in advertising are separated by differing language games. Hackley (2003g) maintained that the divide could also be understood in terms of differing **representational practices** in the two fields. In other words, each field applies quite different criteria to judge the value and contribution of research and consequently research in each field is often described in quite different terms.

Most obviously, professional advertising research has to be justified in terms of outcomes or practical implications in a way that academic research does not. It has to pass the 'so what' test. But academic research has to be justified in theoretical terms. Indeed, much academic advertising research is entirely self-referential, because it makes sense only in terms of its connection to other academic theories. Of the 250 or more advertising research studies reviewed by Vakratsas and Ambler (1999), only a small number derived from, or were used in, practical advertising management.

The exchange of ideas between advertising and academia has, sometimes, been mutual. Academic researchers have drawn on models and techniques developed by advertising people and tested or adapted them to different situations. For example, some of the academic research into creativity and idea-generating techniques has drawn on models originally developed in advertising (Osborn, 1963). In turn, the advertising profession has arguably been more receptive to academic ideas than any other marketing or management field. Most professional advertising research techniques began life in psychological, sociological or anthropological studies, even if the theoretical aspect of academic research is largely ignored by practitioners. As Kover (1995) has pointed out, advertising professionals generally have little time for theory. Hackley (2003d: 319) reported the comments of advertising professionals in top UK and US agencies. One creative professional admitted that 'we hate research', and a senior account planner explained that 'there's an analysis of what a client does, the category of an industry, then starting to see what information is missing and what we might need – we also have a group called the Discovery Group and they do ethnographies'. This quote perhaps illustrates the dual character of practitioner research in advertising. It is pragmatic and driven by the particulars of a client's problem, but it also draws on theoretical concepts from the academic world for its operating vocabulary.

BOX 9.1

Advertising Research and Organizational Politics

It was reported that a new campaign for a carbonated drink brand departed from the usual sip, smile 'n' sing format and took a less obvious narrative route, with the dramatic resolution ('the brand as hero') at the end of the ad. In a copy-test the ad was shown to a group of franchise-holders who were all surprised when the usual image of the brand being consumed by an ecstatic (and attractive) actor did not appear within the first five seconds. The franchisers were not impressed by the agency's creative execution and demanded that the ad be scrapped and replaced by another one in the old format. The client advertising director, who had agreed to the new style, was removed from his post as a result of the bad test results. Many creative professionals deplore this kind of pre-launch testing since, they argue, it does not accurately reflect the environment in which advertising is viewed. Another criticism is that clients are not necessarily the best audience for pre-testing advertising executions since they do not always understand the ways in which promotional communication might motivate a range of consumer segments.

Uses of Advertising Research

Different advertising agencies place different degrees of emphasis on applying research at various stages in the advertising development process. In this section we will look at both the methods and uses of research, since the choice of method is often informed by the purpose for which research is needed. Considering the importance much academic research attributes to advertising there are surprisingly few studies of how advertising is actually developed in agencies. Advertising professionals are pragmatic and intellectually flexible.

They often grasp what academics struggle to articulate: namely, that advertising is a form of communication that is ineluctably social and is responded to emotionally by consumers seeking meaning through consumption. Yet they have also to justify advertising strategy and creative execution decisions to clients, who in turn have to justify the expenditure on promotion to their main board. Research is necessary not only to generate insights which give an evidence base to strategy decisions but also, as noted above, to justify those decisions to third parties. The two aims of research are not always compatible, since the criteria by which research evidence is judged can differ, depending on the educational and experience background of different individuals. Even in ad agency account teams, the three main roles of creative, account planning and account management can bring very different values and world-views to their implicit theories of communication and consumption (Hackley, 2003b, c, f).

Among the published research there is on how advertising agencies develop campaigns, Punyapiroje et al. (2002) offer an account of advertising development in Thai advertising agencies and McCracken (1986: 74–6) describes the creative advertising development process in US agencies. Scott's (1994a: 468) work focuses on the ways agency creatives tap into the symbolic consumer consciousness and refers to the 'shared social milieu' upon which advertising professionals depend for the 'learned cultural/textual conventions' (p. 463) that will mobilize meaning in their ads. Scott and McCracken both refer to the cultural knowledge underlying advertising interpretation which binds both ad maker and ad watcher in a creatively resonant consummation of advertising development. Hackley (2000, 2002) also refers to the cultural knowledge that presupposes not only the understanding of advertising but also the understanding of consumers by communication professionals (see also Svensson, 2007).

The various types of research in the development process are set out in Table 9.0.

Table 9.0 Research in the advertising development process

Stage in the process	Types of research typically undertaken
Client brief	Secondary research into market, business, brand, competitors
Creative research	Primary studies into consumer groups and consumption practices
Creative brief	Anthropological and/or focus group studies of target consumers
Creative development	Focus and/or observational studies of consumer response to creative stimuli
Pre-launch testing	Copy-testing, attitude scaling with finished creative executions
Post-launch testing	Tracking studies, awareness studies, sales response tracking

Research in the Advertising Development Process: Client Brief

We know that advertising agencies use different types of research at different stages of the creative advertising development process. The research process begins with the client brief, which the agency account team needs to investigate thoroughly in order to set the terms of reference for the campaign. Initial research will often be undertaken as soon as the client's brief is received. This will establish basic parameters of knowledge about the brand, its market, its consumers and competitors, and the way that the brand fits in with the client's business. All of this work will inform the communications brief, which is the agency's interpretation of the client brief.

Much of this initial research is likely to rely on secondary data sets, that is, data sets already recorded as part of other studies, such as commercial market reports (like *Mintel*). Professional research organizations produce panel data, for example, recording the purchasing or behaviour of a selected group of consumers over a long timescale. Industry bodies such as Radio Joint Industry Research Limited (or RAJAR) or the Outdoor Advertising Association (OAA) in the UK publish data on audience radio listening habits and outdoor poster coverage respectively. The agency needs to know not only all about the brand, the client and the market conditions, but also about the target consumers. Who are they, and how can they be reached with a communication which means something to them? Advertising agencies will also sometimes undertake their own **primary research** into consumption behaviour in that particular product or service category in order to understand the client and the business fully.

Creative Research and Creative Development

Once the brand and the market are fully understood, creative research will be undertaken in which the thoughts and behaviour of relevant groups of consumers are assessed in relation to the brand and its categories. The aim will be to generate actionable insights that might form the basis for the creative work. This research will often use primary data, such as transcripts of focus or discussion groups, transcripts of in-depth interviews with consumers, or video footage of naturalistic experiments in which consumers are asked to use the product while being observed. How do target consumers relate to the brand? How do they consume it, talk about it, what does it mean to them? Such questions can be answered by relatively open-ended research techniques which will allow the consumers the flexibility to frame their own responses independent of any presuppositions the agency staff might bring to the brief. Sometimes, the creative research uncovers a particular theme or insight which seems to capture the essence of the consumers' engagement with the brand or category, and which can then act as the lynchpin of the creative development, ensuring that the campaign is resonant for target consumers (see Box 9.2). The creative research will often be undertaken before writing the creative brief. As the creative execution develops there may be a need for further, more focused research studies to ascertain the consumer response to particular ideas on copy or visuals.

BOX 9.2

Research Insights Informing Creative Work

Creative research often uses qualitative data to generate insight into the way consumer groups understand a given brand and its positioning. In a European campaign for VW cars, research found two related insights that drove the advertising for the Polo and Golf ranges. Firstly, the research found that consumers thought they were quite knowledgeable about car prices, but in fact they had very little knowledge about actual pricing structures. Secondly, the research found that consumers had an impression that VW cars were more expensive than other cars in their class. In the case of the new VW small car range, this was incorrect. However, the perception clearly held advantages, since it carried an implication of superior quality. The creative problem was compounded because consumers in Europe and the UK were resistant to advertising that emphasized a price benefit. Not only that but creative staff were also bored by a brief that asked them to merely say that 'this price is lower than the others' (called 'a prices brief').

Few creative awards are won on a prices brief. As a solution the agency produced a creative brief that described a need to make ads that were telling but off-beat in their quirky humour. With humour, the campaign could convey the message about price without alienating or boring consumers. The brief resulted in a campaign that ran for over 10 years, based on funny ways to tell consumers that they were wrong about VW pricing. Awards were won and VW increased its market share substantially. The research insight that drove the creative work was derived from qualitative data, interpreted creatively by the agency account planner.

Pre- and Post-Launch Research

Once the agency team and client are happy with a creative execution they might wish to reassure themselves about the response of target consumers to specific aspects, such as the script (or copy), the action, scene and actors (if it is a TV ad) or the combination of colours and copy for a print ad. Ads may be adjusted or even abandoned altogether because of results from a pre-launch 'copy' test. This area is fraught with difficulty (see Box 9.3) because the client may want to approve the creative work even though the agency account team by now feel that they understand communication more acutely and are in a better position to make such judgements. Many a creative execution has been abandoned at pre-launch because of the wishes of the client representative, to the fury of the creative team and the frustration of the account manager.

After the campaign launch, there is a need to assess the effectiveness of the campaign against its objectives so **tracking studies** are undertaken using a combination of research methods. For example, attitude and awareness surveys might be useful to ensure that the right consumers are being targeted in the right way. This might provide opportunities to tweak the media plan or creative work, or in extreme cases to re-evaluate the entire campaign. Finally, when the campaign has finished, the agency will need to provide a detailed assessment of how effective it was. Tracking studies are very important for agencies since they constitute a record of the campaign's evolution and its marketing results. They can provide evidence for clients that the campaign has accomplished the objectives set for it. Case histories that are written up from successful campaigns provide a learning resource and, if they are submitted to awards competitions, can be useful PR for the agency itself.

BOX 9.3

The Limits of Pre-launch Testing*

Valentine Appel, a revered figure in advertising research, once claimed that research of finished commercials could do two things well. One was to eliminate advertising that was really bad. The other was to select advertising that was really good. Often, however, really innovative advertising does not test well because it cannot be captured by the rational measures of much advertising research.

Given the limitations of advertising research to pre-test commercials, one wonders why it is required. The answer is partly political: advertisers need to gain budget approval from many individuals. They therefore need statistical evidence, even if it merely supports the obvious. The other, related reason is that advertisers are highly risk-averse. Advertising research can provide reassurance. It is close to a truism that much advertising is neither good nor bad, just mediocre. Research can test three executions, for example, and show if one is preferred to the others. The advertising manager has the basis for a decision based on concrete numbers, on science, even though the chosen commercial is not really different from the rejected ones. It makes little difference what he or she selects. Cynical? Yes. Reality? Yes. Advertising testing may not be important for decisions but it is necessary for careers.

*This vignette was kindly contributed by Professor Arthur J. Kover, former editor of the *Journal of Advertising Research*.

Types of Research in Advertising

We have already touched upon several different research methods. The following section will discuss these in a little more detail with a focus on the arguments surrounding the relative appropriateness of different methods for different purposes. There is a distinction between qualitative and quantitative research methods which often polarizes these debates. This can be a distraction. At least a third of commercial marketing and advertising research spend goes on qualitative research of all kinds, so there is no sense in the industry that it is a case of either one or the other. Most studies will have elements of both. More fruitful debate surrounds the pragmatic choices of research method in the context of specific research questions.

Experimental Research

Advertising has a long tradition of formal/scientific experimental research. For example, in campaign pre-testing experiments a selected audience might be gathered together to watch an advertisement. The audience presses buttons on their seat arms to indicate whether they like or dislike particular parts of the ad. The results are then presented in a graphical and statistical form. In less technologically enhanced conditions the audience may be given questionnaires to fill out after they have watched the ad, to determine how much or how little they liked it and how well they recalled various components.

This kind of research (as noted above, often known as 'copy-testing') is sometimes conducted according to formulae that will dictate the criteria that an ad has to meet in order for the campaign to be launched. If the results are not favourable then the ad may be changed or scrapped. Many creative staff, incidentally, feel that quasi-experimental copy-testing techniques are based on mistaken assumptions about how audiences engage with advertising and therefore miss the point. For many account managers and clients, though, experimental designs for copy-testing offer a succinct and measurable means of assessing creative executions before incurring the expense of a full campaign launch.

Some experimental advertising research uses biological measures of attention and sensory stimulation. The **psycho-galvanometer tests** measure the activity of sweat glands with carefully placed electrodes and assess the degree of excitement the consumer feels at all times throughout an ad viewing experience. If images in the ad are very uninteresting as judged by the test, they may be changed. The **eye tachistoscope test** tracks the viewer's eye movements across an ad so that the experimenter can judge which bits are the most appealing. They can also see how the eye is drawn through the images. Today the latest trend in biological consumer research involves **magnetic resonance imaging (MRI)** scanners to see which parts of a person's brain are stimulated by particular visual, auditory or other sensual experiences. Since particular parts of the brain can be matched with specific activities and sensations, MRI research holds out the possibility that products and ads could be devised that will stimulate predicted responses. It could be argued, though, that such control over consumers is not attainable given the idiosyncrasy of consumers and the complexity of the consumer–marketing relation. Furthermore, the brain exhibits plasticity in the sense that different brain regions can support the same physiological function in certain circumstances (such as brain injury), so isolating given activities to specified regions of the brain is extremely difficult.

Experimental research designs such as the above can be criticized for their lack of ecological validity. That is, they do not accurately replicate the conditions under which consumers typically engage with advertising (see, for example, Ritson and Elliott, 1999). Naturalistic experiments try to recreate the consumer-advertising environment in the hope of getting more relevant results, for example by setting up a specially-created advertisement for consumers to watch in a group. The spontaneous discussion is rewarded.

BOX 9.4

Research Informs Hovis Campaigns

Hovis, a 115-year-old brown-bread brand owned by Premier Foods, was suffering declining revenue because of an intense downward pressure on price from the competition and also from the power of distribution outlets to discount prices. Volume was growing but profit declining. DDB London conducted primary research in the form of questionnaire surveys in order to fully understand why brand equity was diminishing. The brand was seen as out-of-date and **spontaneous brand awareness** was in decline. Qualitative research had previously found that people described a 'Hovis room' as a warm and inviting kitchen. By 2001 they were describing people standing outside the room looking in: people no longer identified with the traditional, old-fashioned positioning of the brand. This kind of research and the thinking it stimulates informed the advertising strategy. This strategy followed a new advertising approach that emphasized the health goodness of the bread and eschewed the traditional advertising theme that had played up the bread's northern English heritage. The new campaign was drawn in a cartoon style reminiscent of animated TV shows like *The Simpsons*, to distance it from the old advertising filmed on the cobbled streets of northern England. The relaunch also used new packaging, PR and a supporting website. The brand increased sales while also raising the price. The combination of a radical new advertising approach, new packaging and below-the-line support in the form of PR and a website succeeded in repositioning the brand in a contemporary new light. The brand, refreshed, later reached a compromise positioning with a stunning television ad which crossed a century of the brand's history, positioning it in a way which retained a sense of nostalgia but also reinforced its place as a feature of British life in the contemporary age.[2]

Survey Research

Formal/scientific primary research into consumer attitudes may be conducted using questionnaire-based attitude surveys. As with experimental designs, these will often be analysed using quantitative methods such as statistical tests of significance. Questionnaire surveys are often most useful where existing knowledge is to be examined in a larger or new audience. For example, if a consumer discussion group revealed that people felt that their music buying was more important to them than their daily newspaper purchase, this could then be tested on a wider scale with a questionnaire survey. For exploring entirely new areas, qualitative research can often be best because the data are not confined to the precise questions that are asked.

There are other potential problems with questionnaire surveys. They often ask people questions upon which the respondent has never been asked to express an opinion before. The scaled questions encourage a response. This process may create a false circumstance in which an attitude is revealed, for example, which does not exist outside the context of a questionnaire survey. A related problem is that people are notoriously forgetful when reporting their own behaviour. If we are asked about typical purchasing behaviour, weekly expenditure, preferred retail outlets or other factual information, we will often get it wrong. Finally, the sampling issues associated with survey questionnaires are always difficult to resolve. Statistically, results of surveys cannot be **generalized** across a wider population unless the sample is randomly generated. In most social studies researchers make do with samples that are **representative** of the population in which they are interested even though for statistical purists this may mean that the results cannot be generalized across the wider population. Rather, the findings tell us only about the small number of people who filled in the questionnaires.

The survey industry is big: political polls, opinion polls and questionnaire-based market research studies are commissioned daily at great cost. As with all research, questionnaire surveys can only be useful if they are designed carefully to achieve specified outcomes. The interpretation of findings is difficult and must be done in full knowledge of the limitations of these methods.

BOX 9.5

Self-reports as Behavioural Data

While self-reports of feelings and emotions may be sincere, self-reports of actual behaviour can be far less accurate. This was well illustrated in one retail research study in which security cameras were used to monitor shoppers' in-store browsing behaviour. The research aim was

(Cont'd)

to generate insights that might help improve in-store retail design or merchandising techniques. A sign had been erected at the store entrance warning customers that their behaviour might be filmed for research purposes. On exiting from the store researchers approached the consumers to ask them to explain their behaviour. But the exit interviews proved less than informative. When asked why they lingered for so long at one display, or why they moved from display x to display y, most consumers had little recollection of their movements and some insisted that they had not behaved in the way described, even when confronted with the film evidence. We are not very good, as consumers, at remembering our behaviour. We may be better at recalling the general emotions that our consumer behaviour reflects.

Apocryphal stories tell us about some of the limitations of questionnaire surveys. Akio Morita's Sony Walkman, the precursor for modern personal stereos (or CD players), is said to have met with adverse market research results, presumably because the consumers questioned could not grasp the concept of walking around with a hi-fi playing in their ears. Sony had a retail network and marketed the Walkman in spite of the bad survey results, to great success. Truly innovative marketing ideas require creative entrepreneurship and teach consumers new consumption concepts. They are beyond the scope of conventional, market research techniques because consumers have nothing with which they can compare a truly innovative concept. The *Reader's Digest* journal once surveyed its huge readership to find out who readers intended to vote for in the US presidential election. Even though the survey population was very large, the result proved wrong because readers of that publication were not representative of the wider US voting population.

Quantitative and Qualitative Advertising Research

Advantages of Quantitative Research Methods

As we noted above there are debates about the situations in which it is better to use quantitative or qualitative research methods. There can be many advantages to the use of quantitative approaches. For example, advertising effectiveness is sometimes tracked using sales figures in relation to the number of target TV spots that an advertisement hits. Clearly, quantitative measurements such as this are essential in fully understanding the impact of a campaign. Statistical techniques such as multivariate analysis can be useful in separating out possible causal variables that might intervene between an advertisement and a consumer purchase. Results from experiments can be collated and cross-tabulated, and survey questionnaire results can be statistically analysed for significance. Of course, much of the initial research into the brand category and competitive situation will draw on numerical data to establish items such as brand usage frequency, consumer segment demographics, competitive structure, relative sales volume of the market, and so on.

Some agencies will use sophisticated, quantitative data analysis techniques, especially when tracking the effectiveness of ad campaigns and trying to establish a statistically significant link between consumer behaviour (for example, purchasing behaviour) and exposures to an ad. It is usually extremely difficult, though, to isolate ad exposure from other possible causal variables. Agencies will also use basic quantitative skills in conducting an analysis of their client's business to support the client brief and advertising strategy.

The distinction between qual. and quant. is not necessarily clear cut. For example, qualitative data-gathering techniques such as discussion groups or in-depth interviews may have a quantitative element, as the transcripts might be subject to content analysis where categories of event are listed and counted. The researcher could perhaps want to count the number of times a discussion group mentions 'colour' when discussing a confectionery product's packaging, to see whether the colour of the packaging is closely identified with the brand.

The awareness–interest–desire–action (acronym A–I–D–A) model (see Chapter 2) assumes that consumers will go through a linear, sequential process before purchasing a product. This explains the interest by advertising researchers in intermediate measures of advertising effectiveness such as awareness, interest, degree of liking of an ad (signifying the degree of interest in the ad) and, of course, recall. Advertisers are very interested to learn how many exposures to an ad it may take before a consumer can remember their brand or the particular appeal of the ad. The development of Likert scales in attitude research seemed to offer a way of quantifying these variables across large numbers of respondent consumers.

For all the intuitive plausibility of measures of recall or positive attitudes towards the ad as predictors of campaign success, no necessary link with consumer purchasing behaviour has been demonstrated. These are states that do not necessarily reflect how the brand personality has been sustained in an ad. We all remember ads that we like or brands that we do not like. We remember ads that we hate for brands that we like. And we forget much advertising, although our weekly purchases will often reflect a highly brand-conscious buying mentality.

Qualitative Data and Interpretive Techniques

One senior account planner in a major US agency, interviewed by the author, described how ethnographies were becoming more popular than focus groups:

The traditional focus group, while it's been very helpful, doesn't always necessarily get you the insights you're going to need because it's very dependent on whether someone can articulate ... and that tends to be rational ... what you really want to get at are more the emotions people have about things rather than the attitudes ... ethnographies (have) become the consumer research of choice these days.

There is a tendency to use the term 'qualitative research' as if it refers to a commonsense interpretation of naturally occurring social data such as audio recordings of talk or video recordings of behaviour. However, such approaches are more accurately labelled 'interpretive research' because the interpretation of qualitative data is not self-evident: qualitative data are invariably open to a range of interpretations. Qualitative data-gathering methods are largely drawn from traditions of anthropology (especially ethnography) and cultural sociology (Hackley, 2003e) and their rationale is based on those theoretically driven academic traditions. Popular data-gathering techniques such as participant observation, in-depth interviewing and questionnaire surveys also derive from anthropological studies.

BOX 9.6

Qualitative *vs* Quantitative Research

One leading London agency has stated in its own literature that the quantitative approach to creative research often 'looks at aggregated data instead of understanding individuals, and judges advertisements against artificial and often irrelevant criteria ... we prefer the flexibility of qualitative research'. This position on advertising research, well-established and formalized in the role of the account planner, is not universally shared in the advertising industry. Many agencies prefer quantitative data as the research basis for planning decisions.

Qualitative research may involve focus or discussion groups, observation studies or in-depth interviews. Sometimes, qualitative advertising research explicitly draws on anthropology for its theoretical foundation. The US agency Ogilvy and Mather has a discovery team of anthropologists who conduct consumer research studies; account planners at DDB Needham Worldwide in New York have conducted **deprivation studies** drawing on anthropological techniques to determine the value and meaning attached to the possession of particular types of consumer goods (Hackley, 2000). Agencies have used techniques of ethnography to give their qualitative research greater theoretically-driven insight and hence, they hope, greater intellectual weight with clients. However, what agencies claim as ethnography tends to be based on studies of weeks or months rather than the years typically required of ethnography (Elliott and Jankel-Elliott, 2002).

Some agencies have a relatively informal approach to their qualitative research. They regard qualitative research as 'talking to' consumers (Hackley, 2000) and treat the data of videos, transcripts and audio recordings as stimuli for ideas rather than as empirical evidence to support or reject hypotheses. Publicis Thailand is one agency which assimilates a commonsense understanding of consumers they call 'street smarts' throughout the advertising development process (Hackley and Tiwsakul, 2008). Other agencies will have a more explicit, theoretically informed approach to qualitative data interpretation, but most will not. The research skills and sensitivity to nuances of data of experienced planners are relied upon to a great degree, although the interpretations of qualitative research are often hotly debated in the agency account team.

Many agencies have employed trained psychologists for their research expertise in generating insights into consumer reasoning, behaviour and motivation. Consumer psychologists might conduct naturalistic experiments (in a consumption setting) or laboratory experiments measuring attitudes to ad exposures or brand recall. Qualitative research approaches in laboratory settings include **projective techniques** in which a consumer will be given a story-completion task or asked to explain the motivations of a person in a visual consumption setting. The results can generate insights that would not be revealed under more direct forms of interrogation.

Much qualitative/interpretive research focuses on the meaning of consumption, in the hope of generating a fundamental insight that can give the brand personality and the advertising a telling resonance. It does this by seeking methods to understand the lived experience of the group in question. Studies such as Sherry (1983, 1987, 1991) and Holbrook (1995) have shown how consumers seek and find meaning in their lives from their consumption experiences in ways that are non-trivial and far-reaching. The emphasis on the symbolic meaning of consumption rather than the rational/instrumental utility of consumption underlies much qualitative research.

BOX 9.7

Video Data and Qualitative Research

An international qualitative research agency adopted a quasi-anthropological approach in an account with a household cleaning goods manufacturer. They sent a cameraman into a household for two weeks simply filming the housewife doing her cleaning. The video footage makes oddly compelling viewing: after a day or two the presence of the cameraman is forgotten by the householder and the film of the lady unselfconsciously cleaning the kitchen and bathroom reveals the patterns and rituals of product usage in a setting more intimate than any other research method could reveal. The detail of how she holds the scouring sponge or the quantities of cleaning fluid she uses and where it is applied are invaluable pieces of information for the brand manufacturer and indeed for the advertiser.

If consumers' engagement is with the symbolic values portrayed by advertising and marketing, then research techniques are needed which have the subtlety and sensitivity to generate insights that are not necessarily understood fully by the consumers themselves. Ad agencies and marketing organizations need to grasp these elusive insights in order to exploit the underlying motivations for consumer practices.

Informal Research in Advertising

Another aspect of qualitative research concerns the use, more common than professionals will sometimes concede, of individual, subjective experience and reasoning in strategy decision. Research, for some professionals, is not necessarily confined to methods and studies which are formally labelled 'research'. For most people, the term 'research' implies a formal, quasi-scientific activity conducted according to strict rules and procedures. As we have seen, ad agencies do make considerable use of formal research procedures in their research, but there is also much that is *ad hoc* and informal. Advertising professionals often rely on intuition and experience in their everyday judgements and many never conduct research that would be recognized as such by an academic social scientist.

Some creative staff when given a brief will try to gain an intuitive understanding of the brand category by watching or taking part in the consumer practice. Many would maintain that this is all the research they need. Advertising professionals in general, and creative staff in particular, tend to have a lively interest in the world at large. They are curious about many aspects of human behaviour: after all, a career in advertising is essentially based on practical psychology. How people behave, think and act and what they consume are fascinating questions to an informal social scientist such as an advertising person.

One agency that had the account for children's Lego play bricks set up a Lego playroom in the agency so that creative staff could understand the product from the perspective of a user. The staff also brought their own children in and watched them playing with the bricks. Another creative spent some time in a supermarket studying shoppers because he had been given a brief for tea-bags. This kind of informal ethnography will not, of course, tell the agency anything about the market as a whole, but it can act as a powerful source of creative stimulation, sparking ideas and producing novel lines of thinking.

BOX 9.8

Creatives and Research

Although research is a hugely important part of the advertising and marketing industries, some in the industry think that research can have a bad effect on the standard of advertising. Indeed, many creative professionals in advertising would put it much more strongly than this: many are openly hostile to formal research. They feel that creative inspiration is the basis of successful advertising and they see research as a power tool wielded by those who have little understanding of how or why consumers engage with advertising. The following quote is from a copywriter complaining about research in the New York newsletter of the American Marketing Association: 'Don't tell me that ... [your] ... little questions and statistics can pinpoint the complexity and richness of how people respond to my work' (Kover, 1996: RC9). This quote neatly illustrates the conflicts that can arise when research is conceived as a formalized and method-driven technique that offers definitive findings (see 'positivistic' in glossary).

The Account Planning Role and Research

The consumer is an elusive entity, knowledge of whom confers power in the agency. Whoever can make the most plausible claim that he or she knows and understands the consumer will have the most influential voice in designing advertising strategy. Therefore, the person who has authority over the research and its interpretation wields a great deal of power over the advertising development process. Chapter 4 showed that the account planning role was specifically conceived as taking overall charge of research and, in particular, ensuring that the insights of creative research were assimilated into creative advertising development. It would therefore be a politically important role because it would moderate the tension between creative and account management by offering an authoritative voice based on evidence-driven research (Feldwick, 2007).

Traditionally, advertising agencies have been organized hierarchically, with the account executive (also called the account manager) in charge. Research would be commissioned by the account executive and he or she would have the major role in interpreting the findings and deciding what the implications might be for advertising strategy and creative executions. In the 1960s a new role emerged that challenged the authority of the account executive by claiming to be the authoritative voice of the consumer in the agency. At a JWT awayday the new discipline was inappropriately labelled 'account planning'. The label stuck.

Uses of Qualitative Research Insights

There are many examples of products and advertising strategies being developed through qualitative research insights.

Disposable nappies (or diapers) were developed from studies which invited young parents into the agency so that their behaviour when changing their babies could be observed. The techniques they used to unwrap, remove and fasten the nappies, and how they interacted with the infant while doing so, were instrumental in informing the design of disposables such as the Huggies brand.

One Thai ad agency used a technique they called 'street smarts' and observed how consumers used Nestlé Coffee Mate, a very popular brand in Thailand, in the social context of coffee shops, so that their creative work was informed by an intimate understanding of how consumers use the product within a social setting.

It is said that Toyota executives spent time in California before designing the Lexus in order to observe how affluent consumers used their luxury cars. In these and in many other cases qualitative observation provided practical marketing insights.

As noted in Chapter 4, the account planning role evolved to address some of the difficulties faced by agencies that were trying to formally integrate their research into the creative advertising development process. The success of the discipline has been mixed (Hackley, 2003f) but in the agencies which espouse it there tends to be a general acceptance of the value of qualitative insight for guiding creative development. For originators of account planning such as Stephen King at JWT and Stanley Pollitt at BMP (Feldwick, 2007; Pickton and Crosier, 2003; Pollitt, 1979; Steel, 1998), the integration of research into creative advertising development is one of the primary responsibilities of the account planner. The role was also conceived partly to act as a buffer between the account management and creative functions to reduce conflict and promote a better understanding of research within the agency.

The account planning role, as 'the voice of the consumer in the agency', brings the enigma of research under the remit of one person who is charged to design, conduct, interpret and explain research and its implications for creativity throughout the process. Performing the role successfully demands exceptional interpersonal and research skills from the account planner. It also requires an agency ethos that supports the planning task (Hackley, 2000). Those advertising professionals dismissive of account planning question whether a specialist account planning discipline is really necessary to perform the tasks described above. In many agencies account management retains control over the use of research and engages the services of a specialist researcher. However, account planning enthusiasts might counter that account management tends to be too close to the client and too dependent on the quantitative notions of research to be able to independently apply the value of consumer insight-driven creativity.

Debate and Dissent around Research in Advertising

Much misunderstanding about research in advertising occurs because it is not one entity but many. As we have seen, research is conducted for a number of different purposes. First, it is what is done to initially investigate a brand's market category, its role in the client's business and the consumer segments which are current or potential users. Second, it is what account planning staff do to try to generate facts about consumer reality that can give communication a particular resonance. Third, research is what is often done to completed creative work before the campaign is launched, in an effort to predict the likely consumer response. Indeed, in some US agencies research is often regarded as being synonymous with copy-testing. Fourth, research is the process of trying to track the response of consumers to the campaign. Debates around research method in advertising, then, revolve not only around fundamental questions of research philosophy but also around the usefulness of particular methods in given situations. As Kover (1995) and Hackley (2003c) made clear, advertising agencies comprise professionals with very different intellectual backgrounds and equally different implicit theories of practice. These differences are caused by different assumptions about the nature of advertising and consumers.

For example, much research in the field has its basis in the linear information processing model of communication (deriving from, for example, Schramm's (1948) mass communications research) described in Chapter 2. The linear model of communication conceives of advertising as something that acts on individual consumers in social isolation and this assumption has framed much of the research in the field. Some academic researchers (e.g. Mick and Buhl, 1992) have argued that this preoccupation with advertising exposure isolated from its social context risks misconstruing the fundamentally social nature of the interaction between consumers and advertising (but also see Scott, 1994a, for comments on Mick and Buhl, 1992). Consumers usually engage with advertising in a social context and not alone in a viewing booth. Ritson and Elliott (1999, citing Holbrook, 1995: 93; McCracken, 1987: 123, in support) have suggested that advertising cannot properly be understood as if it operates in a social vacuum. Advertising, they argue, is actively consumed, reinterpreted and used for purposes of social positioning and identity formation (Buttle, 1994; O'Donohoe, 1994).

Rationality Versus Emotion in Advertising

The linear information processing tradition of advertising theory also emphasizes conscious and rational information processing. Academic researchers have drawn attention to the symbolic character of advertising communication, suggesting that consumer motivations are not invariably dominated by conscious reasoning. For example, McCracken (1986) has alluded to the deeply symbolic character of consumption and argues that this feature has been marginalized in favour of a rational model of how advertising works. For this researcher cultural meaning has a 'mobile quality' (p. 71) and advertising is an 'instrument of meaning transfer' (p. 74). Mick and Buhl (1992: 314) draw critical attention to the tendency for advertising research to regard ads as 'relatively fixed stimuli' and consumers as 'solitary subjects, without identities, who react to ads through linear stages or limited persuasion routes, for the principal purpose of judging brands'.

Holbrook and O'Shaughnessy (1988: 400) maintain that humans live 'embedded within a shared system of signs based on public language and other symbolic objects'. Advertising can be seen as a major site of signification, taking consumer cultural meanings, placing them in the context of brand marketing and reflecting them back so that consumers can perform cultural practices symbolically through the consumption of marketed brands. The particular signs that carry meaning in a given context for a given **consumer community** are difficult for brand advertisers to ascertain unless they can understand the world in the same way as the group of interest.

For Thompson et al. (1989: 433) 'personal understandings are always situated within a network of culturally-shared knowledge, shared beliefs, ideals and taken-for-granted assumptions about the nature of social life'. The implication is that social research cannot fully appreciate personal understandings without also understanding how they interface with the social context in which they are formed. Qualitative research approaches, particularly those drawing on interpretive traditions of social research, offer one way for advertisers to access these meanings.

Agencies do often try to capture the emotional response of consumers to advertisements by using survey questionnaires to assess the degree to which a consumer rates an ad on a five point scale of how much they like it. Leaving aside the problems of self-reports as research data, there can be a concern over whether liking an ad has any relevance for the client. Many of us like ads which we don't find persuasive. The symbolic element of consumer behaviour is difficult to capture because it is unarticulated. We may not be able to rationalize why we like certain ads. There is a case for measuring emotions and attitudes just because it can be done, and it is more concrete knowledge than none at all. But there is also a case for using more open-ended methods, however messy they may be, if they can sometimes enable consumers to express the underlying symbolism of brand communication.

Against Research in Advertising

Advertising is an area in which art and business collide, often with aesthetically striking and commercially fruitful results. Understandably, there are conflicts resulting from the differing values and mindsets associated with each community. Research is a major site of such conflicts: the way it is used, undertaken and interpreted in agencies can place these conflicts in sharp relief. In sociological terms, research in agencies can be seen as part of a managerial ideology pushing to impose rational efficiency on administrative fields (Lears, 1994). Research methods can provide measureable criteria with which to judge creative advertising. Regardless of whether measurement in consumer research is valid or useful, it does provide the appearance of rational efficiency, just as work study techniques do in labour-intensive manufacturing. In each area there are those who would argue that the net effect of measurement on output quality or efficiency is negative.

The appearance of rational efficiency is perhaps less important for advertising agencies today than it once was. In the early part of the twentieth century it was considered important for the advertising industry to put its disreputable, snake-oil salesman image behind it and win legitimacy by becoming a rational, bureaucratic field of business. Today, the widespread belief that advertisers are knowledgeable about the psychology of consumption and have skills of hidden persuasion (to borrow Vance Packard's term) is part of the mystique of the advertising business.

For many creative professionals the term 'research' is synonymous with formal methods that are used to test and often veto creative executions. The attitude to research expressed by Toscani in Chapter 8 best captures the creative perspective. Toscani never did any research but produced some of the most striking and effective advertising that the industry has seen. Of course, Toscani took creative risks, but professionals would argue that taking such risks improves the quality of advertising. Many feel that an over-reliance on research to test creative executions can make advertising neither offensive nor enchanting, simply conservative. Some creative staff believe that inspiration based on an intuitive understanding of consumers is the best way to produce great advertising. Of course, the intuitive understanding of top creative people is built on wide and eclectic interests. It is also based on characteristics such as a capacity for hard work, an acute sense of observation, high intelligence, intellectual flexibility and the ability to work under pressure (McKeil, 1985; Ogilvy, 1963, cited in Wilmshurst and Mackay, 1999).

Promotional agencies often need to invoke research findings because clients are suspicious of creativity that cannot be clearly justified by a well-founded piece of research. Even within the communications industry, many professionals place creativity in opposition to advertising effectiveness. They argue that too much creativity impairs effectiveness. In some cases the business case for a creative execution can be supported using statistical or other hard data. Graphs and charts based on numerical data can go a long way to reassuring clients that the pretty advertising pictures are part of a robust and coherent business strategy. Statistically-based research approaches invoke the discourse of science in a field that is often characterized by judgmental or intuitive decision-making. The rhetoric of science has a long history as persuasive advertising copy selling detergent, convenience food or toothpaste. It can be just as valuable to account executives who need to persuade clients that a business decision is based on good evidence and rigorous thinking.

Research Ethics

Given the heightened sensitivity over ethical issues in advertising and marketing in general it is worth briefly discussing some issues of research ethics which may impact in advertising contexts. Conducting research with consumers involves prying into their and our attitudes and lifestyles. In some cultures, consumers tend to be very open about this and happy to tell a researcher they have never met before intimate details of their consumer behaviour. In others, it is much less likely that a cold-calling researcher would get a positive response. Where consumers are willing to give of their time to discuss aspects of their consumer experience, it is incumbent on the researcher to treat information as highly confidential and to respect the wishes, feelings and wellbeing of the research participant.

The leading professional bodies have their own ethical standards which they require professionals to adhere to.[3] There are, also, various ethical conventions which are widely accepted as good practice. For example, research participants' names and personal details should normally be anonymized in research reporting. A lot of research is conducted through agencies which keep a roster of consumers who put themselves forward for paid participation in research studies. Even though they have volunteered, their personal details should not be publicized.

Research studies should not cross legal or ethical boundaries in any way. For example, in Box 9.10 the research described was ethically dubious since the researcher did not ask the permission of the university to conduct research on its campus. Of course, research such as this does not seek ethical approval since it would probably not be offered.

Some research studies might wish to use minors (children) in which case detailed procedures of vetting and ethical approval would have to be sought. Research participants in focus groups who are being videoed would need to be reassured that the film would only be used for the precise purpose for which it was being undertaken, and only by officials of the relevant companies involved in the research study. They would also need to be reassured of the integrity and trustworthiness of the researcher.

BOX 9.10

Exploiting Insider Research Sources

A Scotch whisky brand hired a student to be a brand representative on a UK university campus. He was asked to perform various duties such as conducting questionnaire surveys in class and recruiting participants for discussion groups which focused on tasting and talking about the branded whisky. The manufacturers wanted to learn how to gain a foothold for their brand in the student market, given that many drinkers do not begin to drink whisky until they are over 25. The student also promoted the brand by consuming it and setting up promotional posters in the campus bars. For his work, he received some much needed remuneration and some experience in marketing that might help in his future career. The brand owners received far more; unrestricted access to a potentially valuable market segment at a nominal cost. To carry out market research on a student campus a brand manufacturer would normally have to ask for permission and then use designated points of access. An alcohol brand, especially, would have to go through vetting procedures before permission would (or might) be granted. Using a financially embarrassed student is not only cheap, it also means that students are accessed by one of their peers and therefore resistance is circumvented.

Today, most universities and research agencies have ethics codes which research studies have to abide by. These are especially important in cases where studies touch on deeply personal or possibly traumatic events in a participant's life, such as sexual behaviour, alcohol consumption, family trauma and other cases in which the ethical procedure would need to be strictly adhered to in the interests of both the research agency and the participant.

Chapter Summary

Chapter 9 has focused on issues around research in advertising rather than offering a detailed exposition of how to execute certain methods, which would be the subject of another book. Many methods, such as questionnaire surveys, experiments, focus or discussion groups and video ethnographies are well known. Just how to execute them in the most effective way is a complex topic. In advertising, debate focuses around what method is best for a particular purpose. The chapter described how research plays a role in each stage of the creative advertising development process. It explained that many of today's major research agencies began life as advertising agency research departments. It also outlined some of the exchange of ideas which has occurred in the field between academic and industry researchers. Some typical methods of research in advertising were explained, with advantages and disadvantages discussed. The chapter went on to discuss ongoing debates in the industry over the best methods and the best way to execute them for the different purposes of research in advertising. Finally, some issues in research ethics were discussed.

 ■ **Review Questions** ■

1 Place yourself in the position of an account planner trying to understand a new brief from a manufacturer of branded disposable nappies (diapers). What sources and kinds of information will be required? What methods will be useful? Explain your choices in terms of the research priorities such a brief demands.

2 Why is research a source of potential conflict in advertising agencies? Form an account team group commissioned with an account for a brand of your choice. Now role-play the planning discussion to pick out the important preliminary issues. In what ways can you see that each account team member (account management, account planning and creative) approaches the task with quite different interests at stake?

3 Pick three print ads and conduct copy-test experiments with an audience. Devise scaled questionnaires to assess the strength of feeling subjects have towards various components of the ad. What issues arise? How useful are the findings?

4 Convene a focus/discussion group to explore the issue of ethics in advertising. Use a selection of ethically controversial ads as stimulus material. Write up the main findings. Now write a brief assessment of the main problems and uses of this research technique.

5 Outline how a new brief for a brand of fruit-flavoured alcoholic drink might be better understood through informal and qualitative research.

■■■ **CASE** ■■■

'Social Branding' and the Dove 'Campaign for Real Beauty'[4]

Dove is a range of feminine beauty and cleansing products manufactured by Unilever. Dove has become an archetype for 'social' branding because it has gained passionate commitment and engagement from its consumers for its ethos of raising women's self-esteem. At the same time,

Picture 8   This ad forms part of the Dove 'Campaign for Real Beauty' that is linked with the Dove Self-Esteem Foundation, a funded charity concerned with activities and education designed to boost the self-esteem of girls and young women.

Reproduced with kind permission of Ogilvy UK and Unilever.

(See the colour insert near the middle of this book for a full colour image.)

the brand has raised its market share by an estimated 30 per cent (Robinson et al., 2009). The Dove 'Campaign for Real Beauty' began in 2003 with the aim of generating an emotional engagement with the brand from consumers. The key issue which has driven the emotional engagement has been women's self-image and the belief that cosmetic products marketing and advertising should make women feel more, not less, attractive.

'Social' branding is a term that is associated with the cultural status of brands as tools for the production of self and social identity. Social branding initiatives attempt to leverage cultural insights to create marketing initiatives which further socially desirable and ethical ends. This may entail creating shareholder value as well, as with Dove, but often entails social marketing campaigns for public bodies and government health and education agencies related, for example, to reducing cigarette smoking and promoting exercise or reading. The distinguishing feature of social branding is that its force rests on an identification with the target consumers' values and behaviour which will create a sense of personal engagement with the campaign. In one sense there is nothing new in this – good advertising practice has always valued insights into the consumer as hooks for creativity. Social branding articulates this in a new way linked with ethics and social responsibility.

The central insight of the Dove 'Campaign for Real Beauty' is the research finding that most women do not consider themselves beautiful. Furthermore, after reading a fashion magazine full of images of ideal beauty, most women reported that they felt less attractive (Robinson et al., 2009). The Dove campaign subverts the traditional genre of feminine beauty products advertising by using models and creative approaches which are deliberately distanced from idealized images of beauty (see Picture 9). The CEO of cosmetics brand Revlon was reputed to have summed up his company philosophy by saying they didn't sell cosmetics – they sold hope. To put this in a similar aphorism, Dove, in contrast, sells self-esteem.

Intriguingly, the campaign team say that in order to sell the idea to the male, middle-aged senior board they resorted to taking a video of the board members' daughters talking about the way that cosmetic and beauty products advertising made them feel. They echoed the wider research findings and this helped convince the board to support a campaign which took a radically different approach to an important and well-established brand.

One of the most compelling features of the Dove campaign has been its integration of media for different engagement approaches. The press and TV advertising has made a feature of using 'real' women and not professional models, while clever public relations[5] has leveraged the theme of empowering women in Dove advertising rather than encouraging insecurity about body image. The brand values have been portrayed through a long-running and innovative integrated campaign using above-the-line television, press and outdoor advertising, along with a significant presence in online and editorial.

One of the most noted aspects of the Dove campaign has been a viral video made by Ogilvy Toronto which was placed on YouTube.[6] The video, called 'Evolution', shows an 'ordinary' woman being transformed into a model by a makeover and some graphics trickery. Her hair and complexion are changed and her neck digitally lengthened with Photoshop to give her a typical model appearance. The artificial evolution into catwalk model shows that beauty ideals in the media cannot be regarded as authentic. The video has been viewed almost 10 million times and generated a great deal of comment through blogs, media comment and word of mouth (WOM). A follow-up video called 'Onslaught', also by Ogilvy, has already created considerable attention.[7] Other initiatives in the 'Campaign for Real Beauty' have included the Dove self-esteem fund which contributes to groups working with young women and girls to raise self-esteem, and the Dove CRB website which carries product information, news, and interactive games.

Critics have argued that the women Dove uses in its campaign might be 'real' and size 10 or 18 but they are not unattractive and they look good in the ads. Then again, one could argue that this is exactly the point – that women who are not professional models can look attractive if they feel confident and empowered. This sets Dove apart from the majority of beauty campaigns which offer women an airbrushed ideal of feminine beauty, an ideal which women are expected to endorse by consuming the product which they know rationally cannot make them look like the model in the ad. Another criticism is that there is a contradiction in Dove's positioning, since it is, after all, a massively successful beauty products brand.

As an advertising and branding campaign, Dove is an exemplar of astute social branding technique. The campaign has generated extensive debate over all media channels from internet blogs to national press and prime time television shows. Discussion has centred around whether women are complicit in male value judgements about unattainable standards of beauty when they are over-critical of their own physical appearance and that of their friends. This is the tendency which, critics argue, many beauty products' marketing campaigns exploit. Dove has shown that an advertising campaign which subverted the traditional genre for its product category and solicited consumer engagement with a deeply felt personal issue could also be a major commercial success.

 ## ■ Case questions

1 Can you think of any other brand categories which might benefit from a social branding positioning? Justify your choices, giving examples.

2 Why has Dove achieved the success that it has? What, in your opinion, is the key customer benefit in this example of social branding?

3 Look at the Dove CRB material available on the internet. Are there any other initiatives you feel Dove could deploy to leverage the deep sense of engagement its consumers have with the brand?

■ ■ Further Reading ■

De Pelsmacker, P. and Dens, N. (2009) *Advertising Research: Message, Medium and Context*. Antwerp: Garant.

Ehrenberg, A. and Barnard, N. (1997) 'Advertising and product demand', *Admap*, May: 14–18.

Hackley, C. (1998) 'Social constructionism and research in marketing and advertising', *Qualitative Market Research: An International Journal*, 1(3): 125–31.

Jones, J.P. (1990) 'Advertising: strong force or weak force? Two views an ocean apart', *International Journal of Advertising*, 9: 233–46.

Wells, W.D. (ed.) (1997) *Measuring Advertising Effectiveness*. Hillsdale, NJ: Lawrence Erlbaum Associates.

Web-based Resources

Hackley C. (2007) 'Marketing psychology and the hidden persuaders', *The Psychologist*, www.thepsychologist.org.uk/archive/archive_home.cfm? volume ID=20&editionID=150&ArticleID=1228

On the Companion Website

These journal articles are freely available on the companion website (www.sagepub.co.uk/hackley).

Relocating Alcohol Advertising Research: Examining Socially Mediated Relationships with Alcohol
Jane Cherrington, Kerry Chamberlain, and Joe Grixti
Journal of Health Psychology, Mar 2006; vol. 11: pp. 209–222.

Interpretability and Social Power, or, Why Postmodern Advertising Works
Martin Morris
Media, Culture & Society, Sep 2005; vol. 27: pp. 697–718.

How Advertising Works: Alternative Situational and Attitudinal Explanations
Peter W. Reed and Michael T. Ewing
Marketing Theory, Jun 2004; vol. 4: pp. 91–112.

Notes

1 Major European research organization http://www.esomar.org/
2 See the ad at http://www.hovisbakery.co.uk/our-ads/ (accessed 25 June 2009).
3 For example, the ethics code of practice of the Market Research Society, at www.mrs.org.uk/standards/guidelines.htm
4 www.campaignforrealbeauty.co.uk/#/main_landing.aspx/ (accessed 3 May 2009).
5 www.unilever.co.uk/ourbrands/casestudies/dove_casestudy.asp (accessed 3 May 2009).
6 www.digitaltrainingacademy.com/viralmarketing/2007/08/dove_new_models_for_advertisin/ (accessed 3 May 2009).
7 www.youtube.com/watch?v=Ei6JvK0W60I (accessed 4 May 2009).

10 Integrating e-Marketing and Advertising

Chapter Outline

In the converging advertising environment is it increasingly difficult to separate elements of the media mix. Nevertheless, these elements merit discussion in their own right, especially with regard to their often pivotal role in integrated marketing communications campaigns. This chapter picks up some of the issues on new media and integrated communication planning introduced in Chapter 1 to discuss them in the context of other e-marketing issues, including mobile and interactive advertising.

Key chapter content:

- e-Marketing and integration: benefits and scope

- Integration issues

- Mobile advertising.

e-Marketing and Integration: Benefits and Scope

The benefits of integrating different media in campaign planning are tangible. For example, research by the Internet Advertising Bureau has suggested that when an above-the-line media plan was supplemented by online advertising to 10–15 per cent of budget, the overall campaign benefits (however measured) would show increases of 20–30 per cent (Sharma et al., 2008: xiii). This tendency for integration to leverage disproportionately large benefits has been seen in all media mixes. But what particular qualities do e-marketing approaches bring to integrated marketing communication campaigns?

Firstly, it makes sense to examine what is included in the e-marketing category. E-marketing refers broadly to any marketing through electronic media, especially digital media such as the internet, mobile devices and digital television. Examples of some of the marketing communication techniques made possible by e-marketing are listed in Table 10.0. This is the fastest developing area of advertising and promotion since new technology and new applications are emerging very rapidly. The internet, in particular, is the fastest growing advertising medium in terms of reach and share of promotional spend. What is most intriguing about the field, from an advertising point of view, is the rate of convergence between electronic media. It seems likely that mobile devices combining television and the internet will become more and more common with much improved accessibility and quality in the future. Integration then will have moved beyond being a source of strategic advantage in advertising, it will be a technological fact and a compulsory aspect of promotional planning.

Table 10.0   Examples of e-marketing techniques

• viral marketing by email or video	• interactive billboards
• SMS text messaging	• microsites and sales promotions
• podcasting	• advergaming
• weblogs	• online direct marketing
• affiliate marketing	• social networking and buzz marketing
• search engine marketing	• interactive product placement
• online personal selling	• the use of online consumer communities
• online advertising	

The meaning of viral marketing has extended beyond email to video, since video sharing websites have become such popular vehicles for viral advertisements. SMS text messaging can make use of location technology to target mobile device carriers when they are in a specific place, such as a particular shopping area. **Affiliate marketing** refers to co-operative ventures which enable sites to market each other's products or provide direct click-through access to related, affiliated brands. Search engine marketing is the practice of making sure that a particular brand features at the top of category searches by paying search engines and ensuring that search terms are connected with the brand. With online personal selling a pop-up window connects consumers browsing a site with a live sales person. Online advertising includes banner, classified and click-through ads, while many brands will make use of microsites (such as Dove's, discussed in Chapter 9) with brand information, offers and opportunities for consumer engagement. Another way of generating consumer engagement is by producing a game based on the brand, called **advergaming**. Interactive product placement (described in Chapter 6) makes use of a technology which enables viewers watching TV or video online to click on items in the scene to find out how to buy them.

In many cases, techniques such as these emerge from more creative ways of understanding how consumers interact with electronic technology. In others, the techniques are technology-driven. For example, computer games have now evolved beyond hand-held devices so that gestures, speech and body movement can involve gamers in a scenario in which they interact with characters. This virtual world clearly has immense possibilities for deepening consumer engagement in promotional communication. On one level we can simply walk through shopping centres and choose products, or we can become characters in the scenarios depicted on screen. So, say, you could enter a shopping world and have sales people talk to you directly, answering queries you have put to them. Or you could have three-dimensional games designed around a brand.

These are but a few examples in a crowded and rapidly changing area. Part of their appeal is novelty – they are new, and that has an intrinsic appeal, especially to people intrigued by new technology. There are also significant commercial advantages to be gained from using e-marketing communication. Some are listed in Table 10.1.

Table 10.1   Advantages of e-marketing communication

Cost: an e-marketing campaign can be created at relatively little expense when compared to above-the-line media campaigns.

Reach: e-marketing communications can reach huge volumes of potential consumers globally.

Accountability: there is considerable scope for measuring results from direct response mechanisms in e-marketing.

Conversion: e-marketing enables customers to make instant purchases, enabling a good rate of converting browsers into customers.

Engagement through interactivity: e-marketing makes it possible to engage consumers in dialogue or interaction, for example where brand-based websites offer games, blogs, offers, news and competitions.

(Cont'd)

Table 10.1

Segmentation and database management: it is possible to link the customer database with the company website and achieve personalized, targeted offers based on tracking pervious purchases and inquiries.

Relationship management: since people are accessing the internet via increasingly mobile means it is possible to target and interact with individuals in ways which are tailored to their personal lifestyle.

24/7 service: there is no limit on the opening hours of a website.

Creative scope: e-marketing offers a creative palate for advertisers almost without limit. Different media can be combined and enhanced through display and visual technology, generating powerful possibilities for engaging consumers.

It has always been slightly problematic to separate marketing activities and processes from marketing communication (Schultz et al., 1993). There is an interface between the two. For example, the brand positioning, the satisfaction of consumer needs, and indeed the purchase are all predicated on communication, in some sense. E-marketing technology has made the indivisibility of marketing communication all the more evident since it has collapsed sourcing and logistics, order fulfilment and customer service, and promotion, into one entity. The website connects the customer directly with stock control. Of course, behind the scenes there may be many links in the chain. Delivery, for example, is often outsourced to another company, while there may be many stock suppliers, and multi-media advertising and promotion programmes. But the website offers a seamless integration of all these elements from the customer perspective. Not only that but company websites can also generate additional revenue streams by taking advantage of the browsing traffic through affiliate marketing programmes or the trade in customer databases for market segmentation and customer profiling.

┌ BOX 10.0 ┌

Twitter Looks for a Revenue-Generating Business Model[1]

Epitomizing the challenge of new media and advertising is *Twitter*, a service which enables users to communicate instantly in short (150 character) sentences. At the time of writing (July 2009) social networking site *Twitter* had become the fastest growing website in the UK, according to a report in the *Independent* newspaper drawing on data from internet analyst Hitwise. At just over 5 per cent of total visits in June 2009 it is still relatively small compared to *Facebook* (32 per cent of total visits), *MySpace* (29 per cent) and *YouTube* (9.5 per cent).

But its growth trajectory is striking, with a 22-fold increase in a year, ranking it as the 5th most popular social networking site on the internet. Topical news coverage connecting it with world events and celebrity users has helped broaden its appeal. *Twitter* was founded by Biz Stone, Jack Dorsey and Evan Williams in 2006, though most of its growth has occurred in 2009. The problem facing *Twitter*, like all the other social networking sites, is how to generate revenue on the back of its immense consumer traffic. It has rejected the advertising model used by some other sites and instead is hoping to explore partnerships with other companies which need to communicate with customers. One of the advantages of *Twitter* is that it is exceptionally well suited to mobile applications and so may be able to leverage this in its search for a revenue-generating business model.

e-Marketing Planning Issues

Developing an e-marketing plan entails much the same sequence of steps as for a conventional advertising or marketing communication plan (described in Chapter 3). Firstly, there is a need to identify the desired or potential target audience. If there are several potential audiences then they should be ranked in order of importance so that media mix decisions can be made on clear commercial considerations. The next step is objective setting. The objectives can be much the same as for any other kind of advertising, such as increasing the market share of an existing brand, positioning or repositioning, brand launch, change attitudes, reach a new market, building sales through the internet, and so on. Once objectives are established the optimum e-marketing mix has to be decided upon. As in Table 10.0, there are numerous techniques from which to choose, depending on the precise objectives, and target groups. Budget setting might be the next stage, given that the objectives and e-marketing mix ought to give an idea about the potential rate of return. In many cases this doesn't happen and the budget is simply a default figure, what is left after essential costs. But this is a short-sighted way of operating since marketing budgets are an investment which will provide a rate of return. True, in marketing, the rate of return (often called ROI or return on investment) is notoriously difficult to calculate with precision. But of all marketing media, e-marketing offers the most powerful potential for measuring and also for achieving a desired ROI because of its integration with database management and order fulfilment.

The next step in the planning process concerns action, especially tactics. What has to be done to make this plan work? Finally, constant attention to the measurement of results can make it possible to adapt, increase or redirect resources to a particular area where necessary.

Integration Issues

Benefits of Integrated Marketing Communication

As we have already seen in many examples, communications professionals are integrating media in innovative ways. Integrated Marketing Communication, or IMC for short (Belch and Belch, 2008; Schultz and Kitchen, 1997; Schultz et al., 1993), has been a topic of discussion among advertising academics for some time. Integration in this context implies planned, co-ordinated communication conceived from a strategic point of view. Strategic here means that the communication plan commands significant resources and has a carefully conceived purpose which is directly linked with the major objectives of the organization. IMC is the planning and co-ordination of marketing communications in order to portray a coherent brand personality and a consistent communications strategy across all media channels.

The idea that all communications channels might be integrated around the brand is intuitively appealing to brand organizations, which seek control over their operating environment in order to reduce risk and uncertainty. The theory of IMC suggests greater control over the marketing communications environment in which consumers form their preferences and enact their consumption choices. The logic is that if a brand message is received (by a consumer) from more than one channel, the two channels might act to mutually reinforce the message, provided that the message from each channel is consistent. If all channels are operated as distinct entities with differing priorities, tactical objectives and creative executions, such consistency and control are not possible. The integration in IMC implies that all organizational communications are co-ordinated from an holistic, strategic standpoint.

A consumer may, for example, form a particular impression of a brand from a TV ad, which could be contradicted or undermined by another about the same brand received from the press or radio. As consumers we are not discerning about the source of our brand ideas. We neither know nor care whether our overriding impression of brand X was formed from a TV ad, a press story, a conversation with a friend or direct consumption experience. If, as is more likely, our impression of a brand is formed from an accumulation of encounters with it over time from every kind of communication source, then we are not aware of which, if any, particular source was dominant in framing our idea. As Percy et al. (2001) note, to consumers all promotion is 'advertising'.

If brand marketing organizations are able to co-ordinate their communications then the messages they transmit can work with each other synergistically rather than competing against each other to get and keep the consumer's attention and to promote the brand values. The theme of integration emphasizes control over the whole brand image, from corporate communication and imagery all the way through to the brand, product level and even the customer interface through service and merchandising.

Practical Difficulties of Integrated Communications

In practice, the differing disciplinary traditions and practices of the various communications agencies make true integration very difficult for organizations to achieve. It is often more feasible to create a degree of commonality that links the various channels with consistent themes and values while allowing for a variation within the overall theme. In other words, organizations achieve limited yet significant control over the way that their brand is portrayed across communication channels by establishing common themes.

Even this abstract level of integration can be problematic for large organizations. In the communications industry PR, advertising, sales promotion, direct and database marketing, internal communication, and so on, are all regarded as distinct disciplines. Many large corporations are traditionally set up with different officers and departments handling these disciplines. Co-ordination is a difficult task when communications professionals have to liaise with so many different people, each of whom has a different perspective. Even within one organization it is common for different departments to deal with, respectively, brochures and print publicity, public relations, corporate image and customer relations, and brand advertising. These different departments do not necessarily speak to each other on a regular basis.

So integration of communication across channels can be achieved in partial ways: above- and below-the-line channels can be integrated to form 'through-the-line' campaigns. Media channels with different characteristics may be used in tandem with various creative executions in order to portray the brand personality in coherent but varied and mutually reinforcing ways. Full-scale integration of all media channels is much more problematic since it demands a degree of central control that few organizations would deem appropriate or possible. However useful in principle it may be for a consumer to get a consistent message about the brand from telephone conversations with service personnel, TV and press ads, press editorial, company brochures and written material, controlling each of these elements closely is beyond the scope of most organizations. Nevertheless, even partial integration is attractive to organizations because of the potential benefits in terms of control over the brand and influence over consumer perceptions.

Pressures for Integration in the Advertising Business

The structure and priorities of marketing communications agencies are changing. Clients' pressure for integrated, through-the-line communications is changing the priorities of agencies that have traditionally specialized in above-the-line work. Ad agencies are trying to offer expertise in non-advertising dimensions of the communications mix such as sales promotion, web-based communication and digital television, and below-the-line specialists are getting into mainstream advertising. For example, the direct marketing agency Wunderman of London handle internet communications, public relations events, direct mail and also some press ads for clients such as Xerox, M & G, Jaguar cars and Microsoft. What is more, the need for integrated media solutions has increased the importance of media agencies, many of which have in recent years become separate businesses distinct from the advertising agencies of which they were once part.

Now some media agencies are actually moving back into creative work by hiring dedicated creative staff or by sub-contracting creative work to small, independent creative hot shops and boutiques. Although these small independents can offer good creative ideas, some industry professionals argue that they are unlikely to have the resources to nurture a brand in over time. It remains to be seen how the conflicts facing marketing communications agencies will be resolved in the longer term.

Media Pressures on Integration

In spite of the difficulties, partial integration is an increasingly powerful influence in advertising and marketing communications because of the ways in which media channels can dovetail into each other to portray the brand identity. 'Through-the-line' approaches in which different media channels are deployed in one campaign are now common. Furthermore, conventional wisdom about the relative impact of different channels has been upturned. The rapid changes in the media infrastructure have resulted in changes in the marketing power of the differing media. TV remains highly important, but other media channels can perform similar communication functions as well as or better than TV, and often more cheaply. For example, major brands have used PR to raise awareness on brand launches. Others have led their communications strategy with below-the-line approaches such as direct response and direct mail. In fact, below-the-line promotion is now a site of creativity as fertile as that of the display ad. Creative uses and combinations of media channels have assumed more importance as technological developments and audience fragmentation drive marketing communications strategies in media-saturated, advanced economies. This general trend has blurred the disciplinary boundaries of marketing communication somewhat and has led to increased integration. The buzz-phrase 'media-neutral planning' reflects the new order of media relations, with mass media advertising no longer necessarily the senior partner.

BOX 10.2

Internet and Not-So New Media

The increased pressure for cost-effectiveness of media buying has resulted in greater attention being paid to non-traditional media, especially digital and mobile. 'New media' is still a term used in the business although most forms of new media are no longer new at all. It is now common for brand advertisers to set up a dedicated website, to offer a web-based retail interface, to target consumers with SMS text or multi-media messaging or to produce CD-Roms, DVDs or videos for publicity purposes in through-the-line, integrated campaigns which operate across the media mix. Interactive television is another new medium with great marketing potential, but one that has so far proved less popular among TV viewers than the industry expected. The potential for marketing communications with mass coverage and targeted themes is clearly attractive to advertisers. New agencies specializing in SMS text messaging or other aspects of digital communications are emerging, chasing the popularity of mobile phones and their ability to target consumer groups using tailored messages with direct-response potential. The growth of new media opportunities is compounded by a similar rise in ambient media opportunities to insert promotional messages into non-advertising spaces in the consumer environment (Shankar and Horton, 1999).

Evolving New Media

As noted, telecommunications and broadcast technology are developing so quickly that new media do not remain new for very long. The internet is still new only in relation to more traditional print and broadcast advertising media. Digital technology has reduced the cost of producing promotional print brochures, videos, CD-Roms and DVDs for circulation. New technology has produced a growth in agencies specializing in email and SMS text messaging for advertising. Some agencies have attracted a poor reputation for this sector by spamming thousands of messages indiscriminately, often for illegal or ethically dubious products or services. Used with greater discrimination, such methods can target specified consumers with messages tailored to their consumption and leisure interests. The WAP technology in mobile phones makes it possible to track the physical whereabouts of owners at any time (so long as they are carrying their mobile phone). In one experiment mobile phone users were targeted with text message promotional offers as they walked past the relevant store. All they had to do was to walk in to take advantage of the offer.

Mobile telecommunications and electronic payment and data storage have become key aspects of the Integration of Marketing Communications along with logistics and order fulfilment. New media often have the capacity for direct response. For example, the UK national newspaper *The Sunday Times* has used a CD-Rom format to carry promotional offers for many kinds of entertainment product such as music, cinema and theatre tickets, and fashion.[2] This format, given away as a supplement to the newspaper, demonstrates products and services through audio or video clips and can interface with websites (through 'hot links to the online shop') so that users can buy instantly. The CD carries demonstrations and try-outs of movies, computer games, book extracts, TV shows and competitions. It is at once a series of advertisements, an electronic catalogue and an entertainments listings vehicle. The fact that it is given away with a Sunday newspaper means that the audience is pre-segmented: the newspaper marketing team already knows a lot about their readership and can recruit advertisers interested in a preselected audience of active consumers. At the time of writing, advertising in *The Sunday Times* can cost more than £50,000 for a single, one-page ad (more for colour). The CD-Rom format also increases the newspaper's capacity for carrying advertising and selling it at a lower cost to advertisers.

The capacity for marketing communications vehicles to provide an instant purchasing interface is one of the reasons why interactive TV was predicted to become very popular. The consumer take-up of interactive TV has not been as rapid as expected by the industry, but it nevertheless remains an enticing opportunity for brand owners to communicate with individual consumers in a format which offers a purchase capability. The internet is a powerful vehicle for this form of integrated marketing, but so far has proved a difficult medium for marketers to master. Some internet brands such as *Amazon, eBay* and *lastminute.com* have shown the massive sales leverage that an internet presence can offer a brand. The many dotcom failures have shown how difficult it can be to get this form of business right. Many brands hedge their bets in their marketing communication activities by adopting integrated strategies which link interactive websites to mass media and other advertising. A popular ad with a dedicated website can in itself provoke many 'hits' from consumers interested in the ad and/or the brand.

Mobile Advertising

As we have noted, convergence is the theme of the moment. It won't be fully exploited for a long time, decades perhaps, but there is the technological potential for people to carry mobile devices that can serve all their work, communication and entertainment needs. How long it might take consumers to want to carry such devices on a wide scale is another question. It is hugely unlikely that a non-advertising funding model will predominate in this new world of convergence, and highly likely that advertising will be central to it. The current state of mobile advertising is that it is an under-developed market, though there is much interest in the industry. One key element of mobile currently is permission – advertisers cannot legally spam mobile phones with text messages in the same way that they can spam email accounts. The permission of the user has to be granted in order for mobile phones to receive promotional SMS texts, pictorial ads or other promotional material (Barwise and Strong, 2002). Nevertheless, this is a growing market. But, of course, in the future, as convergence progresses, there will be far more to mobile advertising than permission-based SMS text messages. For example, many laptops or netbooks can receive internet TV. This carries placed brands in the scene, even if it doesn't include spot advertising. Access to video material on websites is often preceded by a short advertisement. When the software is invented, mobile devices would carry full internet facilities.

Characteristics of Mobile Phones

Mobile phones have some unique capabilities and characteristics. They are highly personal: people feel that their choice of phone is an intimate part of their lives. In many cases, phones can be fashion statements signifying the social group of the user. Users can make their phones individual by making cosmetic changes to the appearance and by adding their own pictures, voice recordings, music and video selections and home movies, not to mention to-do-lists, personal diaries, and address books. Phones can be used to get us home when we are lost, if we use the satellite navigation and GPS facility. A parent who gives a mobile to a child knows that they can find them if they get lost. They can be used as payment devices. What is more, as well as all these capabilities, mobile phones are perpetually live; many users keep them switched on all the time and take them everywhere. Some even sleep with them by their bedside.[3] Mobile phones have the capacity to transmit video, television or radio. As such they have the capacity to achieve the immediacy of radio, with a much more precise targeting facility. An ad for a snow shovel isn't going to be much use unless it can be targeted regionally, preferably just before or after a snowstorm. Radio can do this, and so can mobile, or at least it can in principle.

BOX 10.3

Value of Mobile Phone Advertising Set to Rise[4]

Estimates of revenue growth in global mobile phone advertising vary between $11 billion and $19 billion by 2011. Although the industry is still relatively under-developed, much work is going into developing a standard platform which will open up the whole market to advertising. Some models under investigation include offering free calls and texts to users willing to accept some advertising. Others include equipping phones to play advertisements when they are inactive. WAP based competitions, SMS text alerts and banners are already in use in some contexts. There is much at stake in developing a truly viable advertising model for mobile.

The extent of mobile internet consumption is dependent not only on the receiving technology, but also on the transmitting technology. In some cases today entire towns have become internet hotspots, making internet access free and ubiquitous. Currently, many mobile phones offer access to mobile internet services, though the quality and richness of the mobile phone internet have limitations, even if the network's coverage is good. Broadband internet access is not universally available, even in-home. So there are limits to the applications which can be delivered in mobile contexts.

The limitations aside, the possibilities for mobile advertising seem powerful. It has been estimated that there are around 3 billion mobile phone users worldwide. On the face of it this represents a sizeable potential for advertising, even though most mobile phone users are not looking for advertisements. Some public phones in the USA force the caller to listen to an advertisement before their call is put though. Mobile phone companies do not yet seem to be using this model, but some have allowed fleeting ads to cut across the screen. Technology is developing though, making the phone a more flexible device. Internet browsing we know about, and music, including ringtones and real tones, has become a multi-billion dollar market for phones within a decade.

According to Sharma et al. (2008: 47), the first mobile advertising was created in Japan in 2001 when the country's largest mobile operator and the advertising agency Dentsu formed the first advertising agency specializing in mobile, calling it D2C. New developments in mobile gaming soon followed. Most phones today have SMS capability and more and more are being equipped with the capacity to access mobile internet services. Internet advertising is the fastest growing category of advertising spend. But technological limitations remain a hindrance for mobile content, including advertising. Mobile phones cannot cut and paste, nor can they easily link with non-mobile internet sites. Mobile video and WAP applications are developing in popularity, opening up greater potential for advertisers.

In sum, mobile devices offer powerful ways of generating consumer engagement. Measuring consumer engagement is not easy, since it evades a slick definition. But the main implication of engagement is that the consumer's attention is active not passive. Whether one is browsing websites, or email, reading or sending text messages, playing mobile games, downloading ringtones, playing music, taking photographs or downloading an application, there is volition and attention present. Neither are necessarily present in other forms of advertising. Whether some of the magic of mobile phone use will be damaged by imposing banner ads or other promotions within the context of mobile phone usage is a difficult question. Clearly, it could. Equally clearly, brands are becoming a taken-for-granted presence in games, videos, television and music. As technology develops and convergence proceeds, the limitations of existing funding models and usage habits for mobile phones will give way to new practices, and it is likely that advertising and promotion will not only be part of these but also that its revenue will be driving the new content.

Chapter Summary

Chapter 10 has taken up themes of integration, media convergence and the development of digital communications technology outlined earlier in the book to examine further the advertising applications of e-marketing and mobile. It reviewed some of the pressures for and possibilities of integration in marketing communication, and suggested that the line where marketing stops and advertising begins is going to be rubbed out altogether when media convergence becomes viable, with multi-application devices for work, communication and entertainment being carried around by everyone. This, though, remains some way off. Meanwhile, more immediate concerns revolve around ways of making mobile advertising more acceptable to phone users. In particular, the mobile phone's capacity for generating user engagement, defined here as volitional and active attention over time, is highlighted as a potentially powerful aspect of mobile advertising.

■ Review Questions

1 What are the key characteristics of mobile phones and how might these be useful to advertisers?

2 Give four examples of consumer engagement elicited by advertisers. How have they managed to motivate consumers to respond in these cases and to what extent might this engagement bring tangible benefits for the brand?

3 Conduct an informal discussion group to ascertain what kinds of advertising your peers might accept on their mobile phones, and under what circumstances. Do their answers suggest the possibility of monetizing this advertising revenue?

4 E-advertising on the internet brings together marketing and communication in a unified entity. Discuss what the implications of this might be for four different industries.

═══ CASE ═══

British Army Recruitment Goes Gaming in a Digital Campaign[5]

The British Armed Forces face the challenge of recruiting 16,000 new recruits per year. The task of reaching potential recruits with a persuasive appeal has changed since the media consumption habits and hobbies of young people have altered in recent years. It is true that audience fragmentation and changing patterns of media consumption have affected all demographic groups, but truer of the 16–24 age group who are, typically, low consumers of daily newspapers and TV shows, but high consumers of internet and mobile media channels. This makes them hard to reach with targeted communication. OTX Research[6] estimates that under-24s spend up to 23 cumulative hours per day texting, emailing, communicating on social networking websites and other digital media. These activities are often conducted simultaneously, hence the high cumulative figure. How can an army reach such a market? One campaign has exploited the familiarity of young males with computer games. The Publicis[7] agency created a campaign called 'Start Thinking Soldier' aimed at recruiting from a (predominantly though not exclusively male) group who have grown up playing computer games. The campaign involved a series of online missions which can be conducted by anyone with a computer and internet access.[8] Early blogging comment (the campaign was launched on 6 April 2009) has expressed some disappointment with the quality of the online game, though such games have to compete with hugely successful and sophisticated computer game products such as *Call of Duty*. However, it has been noted that a similar campaign conducted for the American Army was very successful. The campaign will entail four TV commercials over a four-month period, each unlocking an online mission.

Army recruitment advertising has had a patchy history. Some early campaigns in the UK played on patriotism for queen and country (with a famous slogan of 'Your Country Needs You!') while more modern campaigns sometimes seemed to suggest that the army was a gap year for world travel and skiing, with shots of soldiers having fun and slogans like 'Join the army – see the world'. While these campaigns made army careers look attractive they didn't always attract the right kinds of applicant. In recent years army recruitment campaigns have been trying to increase the conversation ratio of applications to acceptances by improving the quality of applicants through campaigns which emphasized the problem-solving challenges of army life rather than the superficial glamour of army travel.

The current campaign focuses on the problem-solving and IT skills which army life demands. The integration of television with digital media (supported by posters) is designed to engage potential recruits by tapping into their interest in computer games based on war scenarios. It will also serve to target potential recruits who have some IT skills, a current priority for the British army.

 ■ Case Questions

1 Can you describe the rationale behind the integration of media in this case in terms of channel and theme integration?

2 In your opinion, might there be flaws in the rationale behind this campaign? What are they?

3 Do you feel that integration of media channels might be more suited to other kinds of brand offer? Give examples for your answer.

Web-based Resources

Brand Attention, an online marketing agency: www.brandattention.com/mobile-search.html

Internet Advertising Bureau UK: www.iabuk.net/en/1/home.html

Mobile Marketing Association: http://mmaglobal.com/region/europe/united-kingdom

UK Government business advice website: www.businesslink.gov.uk

On the Companion Website

These journal articles are freely available on the companion website (www.sagepub.co.uk/hackley).

Free Advertising: How the Media Amplify Campaign Messages
Travis N. Ridout and Glen R. Smith
Political Research Quarterly, Dec 2008; vol. 61: pp. 598–608.

Click Here: The Impact of New Media on the Encoding of Persuasive Messages in Direct Marketing
Ming Cheung
Discourse Studies, Apr 2008; vol. 10: pp. 161–189.

The Sydney 2000 Olympic Games: How the Australian Tourist Commission Leveraged the Games for Tourism
John Morse
Journal of Vacation Marketing, Apr 2001; vol. 7: pp. 101–107.

Notes

1 'Twitter is named UK's top website for growth', by Nick Clarke, *The Independent*, Business section, Friday 26 June 2009, p. 43.
2 Called 'The Month'.
3 Though it is a good idea to switch them off at night because of the small amount of radiation they emit.
4 'Professional investor: mobile phone advertising, the next big thing', by Makis Katetsis, *The Independent*, 22 September 2007 www.independent.co.uk/money/spend-save/professional-investor-mobile-phone-advertising-the-next-big-thing-464529.html
5 This case has been adapted from 'Calling all computer nerds: 'Your Country Needs You', by Ian Burrell, *The Independent*, Media section, Monday 6 April 2009, p. 42.
6 Reported in *The Independent*, Media section, 6 April 2009, p. 42.
7 www.igniteconversations.com/
8 www.armyjobs.mod.uk/startthinkingsoldier/Pages/Default.aspx

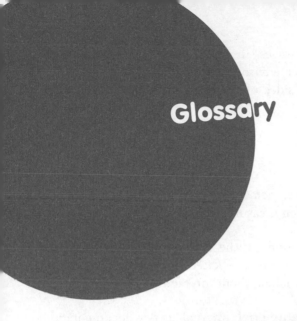

Glossary

Above-the-line, below-the-line, through-the-line: Terms that originate from the UK system of ad agency remuneration (now largely defunct). If a medium generated commission payment to the agency, it was regarded as above-the-line. Above-the-line media included mainstream advertising on press, cinema, commercial radio and TV. Below-the-line media generated no agency commission and included sales promotion, public relations and direct mail. Through-the-line campaigns utilized combinations of above and below-the-line media.

Account manager: The role responsible for client liaison and the general business management of an account.

Account planner: The account team role responsible for research and strategy.

ACORN: A Classification of Residential Neighbourhoods: a form of geodemographic segmentation which categorizes consumers on the basis of the residential neighbourhood where they live (further details on www. caci.co.uk).

Adspend: The monetary expenditure on advertising and promotion.

Advergaming: The use of interactive games via the internet or mobile as an advertising device.

Advertainment: Advertisements which entertain by relating a dramatic narrative or by engaging consumers in an interactive process such as a game.

Affiliate marketing: Co-operative ventures, often e-based, with, for example, host websites carrying other brands' material for click-through business.

Ambient media: Promotional messages inserted into traditionally non-promotional spaces in the consumer environment, such as the back of car parking tickets, farmer's fields, the sides of buildings, and printed on toilet tissue.

Audience: The number of people or households exposed to a given communication in a specified time period.

Awareness: The extent to which consumers have heard of or seen and recall a brand or a particular promotion, often measured by surveys.

Brand engagement: No agreed definition but the concept revolves around the volitional and active attention of consumers, elicited by making promotions more interesting and, especially, by making them interactive.

Client brief/advertising strategy/creative brief: Internal agency documentation charting and guiding the development of communication.

Connote, connotation: A term referring to the subsidiary or secondary meanings that may subsist in a given sign and which depend upon the cultural knowledge and interpretive preference of the viewer. For example, a picture of a motor vehicle in a promotion may demonstrate its comfort, performance and elegance. A particular brand of vehicle pictured in a given lifestyle setting may carry other connotations, just as a BMW Mini connotes movies, Britain, the swinging '60s, rally-car performance and fun for those familiar with the Mini's cultural heritage.

Consequentialist, consequentialism: The doctrine that the ethical status of acts should be judged according to the actual or possible consequences. In other words, if an advertisement may have good consequences, it is judged ethically acceptable. Many charities and public-service campaigns that try to shock people into driving more safely, drinking less alcohol, and so on, are allowed to do so based on these implicit grounds.

Consumer communities: Consumer groups whose only commonality is their mutual interest in a particular set of consumption values or practices. Some advertising agencies use the phrase 'brand communities' to indicate that heterogeneous social groups who share only a mutual interest in a particular brand can be defined as a group on this basis. The 'values' that are integral to the brand are, implicitly, shared by the group. An example might be the Manchester United supporters' club, a widely diverse group in terms of age, sex, ethnicity, nationality and social status, which is united only in their interest in the soccer club (and its merchandise).

Consumer practices (see also **social practices** and **cultural practices**): Consumer behaviour implies that consumers 'behave' according to rules while consumer practice implies that consumers' motivations are more complex. Consumer 'practice' carries a symbolic value in that it can serve the purposes of social positioning and identity formation. For example, from a consumer behaviour perspective a brand might be purchased because the repetitious advertising has created a conditioned response, but from a consumer practice perspective purchasing a particular brand might carry symbolic value for that consumer reflecting lifestyle aspiration and social status.

Copy-testing: A quasi-experimental group of research approaches usually conducted to test creative executions before a campaign launch. Copy-testing measures attitudes towards an advertisement and its different visual or other components.

Cost-per-thousand: The cost per thousand consumers reached through a given medium, e.g. website banner ad, direct mail shot, TV ad.

Covert communication: Covert communication in advertising occurs where the absence of a clearly designated communication source facilitates meanings that are hinted at, suggested or implied.

Creative hot shops/boutiques: It is common in the marketing communications field for successful professionals to break away from their employing agency to form new partnerships known as creative hot shops or boutiques. They are normally small partnerships of experienced professionals who seek a more responsive and rewarding environment than a large agency can offer.

Database mining software: Data mining entails using large databases of customer information to generate new segments to target with direct marketing initiatives. Software packages such as Viper can be useful in allowing marketing analysts to create contact lists of consumers from larger customer databases grouped according to any given criterion.

Deontological, deontology: The doctrine that acts should be judged on their intrinsic rightness or wrongness regardless of the consequences. For example, many consumers objected to Benetton ads on the grounds that they were offensive: this is implicitly a deontological, ethical position.

Deprivation studies: A technique used in anthropological studies that requires research participants to forego an item for a period of time and to record their feelings about its absence in a diary. The feelings of deprivation endured (and expressed) can be a measure of the importance and role of the item in the person's life. One such study conducted for a global audio equipment manufacturer examined the role of audio equipment in people's lives by getting a panel of consumers to do without their audio equipment for a month.

Discourse: Anything that can be described in words: a category of social text that entails accepted or conventional communicative practices.

DRTV: Direct-response television.

Embedded marketing: Marketing initiatives presented in the context of entertainment vehicles such as movies, TV shows or sponsored media events. The key element of embedded marketing is that the audience is not necessarily explicitly aware that the brand exposure is a paid-for promotion.

Ethics: The study of the good life, including the exploration of questions of what good conduct is conducive to living the good life.

Eye tachistoscope test: A technique of advertising research in which a camera device tracks the movement of a viewer's eye over a creative execution.

Fragmentation of media audiences: Audience fragmentation refers to the disintegration of mass media audiences into many smaller groups focused around some of the increasingly specialized and personalized media vehicles.

Frame of reference: One way in which we see and understand the world is by comparing new experiences with old ones stored in our memory. Our vocabulary of stored cultural representations can be seen as a frame of reference which informs and limits our interpretation of new experiences.

Full-service agency: An increasingly rare breed of agency that purports to offer the full range of communications services to clients. In practice most agencies rely to a greater or lesser degree on the sub-contracting of specialist services.

Generalization: Many traditions of advertising research seek findings in the form of simple factual propositions that can hold true for entire populations.

Geodemographics: A technique of consumer segmentation which combines demographic with geographical information.

Glocalization: A coined word referring to the managerial application of local criteria to marketing policy while retaining global themes and values. In marketing communication it might refer to allowing local agencies some licence to design creative tactics that make sense to local people within a controlled set of global brand values represented by particular logos or visual themes.

Guerrilla marketing: Tactics can include placing paid individuals in bars to engage customers in seemingly spontaneous conversation about an alcohol brand, marketers entering internet chatroom conversations under the guise of consumers, illegal fly-posting and graffiti campaigns.

Hierarchy-of-effects theories: Theories of persuasive communication that conceive of a passive and indifferent consumer who must be persuaded to buy the brand by the accumulated effect of a number of ad exposures.

High involvement: Consumers' purchase experience can be categorized as 'high involvement' if it represents a purchase of such importance that it requires a high order of processing, including, for example, an information search and evaluation of alternatives. Purchases such as a house, car or family holiday might be characterized thus. Many purchases that take a lower proportion of disposable income are thought to be more spontaneous and subject to a lower order of rational processing (i.e. low involvement). This binary construct loses its explanatory effectiveness when purchases have a powerful, symbolic value for consumers. The motive behind such purchases lies beyond the reach of the processing metaphor.

Integrated Marketing Communications (IMC): A management initiative to link and coordinate brand communications through all media channels in order to generate a synergy effect. IMC is often only partially achieved because of functional divisions within organizations between, say, public relations, advertising, personal selling and corporate communications.

Integrated solutions: Clients seeking solutions to their marketing and communication problems may require communications strategies that cut across the traditional demarcations of the communications mix of channels. Integrated solutions do not merely use differing channels, but co-ordinate them so that they act in a mutually reinforcing way.

Interpretive community: A group that shares certain cultural reference points and therefore a sense of meaning in some situations. For example, intertextual references in ads to scenes from Hollywood movies or to sports events will be most quickly understood by, respectively, movie buffs and sports fans.

Intertextuality: A characteristic of discourses whereby they adapt, copy or refer to other discourses, for example where ads refer to movies, or movies refer to brands.

Likert scales: The original form of attitude measurement scale; usually in the form of a five-item response scale ranging from 'strongly negative' to 'strongly positive'.

Linear information processing [theories of communication]: Theories (or models) that draw an analogy between human and machine information processing. Humans are assumed to process sensory data in a linear sequence. Also known as Consumer Information Processing (CIP).

Magnetic Resonance Imaging (MRI): A medical technique for scanning the brain also used in consumer research.

Managerial managerialist: The genre of business writing and research devoted to solving the problems of managers without reference to wider social scientific or ethical issues and values.

Marketing mix: Traditionally, the four Ps of marketing management, Price, Product, Promotion and Physical distribution. Subsequent versions have added People and Processes.

Media channels/media vehicles: The term 'media channels' normally refers to the various media that can carry promotional communication, such as TV, radio, cinema theatres, outdoor and press. Word-of-mouth is usually regarded as a non-mediated channel even though it may be utilized deliberately in marketing campaigns. A media vehicle may be a specific newspaper or TV station.

Media planner: A specialist whose responsibility it is to see that a given campaign reaches the largest number of targeted consumers possible within the allocated budget. The media reach of a campaign refers to the size of the audience.

Media-neutral planning: Agencies have historically been biased towards mass advertising in their media planning, partly because mass media advertising tended to earn the most money for agencies under the commission-based remuneration system. As the commission system is breaking down in favour of a billing system of remuneration, agencies are more willing to choose between media on an objective appraisal of their relative effectiveness for the campaign in hand.

'New' media: Technological development and cost reductions have made possible promotional media such as SMS text messaging, email, DVD Roms, internet, and WAP-enabled and G3 mobile telephony.

Operant conditioning: In behavioural psychology operant conditioning changes behaviour in response to repeated stimuli administered by an operator. Advertisements can be conceived of as stimuli which, if repeated often enough, might change consumer behaviour. One flaw in this hypothesis might be that behavioural conditioning demands a closely controlled learning environment while the advertising exposure of an individual consumer cannot easily be controlled.

Ostensive communication: Communication which is explicit and has an identifiable source, usually contrasted with communication that is implied or hinted at.

Panel data: Various marketing research organizations (e.g. AGB, Neilson) compile longitudinal market and consumer research data that they then sell to interested parties. Panel data can include weekly measures of grocery purchasing behaviour, TV viewing or radio listening, each of which are based on a panel of consumers statistically extrapolated to reflect the possible behaviour of whole populations.

Peer group: We refer closely to the views and values of people in our immediate social circle when we form new views. These people form our peer group and they can be influential in our own consumption and other choices.

Penetration: The percentage of a market that is reached by a given medium or an individual promotional communication.

Perception matrix: A spatial technique of conceptualizing brand positioning using two axes based on contrasting polar opposites. For example, in a perceptual map of the positioning of beer brands, the two axes could be dark–light and strong–weak. The axes are drawn to form a cross and the various beer brands plotted on a scale.

Pitching: The pitching or pitch process is the traditional method by which advertising agencies get new business. They 'pitch' their ideas to a prospective client in response to the client's brief, in competition with other agencies.

Polysemy: The capacity of a social text such as an ad to have multiple meanings. The meanings inferred will depend on such things as the cultural context of interpretation and the interpretive strategy of the reader.

POS: Point-of-sale can refer to sales promotions at the cash till of a store or to any in-store promotion such as free sample stalls and LCD screen advertising.

Positioning: A key marketing concept indicating the values or ideas that are associated with a given brand. For example, the Nestlé Kit Kat chocolate confection is positioned (in the UK) as an excuse to have a break (that is, a rest) from work; the Marlboro cigarette brand is associated (through the image of the Marlboro cowboy) with individualism and toughness.

Positivistic: A term borrowed from the philosophy of logical positivism (Ayer, 1936) but referring in management and business research to approaches that model their methods and assumptions on those of natural science. One common form of positivistic research seeks to test hypotheses across large populations in order to generalize findings.

Primary research: The generation of new data. Contrasts with secondary research, which refers to the use of data already in existence.

Product placement: The practice of placing branded products or services in TV, radio, movie or other forms of entertainment.

Projective techniques: A psychological technique used in qualitative consumer research. It can take the form of a story-completion or picture-completion task. It originated in the psychiatric technique of asking a respondent to interpret Rorschach ink blots.

Promotional mix: The combination of differing promotional techniques, including advertising, direct response and direct mail, public relations, sales promotion, personal selling, e-marketing communication, and so forth, used to promote a brand or service. The term 'communications mix' is often used to indicate the differing communication channels that are deployed to reach the targeted audience.

Psycho-galvanometer tests: Tests carried out by a machine that measures the stimulation of the central nervous system by measuring the activity of sweat glands, thereby indicating the degree of interest a viewer has in a creative execution.

Psychographics: A lifestyles and attitudes-based approach to consumer segmentation. Many advertising agencies have devised their own categorization system.

Qualitative: Adjective describing non-numerical research to seek insight into the quality of a group or person's experience of a given phenomenon.

Quantitative: Adjective describing research that generates numerical data.

Reach: The number of individuals or households within a target audience reached by a given promotional communication. Often expressed as a percentage.

Representational practices: A term common in cultural studies simply meaning ways of communicating. The term implies that truth in the world has an element of subjectivity so that, for example, advertising researchers may understand the social world in quite incompatible terms, such as when consumer research is cast in qualitative or quantitative terms. The word 'practice' is important in this phrase since it implies that communication is not confined to meaning-transfer but also fulfils social strategies (see Edwards and Potter, 1992; Potter and Wetherell, 1987). In some agencies quantitative data are regarded as more authoritative as grounds for argument than qualitative data.

Representative: Adjective describing a sample which, for research purposes, is assumed to have the same characteristics as the whole population of interest.

Segmentation: Conventional wisdom in marketing management holds that marketing resources are most effectively deployed if they are aimed at a clearly defined market segment, a group of existing or potential sales prospects.

Semiology: The study of linguistic signs. Associated with the work of Ferdinand de Saussure.

Semiotics: The study of all signs and their meaning in communication.

Signification: Used in this book to indicate the passive communication implicit in marketing signs of all kinds. For example, the 'swoosh' design, indicating the Nike brand and deployed on a huge variety of media, is probably one of the most widely recognized signs in all contemporary culture. The 'swoosh' carries a complex of contrived meanings deriving from Nike promotional activity, including sporting excellence, winning, 'street' style, etc.

Socio-economic group: An approach to classifying groups of individuals based on the occupation of the main household wage earner. Devised by the UK civil service in the late 1940s and still used in audience analysis.

Split-run studies: A technique of measuring advertising effect by comparing two differing executions in demographically similar regions.

Spontaneous brand awareness: Brand awareness is often tested using prompted and unprompted survey measures. Consumers might be asked to list the brands in a given category that they are aware of (unprompted). They might then have a list of brands read to them and are asked to indicate which they have heard of or seen in the last week (prompted).

Sub-culture: A sociological term referring to the way some people seek identity and realization in non-mainstream, group activities. The term has become associated with illicit activities such as street fighting gangs or punk rockers, but might equally apply to any group whose values, activities and social practices lie outside mainstream and establishment culture.

Sub-text: Texts that subsist beneath the main text, in other words, implied meanings, additional or subordinate to the primary meaning of a text.

Synergy: A coined word indicating the mutually reinforcing promotional effect of portraying a brand in a similar style on two or more media channels.

Targeting: The task of reaching the chosen segment of consumers by placing creative executions on carefully chosen media channels.

TGI: Target Group Index. An audience and market research agency (www.bmrb-tgi.co.uk).

Tracking studies: Research studies which track the effect of a campaign after its launch against the objectives set for it.

Traffic controller: An administrative role within agencies responsible for keeping track of the progress of different accounts.

Viral marketing: Originally confined to internet-based techniques of generating publicity (the establishment of Hotmail was the model for viral marketing), it is now sometimes conflated with guerrilla marketing tactics to include any attempt to contrive apparently spontaneous WOM publicity.

WOM: Word-of-mouth (promotion), the spontaneous exchange of ideas within peer groups about a brand or advertisement.

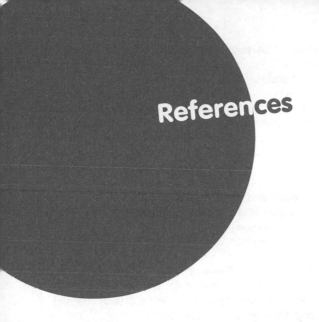

References

Aaker, D., Batra, R. and Myers, J. (1992) *Advertising Management*, 4th edn. Englewood Cliffs, NJ: Prentice-Hall.

Ambler, T. (1996) 'Can alcohol misuse be reduced by banning advertising?', *International Journal of Advertising*, 15(2): 167–74.

Ambler, T. (1998) 'Myths about the mind: time to end some popular beliefs about how advertising works', *International Journal of Advertising*, 17(4): 501–9.

Amis, J., Slack, T. and Berrett, T. (1999) 'Sport sponsorship as distinctive competence', *European Journal of Marketing*, 33(3/4): 250–72.

Arnould, E. and Thompson, C. (2005) 'Consumer Culture Theory (CCT): twenty years of research', *Journal of Consumer Research*, 31: 868–82.

Ayer, A.J. (1936) *Language, Truth and Logic.* London: Victor Gollancz. (Reprinted by Penguin Books, 1990.)

Bagozzi, R., Tybout, A.M., Craig, C.S. and Sternthal, B. (1979) 'The construct validity of the tripartite classification of attitudes', *Journal of Marketing Research*, 16 (February): 88–95.

Bakhtin, M. (1989) 'Discourse in life and discourse in art (concerning sociological poetics)', in R. Davis and R. Schleifler (eds), *Contemporary Literary Criticism*. New York: Longman. pp. 392–410.

Banister, L. (1997) 'Global brands, local contexts', *Admap*, October: 28–30.

Barnard, N. and Ehrenberg, A. (1997) 'Advertising: strongly persuasive or nudging?', *Journal of Advertising Research*, 37(1): 21–31.

Barry, T.E. and Howard, D.J. (1990) 'A review and critique of the hierarchy of effects in advertising', *International Journal of Advertising*, 9: 121–35.

Barthes, R. (2000) *Mythologies.* London: Vintage. (Translation Jonathan Cape 1972.)

Barwise, P. and Strong, C. (2002) 'Permission-based mobile advertising', *Journal of Interactive Marketing*, 16/1: 14–24.

Belch, G. and Belch, M. (2008) *Advertising and Promotion: An Integrated Marketing Communications Perspective*, 8th edn. New York: McGraw Hill.

Belk, R.W. and Pollay, R.W. (1985) 'Images of ourselves: the good life in twentieth century advertising', *Journal of Consumer Research*, 11: 887–97.

Belk, R.W. (1988) 'Possessions and the extended self', *Journal of Consumer Research*, 15(2): 139–68.

Berger, P.L. and Luckman, T. (1966) *The Social Construction of Reality.* London: Penguin.

Billig, M. (1987) *Arguing and Thinking: A Rhetorical Approach to Social Psychology.* Cambridge: Cambridge University Press.

Billig, M. (1991) *Ideology and Opinions.* London: Sage.

Binet, L. (2009) 'Payback calculations: how to make sure you get your sums right', in N. Dawson (ed.), *Advertising Works 17: Proving the Return on Marketing Investment.* Henley-on-Thames, Oxfordshire: World Advertising Research Center. pp. 19–22.

Blake, A., MacRury, I., Nava, M. and Richards, B. (eds) (1996) *Buy This Book: Studies in Advertising and Consumption.* London: Routledge.

Bogart, L. (1966) in Bogart, L. (Ed.) *Psychology in Media Strategy.* Chicago, IL: American Marketing Association.

Broadbent, T. (2009) 'Effectiveness and two-thirds of the human race', in N. Dawson (ed.), *Advertising Works 17: Proving the Return on Marketing Investment.* Henley-on-Thames, Oxfordshire: World Advertising Research Center. pp. 3–6.

Brown, S. and Schau, H.J. (2008) 'Writing Russell Belk: excess all areas', *Marketing Theory*, 8(2): 143–65.

Brown, S., Stevens, L. and Maclaran, P. (1999) 'I Can't Believe It's Not Bakhtin!: literary theory, postmodern advertising, and the gender agenda', *Journal of Advertising*, 28(1): 11–24.

Brownlie, D., Saren, M., Wensley, R. and Whittington, D. (eds) (1999) *Rethinking Marketing: Towards Critical Marketing Accountings.* London: Sage.

Bullmore, J. (1988) *Behind the Scenes in Advertising*, 2nd edn. Henley-on-Thames: Admap.

Burr, V. (1995) *An Introduction to Social Constructionism.* London: Routledge.

Burrell, G. and Morgan, G. (1979) *Sociological Paradigms and Organisational Analysis.* London: Heinemann.

Butterfield, L. (ed.) (1999) *Excellence in Advertising: The IPA Guide to Best Practice.* London: Butterworth-Heinemann.

Buttle, F. (1994) 'Marketing communications theory – what do the texts teach our students?', *International Journal of Advertising*, 14: 297–313.

Calfee, J.E. and Scherage, C. (1994) 'The influence of advertising on alcohol consumption: a literature review and an econometric analysis of four European nations', *International Journal of Advertising*, 13(4): 287–310.

Chada, R. and Husband, P. (2006) *Cult of the Luxury Brand: Inside Aisa's Love Affair with Luxury.* London: Nicholas Brearley.

Chong, D. (2009) *Arts Management.* London: Routledge.

Cook, G. (2001) *The Discourse of Advertising.* London: Routledge.

Cook, W.A. and Kover, A.J. (1997) 'Research and the meaning of advertising effectiveness: mutual misunderstandings', in W.D. Wells (ed.), *Measuring Advertising Effectiveness.* Hillsdale, NJ: Lawrence Erlbaum Associates. pp. 13–20.

Cornelissen, J.P. and Lock, A.R. (2002) 'Advertising research and its influence upon managerial practice: a review of perspectives and approaches', *Journal of Advertising Research*, 42(3): 50–5.

Cova, B., Kozinets, R. and Shankar, A. (2007) *Consumer Tribes.* London: Butterworth-Heinemann.

Croft, R. (1999) 'Audience and environment: measurement and media', in P.J. Kitchen (ed.), *Marketing Communications, Principles and Practice.* London: Thomson Learning. pp. 111–34.

Cronin, A.M. (2008) 'Gender in the making of commercial worlds: creativity, vitalism and the practices of marketing', *Feminist Theory*, 9(3): 293–312.

Crosier, K. (1999) 'Advertising', in P.J. Kitchen (ed.), *Marketing Communications: Principles and Practice.* London: Thomson Learning. pp. 264–88.

Danesi, M. (1994) *Messages and Meanings: An Introduction to Semiotics.* Toronto: Canadian Scholar's Press.

Danesi, M. (2006) *Brands*. London and New York: Routledge.

d'Astous, A. and Seguin, N. (1999) 'Consumer reactions to product placement strategies in television sponsorship', *European Journal of Marketing*, 33(9/10): 896–910.

Dawson, N. (2009) 'The evolution of commercially effective communication', in N. Dawson (ed.), *Advertising Works 17: Proving the Return on Marketing Investment*. Henley-on-Thames, Oxfordshire: World Advertising Research Center. pp. 27–34.

DDB London Works, introduced by Richard Butterworth and Lucy Jameson (2003) Henley-on-Thames: WARC and IPA.

De Pelsmacker, P., Geuens, M. and Van den Bergh, J. (2004) *Marketing Communications: A European Perspective*, 2nd edn. London: Financial Times/Prentice Hall.

Dermody, J. (1999) 'CPM/HEM models of information processing', in P.J. Kitchen (ed.), *Marketing Communications – Principles and Practice*. London: Thomson Learning. pp. 156–71.

De Saussure, F. (1974) *Course in General Linguistics*. London: Collins.

Deuze, M. (2007) *Media Work*. Cambridge: Polity Press.

deWaal Malefyt, T. and Moeran, B. (2003) *Advertising Cultures*. London: Berg.

Dichter, E. (1949) 'A psychological view of advertising effectiveness', *Journal of Marketing*, 14(1): 61–7.

Dichter, E. (1966) 'How word-of-mouth advertising works', *Harvard Business Review*, 44(6): 147–57.

Eagle, L., Kitchen, P.J. and Bulmer, S. (2007) 'Insights into interpreting integrated marketing communications: a two-nation qualitative comparison, *European Journal of Marketing*, 41(7/8): 956–70.

Eagleton, T. (1991) *Ideology*. London: Verso.

Easterby-Smith, M., Thorpe, R. and Lowe, A. (2002) *Management Research: An Introduction*. London: Sage.

Eco, U. (1976) *A Theory of Semiotics*. Bloomington, IN: Indiana University Press.

Eco, U. (1984) *Semiotics and Philosophy of Language*. London: Macmillan.

Edwards, D. and Potter, J. (1992) *Discursive Psychology*. London: Sage.

Ehrenberg, A. and Barnard, N. (1997) 'Advertising and product demand', *Admap*, May: 14–18.

Ehrenberg, A., Barnard, N., Kennedy, R. and Bloom, H. (2002) 'Brand advertising and creative publicity', *Journal of Advertising Research*, 42(4): 7–18.

Elliott, R. (1998) 'A model of emotion-driven choice', *Journal of Marketing Management*, 14: 95–108.

Elliott, R. and Beckmann, S. (eds) (2000) *Interpretive Consumer Research: Paradigms, Methodologies and Applications*. Copenhagen: Copenhagen Business School Press.

Elliott, R. and Jankel-Elliott, N. (2002) 'Using ethnography in strategic consumer research', *Qualitative Market Research: An International Journal*, 6(4): 215–23.

Elliott, R. and Ritson, M. (1997) 'Post-structuralism and the dialectics of advertising: discourse, ideology, resistance', in S. Brown and D. Turley (eds), *Consumer Research: Postcards From the Edge*. London: Routledge. pp. 190–248.

Elliott, R. and Wattanasuwan, K. (1998) 'Brands as symbolic resources for the construction of identity', *International Journal of Advertising*, 17(2): 131–44.

Feldwick, P. (2002a) *What is Brand Equity Anyway?* Henley-on-Thames: World Advertising Research Centre.

Feldwick, P. (ed.) (2002b) *Pollitt on Planning*. Account Planning Group, BMP (DDB). Needham. Henley-on-Thames: Admap.

Feldwick, P. (2007) 'Account planning: its history and significance for ad agencies', in G. Tellis and T. Ambler (eds), *The Sage Handbook of Advertising*. London: Sage. pp.184–98.

Fill, C. (2002) *Marketing Communications: Contexts, Strategies and Applications*, 3rd edn. Essex: Prentice Hall.

Fill, C. (2009) *Marketing Communications: Interactivity, Communities and Content.* London: FT/Prentice Hall.

Forceville, C. (1996) *Pictorial Metaphor in Advertising.* London: Routledge.

Ford, B. (1993) *Television and Sponsorship.* Oxford: Butterworth Heinemann.

Fowles, J. (1996) *Advertising and Popular Culture.* London: Sage.

Fox, S. (1984) *The Mirror Makers: A History of American Advertising and its Creators.* New York: William Morrow.

Foxall, G.R. (2000) 'The psychological basis of marketing', in M.J. Baker (ed.), *Marketing Theory: A Student Text.* London: Thomson Learning. pp. 86–101.

Franzen, G. (1999) *Brands and Advertising: How Advertising Effectiveness Influences Brand Equity.* Henley-on-Thames: Admap.

Gardner, B. and Levy, S. (1955) 'The product and the brand', *Harvard Business Review,* March–April: 33–9.

Griffin, C., Bengry-Howell, A., Hackley, C., Mistral, W. and Szmigin, I. (2009) '"Every time I do it I absolutely annihilate myself": loss of (self)-consciousness and loss of memory in young people's drinking narratives', *Sociology,* 43(3): 457–77.

Gronhaug, K. (2000) 'The sociological basis of marketing', in M.J. Baker (ed.), *Marketing Theory: A Student Text.* London: Thompson Learning.

Hackley, C. (1998) 'Social constructionism and research in marketing and advertising', *Qualitative Market Research: An International Journal,* 1(3): 125–31.

Hackley, C. (1999a) 'The communications process and the semiotic boundary', in P.J. Kitchen (ed.), *Marketing Communications: Principles and Practice.* London: Thomson Learning. pp. 135–55.

Hackley, C. (1999b) 'The meanings of ethics in and of advertising', *Business Ethics: A European Review,* 8(1): 37–42.

Hackley, C. (2000) 'Silent running: tacit, discursive and psychological aspects of management in a top UK advertising agency', *British Journal of Management,* 11(3): 239–54.

Hackley, C. (2001) *Marketing and Social Construction: Exploring the Rhetorics of Marketed Consumption.* London: Routledge.

Hackley, C. (2002) 'The panoptic role of advertising agencies in the production of consumer culture', *Consumption, Markets and Culture,* 5(3): 211–29.

Hackley, C. (2003a) 'IMC and Hollywood: what brand managers need to know', *Admap,* November: 44–7.

Hackley, C. (2003b) 'How divergent beliefs cause account team conflict', *International Journal of Advertising,* 22(3): 313–32.

Hackley, C. (2003c) '"We are all customers now" … rhetorical strategy and ideological control in marketing management texts', *Journal of Management Studies,* 40(5): 1325–52.

Hackley, C. (2003d) 'Divergent representational practices in advertising and consumer research: some thoughts on integration', special issue on representation in consumer research, *Qualitative Market Research: An International Journal,* 6(3): 175–84.

Hackley, C. (2003e) *Doing Research Projects in Marketing, Management and Consumer Research.* London: Routledge.

Hackley, C. (2003f) 'Account planning: current agency perspectives on an advertising enigma', *Journal of Advertising Research,* 43(2): 235–45.

Hackley, C. (2003g) 'From consumer insight to advertising strategy: the account planner's integrative role in creative advertising development', *Marketing Intelligence and Planning,* 21(7): 446–52.

Hackley, C. (2007) 'Marketing psychology and the hidden persuaders', *The Psychologist,* 20(8): 488–90.

Hackley, C. (2008) 'UK alcohol policy and market research: media debates and methodological differences', *International Journal of Market Research,* 50(4): 429–31.

Hackley, C. (2009a) *Marketing – A Critical Introduction.* London: Sage.

Hackley, C. (2009b) 'Parallel universes and disciplinary space: the bifurcation of managerialism and social science in marketing studies', *Journal of Marketing Management*. 25(7–8): 643–59.

Hackley, C. (2009c) 'Is Andy Burnham right to ban product placement on UK Television?', in *Utalk Marketing*. http:www.utalkmarketing.com/Pages/Article.aspx?ArticleID=13378& title=Is%20Andy%20Burnham%20Right%to%20Ban%20Product%20Placement%20 On%20UK%Television

Hackley, C. (2010) 'Theorizing advertising: managerial, scientific and cultural approaches', in P. MacLaran, M. Saren, B. Stern and M. Tadajewski, (eds), *The SAGE Handbook of Marketing Theory*. London: Sage. pp. 89–107.

Hackley, C. and Kitchen, P.J. (1999) 'Ethical perspectives on the postmodern communications Leviathan', *Journal of Business Ethics*, 20(1): 15–26.

Hackley, C. and Kover, A. (2007) 'The trouble with creatives: negotiating creative identity in advertising agencies', *International Journal of Advertising*, 26(1): 63–78.

Hackley, C. and Tiwsakul, R. (2006) 'Entertainment marketing and experiential consumption', *Journal of Marketing Communications*, 12(1): 63–75.

Hackley, C., and Tiwsakul, R. (2008) 'Comparative management practices in international advertising agencies in the UK, Thailand and the USA', in C. Smith, B. McSweeney and R. Fitzgerland, (eds), *Remaking Management: Between Global and Local*. Cambridge: Cambridge University Press. pp. 586–626.

Hackley, C., Tiwsakul, R. and Preuss, R. (2008a) 'An ethical evaluation of product placement – a deceptive practice?' *Business Ethics – A European Review*, 17(April): 109–20.

Hackley, C., Bengry-Howell, A., Griffin, C., Mistral, W. and Szmigin, I. (2008b) 'The discursive constitution of the UK alcohol problem in safe, sensible, social: a discussion of policy implications', *Drugs: Education, Prevention and Policy*, 15(S1): 61–74.

Harbor, C. (2007) 'Pervasive and persuasive: advertisements for concerts in London 1672–1750.' Conference paper. Marketing Theory into Practice: Academy of Marketing conference, Kingston Business School at Royal Holloway University of London, 3–6 July.

Harrison, S. (1995) *Public Relations: An Introduction*. London: Routledge.

Head, V. (1981) *Sponsorship: The Newest Marketing Skill*. Cambridge: Woodhead-Faulkner, in association with the Chartered Institute of Marketing.

Heath, R. and Feldwick, P. (2008) '50 Years using the wrong model of advertising', *International Journal of Advertising*, 50(1): 29–59.

Hedges, A. (1997) *Testing to Destruction – A Critical Look at the Uses of Research in Advertising*. London: Institute of Practitioners in Advertising. (First edition, 1974.)

Hirschman, E. (1986) 'Humanistic inquiry in marketing research: research, philosophy, method and criteria', *Journal of Marketing Research*, 23(August): 237–49.

Holbrook, M. (1995) *Consumer Research: Introspective Essays on the Study of Consumption*. London: Sage.

Holbrook, M. and Hirschman, E. (1982) 'The experiential aspects of consumption: consumer feelings, fantasies and fun', *Journal of Consumer Research*, 9(September): 132–40.

Holbrook, M.B. and O'Shaughnessy, J. (1988) 'On the scientific status of consumer research and the need for an interpretive approach to studying consumption behaviour', *Journal of Consumer Research*, 15: 398–403.

Holt, D. (2002) 'Why do brands cause trouble?', *Journal of Consumer Research*, 29(June): 70–90.

Holt, D. (2004) *How Brands Become Icons: The Principles of Cultural Branding*. Boston, MA: Harvard Business School Press.

Horkheimer, M. and Adorno, T.W. (1944) *The Dialectic of Enlightenment*. New York: Continuum.

Hosany, S. and Hackley, C. (2009) *The Measurement of Emotions in Marketing and Consumer Research*. Unpublished working paper.

Hoy, M., Morrison, M. and Punyapiroje, C. (2000) 'Adver-Thai-sing standardisation: does the Western approach of investigating gender role portrayals transfer to Eastern countries?', *World Communication*, 19(1): 52–68.

Iser, W. (1978) *The Act of Reading.* Baltimore, MD: Johns Hopkins University Press.

Jefkins, F. (2000) *Advertising.* Harlow: Pearson Education.

Jenkins, H. (2008) *Convergence Culture: Where Old and New Media Collide.* New York: New York University Press.

Jones, J.P. (1990) 'Advertising: strong force or weak force? Two views an ocean apart', *International Journal of Advertising*, 9: 233–46.

Jones, J.P. (1999) *The Advertising Business.* Thousand Oaks, CA: Sage.

Katz, H. (2006) *The Media Handbook: A Complete Guide to Advertising Media Selection, Planning, Research and Buying.* Hillsdale, NJ: Lawrence Erlbaum Associates.

Katz, E. and Lazarsfeld, P.F. (1955) *Personal Influence.* Glencoe, IL: Free Press.

Keller, K.L., Heckler, S.E. and Houston, M.J. (1998) 'The effects of brand name suggestiveness on advertising recall', *Journal of Marketing*, 62: 48–57.

Kelly, A., Lawlor, K. and O'Donohoe, S. (2005) 'Encoding advertisements – the creative perspective', *Journal of Marketing Management*, 21: 505–28.

Kelley, L.D. and Jugenheimer, D.W. (2008) *Advertising Media Planning: A Brand Management Approach*, 2nd edn. Armonk, NY: M.E. Sharpe.

Kennedy, John E. (1904) *Reason Why Advertising Plus Intensive Advertising.* Terre Haute, IN: TWI Press, Inc.

Kitchen, P.J. (ed.) (1999) *Marketing Communications: Principles and Practice.* London: Thompson.

Kitchen, P.J. and Hackley, C. (1999) 'Ethical perspectives on the postmodern communications leviathan', *Journal of Business Ethics*, 20(1): 15–26.

Kitson, H.D. (1921) *The Mind of the Buyer.* New York: Macmillan.

Klein, N. (2000) *No Logo.* London: Flamingo.

Kochan, N. (1996) *The World's Greatest Brands.* New York: New York University Press.

Kotler, P. and Roberto, E.L. (1989) *Social Marketing: Strategies for Changing Public Behaviour.* New York: The Free Press.

Kotler, P. and Zaltman, G. (1971) 'Social marketing: an approach to planned social change', *Journal of Marketing*, 35: 3–12.

Kover, A.J. (1995) 'Copywriters' implicit theories of communication: an exploration', *Journal of Consumer Research*, 21(March): 598–611.

Kover, A.J. (1996) 'Why copywriters don't like research – and what kind of research might they accept', *Journal of Advertising Research*, 36(2): RC8–12.

Kover, A.J. and Goldberg, S.M. (1995) 'The games copywriters play: conflict, quasi-control, a new proposal', *Journal of Advertising Research*, 35(4): 52–68.

Lazarsfeld, P.F. (1941) 'Remarks on administrative and critical communications research', *Studies in Philosophy and Science*, 9: 3–16.

Lasswell, H.D. (1948) 'The structure and function of communication in society', in L. Bryson (ed.), *The Communication of Ideas.* New York: Harper.

Lavidge, R.J. and Steiner, G.A. (1961) 'A model for predictive measurements of advertising effectiveness', *Journal of Marketing*, 24(October): 59–62.

Lears, J. (1994) *Fables of Abundance: A Cultural History of Advertising in America.* New York: Basic Books.

Lee, N. and Lings, I. (2008) *Doing Business Research: A Guide to Theory and Practice.* London: Sage.

Lehu, J.M. (2007) *Branded Entertainment: Product Placement and Brand Strategy in the Entertainment Business.* London: Kogan Page.

Leiss, W., Kline, S. and Jhally, S. (1997) *Social Communication in Advertising: Persons, Products and Images of Well-Being.* London: Routledge.

Leiss, W., Kline, S., Jhally, S. and Botterill, J. (2005) *Social Communication in Advertising: Consumption in the Mediated Marketplace.* London: Routledge.

Lemle, R. and Mishkind, M. (1989) 'Alcohol and masculinity', *Journal of Substance Abuse Treatment*, 6: 213–22.

Levitt, T. (1983) 'The globalisation of markets', *Harvard Business Review*, April/May: 92–107.

Levy, S. (1959) 'Symbols for sale', *Harvard Business Review*, 37(July): 117–24.

Lutz, R.J. (1977) 'An experimental investigation of causal relations among cognitions: affect and behavioural intention', *Journal of Consumer Research* 3(March): 197–208.

McCracken, G. (1986) 'Culture and consumption: a theoretical account of the structure and movement of the cultural meaning of consumer goods', *Journal of Consumer Research*, 13(1): 71–84.

McCracken, G. (1987) 'Advertising – meaning or information?', in M. Wallendorf and P. Anderson (eds), *Advances in Consumer Research,* Vol. 14. Provo, UT: Association for Consumer Research. pp. 121–4.

McCracken, G. (1990) *Culture and Consumption: New Approaches to the Symbolic Character of Consumer Goods and Activities.* Bloomington, IN; Indiana University Press.

McCracken, G. (2005) *Culture and Consumption 11: Markets, Meaning and Brand Management.* Bloomington, IN: Indiana University Press.

McDonald, C. and Scott, J. (2007) 'A brief history of advertising', in G. Tellis and T. Ambler (eds), *The Sage Handbook of Advertising.* London: Sage. pp. 17–34.

McFall, L. (2004) *Advertising: A Cultural Economy.* London: Sage.

McKeil, J. (1985) *The Creative Mystique.* London: John Wiley and Sons.

McLeod, C., O'Donohoe, S. and Townley, B. (2009) 'The elephant in the room? Class and creative careers in British advertising agencies', *Human Relations*, 62(7): 1011–39.

McLuhan, M. (1964) 'Keeping upset with the Joneses', in *Understanding Media.* London: Routledge and Kegan Paul. pp. 226–33.

MacInnis, D.J. and Jaworski B.J. (1989) 'Information processing from advertisements: toward an integrative framework', *Journal of Marketing*, 53: 1–23.

Macklin, M.C. and Carlson, L. (eds) (1999) *Advertising to Children: Concepts and Controversies.* Thousand Oaks, CA: Sage.

Malhotra, N. and Birks, D. (2003) *Marketing Research: An Applied Approach.* London: FT/Prentice Hall.

Manchanda, R.V., Dahl, D.W. and Frankenberger, K.D. (2003) 'Does it pay to shock? Reactions to shocking and nonshocking advertising content among university students', *Journal of Advertising Research*, 43(3): 268–79.

Manning, N. (2009) 'The new media communications model: a progress report', in N. Dawson (ed.), *Advertising Works 17: Proving the Return on Marketing Investment.* Henley-on-Thames Oxfordshire: World Advertising Center. pp. 7–14.

Marchand, R. (1985) *Advertising and the American Dream: Making Way for Modernity 1920–1940.* Berkeley, CA: University of California Press.

Marchand, R. (1998) *Creating the Corporate Soul: The Rise of Public Relations and Corporate Imagery in American Big Business.* Berkeley, CA: University of California Press.

Measham, F. (2004a) 'The decline of ecstasy, the rise of 'binge' drinking and the persistence of pleasure', *Probation Journal*, 5(4): 309–26.

Measham, F. (2004b) 'Play space: historical and socio-cultural reflections on drugs, licensed leisure locations, commercialisation and control', *International Journal of Drug Policy*, 15: 337–45.

Measham, F. (2006) 'The new policy mix: alcohol, harm minimisation, and determined drunkenness in contemporary society', *International Journal of Drug Policy*, 17: 258–68.

Meenaghan, T. (1991) 'Sponsorship: legitimising the medium', *European Journal of Marketing*, 25(11): 5–10.

Meenaghan, T. and Shipley, D. (1999) 'Media affecting sponsorship', *European Journal of Marketing,* 33(3/4): 328–47.

Melewar, T.C. (2003) 'Determinants of the corporate identity construct: a review of literature', *Journal of Marketing Communications,* 9(4): 195–220.

Melewar, T.C. and Wooldridge, A. (2001) 'The dynamics of corporate identity: a review of a process model, *Journal of Communication Management,* 5(4): 327–40.

Mick, D.G. (1986) 'Consumer research and semiotics: exploring the morphology of signs, symbols and significance', *Journal of Consumer Research,* 13: 196–213.

Mick, D.G. and Buhl, K. (1992) 'A meaning based model of advertising', *Journal of Consumer Research,* 19 (December): 317–38.

Moeran, B. (2009) 'The organization of creativity in Japanese advertising production', *Human Relations,* 62 (July): 963–85.

Motion, J., Leitch, S. and Brodie, R. (2003) 'Equity in co-branded identity – the case of Adidas and the All Blacks', *European Journal of Marketing,* 37(7/8): 1080–94.

Mulder, N. (1996) *Inside Thai Society: Interpretations of Everyday Life.* Amsterdam: The Pepin Press.

Nava, M., Blake A., MacRury, I. and Richards, B. (eds) (1996) *Buy This Book.* London: Routledge.

Nelson, J.P. and Young, D.J. (2001) 'Do advertising bans work? An international comparison', *International Journal of Advertising,* 20: 273–96.

Nightingale, D.J. and Cromby, J. (eds) (1999) *Social Constructionist Psychology: A Critical Analysis of Theory and Practice.* Buckingham: Open University Press.

Nixon, S. (2003) 'Re-imagining the advertising agency: the cultural connotations of economic forms', in P. DuGay and M. Pryke (eds), *Cultural Economy.* London: Sage.

O'Donohoe, S. (1994) 'Advertising uses and gratifications', *European Journal of Marketing,* 28(8/9): 52–75.

O'Donohoe, S. (1997) 'Raiding the postmodern pantry – advertising intertextuality and the young adult audience', *European Journal of Marketing,* 31(34): 234–53.

Ogilvy, D. (1963) *Confessions of an Advertising Man.* New York: Atheneum.

Ogilvy, D. (1983) *Ogilvy on Advertising,* 2nd edn. London: Multimedia Books.

Osborn, A. (1963) *Applied Imagination – Principles and Procedures of Creative Problem Solving.* New York: Charles Scribner's Sons.

O'Shaughnessy, J. (1997) 'Temerarious directions for marketing', *European Journal of Marketing,* 31(9/10): 677–705.

O'Shaughnessy, N. and O'Shaughnessy, J. (2004) *Persuasion in Advertising.* London: Routledge.

Packard, V. (1957) *The Hidden Persuaders.* New York: McKay.

Parsons, E. and Maclaran, P. (2009) *Contemporary Issues in Marketing and Consumer Behaviour.* London: Elsevier.

Pateman, T. (1980) 'How to do things with images: an essay on the pragmatics of advertising', in T. Pateman (ed.), *Language, Truth and Politics.* East Sussex: Jean Stroud. pp. 215–37.

Pateman, T. (1983) 'How is understanding an advertisement possible?', in H. Davis and P. Walton (eds), *Language, Image, Media.* Oxford: Blackwell. pp. 187–204.

Peirce, C.S. (1958) *Collected Papers.* Cambridge, MA: Harvard University Press.

Peng, N. and Hackley, C. (2007) 'Political marketing communications planning in the UK and Taiwan – comparative insights from leading practitioners', *Marketing Intelligence and Planning,* 25(5): 483–98.

Peng, N. and Hackley, C. (2009) 'Are voters, consumers? A qualitative exploration of the voter–consumer analogy in political marketing', *Qualitative Market Research: An International Journal,* 12(2): 171–86.

Percy, L. and Elliott, R. (2009) *Strategic Advertising Management,* 3rd edn. Oxford: Oxford University Press.

Percy, L. Rossiter, J.R. and Elliott, R. (2001) *Strategic Advertising Management*. Oxford: Oxford University Press.

Pickton, D. and Broderick, A. (2000) *Integrated Marketing Communications*. London: Pearson Education.

Pickton, D. and Broderick, A. (2005) *Integrated Marketing Communications*. London: FT Books.

Pickton, D. and Crosier, K. (2003) 'Marketing intelligence and planning', *Account Planning*, special issue, 21(7): 410–15.

Pollay, R.W. (1986) 'The distorted mirror – reflections on the unintended consequences of advertising', *Journal of Marketing*, 50(April): 18–36.

Pollitt, S. (1979) 'How I started account planning in agencies', *Campaign*, 20(April): 29–30.

Potter, J. and Wetherell, M. (1987) *Discourse and Social Psychology: Beyond Attitudes and Behaviour*. London: Sage.

Punyapiroje, C., Morrison, M. and Hoy, M. (2002) 'A nation under the influence: the creative strategy process for advertising in Thailand', *Journal of Current Issues and Research in Advertising*, 24(2): 51–65.

Quickenden, K. and Kover, A.J. (2007) 'Did Boulton sell silver plate to the middle class? A quantitative study of luxury marketing in late eighteenth-century Britain', *Journal of Macromarketing*, 27(March): 51–64.

Richards, B., MacRury, I. and Botterill, J. (2000) *The Dynamics of Advertising*. London: Routledge.

Ritson, M. and Elliott, R. (1999) 'The social uses of advertising: an ethnographic study of adolescent advertising audiences', *Journal of Consumer Research*, 26(3): 260–77.

Ritzer, G. (2000) *The McDonaldization of Society*. New century edition. Thousand Oaks, CA: Pine Forge Press and Sage.

Robinson, N., McWilliams, H., Bullinger, F. and Schouest, C. (2009) 'Dove's big ideal: from real curves to growth curves', in N. Dawson (ed.), *Advertising Works 17: Proving the Payback on Marketing Investment*. Henley-on-Thames: IPA/WARC, World Advertisng Research Centre. pp. 335–70.

Rosch, E. (1977) 'Human categorization', in N. Warren (ed.), *Advances in Cross Cultural Psychology*, Vol. 1. New York: Academic Press. pp. 1–49.

Rossiter, J.R., Percy, L. and Donovan, R.J. (1991) 'A better advertising planning grid', *Journal of Advertising Research*, October–November: 11–12.

Russell, C.A. (1998) 'Towards a framework of product placement: theoretical propositions', *Advances in Consumer Research*, 25: 357–62.

Sawchuck, K. (1995) 'Semiotics, cybernetics and the ecstasy of marketing communication', in D. Kellner (ed.), *Baudrillard: A Critical Reader*. Oxford: Blackwell. pp. 89–116.

Schlosser, E. (2001) *Fast Food Nation: The Dark Side of the All-American Meal*. London: HarperCollins.

Schor, J. (1998) *The Overspent American: Upscaling, Downshifting and the New Consumer*. New York: Basic Books.

Schramm, W. (1948) *Mass Communication*. Urbana, IL: University of Illinois Press.

Schroeder, J.E. (2002) *Visual Consumption*. London: Routledge.

Schroeder, J.E. (2004) 'Visual consumption in an image economy', in K. Ekstrom and H. Brembeck (eds), *Elusive Consumption*. Stockholm: Berg.

Schroeder, J.E. (2005) 'The artist and the brand', *European Journal of Marketing*, 39(11/12): 1291–305.

Schultz, D. (2003) *IMC – The Next Generation*. New York: McGraw-Hill.

Schultz, D. and Kitchen, P. (1997) 'Integrated marketing communications in US advertising agencies: an exploratory study', *Journal of Advertising Research*, September/October: 7–18.

Schultz, D.E., Martin, D. and Brown, W.P. (1987) *Strategic Advertising Campaigns*, 2nd edn. Lincolnwood, IL: NTC Business Books.

Schultz, D.E., Tannenbaum, S.I. and Lauterborn, R.F. (1993) *Integrated Marketing Communications*. Lincolnwood, IL: NTC Publishing Group.

Scott, L. (1990) 'Understanding jingles and needledrop: a rhetorical approach to music in advertising', *Journal of Conusmer Research*, 17(September): 223–36.

Scott, L. (1994a) 'The bridge from text to mind: adapting reader-response theory to consumer research', *Journal of Consumer Research*, 21: 461–80.

Scott, L. (1994b) 'Images in advertising: the need for a theory of visual rhetoric', *Journal of Consumer Research*, 21: 252–73.

Shankar, A. (2000) 'Lost in music? Subjective personal introspection and popular music consumption', *Research: An International Journal*, 3(1): 27–37.

Shankar, A. and Horton, B. (1999) 'Ambient media – advertising's new media opportunity?', *International Journal of Advertising*, 18(3): 305–21.

Shannon, C.E. (1948) 'A mathematical theory of communication', *Bell System Technical Journal*, 27 (July and October): 379–423, 623–56. http://plan9.bell-labs.com/cm/ms/what/shannonday/shannon1948.pdf

Sharma, C., Herzog, J. and Melfi, V. (2008) *Mobile Advertising – Supercharge your Brand in the Exploding Wireless Market*. Hoboken, NJ: Wiley.

Sherer, P.M. (1995) 'Selling the sizzle: Thai advertising crackles with creativity as industry continues to grow', *The Asian Wall Street Journal Weekly*, 1: 6–7.

Sherry, J.E. (1983) 'Gift giving in anthropological perspective', *Journal of Consumer Research*, 10(September): 157–68.

Sherry, J.F. (1987) 'Advertising as cultural system', in J. Umiker-Sebeok (ed.), *Marketing and Semiotics*. Berlin: Mouton. pp. 441–62.

Sherry, J.F. (1991) 'Postmodern alternatives – the interpretive turn in consumer research', in T.S. Robertson and H.H. Kasserjian (eds), *Handbook of Consumer Behaviour*. Englewood Cliffs, NJ: Prentice-Hall. pp. 548–91.

Shimp, T.A. (2009) *Integrated Marketing Communications in Advertising and Promotion*, international edition. South Western College.

Sperber, D. and Wilson, D. (1986) *Relevance: Communication and Cognition*. Oxford: Blackwell.

Steel, J. (1998) *Truth, Lies and Advertising: The Art of Account Planning*. New York: John Wiley and Sons.

Stern, B.B.(1993a) 'A revised communication model for advertising: multiple dimensions of the source, the message and the recipient', *Journal of Advertising*, 23: 25–16.

Stern, B.B. (1993b) 'Feminist literary criticism and the deconstruction of ads: a postmodern view of advertising and consumer responses', *Journal of Consumer Research*, 19: 556–66.

Stern, B.B. (ed.) (1998) *Representing Consumers: Voices, Views and Visions*. London: Routledge.

Stevens, R. (1996) 'Ten ways of distinguishing between theories in social psychology' and 'Trimodal theory as a model for interrelating perspectives in psychology', in R. Sapsford (ed.), *Issues for Social Psychology*. Milton Keynes: Open University. pp. 45–66, 77–84.

Strong, E.K. (1925) *The Psychology of Selling and Advertising*. Chicago: American Library Association.

Stuart, G. (2008) 'Foreword', in C., Sharma, J. Herzog and V. Melfi (eds), *Mobile Advertising: Supercharge your Brand in the Exploding Wireless Market*. Hoboken, NJ: Wiley.

Supharp, S. (1993) *Thai Culture and Society: Values, Family, Religion and Tradition*, 8th edn. Bangkok: Thai Watanapanich (in Thai).

Svensson, S. (2007) 'Producing marketing: towards a social-phenomenology of marketing work', *Marketing Theory,* 7: 271–90.

Szmigin, I. (2003) *Understanding the Consumer*. London: Sage.

Szmigin, I., Griffin, C., Mistral, W., Bengry-Howell, A., Weale, L. and Hackley, C. (2008) 'Re-framing "binge drinking" as calculated hedonism: empirical evidence from the UK', *International Journal of Drug Policy*, 19(5): 359–66.

Tanaka, K. (1994) *Advertising Language: A Pragmatic Approach to Advertisements in Britain and Japan*. London: Routledge.

Thompson, C.J., Locander, W. and Pollio, H. (1989) 'Putting consumer experience back into consumer research: the philosophy and method of existential phenomenology', *Journal of Consumer Research*, 17: 133–47.

Thompson, C., Pollio, H. and Locander, W. (1994) 'The spoken and the unspoken: a hermeneutic approach to the understanding the cultural viewpoints that underlie consumers expressed meanings', *Journal of Consumer Research*, 21: 431–53.

Tirakhunkovit, V. (1980) 'Why Thais do not like Thai products', *Monthly Business Journal*, February: 22–9.

Tiwsakul, R. (2008) 'The meaning of Kod-sa-na-faeng: an interpretive exploration of consumers' experiences of television product placement in the United Kingdom and Thailand', PhD Thesis, University of London, Royal Holloway and Bedford New College.

Tiwsakul, R. and Hackley, C. (2006) 'Young Thai and UK consumers' experiences of television product placement-engagement, resistance and objectification', in M. Craig-Lees, G. Gregory, and T. Davis (eds), *Borderless Consumption: Asia Pacific Advances in Counsumer Research, Volume 7*. Duluth, MN: Association for Counsumer Research. pp. 371–76.

Tiwsakul, R. and Hackley, C. (2008) 'Television product placement in Thailand and the UK: implications for international brand communications management'. Paper presented at ICORIA annual conference, Antwerp, Belgium, June.

Tiwsakul, R. and Hackley, C. (2009) 'The meaning of 'Kod-sa-na-faeng' – young adults' experiences of television product placement in the UK and Thailand', in A.L. McGill and S. Shavitt (eds), *Advances in Consumer Research, Volume 36*. San Francisco, CA: Proceedings of the Association of the Consumer Research (October). pp. 584–86.

Tiwsakul, R., Hackley, C. and Szmigin, I. (2005) 'Explicit, non-integrated product placement in British television programmes', *International Journal of Advertising*, 24(1): 95–111.

Umiker-Sebeok, J. (ed.) (1997) *Marketing and Semiotics*. Amsterdam: Mouton de Gruyter.

Usunier, J.-C. (1993) *International Marketing – A Cultural Approach*. New York: Prentice-Hall.

Vakratsas, D. and Ambler, T. (1999) 'How advertising works: what do we really know?', *Journal of Marketing*, 63(January): 26–43.

van Raaij, W.F. (1989) 'How consumers react to advertising', *International Journal of Advertising*, 8: 261–73.

van Raaij, W.F. (1998) 'Interactive communication: consumer power and initiative', *Journal of Marketing Communications*, 4(1): 1–8.

Van Riel, C. (1995) *Principles of Corporate Communication*. London: Prentice-Hall.

Varey, R.J. (2000) *Corporate Communication Management: A Relationship Perspective*. London: Routledge.

Varey, R.J. (2002) *Marketing Communication: Principles and Practice*. London: Routledge.

Vaughn, R. (1986) 'How advertising works – a planning model revisited', *Journal of Advertising Research* (February–March): 57–66.

Veblen, T. ([1899] 1970) *The Theory of the Leisure Class*. London: Unwin Books.

Watson, J. (1924) *Behaviorism*. Chicago: University of Chicago Press.

Weaver, W. and Shannon, C.E. (1963). *The Mathematical Theory of Communication*. Champaign, IL: University of Illinois Press.

Webley, P., Burgoyne, C.B., Lea, S.E.G. and Young, B.M. (2001) *The Economic Psychology of Everyday Life*. Hove: Psychology Press.

Wells, W.D. (1975) 'Psychographics: a critical review', *Journal of Marketing Research*, 12(May): 196–213.

Wells, W.D. (ed.) (1997) *Measuring Advertising Effectiveness.* Hillsdale, NJ: Lawrence Erlbaum Associates.

Wernick, A. (1991) *Promotional Culture – Advertising, Ideology and Symbolic Expression.* London: Sage.

West, D.C. and Paliwoda, S.J. (1996) 'Advertising client-agency relationships: the decision-making structure of clients', *European Journal of Marketing*, 30(8): 22–39.

West, D. (1993) 'Cross-national creative personalities, processes and agency philosophies', *Journal of Advertising Research*, 33(5): 53–62.

West, D. and Ford, J. (2001) 'Advertising agency philosophies and employee risk taking', *Journal of Advertising*, 30(1): 77–91.

Williamson, J. (1978) *The Semiotics of Advertising.* London: Sage.

Wilmshurst, J. and Mackay, A. (1999) *The Fundamentals of Advertising*, 2nd edn. Oxford: Butterworth Heinemann.

Wilmshurst, J. and Mackay, A. (2000) *The Fundamentals of Advertising.* Oxford: Butterworth-Heinemann, in association with ISBA.

Wolf, M. (1999) *The Entertainment Economy: How Mega-media Forces are Shaping our Lives.* New York: Crown Business Books.

World Health Organization (WHO) (1988) *Alcohol and the Mass Media.* Copenhagen: WHO.

Yeshin, T. (2000) *Integrated Marketing Communications.* Oxford: Butterworth Heinemann.

Young, M. (1995) 'Getting legless, falling down pissy-arsed drunk', *Journal of Gender Studies*, 4(1): 47–61.

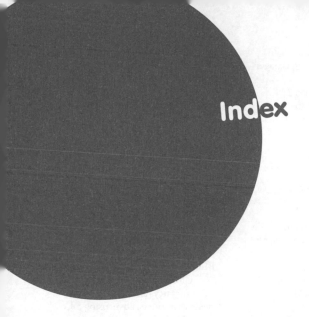

Index

Please note that page references to boxes, cases, pictures and tables will be in *italic* print.

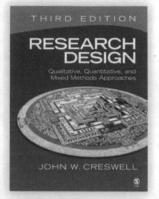
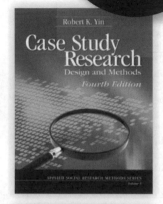

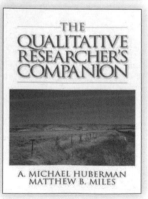
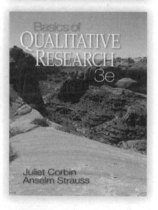